RIGHT VERSUS PRIVILEGE

RIGHT
VERSUS
PRIVILEGE

*The Open-Admissions Experiment
at the City University of New York*

David E. Lavin

Richard D. Alba

Richard A. Silberstein

THE FREE PRESS
A Division of Macmillan Publishing Co., Inc.
NEW YORK

Collier Macmillan Publishers
LONDON

The Free Press
A Division of Macmillan Publishing Co., Inc.
866 Third Avenue, New York, N. Y. 10022

Collier Macmillan Canada, Ltd.

Library of Congress Catalog Card Number: 80-69571

Printed in the United States of America

printing number
1 2 3 4 5 6 7 8 9 10

Library of Congress Cataloging in Publication Data
Lavin, David E.
  Right versus privilege.

  Includes index.
  1. New York (City).   City University of New
York—Open admission—Case studies.   I. Alba,
Richard D., joint author.   II. Silberstein,
Richard A., joint author.   III. Title.
LD3835.L38   378'.105'097471   80-69571
ISBN 0-02-918080-5

Contents

Preface   *vii*

1. Reaction to Confrontation: Let Everyone In   *1*

2. Open Access: Issues and Perspectives   *28*

3. Research Background and Procedures   *46*

4. Access to Educational Opportunity under Open Admissions   *60*

5. Who Were the Open-Admission Students?   *91*

6. Academic Progress, Dropout, and Graduation I: What Happened   *119*

7. Academic Progress, Dropout, and Graduation II: How It Happened   *159*

8. Community Colleges and Stratification in Higher Education   *201*

9. Equipping the Underprepared Student: The Effects of Remediation   *229*

10. The Success of Open Admissions: Conclusions   *265*

11. New York City's Fiscal Crisis and the Fate of Open Admissions   *289*

Appendix A: Quality of the Sample Data   *313*

Appendix B: Reading the Results of Regression Analysis   *318*

Name Index   *327*

Subject Index   *331*

Preface

Equalization of social and economic opportunity has been a major concern of American society during the second half of the twentieth century, and educational institutions have been viewed as primary arenas for efforts to broaden such opportunities. Nowhere have these efforts been more visible than at the City University of New York (CUNY), the nation's third largest higher education system. Breaking sharply with its earlier policies by launching an open-admissions program in fall 1970, the University in one stroke carved a broad path that allowed many thousands of previously ineligible students to attend one of the seventeen four- and two-year colleges comprising its system. The open-admissions policy received wide national attention because it resonated with a number of broad issues and controversies surrounding efforts to expand educational opportunity. Questions concerning who should be educated, debates about "merit" versus "quotas," and concern for academic standards were themes that made open admissions an event of national importance.

This book describes and analyzes the results of that policy, considering which students came, how they were placed in the University, and how they fared academically. In essence, the volume addresses this question: how successful was the open-admissions policy in facilitating educational opportunity, gauged not only by the access it created but also by the results for different groups, especially minorities?

In cases of multiple authorship, recognition is not always allocated fairly among the collaborators, and it is helpful to describe the roles played by each as the study developed. The project had a lengthy and complex history. In 1970 CUNY had no centralized capability for conducting a long-term study of open admissions across its multicampus system. The University's central administration asked Lavin to oversee the development of such a capability. The major initial tasks were to create a student data system and to use such data to produce reports describing some primary academic results under the new policy. Additionally, for large samples, Lavin collected data on student socioeconomic background, attitudes, and aspirations, and he directed fieldwork in which interview data were collected from administrators and faculty on each CUNY campus, describing the special support services (remediation and counseling, for example) that each college developed in the open-admissions effort.

By the end of 1976 all of the data for the research had been collected, Alba joined the project, and the work reported in this volume began in earnest. Alba helped to focus the analysis on ethnicity and took the leadership role in planning the statistical analyses that appear in the book. The manuscript was written by Alba and Lavin and represents an equal collaboration between them. Alba prepared chapters 4, 5, 7, and 8. Lavin prepared chapters 1, 3, 6, 9, and 11. Chapters 2 and 10 were written jointly by them.

Silberstein had joined the project in 1973, and his major initial responsibility was to create an integrated data set from the diverse and unusually complex files that existed at the time. He also developed procedures for evaluating the quality of the student academic performance data. Subsequently, he carried out the major computer work for our data analyses.

Florence Neumann did extensive work for chapter 1, pulling together many of the diverse original source materials and writing an initial draft of the section dealing with the 1969 uprising at City College. For this reason she is identified as co-author of that chapter.

No study that spanned almost a decade and focused upon an institution as large and complex as the City University could have been completed successfully without the help of a large number of people. While it is impossible to acknowledge our debt to all of them, many provided especially critical support.

During the early phase of the project, former Vice-Chancellor Timothy S. Healy provided Lavin with a stimulating and nonbureaucratic atmosphere in which to begin thinking about research on open admissions. Seymour C. Hyman, then Deputy Chancellor, recognized the importance to the University of establishing a routinized student data system. After the major information needs of the project had been defined, his efforts greatly facilitated the success of the initial data collection. The early computer work to establish standardized student performance files was carried out by Marianne Williams.

Barbara Jacobson Kendrick made important contributions to the research. She collaborated with Lavin in producing a first detailed report for the University on student academic achievements, and she played a major role in the field research designed to assess responses of the CUNY colleges to the new policy. Irene Shrier also worked closely with Lavin on this fieldwork.

CUNY Chancellor Robert J. Kibbee facilitated our work in various ways, particularly in providing Lavin with released time to work on the project, not only during the period when the research was geared to the University's immediate needs to monitor the results of the open-admissions policy but also later, when we turned to our broader analyses. Deputy Chancellor Egon Brenner was also generous in his efforts to enhance our progress.

Special thanks go to President Leonard Lief of Lehman College and to Lavin's colleagues in the sociology department there for their cooperation and forbearance during the years when his teaching duties were minimal. Cornell University's sociology department generously extended computer time and other resources to Alba.

A number of other friends and colleagues gave us valuable advice and encouragement along the way. We are especially indebted to Joe Meng, former vice-chancellor for administrative affairs, who was supportive of the project in ways that went well beyond his official duties. Were it not for his many positive interventions on our behalf, it is conceivable that the project would not have been completed. Beth Taylor, head of CUNY's Office of Planning, shared with us many thoughts about equity in higher education and helped sharpen our thinking about the ramifications of the open-admissions policy. Max Weiner gave much helpful advice and steadfast support over the years. President Harold Proshansky, of CUNY's Graduate School, provided important counsel, especially in the early stages of the research, when Lavin was familiarizing himself with the University and the sometimes mysterious ways of its central administration. The Graduate School also housed the project when the manuscript was in preparation, and the Center for Advanced Study in Education provided crucial administrative services.

We benefited from discussions with Paul Allison, Ed Borgatta, Jerry Karabel, Rolf Meyersohn, Mary Lea Meyersohn, and Ray Rist, all of whom read portions of the manuscript and made useful suggestions. Harold Bershady, Frank Furstenberg, Barry Kaufman, Marguerite Lavin, and Caroline Persell read all, or most, of the manuscript in its later stages. Their perceptive responses improved its quality.

The typing of the manuscript was handled ably and expeditiously by Denise Keegan at CUNY and by Sue Hawk, Anne Plescia, and Donna Vose at Cornell. Some of the statistical tabulations were run by Penny Orwick.

Exxon Education Foundation provided the major external funding for our work. Ford Foundation provided a grant that aided in completion of "Open Admissions and Equal Access: A Study of Ethnic Groups in the City University of New York" (*Harvard Educational Review* 49 [February 1979]: 53–92). Permission to reprint some of the material from this article was kindly provided by that journal. We were helped also by grants from the CUNY Faculty Research Award Program and from Cornell University.

1. Reaction to Confrontation: Let Everyone In

THE 1960s WITNESSED intense concern with equality, ranging in expression from civil disobedience to strident demonstrations and riots, from Watts at one end of the country to Ocean Hill–Brownsville at the other. One of the decade's many sparks exploded in spring 1969 in a series of angry and ominous confrontations on the campus of the City College of New York (CCNY), the oldest and most famous of the fifteen two- and four-year colleges then comprising the City University of New York (CUNY). The confrontations focused on a list of demands issued by groups wanting increased access to City College for educationally disadvantaged students, notably blacks and Hispanics. The demands had a forceful logic not only in the egalitarian concerns of the sixties but also in the history of City University.

The University had been in the vanguard of the development of public higher education for the urban poor. Its origins lay in the second quarter of the nineteenth century, when there was considerable political agitation for an expansion of free public education.[1] While progress had been made toward development of free common (elementary) schools, at the beginning of the 1840s further education could be obtained only in private academies and colleges, available to those with the means to pay.[2] Pressures to extend public education led to a referendum in June 1847 in which New York's citizens voted overwhelmingly to establish the Free Academy (renamed the College of the City of New York in 1866), the first tuition-free public insti-

Florence M. Neumann co-authored this chapter.

1

tution of higher education in the United States.[3] At formal opening ceremonies in 1849, the head of the new institution set forth its mission:

> The Free Academy is now to go into operation. The experiment is to be tried, whether the highest education can be given to the masses; whether the children of the whole people can be educated; and whether an institution of learning, of the highest grade, can be successfully controlled by the popular will, not by the privileged few, but by the privileged many.[4]

The Free Academy offered admission to all those who had been pupils in the common schools of the city for at least one year and who could pass an entrance examination.[5] Of the 272 applicants to the first class, 143 passed the exam, an acceptance rate of better than 50 percent.[6]

In the early years the student body consisted largely of native-born Protestants. There were only a few Irish and German immigrants and even fewer Jews.[7] While the sons of poor workers did enroll, students typically came from the families of merchants, clerks, small tradesmen, and professionals.[8] In the late 1870s controversy arose over the fact that only graduates of public schools were eligible for admission. Irish Catholics, who had been unable to obtain public funds for support of parochial schools, especially resented being taxed to support a college that excluded parochial school graduates. In 1882 eligibility to both City College and the Normal School (an academy for women oriented mainly toward training teachers, established in 1870, and renamed Hunter College in 1914) was extended to private school pupils.[9] This broadening of access seems to have been mainly symbolic since few parochial school graduates were added to the rolls of the College,[10] undoubtedly because several Catholic colleges had already been established in New York City.[11]

Rates of graduation from City College were astoundingly low by present-day standards. Over its first fifty years, about thirty thousand students entered; only 2,730 graduated, a graduation rate of less than 10 percent.[12] These low rates had a significance quite different from what they would have had if they had occurred in the second half of this century. Some students dropped out because their families could not continue to support them while in school, and others left because a career in business, teaching, or even medicine and law did not require four years of college.[13] To provide even some college work was part of the mission of the College. That most students did not graduate was not deemed an institutional failure or even a personal deficiency on the part of the students.

Around the turn of the century a dramatic change occurred in the composition of the student body. Beginning in the 1880s and gaining momentum during the ensuing few decades, there was a vast immigration of poor Jews from eastern Europe, notably from Russia.[14] Given their penchant for education, they were drawn to City College in substantial numbers. Though faculty were impressed by the scholarly capability and strong commitment to learning shown by these new students, the Jewish presence initially aroused ethnic conflict (though not of the scale or complexity of late 1960s strife). Eventually, as a result of the Jewish influx "the families of Anglo-Saxon, Dutch, German, and Huguenot descent, who had been accustomed to register their boys in the College in the old days, sent them elsewhere for a college education."[15] While a few members of these earlier groups remained and were joined by students from the city's two major Catholic groups, the Irish and the Italians,[16] by 1905 Jews constituted about 75 percent of the student body.

By the 1920s and the 1930s, City College students were regarded as among the most able in the nation, and the College was often referred to as the "proletarian Harvard." The list of its graduates' accomplishments—in academia, in business, and in public life—read like a selection from *Who's Who in America*, contributing to faith in the College as an open door to the middle class.

The transformation of the College's ethnic composition was not the only change that occurred at the turn of the century. During this period there was also an increase in the number of students who wanted to attend CCNY, an increase that at first it was able to accommodate.[17] This growth was not solely the result of the Jewish passion for education. Other factors were at work to accelerate interest in college-going. One was that professional schools were beginning to demand more education as a prerequisite for admission.[18] Moreover, by 1911 there had been an enormous growth in the number of high schools in the city, and even though the proportion of graduates was very small, they increased the potential pool of students for the College.[19] This expansion of public education in the city created a large arena for employment: the school system itself. As a result of these developments, the number of applicants for CCNY began to outdistance its facilities, and in 1924 entrance requirements were stiffened. For the first time a high school average cutoff point was introduced; in that year an average of at least 72 was required for admission.[20]

Continued growth in the demand for college led the CCNY trustees in 1917 to establish a branch institution in Brooklyn, the city's most populous borough, located far from the main campus in uptown Manhattan. Another branch was established a few years later in Queens. In recognition of the need for a centralized body to oversee the expansion of higher educational facilities throughout the city, the New York state legislature in 1926 abolished the CCNY trustees and created the Board of Higher Education (BHE). Continued overcrowding led the BHE to establish a branch of Hunter College in the Bronx in 1929 and to found an independent Brooklyn College in 1930. Another new college—this time in Queens—opened its doors in 1937.[21]

In spite of these expansions, the municipal colleges were hard pressed to meet the growing demand for higher education, especially after World War

II, thus leading to an increase in the high school average required for admission.[22] A report to the BHE projected that by 1950 there would be almost fifty-thousand students capable of attending college who could not be accommodated by current facilities. The report also noted that the occupational structure of the city was changing, increasing the demand for workers with at least some college education.[23] These developments led to the founding of three community colleges during the 1950s, but still the system was unable to keep pace with the demand. In an explicit effort to maintain a balance between enrollments and facilities in the four-year colleges, high school average cutoff points were again raised.[24] As a result, between 1952 and 1961 the number of new admissions to baccalaureate programs actually declined from 8,859, or 17 percent of high school graduates in the city, to 8,563, or 13 percent of the graduates.[25] Even the admissions requirements for the community colleges were quite stringent.[26] In short, admission to the municipal college system was becoming ever more difficult as demand was growing, and serious questions were being raised about the appropriateness of such a policy in a publicly supported university.[27]

Despite the increasingly stringent entrance requirements, enrollments in the municipal colleges were becoming ethnically more diversified in some respects, although not in others, during the post–World War II period. Throughout the century the heavy representation of Jewish students continued, both at City College and at the schools subsequently established.[28] But it was only after the war that Irish and Italian Catholics began to attend the municipal institutions in large numbers. For two reasons, they had been sharply underrepresented before then. One was that the church discouraged attendance at secular institutions; numerous Catholic colleges in the New York metropolitan area undoubtedly attracted a substantial portion of those Catholic youths who went to college, especially the Irish. In addition, the ethnic cultures of these groups, particularly the Italians, did not place the heavy emphasis upon higher education that was displayed among Jews. Indeed, among those of southern Italian origin (who constituted the overwhelming proportion of Italian immigrants to the city), educational aspirations were thwarted by cultural values, such as an emphasis on loyalty to the family above all else, that were finely tuned to the needs of a rural folk society but were very dysfunctional in a highly industrialized urban setting.[29] Yet the forces of assimilation made themselves felt in the postwar period.[30] Italian Catholics began to attend Catholic colleges in sizable numbers, constituting half the student body at the city's best Catholic college, Fordham, by 1960.[31] And Catholics began appearing at the city's public colleges: by the mid to late 1960s they comprised almost a third, and at some of the municipal colleges about 40 percent, of the entering classes.[32]

But what the municipal colleges had done for these earlier groups arriving from Europe (for Jews earlier and for Catholics much later), they had failed to do for the new arrivals from the American South and the Caribbean. During the 1950s the population of New York City remained almost constant, but about 700,000 blacks and Puerto Ricans replaced a similar number of whites who left over that period.[33] In that decade the percentage of minority students in the high school graduating classes remained around 13 percent, but in 1960 they comprised only 5 percent of the enrollment in the municipal colleges, the same percentage as in 1950.[34] During the 1960s, entrance requirements at the four-year institutions stiffened even more, which exacerbated the underrepresentation of minority students, who typically had lower high school averages and could not meet these standards. Moreover, minority high school graduates were far less likely than whites to have received college preparatory academic diplomas, thus limiting even further the number who could qualify for traditional college programs.[35] So on the eve of open admissions, it was apparent that the municipal colleges were serving different groups in very unequal ways.

The Movement to Expand Educational Opportunity

In 1963, with the arrival in New York of Albert H. Bowker, the municipal colleges began to move in a new direction. To coordinate the varied activities and policies of the semi-autonomous city colleges, the system was designated the City University of New York (CUNY) in 1961, and Bowker left his post as dean of Stanford University's Graduate School to become CUNY chancellor. The appointment was to bring about centralization of policymaking functions and a renewal of the University's mission by serving a much broader spectrum of the city's population. Paradoxically, one of the main reasons Bowker was brought in was to oversee the development of a centralized program of doctoral studies in all major academic areas (which he did). But early on he was struck by CUNY's unresponsiveness to the burgeoning college-age population and to the changed ethnic composition of the city.

Under Bowker's leadership the movement toward a more inclusive CUNY was begun. The impetus came from several sources. Broadly speaking, the 1960s was a time of rising expectations and growing militancy among minority groups throughout the nation. Those expecations were both a source and a result of the belief of liberals that much more should and could be done to reduce poverty and to increase the opportunities of minorities to improve their economic and political status. Having come from California, where the public sector already had in operation a system of universal access to higher education, and possessing a strong liberal social consciousness, Bowker was a man in tune with the times. He was also pragmatic. Recognizing the major demographic changes that had taken place in the city, he perceived that the University's political support might erode if it continued its highly selective admissions policies. He saw the long-run interests of CUNY as requiring a major expansion—one that included a break with traditional admissions standards.[36]

The transition from the exclusive admissions practices of 1960 to the open-admissions policy of 1970 began modestly enough. In an initial effort to increase the enrollment of minority students, Bowker in 1963 was able to obtain a commitment of funds from the state to set up an experimental admissions program in the community colleges. This program, known as College Discovery, started in 1964.[37] At the senior-college level, a special prebaccalaureate course of study was offered at City College during the 1965–1966 academic year.[38] About one hundred students were drawn, outside the admissions criteria then in force, from the Harlem neighborhood immediately surrounding the College. The intent was to provide compensatory work preparatory to the entry of these students into traditional college programs.

These initial efforts were mainly symbolic: while they indicated CUNY's intention to expand opportunity for minority students, they made no real dent in increasing the minority presence in the University. More broadly, they did not come to grips with the consequences of the postwar baby boom. High school graduating classes had become larger than they had been in the 1950s, and without an expansion of enrollments, an elevation of entrance requirements at some CUNY colleges to a 90 high school average was foreseen for 1966. To expand enrollments and provide greater minority access would require a major increase in the University's funding, covering not only operating costs but also physical plant expansion. The chancellor perceived the city's ability to support a larger CUNY as limited, and he concluded that growth would depend on greater state support.[39] Bowker's efforts to secure that support were ultimately successful. Early in the summer of 1966 the state legislature passed a bill providing for an expanded freshman class in the fall, establishing a construction fund for future growth, and allocating monies for a special minority admissions program in the four-year colleges.[40] This program, known by the acronym SEEK (Search for Education, Elevation, and Knowledge), began that fall with a thousand students. It immediately became the major avenue of minority entry to CUNY's senior colleges.

This larger commitment from the state gave momentum to the drive for broader access to the University. Early in 1966 Bowker had convinced the BHE to approve a general statement of the University's intention to offer 100 percent admission.[41] This aim was further specified in a revision of CUNY's 1964 master plan and reaffirmed in its 1968 plan.[42] The plan noted that the large influx of unskilled migrants from the South and from Puerto Rico had come at a time when unskilled jobs were a shrinking sector of the labor market. To improve the prospects of these groups and to meet the broad demand for college, the University proposed that by 1975 a place be provided for every high school graduate according to the following stratified scheme: (1) the top 25 percent of high school graduates would be offered admission to a senior-college baccalaureate program; (2) the top two-thirds of graduates would qualify for community colleges (the top half would be eligible for transfer programs, while the rest would qualify for career programs); (3) about 6 percent would be admitted to senior colleges via the SEEK program—and thus outside the regular admissions procedure—and about 4 percent would be admitted to community colleges via the College Discovery program; (4) all others could enroll in "educational skills centers" that would provide job-oriented technical training. These centers also were to offer "college adapter" courses that would help identify students with potential for community-college career programs.[43] Even with its highly stratified admissions criteria, this proposal took a great stride forward, relative to CUNY's selectivity of the late 1950s and early 1960s. But in light of what was to come, it would appear quite modest. Indeed, Bowker's forward to the master plan was prophetic: "Change, however well anticipated, has a way of making the most forward looking plans obsolete. This plan is not likely to be an exception."[44]

External pressures on the University to admit more minority students were increasing,[45] and what CUNY planned to do in 1975 seemed remote in the spring and summer of 1968. Nationally the political ferment in minority communities had changed from the nonviolent tactics of the civil rights movement to greater militance and even riots. Martin Luther King had just been assassinated. Largely in response to that event, minority students demonstrated on some CUNY campuses,[46] and the city had just witnessed one of the bloodiest of the campus-police conflicts of the sixties—the student rebellion at Columbia. It was in this climate that Bowker brought the BHE together in August 1968 to consider the question of further expansion of minority enrollment. An important outcome of the board's deliberations was a proposal for a "Top 100 Scholars Program"[47] under which those who ranked among the top one hundred graduates of their high school class would be admitted to one of the CUNY senior colleges. For this group high school average would be ignored in the admissions process. This stipulation was made in recognition of the fact that students in the city's ghetto high schools typically earned lower averages than did students holding the same class rank in nonghetto schools. Thus, students in the heavily minority schools would be admitted even if they had not attained the average currently required for admission. Moreover, because minority students were far less likely than whites to receive college preparatory diplomas, the program also stipulated that students ranking in the top one hundred would be admitted regardless of the type of diploma they had earned.[48]

In setting forth this program, the board stated its ultimate intent: minority groups should be represented at CUNY "in the same proportion as they are represented among all high school graduates of the City."[49] This statement served to crystallize what had been a growing concern among whites in the city, particularly those who formed the traditional Jewish constituency of CUNY; namely, during a period when admission to the University was highly selective, places were increasingly being allocated to students who did not meet traditional criteria—at the expense of other qualified students. The board's reference to "proportion" irritated a particularly sensitive nerve in the Jewish community: the noxious concept of the quota, which private colleges had once used against them.[50]

At the same time it did not appear that CUNY's efforts to increase the minority presence evoked the gratitude some might have expected. Indeed, a proposal by the board to establish a community college in Harlem was opposed by Manhattan Borough President Percy Sutton, a black, who objected that to establish only a two-year college would be patronizing.[51] A later effort to establish such a college in the Bedford-Stuyvesant section of Brooklyn received a negative reception from community leaders there, with the result that the plan was ultimately modifed to project a four-year senior college for the area.[52]

That there were conflicting views about the direction the University should take was only one manifestation of a broader pattern of increasing racial tension in the city. In 1966 the creation of a Civilian Review Board to assess independently charges of police brutality was the subject of a referendum that precipitated heated debate. Many whites saw this proposed board as an encouragement to lawbreakers and thus as an interference with the police, who already had a difficult enough time preventing "crime in the streets." The controversy had undeniably racial overtones: blacks and, to a lesser extent, Puerto Ricans were seen as the criminals and whites as their victims.[53] Subsequently, there were bitter confrontations between blacks and the Jewish-dominated teachers' union over the issue of school decentralization (a decentralization policy was supported by Mayor Lindsay). The outrage of blacks over the difficulties of minority pupils was often couched in anti-Semitic terms, as the teachers were accused of responsibility for educational failure.[54] These occurrences bred a sense among middle- and working-class whites that government had abandoned them in its efforts to advance the situation of minorities.

Racial tension was exacerbated in late 1968 and early 1969 when it became clear that the city and state were planning to reduce the University's budget request for the next academic year.[55] If implemented, such cuts could have necessitated a reduction in the size of the next freshman class. Such a possibility promised to increase minority resentment that not enough was being done to broaden access to CUNY, and at the same time it would heighten Jewish concern that special admissions programs were shrinking the number of seats available to students with strong academic credentials.

> Bowker himself, with a mix of genuine concern and political instinct, warned that tensions might "explode" if budget limitations were allowed to cut the size of the freshman class. He argued that the University would be forced to either

cut regular admissions or to reduce the size of the SEEK and College Discovery programs, pointing out as he did so that hundreds of Jewish parents had urged that the minority group programs be reduced in size. Tensions were running very high at the time, and Bowker was accused by the influential American Jewish Congress of "fomenting racial and religious tension by predicting it."[56]

At this point there seemed no obvious way out of the University's dilemma: whatever might benefit one group would be perceived as a loss by the other. As events unfolded, every action of CUNY appeared as a choice between "merit" and "quotas." But if an impasse had developed at the Board of Higher Education, other parts of CUNY were generating their own action. Particularly at CCNY, a crisis was brewing that promised to push the entire University into a new trajectory.

From Impasse to Crisis: The City College Confrontation

Notwithstanding the concrete actions and stated intentions of the previous few years, blacks and Hispanics continued to be underrepresented at the University.[57] The situation was symbolized by City College. Sitting high on a hill in the middle of Harlem, CCNY's Gothic buildings had the look of a medieval fortress, insulated from the hopes and dreams of the people below. So it seemed fitting that the institution that had spawned the largest urban college system in the nation should be the cauldron from which an open-admissions policy would emerge.

The immediate stimulus for change came from within the CCNY student body. In 1968–1969 CCNY students represented a fairly wide range of political shadings, from the relatively conservative, professionally commited engineering students to various leftist groups of predominantly white membership such as Students for a Democratic Society (SDS). In addition there were a number of minority-group clubs and organizations, which for the most part operated independently of the left-oriented white groups.

The first inkling of what was coming occurred in November 1968, when the Marxist and predominantly black DuBois Club circulated a petition among the student body. Stating that nearly 55 percent of pupils in the public schools were black and Puerto Rican, compared with less than 10 percent in CUNY's senior colleges, the petition contained a list of demands, the key ones being that the racial composition of future entering classes reflect that of the high school graduating classes in the city; that the SEEK program be quadrupled by January 1969 and include students without high school diplomas; and that within the next two years, facilities be built to accommodate all students graduating from high school. About fifteen hundred students (around 10 percent of CCNY's student body) signed the petition, which was addressed to City College President Buell Gallagher.[58] He responded by letter, expressing agreement with the aims of the petitioners but noting that CUNY was already committed to greater ethnic representativeness and that expansion of programs and facilities was largely a matter of money.[59] At the time it appeared that the DuBois Club had engaged in a one-shot episode: the matter remained dormant from November through the December holiday period and final examinations in January 1969.

However, in early February a new minority organization surfaced. The Committee of Ten, representing a coalition of black and Puerto Rican students, called upon the CUNY administration to alleviate "conditions that deny the very existence of the Black and Puerto Rican community."[60] The students issued five demands and insisted that Gallagher "utilize whatever means necessary" to meet them. These demands, listed here, became the agenda for negotiations in the confrontation that was to come.

1. A separate school of black and Puerto Rican studies.
2. A separate orientation program for black and Puerto Rican freshmen.
3. A voice for students in the setting of guidelines for the SEEK program, including the hiring and firing of personnel.
4. That the racial composition of all entering classes reflect the black and Puerto Rican population of the New York City high schools.
5. That black and Puerto Rican history and the Spanish language be a requirement for all education majors.[61]

President Gallagher met with the committee, but no specific agreements were reached, and the group, apparently angered by the response, occupied a major part of the administration building for several hours in an effort to show that it could shut down the College if it so decided.[62]

Later in February a second event indicated the increasing activity of the black and Puerto Rican constituency. For the upcoming student government elections, blacks and Puerto Ricans formed a new party, called the New World Coalition (NWC).[63] Apparently in an effort to broaden its constituency to include whites, the NWC included in its platform a demand for "universal free higher education."[64] In the election, this party made a strong showing, coming in second in the overall voting.[65] But a split existed within the student body: among engineering and natural science students, the NWC did very poorly; among humanities and social science students, it came in first, indicating broad support among the latter for an expansion of access to the College.[66]

In March the University's budget crisis intruded upon events at CCNY. The fact that the University faced a budget reduction for the coming academic year highlighted a dilemma: student demands for broader access were being made at exactly the time when the prospect of enrollment cuts loomed large. As we noted earlier, Bowker initially had suggested that proposed cuts could exacerbate racial tension. In his efforts to build political pressure, he later modified his position, stating that if adequate funds were not forthcoming, there would be no freshman class in the fall. Throughout CUNY this had the effect of coalescing various student and community groups and focusing their attention upon Albany.[67] At City College a minority organization, now identified as the BPRSC (Black and Puerto Rican Student Community—an outgrowth of the Committee of Ten, which had issued the five demands), announced its willingness to join white student groups to fight the budget cuts.[68] The result was a series of massive demonstrations, the most dramatic being a rally of thirteen thousand CUNY students in Albany on March 18.[69] Delegations met with various legislators and with Governor Rockefeller, who claimed that CUNY officials had overestimated the impact of reduced state aid.[70]

The flurry of collective activity subsided as City College broke for spring vacation on April 1. Shortly after school resumed, there was news that although the state allocation would be higher than that given to CUNY in 1968, it was still about $20 million less than had been requested. Bowker reiterated his warning that there would be no freshman class,[71] and President Gallagher submitted his resignation (effective June 1970) in response to the budget cuts. In his letter of resignation he stated:

> I am now asked . . . to stand in the door and keep students out. I shall not accede. I will not do it. I will not turn my back on the poor of all races. . . .
>   My hope, however, is that my departure may serve to symbolize the public outrage which echoes from the brutal and insulting slamming of the college-entrance door.[72]

Adding to a sense of the legitimacy of student demands for broader access, twenty-three of the twenty-seven department chairs supported Gallagher by tendering their resignations "unless a budget adequate to the functioning and development of the City University is provided."[73] The BPRSC, fearing that the budget shortfall would result in "virtually no Black or Puerto Rican students in the University," called for a strike of classes in support of the five demands on April 21. The boycott was reported as 30 percent effective and about one thousand persons, including high school students, rallied on the campus. As one might expect given the earlier student election results, support for the strike was greater among social science and humanities students than among science and engineering students.[74]

In the early morning of the next day, some two hundred members of the BPRSC entered the south campus (where the social sciences and humanities were housed), evicted whomever was already on campus for an early class, chained off the gates, and posted "sentries"—sealing off half the College's territory and eight of its twenty-two buildings.[75] The demonstrators announced that the "University of Harlem" (the south campus) would remain sealed off until the administration met the five demands that had been presented by the Committee of Ten in Feburary. Meanwhile, in the science and engineering buildings of the north campus, classes continued. Reactions of white students were mixed. Radicals were supportive, while others, especially in science and engineering, were outraged at the seizure. On the following day a white group took over another building in a show of support for the BPRSC.[76] President Gallagher stated that no police would be called to the campus,[77] and he announced that representatives of the administration, faculty, and the occupants of the south campus would commence negotiations. He also ordered classes suspended on the north campus, an act that so incensed engineering students that there was talk of the school's imminent "secession" from CCNY.[78] Not only was the College closed, it was polarized.[79]

The propriety of closing the College quickly became an issue in the campaign for the upcoming mayoral primary in which Mayor Lindsay sought renomination. His power base consisted of blacks, Puerto Ricans to a smaller degree, and a good number of Manhattan-based, high-status Jews and Protestants, along with a sprinkling of affluent Catholics. Lindsay's main rival, New York City Comptroller Mario Procaccino (a CCNY alumnus), attracted working-class and lower middle-class Irish, Italians, and Jews, residing largely in the boroughs outside Manhattan.[80] The campaign had one overwhelming issue:

> Had Mayor Lindsay done too much for Negroes, and in lesser degree, Puerto Ricans? Could this charge be pinned on him, not directly, but by the fairly unsubtle messages that political candidates . . . will use: Had he favored Manhattan over Brooklyn and the Bronx, what had he done about crime in the streets, what was his role in the teachers' strike [over school decentralization], and even more directly, had his tenure in office increased racial and ethnic hostility?[81]

In short, did his policies favor poor blacks at the expense of working- and lower middle-class whites?

Responses to the CCNY confrontation were aligned with positions on this larger question. Lindsay supported the closing of the College and Gallagher's conciliatory efforts. Others saw the closing as "appeasement." On May 1 Congressman Mario Biaggi, representing a white working-class constituency, and the militant Jewish Defense League obtained show cause orders against the College for shutting down. Procaccino won a court order setting May 5 as the date for reopening the campus.[82] In the opposing camp, Congressman Adam Clayton Powell of Harlem urged the insurgents to defy the injunction.[83] But by the early afternoon of May 5, white radicals departed from the building that they had occupied in support of the BPRSC. In the evening the black and Puerto Rican students also left the buildings that they had been holding.[84]

What had been a tense but "orderly" confrontation to this point now became violent and chaotic. With the College reopened, there were incidents ranging from false fire alarms and class disruptions to fistfights, assaults, bottle and rock throwing, and mass demonstrations. While some of the clashes threw minority students against whites, there were also eruptions between conservative and radical white factions, each of which had different views about the reopening of the College and about minority demands. Over the next three days a new pattern prevailed: students would arrive for class, violence would break out, and Gallagher would close the College until the next morning. Between one and three hundred police in riot gear appeared on the campus every day in order to clear buildings. The event that drew the most attention was the burning on May 8 of the auditorium of the College's main student center.[85] In a sense this may have been the event that settled the eventual outcome: the then deputy chancellor of the University, Seymour H. Hyman (a City College alumnus), reportedly rushed to the campus after hearing reports of the fire. He was so shaken that at a meeting with Bowker and other staff that night he said, "I was telling people about what I felt when I saw that smoke coming out of that building, and the only question in my mind was, How can we save City College? And the only answer was, Hell, let everybody in."[86]

With the College seemingly in a state of siege, negotiations between Gallagher and the BPRSC were brought to a standstill. His efforts to effect an orderly conciliation now a shambles, the president asked to be relieved of his duties immediately. His letter of resignation reflected his sympathy with the demonstrators and his anger at "the intrusion of politically motivated outside forces [which made it] impossible to carry on the processes of reason and persuasion."[87]

On May 12, Joseph Copeland, a CCNY faculty member who had been a member of Gallagher's negotiating team, was designated acting president by the BHE. The BPRSC agreed to meet with a new negotiating team if police were removed from the campus. Copeland assented. On May 23, the City College Faculty Senate received for approval a document representing the results of the negotiating sessions. It proposed what was, in effect, an ethnically based "dual admissions" plan: 50 percent of CCNY's entering class, beginning in fall 1970, would be drawn from poverty areas or designated ghetto high schools. The other 50 percent were to be admitted under traditional competitive criteria (high school grades and Scholastic Aptitude Test scores).[88]

Even before the Faculty Senate had the chance to discuss the agreement, public reaction was scathing. All major mayoral candidates vehemently attacked the dual admissions proposal. Procaccino threatened to initiate legal action to prevent implementation of the plan, claiming that it was "unfair and discriminatory" and would exclude "intelligent, qualified and ambitious students" from CUNY.[89] Bronx Borough President Herman Badillo, a Puerto Rican, claimed that the proposal "would merely constitute an extension of the educational disaster of New York City public schools into the system of higher education, with no benefits to the children involved, whether they be white, black or Puerto Rican."[90] Mayor Lindsay, initially noncommittal, later asserted that "if this is a quota system, I am against it."[91] The next day he came out in clear opposition to the agreement, which he expressed in a letter to the chairman of the BHE: "We supply substantial amounts of money to the Board and, therefore, we have a real voice in the use of these monies."[92]

On June 2, the Faculty Senate voted to reject the dual admissions plan. It recommended instead the admission of a few hundred additional students from "disadvantaged areas" during the next two semesters. These students were not to take the place of any students who would have qualified for admission under the competitive criteria.[93] But the senate, in transmitting its recommendation to the BHE, also noted:

> A large disadvantaged segment of the City population, for social, economic and educational reasons, has been unable to receive these benefits (of higher education). The most equitable way to attain this stated goal is by a system of "open enrollment" financially supported by the City, State, and Federal Governments.[94]

In June, Bowker and the BHE again took center stage. Their task was to make a final policy decision on the admissions question. During the month the board held a number of public sessions designed to elicit opinions from student, faculty, and community groups. Some favored the maintenance of traditional admissions criteria or at least opposed both the dual admissions plan and the Faculty Senate compromise proposal. This camp included the CCNY Alumni Association, the School of Engineering at City College, the Jewish Defense League, and the CCNY Student Senate. CCNY faculty and the CUNY-wide faculty union supported the CCNY Faculty Senate recommendation, arguing that only this middle ground between the status quo and the dual admissions formula was "socially meaningful and academically responsible." Support for the dual admissions plan came from the BPRSC, other CCNY faculty, and the National Lawyers Guild. The guild argued that the dual admissions system was not a quota system and that institutions have the responsibility to correct situations of inequality and discrimination.[95]

These positions were simply reiterations of prior alternatives, each of which already had generated the unalterable opposition of one group or another. But as June wore on, resolution of the crisis began to crystallize. Particularly influential in this process was the powerful New York City Central Labor Council and its head, Harry Van Arsdale. None of the proposals under discussion at the time appeared to offer anything to a large segment of the New York population: the non-Jewish, white ethnic working classes, largely Irish and Italian Catholics. Many of these people belonged to the trade unions represented by Van Arsdale. Even though it was true (as noted earlier) that by the late 1960s Catholics comprised a third or more of the entering classes at some of CUNY's senior colleges, stereotypes dominated perceptions of who attended the University. A common view, apparently shared by the Labor Council, was that the proportion of Catholics in the student body was trivial at most and that

> the youngsters of this group would have neither the grade point average to compete with the students (predominantly, Jews) taking the conventional admissions route, nor the poverty status or residence to qualify for the "special" admissions procedures.[96]

Though this view was an exaggeration, its consequences were real: Central Labor Council representatives argued that the only proper plan was one that would guarantee admissions to all.[97] The other plans suffered from fatal flaws. Only the open-admissions notion offered something to everyone and seemed to lay to rest the specter that increased representation of some groups would come at the expense of other groups. Both within and outside the University, a consensus began to form around the idea of letting everyone in. Support came from organizations such as the United Federation of College Teachers, the City College Alumni Association, the CUNY University Senate, and the prestigious Public Education Association.[98] By the end of June, Bowker and his staff had decided that an open-admissions program was the solution to the impasse over the expansion of access to the University and that the long-range goal of 100 percent admissions targeted for 1975 should be moved up to fall 1970. This decision was ratified by the BHE in its historic resolution of July 9, 1969. The proposed open-admissions plan contained the following provisions:

> It shall offer admission to some University program to all high school graduates of the City.
> It shall provide for remedial and other supportive services for all students requiring them.
> It shall maintain and enhance the standards of academic excellence of the colleges of the University.
> It shall result in the ethnic integration of the colleges.
> It shall provide for mobility for students between various programs and units of the University.
> It shall assure that all students who would have been admitted to specific community or senior colleges under the admissions criteria which we have used in the past shall still be so admitted. In increasing educational opportunity for all, attention shall also be paid to retaining the opportunities for students now eligible under present Board policies and practices.[99]

In offering places spread throughout the University to all applicants, the board went far beyond the demands of the minority students who had been demanding an increase in minority representation at City College. Thus, the resolution provided not only a way out of the conflict over admissions but also a mechanism for a huge expansion of the University. Perhaps the outcome was not so surprising. Bowker, after all, had been pushing for broader access to CUNY almost from his first day as chancellor. In this light, neither he nor the board had their backs pressed to the wall by the City College crisis. Indeed, that crisis provided just the opportunity that was needed to create what Bowker had favored for a long time.

Curiously, given CUNY's recent budget difficulties with the city and state, neither the mayor nor the governor was consulted about funding possibilities until *after* the July 9 resolution.[100] Undoubtedly, Bowker did not want to give them a chance to bargain and thus deflect the University from the course to which it was now firmly committed.[101] In using this strategy, he seemed on firm ground. No major group in the city opposed the principle of open admissions and Lindsay was running for reelection. Although within his administration there was concern about the fiscal implications—it was feared that after three or four years of large entering classes, the financial commitment might become staggering—key Lindsay staff people urged support of open admissions as an important social priority, and the mayor, both by inclination and in terms of his need for strong support from the minority community in his campaign, came down on the side of the new program. Governor Rockefeller, however, was initially opposed. He felt that the program had been hastily conceived, and since he had wanted to see tuition charged at CUNY (as it was then at SUNY, the state university system), he resented being asked to support a policy of open admissions without receiving in turn an agreement for CUNY tuition.[102] But Rockefeller faced reelection the following year, and as all major groups in the city were behind the plan, he did not want to stand out as the only major political figure against it.

The board's resolution left a major item unresolved: the criteria for allocating students to the various CUNY colleges. In the BHE's 1968 master plan the allocation scheme for its 100 percent admissions program was a highly stratified one that would have directed the great majority of newly eligible students to either a community college or an educational skills center. But given the stormy events of the preceding months, this plan would clearly not be acceptable. The board had earlier established a University Commission on Admissions, which now received the task of developing a set of criteria. This effort was to bring new conflict.

The commission consisted of CUNY faculty, students, and administrators, along with outside civic and alumni groups. Broadly speaking, the body represented three social clusters: minority-group members whose first concern was to increase the representation of minority students in the University; whites who generally supported the objectives of the minority members over other objectives; and other whites who agreed that ethnic representativeness was an important principle but who were equally, if not more, concerned with protecting the traditional concept of merit in the admissions process (in general this position was held by those groups—largely Jewish—

that had been the prime beneficiaries of the earlier highly competitive admissions system).

The commission was largely in agreement that a new admissions policy should not only provide for an expansion of access to the senior colleges but also result in their ethnic integration. Integration was defined as a proportion of minority students in the senior-college freshman class equal to that in the community-college freshman class—the commission was concerned that community colleges not become educational ghettoes. However, given the diversity of this body, it was unable to achieve consensus on senior-college admissions criteria. Instead, the commission presented three plans for the board's consideration.[103] The first would have admitted the major part of the freshman class on the basis of rank in the student's high school. As in the Top 100 Scholars program, the use of rank as an admissions criterion promised to increase minority representation because students in ghetto high schools tended to have lower averages than did students of equivalent rank in academically strong (and mostly white) high schools. The remainder of the seats would be reserved for students entering under the SEEK program, with the number to be determined in accordance with the principle of ethnic balance. The second proposal was to admit 60 percent of the freshmen on the basis of high school rank and about 15 percent under the SEEK program. The remaining 25 percent were to be admitted strictly on the basis of student preference with the proviso that if the number of preferences for a given college exceeded the number of seats available, then those places would be assigned by lottery. This provision sought to increase the chances for admission to a senior college of students from the lower ranks of their graduating classes. The third plan was the only one that attempted to preserve high school average as a factor in the admissions process. It would have reserved places to insure that students previously admitted (under the criteria in force in 1968) would still be so admitted; it also provided for enough seats in the SEEK program to achieve ethnic balance; finally, it proposed that the *major* portion of the freshman class be admitted on the basis of high school rank, a provision that in practice might have been impossible to implement if all students admitted under the old standards were still to be accepted.

While all three plans used high school rank and the SEEK program as means for increasing the minority presence in the senior colleges, they differed in emphasis. The third plan went furthest toward preserving the traditional admissions criteria (especially high school average) and attracted support from whites, especially Jews. Minority members of the commission strongly favored the second plan since they believed its lottery component would do most to increase minority representation in the four-year schools, thus minimizing "tracking" into the community colleges.[104]

When the commission's report was presented to the BHE on October 7, it elicited mainly negative public reaction. The objection was that none of the three proposals sufficiently took the concept of academic merit into account. For example, under any of the three, a student ranking in the fortieth percentile of the class at one of the city's academically elite high schools might have a worse chance of admission to his or her first-choice college than would a student ranking in the twentieth percentile at a ghetto high school, although the first student was likely to be academically stronger than the second. On this ground, the *New York Times*, the major Jewish organizations, and the mayoral candidates, including John Lindsay (who at this late stage of the campaign could ill afford to support a policy that appeared to favor nonwhites at the expense of whites), attacked the report.[105] This objection was echoed by a host of individuals and groups at two large public hearings held by the board in October and November.[106] So, several months after the CCNY confrontation, the ethnic cleavage over the admissions question still remained—the values of merit and equality of opportunity appeared irreconcilable.

This conflict underscored for Bowker and his staff the need to achieve a compromise that simultaneously recognized the twin criteria of high school rank and high school average. They formulated a plan that appeared responsive to the concerns of the conflicting factions. Simply put, the plan guaranteed students who graduated from high school with at least an 80 average (in academic, college preparatory courses) *or* who ranked in the top 50 percent of their high school graduating class a place in a senior college, if that was their preference; all others could enroll in a community college.[107] In short, the twin criteria of rank and average generated two pools of students. The primary function of high school rank was to ease entry to the senior-college pool. Once these two pools were established, the admissions plan was designed to work in the following way: if there were more students who picked a certain college than there were places available at that school, the available seats would go to those with the higher averages. This use of average was designed to preserve the key criterion of the old admissions scheme. Students who were not admitted to their first-choice college as a result of this competition would then be put in a pool for their second-choice school and the competitive process would begin again if the demand for places exceeded the supply.[108] Thus, the new criteria broadened eligibility for senior colleges, but they did not guarantee admission to the first-choice college.

In addition, the board authorized an expansion of the SEEK program so as to increase further the minority presence in senior colleges. Both facets, the admissions model and the SEEK expansion, represented an attempt to accommodate the traditionalist and egalitarian constituencies.

The attempt was successful. Support for the plan was widespread, and it was ratified by the board in November, just after Lindsay's reelection. His approval was forthcoming, as was Rockefeller's somewhat later.[109] A BHE task force appointed earlier was working to coordinate the implementation of open admissions.[110] Each college submitted a plan outlining its concept of open admissions, and such plans were modified in a complex and difficult process of negotiation with the task force.[111]

Open Admissions and Mass Higher Education

In September 1970 a freshman class of almost thirty-five thousand students took their places at CUNY—a 75 percent increase over the previous year's entering class. This new era of open admissions was accompanied by a glare of media publicity, both national and local. That the CUNY policy received such wide national attention may seem curious since open access higher education is hardly new in the United States. Indeed, its roots go back to the middle of the nineteenth century, when the land-grant colleges were established under the first Morrill Act of 1862. These colleges, found particularly in the Midwest, offered admission to all high school graduates. More recently, the California public higher education system had attracted much notice over its so-called differential access version of open admissions. In part, the attention given to CUNY derived from the fact that the events leading to open admissions reflected so clearly the political and racial conflict that reverberated throughout American society for most of the 1960s. Also striking was the abruptness of the change: no major university system had ever moved, almost overnight, from a rigorously selective admissions standard to a policy of guaranteed admission for all high school graduates.

The CUNY plan had additional unique features. One of these was the actual admissions criteria. In 1970 CUNY consisted of eight four-year senior colleges and seven two-year community colleges (by the following year another four-year and another two-year college had begun). In guaranteeing senior-college entry to students having an 80 high school average or ranking in the top half of their graduating class, the CUNY plan was, on the face of it, less stratified than the widely known three-tier California model —in which the university level accepts only the top 12.5 percent of high school graduates, the state colleges accept the top third, and the two-year (junior) colleges accept all others.[112] The CUNY system formally distinguished only two- and four-year colleges, thus constituting a two-tier system. The use of either high school average or rank to admit a student to the upper CUNY tier was designed to generate a less rigid sorting of students between senior and community colleges than the California system allowed. And as we know, it was especially intended to increase minority enrollment in senior colleges.

The goal of increased opportunity was apparent in a second major feature of the policy: mobility between two-and four-year colleges. A place in one of the senior colleges was guaranteed for any graduate of a community college. At least on paper, then, the community colleges were not dead-end institutions whose primary function was to provide terminal vocational education.

There was a third unique aspect to the CUNY plan. Other open enrollment systems were characterized by early and high dropout rates. Jencks and Riesman[113] have pointed out that in colleges with unselective admissions criteria, the faculty tends to be hostile toward freshmen, viewing them as inept until shown otherwise. The result is an exodus of the "misfits" by the end of the first year. In contrast, CUNY aimed to stop or at least to slow the revolving door. As the board put it in its resolution of July 1969, "We do not want to provide the illusion of an open door to higher education which in reality is only a revolving door, admitting everyone but leading to a high proportion of student failure after one semester."[114] The primary means for achieving this aim was the development of large programs of remediation, supportive counseling, and related services. In addition, the University decided that no student should be dismissed for academic reasons during the grace period of the freshman year. Other open access programs have defined their obligation as the creation of access, but the responsibility for academic success belongs to the students: those who drop out bring no discredit to the institution. At CUNY the failure of the student was to a significant degree to be considered also as a failure of the institution.

Thus, the CUNY program was alone in its attempt to provide equality of educational opportunity encompassing not only access but also outcome. Adding to its uniqueness was the political context in which it arose. While open enrollment programs at other universities were begun basically on the initiative of a policymaking establishment, the CUNY plan had, as an essential catalyst, the initiative of those minority constituencies who were its intended beneficiaries. The University's original open enrollment plan, with its 1975 starting date, provided for 100 percent access—but primarily into the community colleges and educational skills centers. The City College confrontation succeeded in changing both the timing and the conception of open admissions. Yet it did so in part because the leaders of the University saw the confrontation not only as a crisis but also as an opportunity for major educational change. How that change affected access for various groups and how they fared after entry forms the substance of this book.

Notes

1. In the late 1820s the Workingmen's party supported universal education as a way of protecting workers from a hardening of class lines, which it thought would result from industrialization. See Diane Ravitch, *The Great School Wars: New York City, 1805–1973* (New York: Basic Books, 1974), p. 23; see also S. Willis Rudy, *The College of the City of New York: A History, 1847–1947* (New York: City College Press, 1949), chap. 1.

2. At that time in New York City there were two private colleges, each with its own grammar (secondary) school, Columbia College and the University of the City of New York (later New York University); see Rudy, pp. 6–8.

3. Mario E.Cosenza, *The Establishment of the College of the City of New York as the Free Academy in 1847* (New York: Associated Alumni of the College of the City of New York, 1925). Rudy, pp. 3–4, noted that the College of Charleston was chartered in 1785 as a private institution and became a municipal college in 1837, charging a substantial tuition fee. The city of Louisville also chartered a municipal institution in 1846, but it was not until 1907 that a "college department" was created—before then the school was a medical institute.

4. Rudy, p. 29.

5. Rudy, p. 31.

6. Rudy, p. 29.

7. Rudy, p. 68.

8. Rudy, p. 68–69.

9. Rudy, pp.124–126, 173–174.

10. In 1882, out of 807 "tickets" issued for admission to the College, only twenty-three went to private school students; see Rudy, p. 126..

11. The city's major Catholic college, Fordham, was established in 1841, even before the Free Academy. Manhattan College was established in 1853, St. John's in 1870, and St. Francis in 1882. See *Barron's Profiles of American Colleges*, (Woodbury: Barron's 10th ed. 1976).

12. Sherry Gorelick, "Social Control, Social Mobility, and the Eastern European Jews: An Analysis of Public Education in New York City, 1880–1924" (Ph.D. diss., Columbia University, 1975), p. 67.

13. Gorelick, p. 67.

14. See Nathan Glazer and Daniel P. Moynihan, *Beyond the Melting Pot*, 2nd ed. (Cambridge: M.I.T. Press, 1970), pp. 138–139; also Maldwyn Allen Jones, *American Immigration* (Chicago: University of Chicago Press, 1960).

15. Rudy, pp. 292–293.

16. That some Irish and Italians were present is clear from an examination of college yearbooks during the early years of the twentieth century. They show the presence of a Newman Club whose members almost all had Irish names and an Italian club called Il Circolo Dante Alighieri, whose membership consisted almost entirely of Italians.

17. This increase can be gauged from the changes in the numbers in succeeding classes. There were 77 members of the class of 1890, 98 members of the class of 1895, and 263 members of the class of 1900, as indicated in Donald A. Roberts (ed.), *CCNY Alumni Register, 1853–1931* (New York: Associated Alumni of the City College of New York, 1932), p. 328.

18. In 1900 only two medical schools, Johns Hopkins and Harvard, required any college training before entry, and only Harvard and Columbia required college preparation for law school. See Frederick Rudolph, *Curriculum: A History of the American Undergraduate Course of Study since 1636* (San Francisco: Jossey-Bass, 1977), pp. 178–179. In the development of the link between undergraduate and professional studies, a major role was played by Nicholas Murray Butler of Columbia. See Harold S. Wechsler, *The Qualified Student* (New York: Wiley, 1977), chap. 4.

19. While there were no high schools in the city in the 1890s, there were nineteen by 1911. Among a sample who entered high school in 1906, it has been estimated that about 12 percent graduated. Only about 2 percent of high school entrants enrolled in college. See Gorelick, pp. 98, 101–103.

20. Women's City Club of New York, *The Privileged Many: A Study of the City University's Open Admissions Policy, 1970–1975* (New York: Women's City Club, 1975), p. 14.

21. These expansions were described in some detail in Rudy, pp. 382–389.

22. Wechsler, p. 262. At the same time, aptitude test scores were introduced as admissions criteria. Students whose high school averages were below the cutoff point could be admitted if their test scores were high enough.

23. Donald P. Cottrell, Adrian Rondileau, and Leo S. Schumer, *Public Higher Education in the City of New York: Report of the Master Plan Study* (New York: Board of Higher Education, 1950).

24. Thomas C. Holy, *A Long Range Plan for the City University of New York, 1961–1975* (New York: Board of Higher Education, 1962).

25. Holy, table 10, p. 91. The Holy report shows that expansion of the municipal colleges occurred entirely in two-year programs. In 1952 new admissions to B.A. programs were 67 percent of all new admissions. By 1961 they were only 39 percent of new admissions.

26. Community-college students had to have taken the same high school courses required for admission to a senior college if they were to qualify for transfer programs. By the early 1960s acceptance in these transfer programs required a high school average in the upper seventies. For an excellent analysis of the postwar history of CUNY see Sheila C. Gordon, *"The Transformation of the City University of New York, 1945–1970"* (Ph.D. diss., Columbia University, 1975).

27. Holy, pp. 73, 127–128, 68–69.

28. In the early 1940s, Jewish enrollment in the four municipal colleges was estimated at 80 percent. New York (State) Joint Legislative Committee on the State Education System, *Report of the New York City Sub-committee Concerning Administration and Financing of the Public Education System of the City of New York* (Albany, 1944).

29. Glazer and Moynihan, p. 199; see also Richard Gambino, *Blood of my Blood: The Dilemma of the Italian Americans* (New York: Doubleday, 1974); Leonard Covello, *The Social Background of the Italo-American School Child* (Leiden: Brill, 1967).

30. A rather recent study of assimilation among Catholic ethnic groups is Richard D. Alba, "Social Assimilation among American Catholic National-Origin Groups," *American Sociological Review* 41 (December 1976):1030–1046. See also Rudolph Vecoli, "The Coming of Age of the Italian Americans, 1945–1974," *Ethnicity* 5 (May 1978):119–147. A detailed study of the education of Catholics is found in Andrew M. Greeley and Peter Rossi, *The Education of Catholic Americans* (Chicago: Aldine, 1966). Further information is given in Andrew M. Greeley, *The American Catholic* (New York: Basic Books, 1977).

31. Glazer and Moynihan, p. 202.

32. In the class of 1930 at City College, less than 3 percent of graduates had Italian surnames (calculated from Roberts). By 1960 this had doubled to 6 percent,

still below their representation in the city's population (Glazer and Moyni-han). The substantial increase in the mid to late 1960s was documented in Jack E. Rossman, Helen S. Astin, Alexander W. Astin, and Elaine H. El-Khawas, *Open Admissions at City University of New York: An Analysis of the First Year* (Englewood Cliffs: Prentice-Hall, 1975), tables 3.4–3.6, pp. 35–37.

33. The estimate of the constancy of the population and of the numbers of blacks and Puerto Ricans were made from figures provided by Glazer and Moynihan, pp. 25–29, 91–94, and table 3.

34. Gordon, pp. 161–162.

35. In New York City high schools at that time, several different types of diplo-mas were given. Vocational and technical diplomas were given to those who attended specialized vocational high schools. In academic high schools weaker students frequently received general diplomas. Only the college preparatory diploma qualified students for baccalaureate programs in the four-year col-leges and for liberal arts transfer programs in the community colleges. See Board of Higher Education, *Master Plan for the City University of New York, 1968* (New York: City University of New York, 1968), chap. 2.

36. Bowker's inclinations were not a source of enthusiasm for the largely conser-vative BHE. His definition of the role of chancellor, his position about the breadth of the population CUNY should serve, and his view that expansion would require a much broader involvement of New York State in the Universi-ty's fiscal support brought him into protracted and at times bitter conflict with the board, particularly its chairman, Gustave Rosenberg. In this conflict Bow-ker triumphed—almost totally—with regard to the definitions of his role and the University's goals. Details of these complex and fascinating events are available in Gordon, pp.178–193, and in Wechsler, pp. 268–274.

37. Wechsler, p. 275.

38. Gordon, p. 207.

39. This was noted in a staff paper put out by the chancellor's office in 1965. As Gordon, p. 184, noted: "It outlined the history of CUNY financing, from what had essentially been 100 percent financing from City tax revenues in 1946 to a 50-50 (City-State) financing arrangement for 1965–66. The paper noted bleakly the 'continuous pressure for funds to cover welfare, health, and ele-mentary and secondary education, coupled with the City's very limited tax base,' which made it 'difficult to be optimistic about the City's continued abil-ity to finance the growth of higher education.' Under these circumstances, CUNY would have to rely more heavily upon State financing if . . . anticipated future enrollments [were to be] accommodated."

40. These efforts threw the University into a crisis. The prospect of increased state funding implied greater state influence on CUNY policy, an influence that alarmed a large part of CUNY's constituency (including most of its board) not only because many opposed any diminution of local control but also because it threatened the continuation of the free tuition policy. Under Governor Rocke-feller's leadership, the state was heavily involved in building a major state uni-versity system, which charged tuition, and his administration was demanding the end of free tuition at CUNY in return for increased state aid. For his part, Bowker appeared willing to pay the price when he said of free tuition: "It is time that the young men and women of New York City cease being short-

changed of their proper share of State and Federal financing by a sentimental and nostalgic continuance of an outworn procedure" (Gordon, p. 186). In an effort to outflank the traditionalist CUNY board, which venerated free tuition, Bowker made this statement publicly, perhaps hoping that it would find support in the minority community, some of whose representatives felt that free tuition was being used to maintain high admissions standards, thus excluding minority students. Ultimately Bowker moved away from this position, and the legislation providing more state funding was passed, with the minority admissions component tacked on as an accommodation to minority members of the legislature. This theme of the racial consequences of the free tuition policy was to be a major ingredient of the bitter conflict accompanying the 1975–1976 fiscal crisis (discussed in chapter 11).

41. Wechsler, p. 274.
42. Board of Higher Education, *Second Interim Revision, 1964 Master Plan* (New York: City University of New York, 1966), chap. 6; *1968 Master Plan*, chap. 2.
43. *1968 Master Plan*, pp. 8–14.
44. *1968 Master Plan*, p. vii.
45. Gordon, p. 208.
46. Wechsler, p. 278.
47. Gordon, pp. 208–209.
48. The rationale and implementation of this plan were described in *1969 First Revision, Master Plan for the City University of New York, 1968* (New York: City University of New York, 1969), pp. 1–5.
49. Board of Higher Education, "Minutes of Meeting," August 1, 1968, p. 182.
50. The Jewish experience with exclusionary quotas was described in Stephen Steinberg, *The Academic Melting Pot* (New York: McGraw-Hill, 1972), chap. 1. For a detailed study of the efforts of Columbia University to exclude Jews see Wechsler, especially chap. 7.
51. Gordon, p. 210.
52. Gordon, pp. 211–212.
53. The opposition of white groups to the Civilian Review Board was described in Glazer and Moynihan, pp. vii–xcv.
54. The significance of the confrontation was noted in Glazer and Moynihan; for a detailed description see Ravitch.
55. The planned budget cuts were noted in Wechsler, p. 280.
56. Gordon, p. 214.
57. As Wechsler, p. 278, noted, in the late 1960s nonwhite students still did not gain admission to CUNY in proportion to their representation in the city's high school graduating classes. Moreover, "if it had not been for the SEEK Program, the percentage of nonwhite enrollment in the senior colleges would have declined from 6.1% to 4.7% between 1967 and 1968, and the total nonwhite enrollment at CUNY would have declined from 8.9% to 8.0%."
58. W. E. B. DuBois Club of City College, "End Racism at CCNY," *The Campus*, November 14, 1968.
59. Buell G. Gallagher, "Reply to Petition," CCNY Presidential Files, 4.41.8 (November 26, 1968).
60. "Blacks and Puerto Ricans Demand That BGG End Racism at College," *Observation Post,* February 7, 1969.

61. "Blacks and Puerto Ricans Demand."
62. Jonathan Penzer, "BPR Seize Building after Seeing BGG," *Observation Post*, February 14, 1969.
63. Jonathan Penzer, "Third World Students Awakening," *Observation Post*, February 7, 1969.
64. Marc Beallor, "Anti-racist Slate at CCNY," *Daily World*, February 7, 1969.
65. Howard Reis, "Albert Vasquez Defeats Henry Arce," *Observation Post*, March 7, 1969.
66. The engineering and natural science departments were physically clustered in the north section of the campus, while humanities and social sciences clustered in the south. Because balloting took place on both campuses, voting results could be separately tabulated.
67. Gordon, p. 215.
68. BPRSC press release, March 6, 1969.
69. John Kifner, "13,000 Students Fight City U. Cuts," *New York Times*, March 19, 1969.
70. "A Letter from the Governor to the Students of New York City" (Albany: Office of the Governor, March 18, 1969); see also Kifner.
71. Gordon, p. 215.
72. Buell G. Gallagher, letter to Porter Chandler, chairman, and members of the Board of Higher Education, March 31, 1969.
73. *Observation Post*, April 18, 1969.
74. *The Campus*, April 22, 1969.
75. Tom Ackerman, "The South Campus Seizure," *Alumnus Magazine* (no. 1): p. 16.
76. Ackerman, pp. 13–15.
77. Gallagher's decision not to call in police was determined in part by an incident that had occurred earlier in the academic year. In November, radical left white groups had provided sanctuary for an AWOL soldier protesting the war. After a week, without consulting students or faculty, the president called in the police, which resulted in the midnight arrest of 171 students. Many faculty and students were incensed by the incident, and their reactions undoubtedly had a constraining effect when the south campus seizure occurred.
78. Ackerman, p. 16; see also Faculty of the School of Engineering, "Resolution and Advisory Deploring the Closing of Entire College," April 29, 1969.
79. The faculty voted to support the closing after lengthy debate had revealed a sharp split between tenured and nontenured faculty. The former wanted the college reopened, while the latter supported the closing. In an informal vote at an earlier point in the debate, tenured faculty voted 136–121 to reopen; the nontenured group supported the closing by the wide margin of 105–43. By day's end, with the gathering much depleted, the final vote ran overwhelmingly in support of Gallagher's action. See *New York Times*, April 28, 1969, and Ackerman, p. 17. About six days after the seizure, Bowker won a commitment from Lindsay for additional funding, and he withdrew his threat of "no freshman class" the following fall. But by this time the confrontation had acquired its own momentum.
80. These political alliances are described in Glazer and Moynihan, pp. xxvi–xxvii.
81. Glazer and Moynihan, pp. xxviii–xxix.

82. Karen DeWitt and William Greaves, "Court Orders CCNY Reopened," *New York Post*, May 2, 1969.
83. Gordon, p. 217
84. Ackerman, p. 21; also *New York Times*, May 5, 1969.
85. *New York Times*, May 8, 1969.
86. Martin Mayer, "Higher Education for All?: The Case of Open Admissions," *Commentary* (February 1973): 40.
87. *New York Times*, May 10, 1969.
88. Board of Higher Education, *"Minutes of Meeting,"* June 30, 1969, attachment F. Also *New York Times*, May 23 and 24, 1969.
89. Joseph McNamara, "Proc Blasts CCNY Pact, Will Fight It in the Courts," *New York Daily News*, May 26, 1969; Sylvan Fox, "Candidates Score Dual Admissions for City College," *New York Times*, May 26, 1969.
90. McNamara; Fox.
91. McNamara; Fox; Arthur Greenspan, "CCNY's in the Campaign Now," *New York Post*, May 26, 1969.
92. Murray Schumach, "Lindsay Attacks Dual Admissions for City College," *New York Times*, May 28, 1969; Stephen Elliot and Joseph McNamara, "Lindsay Raps CCNY Plan, Notes City Pays the Bills," *Daily News*, May 28, 1969.
93. Sylvan Fox, "Faculty Rejects CCNY Dual Plan," *New York Times*, May 30, 1969, and "400 from Slums Urged for CCNY," *New York Times*, June 2, 1969.
94. Faculty Senate, "Text of the Negotiated Agreement on Admissions Policy as Revised by the City College Faculty Senate," June 1969, point 1, p. 1.
95. The major positions and their supporters were recorded in scratch notes of the BHE sessions by staff members of the BHE for the sessions of June 10, 16, and 18, 1969.
96. Gordon, p. 220.
97. Scratch notes for the Board of Higher Education executive session, June 16, 1969. The misperception of the Catholic presence in CUNY arose in part because the data (collected by Alexander W. Astin in annual surveys under the auspices of the American Council on Education) were not available to the public. For that matter, most within the University were probably unaware of them. However, it was undoubtedly true that many whites, Jews as well as Catholics, did not meet the traditional admissions standards and thus would have benefited from a policy of open enrollment. The extent to which different groups actually benefited is shown in chapter 4.
98. Scratch notes; Gordon, pp. 223–224.
99. Board of Higher Education, *"Statement of Policy,"* July 9, 1969, item 4.
100. Gordon, p. 227.
101. Gordon, p. 227.
102. Gordon, p. 229.
103. University Commission on Admissions, *"Report and Recommendations to the Board of Higher Education,"* October 7, 1969.
104. Without question the minority members of the commission were very disturbed about the possible overrepresentation of minority students in community colleges, which they considered inferior. To those who attacked the lot-

tery principle, they responded: "Less than fifty percent of Black and Puerto Rican students who enter high school graduate; the majority of the survivors fall in the bottom halves of their classes, with large numbers graduating with averages below seventy (70). What, one must ask, will be their earning capacities and ability to provide for their families twenty years hence, in competition with their white contemporaries who will have gone to the senior colleges and graduate schools? What will be their relative earning capacities even if they finish two-year career programs in community colleges and go on to become X-Ray technicians and low-level managers in factories? In short, we see unending societal clash unless this vicious educational cycle is smashed. We propose to do this . . . by giving *all* high school graduates a fair and equal chance to achieve a B.A. degree" (University Commission on Admissions, p. 62).

105. Gordon, pp. 235–236.
106. Board of Higher Education, "Summary of Public Hearings before the Board of Higher Education on the Report of the Commission on Admissions," October 22, 1969; November 5, 1969.
107. Board of Higher Education, "Statement of Admissions Policy Adopted by the BHE November 10, 1969.
108. On their applications, students were asked to list six CUNY colleges in order of preference. Some students whose first choice was a senior college nevertheless were allocated to a community college. This would happen if the student's high school average was not high enough to place him or her in that senior college and the student had listed a community college as the second choice.
109. City of New York, Office of the Mayor, "Letter to the Governor of the State of New York," December 1, 1969; Executive Chamber, Statement by Governor Nelson A. Rockefeller, December 2, 1969.
110. This task force was created on September 23, 1969.
111. The task force issued a progress report in December; Board of Higher Education, "Progress Report, 9/25–12/5/69."
112. A more detailed description of the California system was presented by Abraham Jaffe and Walter Adams, "Two Models of Open Enrollment," in *Universal Higher Education: Costs and Benefits* (Washington: American Council on Education, 1971); see also David Rosen, Seth Brunner, and Steve Fowler, *Open Admissions: The Promise and the Lie of Open Access to American Higher Education* (Lincoln: University of Nebraska Press, 1973).
113. Christopher Jencks and David Riesman, *The Academic Revolution* (New York: Doubleday, 1968), p. 280.
114. Board of Higher Education, "Statement of Policy," July 9, 1969.

2. Open Access: Issues and Perspectives

DESPITE THE INTENSITY of the controversies from which it arose, open admissions at the City University can be seen as an extension of developments that began earlier in the century. In the United States and other industrial nations, the twentieth century has been marked by dramatic increases in levels of education and in access to higher education. In 1900, for example, only 6 percent of young Americans had graduated from high school; by 1969, the year before open admissions began, over 75 percent had.[1] Increases in the proportions entering college have also been striking. Accurate estimates of the numbers of students in given age groups entering college around the turn of the century are hard to come by,[2] but clearly only a small proportion could have entered since so few graduated from high school. Nevertheless, by the mid 1960s, over one-third of eighteen and nineteen year olds were enrolled in college.[3] The entry of their children into college had become a sign for many families of their entry into America's middle class.

The role of education in a society like that of the United States has long been a subject for study by social scientists, and a review of their thinking will help us to unravel the meaning of the open-admissions experiment. In particular, there are two fundamental perspectives on the role of education in a society like our own. Although there is not an exact opposition between them, each highlights distinct aspects of educational systems and their relation to the societies of which they are a part.[4] Furthermore, they inspire conflicting views of open admissions. One implies that the extension of educational opportunity to greatly disadvantaged groups will erode social inequalities, while the other suggests that these inequalities will carry over into

28

open admissions and be preserved even in the face of such a change. A comparison of these two perspectives forms a natural backdrop to the empirical analyses that appear in subsequent chapters and gives interpretive depth to the specific findings that occupy the foreground of our portrayal.

Education and the Thesis of Industrialism[5]

One important view of the increasing levels of education in the United States and other industrial societies sees those increases as but one part, albeit a key one, of larger social trends. The driving force is held to be industrialization, which vastly reshapes the social structure and makes the positions of men and women in the labor market, i.e., their occupations, a central element in their social beings. Essential to an industrial society is a shift in the criteria for the allocation of individuals to occupational roles—away from particularism, which is keyed to aspects of birth such as kinship and ethnicity, and toward universalism, keyed to meritocratic standards that in principle can be satisfied by anyone regardless of social origin.[6] Education is a major mechanism by which this shift is accomplished. For a growing proportion of the population, education provides access to the technical and social skills needed for participation in a complexly organized work force and certifies the successful acquisition of such skills. At the same time, education helps to assimilate culturally marginal groups, whether based on social class, ethnicity, or region, to the majority culture and thereby to erode fundamental social cleavages.

This thesis of industrialism, which sees education as playing a similar role in all industrial societies, emphasizes education's importance in loosening the linkage between the status of the family into which an individual is born and his or her own adult status. With obvious implications for open admissions, the thesis thereby emphasizes the independent effects of education on the status of the individual—independent, that is, of his or her social origin—and its potency for social mobility. These emphases can be seen clearly in an important formalization of the industrialism thesis into a number of hypotheses.[7] For example:

1. The more industrialized a society, the smaller the direct influence of father's occupational status on son's occupational status.
2. The more industrialized a society, the greater the direct influence of educational attainment on occupational attainment.[8]

Some of the most important studies of social stratification in American society tend to support these hypotheses. In the most authoritative such work to date, *The American Occupational Structure*, Blau and Duncan[9] have developed a model of the process of status attainment. Analyzing the occupations of American men in terms of their educational accomplishments and their social origins, indexed by the occupational and educational levels of their fathers, Blau and Duncan find that education explains a considerable part of the occupational variation among men and that the impact of social origins among men with equal educational attainment is comparatively small. These findings do not imply that social origins are unrelated to occupational position; to the contrary, they are and importantly so. But in the main the correlation between social origin and occupational position rests on the influence of social origin on educational attainment. The latter is the more direct cause of occupational standing, implying that an individual who achieves a certain level of education is likely to achieve a specific level of occupational standing as well, regardless of social origin.

Additional support is lent by a recent replication of the Blau and Duncan study by Featherman and Hauser, *Opportunity and Change*. Replicating Blau and Duncan's data collection procedures eleven years later, Featherman and Hauser find that, at the later date when their data were collected, education played an even larger role in the occupational attainment of men and, correspondingly, that the role of social origin was diminishing.[10]

The thesis of industrialism sees education generally as growing in importance, but the increasing importance of college education in particular has been linked to a further transformation of the economic foundation of American society—the "coming of post-industrial society," in the words of Bell.[11] Bell foresees the emergence of postindustrialism in the decline of manufacturing and in the expansion of service occupations in American society. Most important among these latter are the professional and technical occupations, symbolized by the computer specialist, which usually require some college education. Their numbers have increased dramatically in this century: at the turn of the century, only one in thirty men worked at such occupations, but by 1970 one in four did so.[12] Professional and technical workers and especially scientists and researchers are paragons of postindustrial man in Bell's view since the central problems of postindustrial society are ones of control and coordination of complex systems, requiring the production of knowledge and information by larger and larger proportions of the work force.

With respect to higher education, the analyses of Featherman and Hauser corroborate elements of the postindustrial thesis. In particular, higher education appears to provide fundamental leverage in the social stratification system of American society. Comparing the benefits derived from each year of higher education to those derived from each year of grammar and secondary school education, Featherman and Hauser find that generally each year invested in higher education brings greater occupational rewards than each additional year spent in school otherwise. For the men in their study, each year of college brought three times the increase in occupational standing produced by each additional year of education before college, even when social background influences on occupational position were taken into account.[13]

Of course, some, particularly Freeman,[14] have noted the sharp downturn in job market prospects for college graduates that occurred at the outset of the 1970s. But as Freeman himself has observed, the college trained continued to have greater earnings and employment prospects than did high school graduates. Indeed, the relative oversupply of college educated workers probably reduced the prospects of high school graduates in major segments of the job market.[15] Moreover, it is not clear that the decline in socioeconomic returns to higher education will endure. As Featherman and Hauser note, "Historical experiences of the cohort whose college-trained members encountered the full force of the Great Depression as they embarked on their careers suggest that early deficits in the value of college may be quite transitory."[16] Because unanticipated changes in demand may occur, it is premature to conclude that the labor market value of a college education has declined.

So far, all of this seems in accord with the common wisdom, but one fact that flies in its face is that some of the primary benefits of college attendance appear to be roughly the same regardless of *which* college is attended. In the popular mind at least, there exists a definite ranking of colleges in terms of prestige, corresponding closely with the social origins of the students who attend them, that is believed to affect the benefits a student derives from attending college no matter what his or her social origin is. Thus, it is widely believed that going to Harvard is likely to lead to "greater things" than going to Podunk State. And attendance at one college rather than another in fact may exert some influence on the success of the student after college. For instance, it may determine the specific professional school a student attends, and there is some evidence to suggest that this affects his or her professional options—whether a lawyer engages in solo practice or works for a large firm, for example.[17] But in terms either of whether the student goes on to professional school or of the occupation he or she ultimately pursues, such "college effects" appear small. Once the social and academic characteristics of their students are taken into account, it appears that colleges exert only a modest independent effect on student success.[18]

In terms of what college does for an individual, what matters most is how long a student attends and whether he or she graduates. For example, the economic benefits of college do not accumulate in linear fashion; the return per year of schooling is greater for the student with a bachelor's degree than for the student without one.[19] Moreover, there is some evidence that the cognitive benefits of college are greater for those who graduate than for those with only partial exposure.[20] This analysis of college effects gives some reason to believe that the socioeconomic benefits of an open-admissions program would be substantial for those who were able to attend college as a result.

The socioeconomic benefits of college attendance take on added significance in light of the persisting advantages held by those with more favored social origins in the chance to attend college. Despite the increasing frequency of college attendance, the disparity in college attendance between those with more favored and those with less favored social origins has not diminished. To be sure, access to college by those from less favored families has increased over this century, but so has access by students from more favored families and by proportionately just as much. As Jencks and Riesman note:

> If we look, for example, at those whose fathers had less than eight years of schooling, we find that they had about 8 chances out of 100 of entering college in 1915–25, compared to 14 in 100 thirty years later. If we then turn to those whose fathers had entered college, we find that their chances of entering college were 47 in 100 in 1915–25, compared to 78 in 100 thirty years later. The increase, in other words, was roughly proportionate.[21]

More recent data continue to show an advantage in college attendance in favor of those from more affluent families. In 1973, for example, under 30 percent of the previous year's high school graduates from the poorest families, those with under $3,000 in annual income, were pursuing some form of postsecondary education; nearly two-thirds of those from the most affluent families, those with $18,000 or more in annual income, were continuing their educations.[22] And racial disparities have actually increased as overall rates of college attendance have grown. In 1969, the year before open admissions began, 36 percent of young white men were enrolled in college, but only 16 percent of young black men were. This racial difference was twice as large as that in 1950.[23] In an era when the vast majority of young persons receive at least a high school diploma, the cutting edge of social privilege has moved from high school to college.

Open admissions, then, can be seen as an attempt to right imbalances in access to higher education, an attempt to extend the opportunity for college entry to disadvantaged students who would constitute a first generation of college goers from their families and communities. As such, this policy is in line with a widely shared belief in equality of opportunity for all, regardless of social origin. Such equality does not require the elimination of inequality or even its reduction; rather, it requires the substitution of individual talent for family status as the basis for inequality. The fact that individuals are rewarded very differently is consistent with equality of opportunity as long as all have basically the same chance to reach for the highest rewards.

But, obviously, one would expect equalization of the opportunity for higher education to lower further the correspondence between social origin and adult position. Insofar as the privilege of affluent families is expressed in their ability to send their children to college, equalizing access should lower their ability to confer an advantage on their children in the competition for adult success. In New York City, with its large, educationally disadvantaged minority populations, equalizing access should allow many black and Hispanic students to pursue higher education for the first time and to obtain the great socioeconomic benefits such education provides. Consequently, open admissions should spur the assimilation of these ethnic groups and reduce social inequalities.

A Critical Perspective on Education

The view of education that we have presented so far, with its optimistic implications for open admissions, is very common in American social science. (But not all who share its basic premises would agree with what we take as its implications for the open-admissions experiment.) Essentially, this view emphasizes the independent effects of education, the benefits it confers on individuals regardless of their social origins. But there is another view of education in American society, one with considerably less optimistic implications for open admissions. In this view, education is not so much an independent force as an intermediate one, standing in between the status of the family into which an individual is born and his or her adult status. This view emphasizes the role of education in transmitting inequality from one generation to the next.

The roots of this more critical view reach back in part to the Coleman Report,[24] whose publication in 1966 initiated a continuing debate over education. In terms of the development of the critical view, one important effect of the Coleman Report and some other works—most notably Jencks and his co-workers' *Inequality*[25]—was to undermine confidence in the independent effects of schooling. The Coleman Report concluded that the characteristics of the schools students attended and presumably the quality of the education they received in them seemed remarkably ineffective in accounting for academic success. In particular, differences between races in test results could not be explained by the characteristics of schools. The analysis by Jencks and his co-workers not only supported these conclusions but also indicated that school characteristics explain little of the subsequent inequalities in occupational status and income.

Responding in part to the findings of Coleman and Jencks, a number of social theorists began to examine the functions of the educational system from a critical perspective. Perhaps the most prominent of these critics were Bowles and Gintis, whose *Schooling in Capitalist America*[26] emphasized education's functions in reinforcing the existing system of social stratification. In their view, education is closely harnessed to the needs of American capitalism and serves its hierarchical division of labor. Rather than conferring benefits on students independently of their social origins, schools are seen as conveying students toward adult positions in accordance with their social origins.

The critical perspective lends itself to a view of schools as a series of channels linked at one end to the characteristics of families from which students come. A central feature of this perspective is the differentiation within educational systems. At the elementary school level, especially in urban school districts, ability grouping is a rather widespread means of differentiation (and it is worth noting that despite decades of research,[27] there is still no evidence that segregation of students by ability has any clear educational benefits, though it undoubtedly succeeds in segregating students by race and class). In high school an important distinction is between the college preparatory and the vocational curriculum. And in higher education there is a major distinction between four-year and two-year colleges.

These structural differences at each level of the educational system are often referred to as tracks.[28] The metaphor is apt because they do indeed lead to different destinations, some of greater value than others. And therein lies their importance: an individual's placement within any given level affects that student's chances of entry into and/or placement within the next stage of the system. Thus, students in the lowest ability classes in elementary school are more likely to be placed in the vocational than in the college preparatory track in high school. Students in college preparatory tracks are more likely to attend college than are students in vocational tracks, and if the latter do go on, they are more likely to find themselves in two-year colleges. Similarly, students who enter four-year colleges are more likely to qualify for graduate school and the professions than are students who begin at the community-college level.

This channeling of students, which makes it especially difficult for those placed in lower tracks to move to higher ones, is believed to occur by virtue of the curricula tracks offer, their distinctive paces of learning, and the expectations teachers hold of the students in them. Students placed in vocational curricula in junior and senior high school are hampered in their ability to enter college because they are not exposed to subject matter thought to be prerequisite to college education. Even when tracks offer the same curricula, however, they differ in pace and in the level of difficulty of the material used in instruction, so that the cognitive distance between students placed in faster tracks and those placed in slower tracks grows. As important as both of these track effects is that of teacher expectations. It appears that teachers expect very different things of students in different tracks and communicate these expectations to them. One researcher documented the blatant insults directed at lower track students by teachers and administrators:

> The reader must feel some skepticism, as I did, at reports of teachers' expressing such degrading insults in front of students. Yet a dozen students report receiving

this kind of comment. I heard such comments myself. One of the younger teachers with a more "liberal" reputation told me, "You're wasting your time asking these kids for their opinions. There's not an idea in any of their heads." This comment was not expressed in the privacy of the teacher's room: it was said at a normal volume in a quiet classroom full of students![29]

Thus, one of the most important potential effects of tracking is damage to the self-image and self-esteem of students and indirectly the lowering of their educational aspirations.

Tracking derives its fullest significance from its correspondence at one end with the social origins of students and at the other with the occupational slots toward which it channels them. Students are not placed in tracks simply on the basis of their ability. The formal mechanisms for placing students include teacher evaluations as well as scores on standardized tests.[30] In both cases, the cultural manifestations of different ethnic and class groups are thought to be essential to the placement process. For one, groups differ in their acquaintance with the middle-class culture that frequently forms the basis for standardized tests. For another, groups differ in their "cultural capital"—in their possession of traits (such as styles of language use and manner) that can be converted through the educational system into socio-economic value.[31] Cultural capital is converted in part by teacher evaluations, which generally are dependent on cultural cues biased against non-white and lower-class students. (It should be noted here that there is another point of view about tracking, one that is consistent with the earlier perspective. For those who presume that standardized tests are reasonably objective measures of ability, tracking is compatible with the belief that ability plays the preeminent role in educational attainment.)

The correspondence between tracks and occupational slots comes about in part because tracks differ in formal curricula. But they also differ in terms of a "hidden curriculum" that has occupational consequences. The hidden curriculum instills values that are compatible with particular occupational strata. Whether, for example, instruction emphasizes the rote learning of cold facts or the exploration of different perspectives on broad questions, whether students are expected to show their knowledge by answering multiple-choice questions or writing subjective essays, students are being prepared to fit into distinct occupational worlds. The instruction of some students prepares them to conform with the strictures of external authority and thereby prepares them for the experiences of many working class occupations. The instruction of others prepares them to deal autonomously with the complexities and ambiguities involved in some middle-class occupations.[32]

Applied to higher education, the critical interpretation implies that open access does not increase equality of opportunity because increases in access are offset by increases in internal stratification.[33] Higher, as well as lower, educational systems are divided into tracks distinguished by the curricula

they provide and the occupations for which they destine students. And social classes and ethnic groups are differentially allocated within higher education. This differential allocation is seen as having lifelong consequences
for postcollege attainment, particularly with respect to occupation and income.

The most important track distinction within higher education is between
two-year, or community, colleges and four-year schools. The community
colleges are frequently regarded as dead-end institutions that subject the
student to a process of "cooling out."[34] These colleges generally have a
two-track curriculum: the liberal arts transfer and the terminal, technical-
vocational career program. The cooling out process is accomplished in two
ways. First, many students are channeled from the start into technical and
vocational rather than liberal arts curricula, and this diminishes their
chances for transfer to a four-year college. Second, many students who begin in liberal arts perform poorly and either transfer to a vocational program or become discouraged and drop out. These dropouts are especially
"cooled out" since their departure is voluntary; thus, their failure appears
to be their own responsibility. Rates of transfer from two-year to four-year
colleges are believed to be low. For those who argue that open access higher
education functions to reinforce the existing system of social stratification,
the community colleges play a major role—for it is the case that the expansion of rates of college-going during the postwar period has been accomplished primarily through the growth of two-year institutions.[35] Indeed,
during this period, the number of such institutions more than doubled—a
far greater rate of growth than has occurred for four-year colleges.[36]

The expansion of access to higher education is seen by some as an adap-
tive response to the political conflict generated by the struggle of different
social groups for improvements in their status.[37] As happened to Tantalus,
however, the fruits sought by the members of disadvantaged groups recede
from them even as they are permitted to reach out. The new students allowed to pursue higher education during an expansion of access are believed
to be tracked into the two-year colleges. Because lower-class and minority
students tend to do less well in high school, are less likely to have been enrolled in college preparatory curricula, and tend to score lower on standardized tests such as the Scholastic Aptitude Test, such students, if they attend
college at all, are seen as confined largely to the community colleges, doom-
ing them to clerical and technical jobs near the bottom of the white-collar
world. Middle-class white students, on the other hand, continue to be
placed in four-year colleges with liberal arts curricula, runways for takeoff
into professional careers. From the critical perspective, open admissions
may strengthen rather than alleviate inequality by providing the illusion of
equal opportunity to those destined for the lowest level of white-collar jobs.

We must note here that whatever the social distinction between two-year
and four-year schools, the assumptions that the senior-college track is more

desirable than the community-college and that, within the latter, the liberal arts curriculum is more desirable than the vocational are debatable. A student whose parents are unskilled and perhaps marginally employed or whose childhood has been supported by public assistance might well regard regular employment as, say, a medical laboratory technician to be a step up and might consciously choose a community-college vocational program to achieve this goal. The result from the student's point of view is a considerable improvement in socioeconomic standing. The fact that individuals might opt for lower tracks as in accord with their interests does not, however, diminish the critical interpretation since the interests of individuals have been shaped by unequal circumstances.

To summarize, the perspective that emphasizes the independent effects of education suggests that open admissions will help create equality of opportunity for socially and economically marginal groups. The perspective that emphasizes the dependence of educational attainment on social origin leads to another view: higher education will adapt to open admissions by absorbing the new students in a lower track (namely, community-college vocational programs) and thereby will preserve class and ethnic privilege in the face of changes purporting to further equality of opportunity. There is yet another point of view—one that does not represent an entirely different perspective on education but rather elaborates on the many negative reactions that have greeted open admissions.

Open Admissions and the Decline in Standards

In contemplating the CUNY open-admissions policy a broad segment of the public has expressed reactions ranging from skepticism to alarm. In their extreme form, these reactions have had an apocalyptic character, seeing in open admissions the destruction of the City University and even an omen of the decline of American civilization.[38] Mayer has described the threat implicit in open admissions:

> Though I know many brilliant people I would not care to have as my doctor or my lawyer or my children's teacher, it is undoubtedly true that a unidimensional measure of academic excellence can be used to set a special, higher floor for many occupations and professions. The ardently egalitarian . . . are fundamentally unconvincing: one can dismiss them with the curse that they should cross the river on a bridge designed by an engineer from an engineering school where students were admitted by lottery; and that their injuries should then be treated by a doctor from a medical school where students were admitted by lottery; and that their heirs' malpractice suit should then be tried by a lawyer from a law school where students were admitted by lottery.[39]

The focus of these reactions has been the issue of academic standards. This issue has probably generated more heat than any other surrounding the policy. Before open admissions began, there were gloomy prophesies about the plan's prospects for success. Some feared that open-admissions students, with their weaker high school records, would stand little chance of performing satisfactorily. Others felt that despite the University's commitment to large-scale programs of remediation, the political pressures stemming from the open-admissions effort would lead to a dilution of academic standards with the veneer of academic success concealing an underlying deterioration of rigor. The University thus found itself in a no-win situation. If students succeeded beyond expectations, it would be accused of lowering standards. If they failed, the gloomy prophets would, happily or not, see their fears confirmed.

If the intensity of concern over academic standards is unquestionable, so is the ambiguity of the concept. Perhaps this is why discussions of the impact of open admissions upon standards have generated much heat but little illumination. Some who assert that open admissions has led to a decline in standards seem to refer to the criteria for *admission*. That admission became less selective is true by definition—so from this perspective it is undeniable that "standards" declined. Others, however, refer to the academic quality of instruction at CUNY and the rigor of the standards used to evaluate student performance.

Many saw the new students as demanding that the curriculum be remade to suit their needs, especially in the creation of ethnic studies departments.[40] The result was viewed as a watering down of the curriculum—"standards of excellence" had given way to a smorgasbord of undemanding courses. Even worse, the new students' lack of academic preparation had debased the level of instruction in many courses. It was feared that students would no longer be expected to read as much or at the same level of difficulty as they had formerly. A further consequence would be a decline in the rigor of grading: B under open admissions would not be what it had been before.

In the long run, large numbers of underprepared students would degrade the learning environment of the students who would have qualified for a senior college of CUNY even in the absence of open admissions. There was concern that because of a changed intellectual atmosphere, these students would suffer and, over time, would no longer attend CUNY. An ultimate concern was with the value of the CUNY diploma. It goes almost without saying that for those who felt that academic standards would collapse because of open admissions, the diploma would become worthless in the long run.

It is best to acknowledge at the outset that we cannot say anything definitive about the standards issue, and we are not certain that it is the right issue. There is a different way to evaluate an educational system: one can look at the "value" it adds to students. By this yardstick, it is not the quality of students at entry or even their quality at exit that matters. Rather, it is the extent to which they *change* intellectually, socially, and otherwise.[41] By either yardstick, we would need data that we presently lack to pass judgment. Except for the trivial view of the standards issue, which sees their decline in changed admissions standards, we would need data about the academic quality of students after they had attended CUNY for some period of time (we already have such data about entering students) in order to judge both the maintenance of standards and the educational value added. But in order to know whether standards declined *as a result* of open admissions, we would need similar data for students at CUNY before open admissions. And to separate the specific consequences of open admissions from more general trends, we would also need comparable data from colleges nationwide. The issue of academic standards is not limited to CUNY. The topic of grade inflation has been widely discussed as a national phenomenon.[42]

We do suspect that standards in the sense of grading rigor may have declined somewhat as a result of open admissions. One City University study looked at the effects of open admissions on grading at selected CUNY campuses. Kramer, Kaufman, and Podell found that the grades handed out by faculty were lower at some campuses after open admissions began but higher at others.[43] Since many students with weak high school backgrounds were admitted under the policy, we would have expected to see a more definite pattern of lower grades if standards had been maintained. But more important, we also suspect that some of the concern about standards stems from the shock of nonacademic changes under open admissions. As we will show in a later chapter, overnight the policy allowed many black and Hispanic students into colleges where few had been before. The ethnic newcomers were different from traditional CUNY students in many ways, not all of which were intrinsically related to educational achievement but which served to brand the newcomers as strangers nevertheless. The newcomers also challenged what some saw as the most basic prerogative of the faculty: to define the cultural standard to which students would have to assimilate. The arrival of many nonwhite students was accompanied by frequent rejections of the traditional curriculum as a form of cultural imperialism. In seeking to define their own heritages as unique and valuable, the new students also sought legitimation in the recognition of these heritages as worthy of incorporation in the curriculum. Their demands for change, particularly in the establishment of ethnic studies departments, threatened the University in a fundamental way, especially by comparison with earlier groups that had entered in large numbers for the first time. While these white predecessors shared one thing with the new minority students—they were poor—they differed by seeing college as an important stage in their assimilation.

In our view, the concern over standards is at least partly explicable in terms of the status competition among ethnic groups. In many situations of ethnic change, when less privileged groups gain sudden access to spheres from which they previously have been excluded, they are seen as a direct threat to those who are already there. The more privileged groups attempt to maintain their advantaged positions by seeking to enforce their cultural standards as the ones to which the newcomers must accommodate themselves, and this attempt is sometimes couched in language expressing a sense of cultural pollution brought by the newcomers. Thereby, the more privileged derogate the newcomers while symbolically elevating themselves. Moreover, insofar as they are successful in forcing their own cultural standards on the newcomers, the more privileged groups place the newcomers at a disadvantage since the newcomers are less familiar with the cultural traits that lead to success.[44]

When Jews began attending City College and the University of Pennsylvania in substantial numbers, the reputation of each institution suffered, though to be sure not on the ground of the debasement of academic standards. City College was stigmatized the "Jewish University of America" and the University of Pennsylvania was disparaged as having the "democracy of the street car."[45] Given the stereotype of blacks as poor performers educationally and the common view of them as having no substantial heritage of intellectual contributions and considering their low socioeconomic status and location outside the cultural "mainstream," it is not hard to imagine that the anticipation of their greatly increased presence in CUNY represented a status threat not drastically different from the one perceived by upper-class Protestants when, earlier in the century, they began sharing "their" colleges with Jews who did not know how to "act."

The Plan of the Book

Even though there is not an exact opposition between the two perspectives with which we opened this chapter, they do suggest a series of questions about open admissions. To an important degree, these questions concern the articulation between the educational system and the occupational structure, and fully answering them would require an investigation of the occupational fortunes of open-admissions students. At this point, we lack the data for that effort. But they also concern the equality of educational opportunity afforded by the policy, and our examination will focus on this issue. We will attempt to answer three basic questions. Who came? How were they placed? How did they do?

With respect to the first question, the program aimed to provide increased opportunity for minority students, specifically blacks and Hispanics. Nonetheless, to a degree not generally recognized, whites were also beneficiaries. The open-admissions program attracted substantial numbers of working- and middle-class Jewish and Catholic students, the former predominantly of eastern European origin and the latter frequently of Irish or Italian descent. Thus, the consequences of open admissions for the ethnic representativeness of the University's student body require careful examination.

But ethnicity is not the only criterion by which to assess the increase in access to higher education. We will assess as well the extent to which open-admissions students were different from regular-admissions students in a variety of ways, such as their social class background and their orientation toward higher education. These comparisons will help us evaluate the extent to which open-admissions students were truly a new kind of student in higher education, one who needed a new model of higher education, as many concerned over declining standards feared. The question of who came will be a focus of chapters 4 and 5.

The placement of students is of obvious concern to the two perspectives we have outlined. An answer to the second question will go a long way toward answering the suspicion that the apparent opportunity provided by open admissions would be offset by the increasing internal stratification of the University, visible in the assignment of different social classes and ethnic groups to distinct levels of the University or to distinct colleges within those levels. We will seek to determine not only the degrees of stratification and of segregation of the campuses but also, if they exist, the processes from which they arose. These determinations will be a focus of chapter 4.

The third question is simply, Were students able to capitalize on the opportunity presented by open admissions? How well did they do academically? No matter how students were placed, the benefits they were able to draw from the opportunity to attend college were affected substantially by their academic performance. To some extent, this is a matter of persistence and graduation. Considerable research has shown that the benefits of college attendance depend on the number of years the student completes and whether or not a degree is earned. But how well the student does, in terms of both grades and credits per semester, is also consequential. The better a student does, the more likely he or she will be to continue education beyond college. An answer to the third question, then, will help us determine whether open admissions led to any reduction of inequality among social classes and ethnic groups in the attainment of the educational credentials required for middle-class occupational careers.

Chapter 6 will describe how academic success varied among important groups, and chapter 7 will analyze the processes that led to these variations. Chapter 8 will examine the success of community-college students in transferring to the senior colleges and thus gaining the opportunity to earn the bachelor's degree. Chapter 9 will assess the success of remediation efforts to prepare the academically deficient student for the demands of college education.

Finally, chapter 10 will summarize our assessment of open admissions, and chapter 11 will describe the turmoil in the wake of New York City's fiscal crisis, which led to changes in the nature and the promise of the open-admissions program. We turn now to a brief description of our data sources.

Notes

1. U.S. Department of Commerce, *Historical Statistics of the United States, Colonial Times to 1970*, vol. 1 (Washington: U.S. Government Printing Office, 1975), p. 379.
2. See the discussion by Christopher Jencks and David Riesman, *The Academic Revolution* (Chicago: University of Chicago Press, 1968), pp. 77–78.
3. U.S. Department of Commerce, *Social Indicators, 1976* (Washington: U.S. Government Printing Office, 1977), p. 301. A detailed analysis of the transformations occurring in the secondary and higher education systems is found in Martin Trow, "The Second Transformation of American Secondary Education," *International Journal of Comparative Sociology* 2 (September 1961): 144–165.
4. An outstanding review of different perspectives on education and the research used in support of them is found in Christopher J. Hurn, *The Limits and Possibilities of Schooling: An Introduction to the Sociology of Education* (Boston: Allyn & Bacon, 1978).
5. We have borrowed the term "thesis of industrialism" from David Featherman and Robert Hauser, *Opportunity and Change* (New York: Academic, 1978), pp. 11–15.
6. This statement of the thesis has deep roots in social theory, extending back to the European thinkers of the nineteenth and early twentieth centuries. As Herbert Gintis observed in a review of Featherman and Hauser's *Opportunity and Change*: "If we avoid quibbling about details, the most striking peculiarity of the 'thesis of industrialization' [sic] is how uniformly it has been accepted. From Pareto to Weber to Parsons, from Adam Smith to Milton Friedman, and for Marxists as well, the shift from ascription to achievement has been a cornerstone of social theory." (*Contemporary Sociology* 9 [January 1980]: 12).
7. The gender language of these hypotheses betrays an unfortunate aspect of the entire empirical literature on social stratification—an exclusive focus on stratification processes as they affect men. A crisp review of the limits imposed by that focus is Joan R. Acker, "Women and Stratification: A Review of Recent Literature," *Contemporary Sociology* 9 (January 1980): 25–35.
8. Donald Treiman, "Industrialization and Social Stratification," *Sociological Inquiry* 40 (Spring 1970): 207–234.
9. Peter Blau and Otis Dudley Duncan, *The American Occupational Structure* (New York: Wiley, 1967).
10. Featherman and Hauser, pp. 254–262. In fairness to the authors we must note that although their work is generally consistent with the thesis of industrialism, they are unwilling in the end to state definitely that the thesis holds. Featherman and Hauser end a meticulous empirical analysis by cautioning that "one

could infer from our discussion of trend in socioeconomic achievement in terms of the 'thesis of industrialism' that . . . the process of stratification has been altered in a more universalistic direction. We believe such one-sided inferences about cause and effect may not safely be drawn from our work'' (p. 482).

11. Daniel Bell, *The Coming of Post-industrial Society* (New York: Basic Books, 1973).
12. Featherman and Hauser, p. 49.
13. Featherman and Hauser, p. 261. That greater socioeconomic benefits accrue from higher education is confirmed persuasively by Christopher Jencks, Susan Bartlett, Mary Corcoran, James Crouse, David Eaglesfield, Gregory Jackson, Kent McClelland, Peter Mueser, Michael Olneck, Joseph Schwartz, Sherry Ward, and Jill Williams, *Who Gets Ahead?* (New York: Basic Books, 1979), chap. 6. They also assert that this effect is especially large for blacks.
14. Richard B. Freeman, *The Over-educated American* (New York: Academic, 1976).
15. Freeman, p. 187.
16. Featherman and Hauser, p. 310.
17. Some evidence to this effect is cited by Randall Collins, "Functional and Conflict Theories of Educational Stratification," *American Sociological Review* 36 (December 1971): 1002–1019.
18. Duane Alwin, "College Effects on Educational and Occupational Attainments," *American Sociological Review* 39 (April 1974): 210–223; Duane Alwin, "Socioeconomic Background, Colleges, and Post-collegiate Achievements," in William Sewell, Robert Hauser, and David Featherman (eds.), *Schooling and Achievement in American Society* (New York: Academic, 1976). The recent analyses of Jencks and his colleagues in *Who Gets Ahead?* confirm the absence of a college effect on occupation but suggest, although not very definitively, that college quality may affect earnings.
19. Robert Hauser and Thomas Daymont, "Schooling, Ability, and Earnings: Cross-sectional Findings 8 to 14 Years after High School Graduation," *Sociology of Education* 50 (July 1977): 182–205; also see Jencks et al., chap. 6.
20. Herbert Hyman, Charles Wright, and John Shelton Reed, *The Enduring Effects of Education* (Chicago: University of Chicago Press, 1975), pp. 52–53.
21. Jencks and Riesman, p. 96.
22. U.S. Department of Commerce, *Social Indicators, 1976*, p. 300. Further evidence is presented by David E. Lavin, "Selection Processes for Higher Education," *Encyclopedia of Education* (New York: Macmillan and Free Press, 1971), pp. 181–188. A cogent statement of the influence of social origins on college attendance and also college graduation is William H. Sewell, "Inequality of Opportunity for Higher Education," *American Sociological Review* 36 (October 1971): 793–809.
23. Reynolds Farley, "Trends in Racial Inequalities: Have the Gains of the 1960s Disappeared in the 1970s?" *American Sociological Review* 42 (April 1977): 189–208. It should be noted that the increasing racial gap in college attendance during the fifties and sixties is consistent with the decreasing racial gap in educational attainment overall since the latter is due to the rising floor in educational attainment, i.e., the universality of high school attendance and graduation.

24. James Coleman, Ernest Q. Campbell, Carol J. Hobson, James McPartland, Alexander M. Mood, Frederic D. Weinfeld, and Robert L. York, *Equality of Educational Opportunity* (Washington: U.S. Government Printing Office, 1966).
25. Christopher Jencks, Marshall Smith, Henry Acland, Mary Jo Bane, David Cohen, Herbert Gintis, Barbara Heyns, and Stephan Michelson, *Inequality: A Reassessment of Family and Schooling in America* (New York: Basic Books, 1972).
26. Samuel Bowles and Herbert Gintis, *Schooling in Capitalist America* (New York: Basic Books, 1976).
27. A good summary is presented by Sarane Boocock, *An Introduction to the Sociology of Learning* (Boston: Houghton Mifflin, 1972), pp. 158–162.
28. For a discussion of tracking that reviews much of the literature, primarily at the elementary and secondary levels, see Caroline Persell, *Education and Inequality: The Roots of Stratification in America's Schools* (New York: Free Press, 1977). For detailed recent studies see James Rosenbaum, *Making Inequality: The Hidden Curriculum of High School Tracking* (New York: Wiley, 1976); and Karl Alexander, Martha Cook, and Edward McDill, "Curriculum Tracking and Educational Stratification: Some Further Evidence," *American Sociological Review* 43 (February 1978): 47–66.
29. Rosenbaum, pp. 179–180.
30. See Persell, pp. 85–89.
31. The concept of cultural capital has been developed by the French sociologist Pierre Bourdieu. His work is now becoming available in English. For example, Pierre Bourdieu and Jean-Claude Passeron, *Reproduction: In Education, Society, and Culture* (Beverly Hills: Sage, 1977). The importance of linguistic styles to cultural capital has been stressed by Basil Bernstein; see his *Class, Codes, and Control*, vol. 1 (London: Routledge & Kegan Paul, 1973). A recent reader compiled by Jerome Karabel and A. H. Halsey, *Power and Ideology in Education* (New York: Oxford University Press, 1976), contains several selections relevant to cultural capital and its role in education.
32. This point is developed extensively in Bowles and Gintis, chap. 5.
33. Bowles and Gintis; Jerome Karabel, "Community Colleges and Social Stratification," *Harvard Educational Review* 42 (November 1972): 521–562; Murray Milner, *The Illusion of Equality* (San Francisco: Jossey-Bass, 1972); Ellen Kay Trimberger, "Open Admissions: A New Form of Tracking?" *Insurgent Sociologist* 4 (Fall 1973): 29–43.
34. The process is described in the well-known article by Burton Clark, "The Cooling Out Function in Higher Education," *American Journal of Sociology* 65 (May 1960): 569–576.
35. Karabel.
36. U.S. Bureau of the Census, *Statistical Abstract of the United States*, 97th ed. (Washington: U.S. Government Printing Office, 1976), p. 141.
37. Collins; Randall Collins, "Some Comparative Principles of Educational Stratification," *Harvard Educational Review* 47 (February 1977): 1–27.
38. Two books illustrate these apocalyptic perceptions: Louis G. Heller, *The Death of the American University: With Special Reference to the Collapse of the City College of New York* (New Rochelle: Arlington House, 1973); Geoffrey Wag-

ner, *The End of Education: The Experience of the City University of New York with Open Enrollment and the Threat to Higher Education in America* (Cranbury: Barnes, 1976).
39. Martin Mayer, "Higher Education for All?: The Case of Open Admissions," *Commentary* 54 (February 1973): 47.
40. Theodore Gross summarizes many of the fears about academic dilution under open admissions in "How to Kill a College: The Private Papers of a Campus Dean," *Saturday Review*, February 4, 1978, pp. 12–20.
41. The value added concept of education is proposed as a standard for evaluating open admissions by Jerome Karabel, "Perspectives on Open Admissions," *Educational Record* 33 (Winter 1972): 30–44. See also Jack E. Rossman, Helen S. Astin, Alexander W. Astin, and Elaine H. El-Khawas, *Open Admissions at City University of New York: An Analysis of the First Year* (Englewood Cliffs: Prentice-Hall, 1975), pp. 2–3.
42. The degree of grade inflation was documented for the national scene by Arvo E. Juola, *Grade Inflation, 1960–1973): A Preliminary Report* (East Lansing: Office of Evaluation Services, Michigan State University, 1974); further discussion is found in Malcolm G. Scully, "Crackdown on 'Grade Inflation,' " *Chronicle of Higher Education*, December 22, 1975, pp. 1, 12.
43. Rena Kramer, Barry Kaufman, and Lawrence Podell, *Distribution of Grades, 1972* (New York: Office of Program and Policy Research, City University of New York, 1974).
44. Though this process has been observed many times, it has not often been described in these terms. An exception is Joseph Gusfield, *Symbolic Crusade* (Urbana: University of Illinois Press, 1963). Some of the most telling instances of status competition occurred when the social arrival of American Jews engendered acute status anxiety among upper-class Protestant Americans. See E. Digby Baltzell, *The Protestant Establishment: Aristocracy and Caste in America* (New York: Random House, Vintage, 1964); Stephen Steinberg, *The Academic Melting Pot* (New York: McGraw-Hill, 1974), chap. 1.
45. Lawrence Vesey, *The Emergence of the American University* (Chicago: University of Chicago Press, 1965), p. 288.

3. Research Background and Procedures

As THE NATION'S most ambitious and controversial effort at expanding higher educational opportunity, CUNY's open-admissions policy was subject to intense scrutiny. Because the University recognized that it would be asked to respond to the many questions raised about that policy and indeed having many questions itself, CUNY provided for a research effort that would document the results and furnish a basis for evaluation.[1]

What should be studied was not defined explicitly by the University in the sense of formulating a precise set of research objectives, but from public discussion and from various statements of the aims of the program issued by the CUNY board (noted in chapter 1), the main research questions were apparent. These were the questions raised in chapter 2: who came to CUNY as a result of open admissions; where and how were they placed in the University; and how did they fare academically?

Data Sets: The CUNY Census

Our analyses of these questions utilize three sources of data. The first is an annual census that is conducted by the University. At fall registration each student is asked to complete a brief form concerning ethnicity, college of enrollment, sex, class in college, and the like. The form is anonymous and the information collected therefore cannot be directly integrated with other data. Although this census does not provide for ethnic distinctions among whites (e.g., Irish Catholics, Italian Catholics, Jews), it does distinguish whites from blacks and Hispanics, thus furnishing the basis for a very important set of trend analyses of the impact of open admissions upon the enrollment of minority students at CUNY. These analyses, presented in chapter 4, cover the period from the last year before open admissions, 1969, through 1975. The census data also allow us to analyze changes in ethnic composition from 1975 through 1978, years when the University was hard hit by New York City's fiscal crisis and the open-admissions policy was modified (see chapter 11).

Academic Data

A second data source allows us to go well beyond aggregate census tabulations of minority enrollment. This consists of official University student data files, which include educational background and academic performance information for the first three freshmen classes entering after open admissions began (the 1970, 1971, and 1972 freshmen). These three cohorts provide the basis for all of our major analyses of the academic outcomes of the open-admissions experiment. The files cover the period from fall 1970 through spring 1975; they include five years of academic performance data for the 1970 freshmen, four years for the 1971 group, and three years for the 1972 cohort. For each cohort the files provide information on the entire population of first-time entering freshmen. The records include data pertaining to four major areas: high school background, scores on standardized tests of basic skills in reading and math, the CUNY colleges and curricula to which students applied and were allocated, and students' academic records at CUNY. The files represent an integration of data gathered from different sources and by different procedures.

Educational Background

CUNY's centralized admissions office collects high school transcript data, which constitute part of the files of students who apply to the University. The high school record contains information on numerous variables; three are used in this study as major indicators of educational background.

1. *High school average.* This measure is the average of the student's grades in all academic courses deemed by the University to be college preparatory in nature (e.g., English, mathematics, science). The variable is of critical importance in this study for it distinguishes those whose entry to the University was made possible by open admissions from those who would have qualified even without the policy. Throughout, we shall refer to the first group as open-admissions students and to the second group as regular students. In the senior colleges open-admissions students are those who en-

tered with high school averages of less than 80. In community colleges open-admissions students are those with high school averages of less than 75. These cutoff points reflect the fact that prior to open admissions an average of 80 or better was generally needed for entry to a four-year college and one of 75 or better was needed for admission to a community college. These constitute the official University definitions of an open-admissions student.

2. *High school rank.* This measure indicates a student's standing relative to other students in the same high school graduating class. Along with high school average this criterion determined eligibility for a senior college under the open-admissions program.

3. *Number of college preparatory courses taken.* These are the courses that CUNY, and indeed most universities, consider academic and thus comprising the core of college preparatory work. Courses in English, mathematics, foreign languages, history, and social studies are illustrative. Physical education, vocational, or technical courses (e.g., typing, "shop," or automotive technology) are not included in the college preparatory category. This variable is significant because it reflects the high school track from which students entered CUNY, and not only in terms of a crude distinction between academic and nonacademic tracks. Even within academic high schools, some of the nominally academic tracks were diluted in the sense that students in them were exposed to less college preparatory work.

Tests of Basic Academic Skills: The Open Admissions Test

To obtain an overview of entering students' academic preparedness, and thus an indication of the need for remedial services, CUNY administered universitywide tests of academic skills to graduating high school seniors in spring 1970 and 1971 (1972 high school seniors did not take these tests). Two tests were used: the first measured reading comprehension; the second assessed numerical skills. The two instruments are referred to as the Open-Admissions Test.[2] The files contain students' raw scores on each test. At the time of administration students were asked whether they felt they needed help in English, reading, and mathematics. These responses are also included in the record. Both the test data and the self-reports are used extensively in chapter 9, where we evaluate the University's remedial effort.

Application and Admissions Data

Applications for admission to the University are processed by CUNY's central admissions office. These applications ask the student to list six

CUNY colleges in order of preference. Our student files indicate each student's first-choice college. They also indicate the college to which the student was actually allocated as well as the choice number of that college. These college choice and allocation data provide the basis for analyses of placement in different levels of the University (described in chapter 4). Additionally, the files show the curricula that students preferred, as well as the ones to which they were actually allocated. These data allow us to undertake an important set of analyses of the determinants of placement into community-college liberal arts transfer and career programs (see chapter 4). They also are used in analyses of the determinants of transfer from community to senior college (see chapter 8).

The Academic Record

After each semester, including summer sessions, the CUNY campuses transmitted to the University's central office computer tapes containing information on the courses students took, the grades they earned, and the number of credits each course carried. After undergoing numerous editing procedures, these raw data were converted into summary measures and merged with the other student data described above. This information, covering the period from fall 1970 through spring 1975, provides a longitudinal record of performance for each semester and summer session, as well as a record of the student's cumulative academic achievement from the beginning of college through each subsequent semester. For example, after the third semester, the record shows students' academic performance in that term as well as their cumulative performance over those three semesters (the cumulative indices also include data for students attending summer sessions). These data form one basis for our analyses of academic achievement in chapters 6 through 9. The file includes the following variables:

1. *College in which enrolled.* During each semester, the record shows whether a student was enrolled in a CUNY college and the specific college he or she attended. These data allow us to analyze persistence and dropout, stopout (e.g., interrupted attendance followed by reenrollment), and transfer within CUNY.

2. *Credits and grades.* In every semester the file shows the number of credits a student was taking,[3] the number earned, and the grade point average. Student grades in each course taken are reported as a letter (A through F) that has a numeric value (A = 4, B = 3, C = 2, D = 1, and F = 0).[4] These values are used to calculate the grade point average for that semester. As noted, the student's record also shows the cumulative credits attempted and earned and the cumulative grade point average after each semester.

3. *Graduation data.* For all three cohorts the files indicate whether a student had graduated by June 1975. For graduates the records also indicate

the type of degree earned, the semester in which it was earned, and the college that granted the degree. Some students earned more than one degree. The typical case was the student who received the associate degree from a community college, transferred to a senior college, and earned a bachelor's degree. If students received more than one degree, all are indicated.

4. *Remediation data.* A subfile of remedial courses was created from the raw course data transmitted from the colleges to the central office. The definition of courses as remedial was based upon information compiled from three sources: college catalogues, registrars, and our interviews with key administrators and faculty involved in each school's remedial effort. This subfile lists each remedial course taken by a student, the skills that it covered (reading and study skills, writing, and mathematics were the major areas), the number of credits the course carried (if any), the grade the student received, and the semester the course was taken. From these data we created a number of summary indices that were used to assess the impact of the remedial effort (see chapter 9).

Quality of the Academic Performance Data

We made numerous assessments of the quality of the data in these population files and found one important shortcoming: the records underreport the number of credits that many students earned. We determined that credits are underreported because the number that many graduates are shown as having earned is lower than the number required for graduation. In the senior colleges, where 128 credits typically are required for graduation, 47 percent of the graduates in the 1970 cohort and 62 percent of the 1971 group showed fewer than 128 credits in their records.[5] However, the extent of credit underreporting was not large: the average number of credits reported as earned by graduates was 124 among the 1970 entrants and 119 among the 1971 cohort. In the community colleges, where sixty-four credits typically are required for graduation,[6] about one-third of graduates in each of the three cohorts showed less than this number in their records: the mean for graduates of the 1970 cohort was sixty-two credits, for 1971 entrants it was sixty credits, and for 1972 entrants it was sixty-two credits. Because these credit shortages occur for graduates, we are certain that they are a general condition applying as well to students who had not graduated by June 1975. This underreporting resulted mainly because incompletes were not always updated in the records transmitted by the colleges. For the most part this condition does not affect the results of our analyses, which are usually concerned not with the absolute numbers of credits earned by students but rather with group comparisons (e.g., regular students versus open-admissions students). However, in chapter 6 we do sometimes focus upon absolute numbers of credits; these instances are subject to qualification, as we shall note.[7]

Student Surveys

Our third data source consists of questionnaires administered to the 1970, 1971, and 1972 freshman classes. The questionnaires requested a wide range of information about student social origins, attitudes, and aspiration. The 1970 survey, administered under the auspices of the American Council on Education, was directed by Alexander W. Astin.[8] The 1971 and 1972 questionnaires were developed and administered under Lavin's direction.

For the most part the questionnaires were administered either at registration or in required freshmen courses, especially English classes. Because a sampling design would have required considerable effort at the campuses and their capacity to implement any sampling procedure was very limited, we decided that it would be easier to attempt administering the questionnaire to all freshmen. Of course, many students did not respond or were in class sections in which questionnaires were not handed out. Moreover, for a variety of reasons, not all colleges administered the survey each year,[9] and in all three years (especially 1971) one or more schools distributed them late (toward the middle or end of a fall semester).[10] Also, students from the SEEK and College Discovery programs are not included in the survey data. However, this is not such a disadvantage since it would be inappropriate to include them in analyses of students' academic outcomes; these special students received services and financial stipends at a level not offered to open-admissions students. The numbers of students in the sample surveys for each year are as follows: 1970, 13,525; 1971, 8,527; 1972, 12,725. These samples represent the following percentages of each year's entering freshmen (excluding special program students): 43 percent (1970), 24 percent (1971), and 36 percent (1972).[11]

The surveys include two major sets of variables. The first pertain to social origins and demographic characteristics, while the second refer to aspirations and attitudes.[12] The social origins and demographic variables are as follows:

1. *Age at entry to CUNY*.
2. *Gender*.
3. *Family income*, ranging from less than $4,000[13] to $15,000 or more.
4. *Educational attainment of mother and father*, ranging from less than grammar school through postgraduate degree.
5. *Ethnicity*. For the 1970 and 1971 cohorts, four major ethnic categories are used: black, Hispanic, Catholic, and Jewish.[14] The rationale for distinguishing these groups is described in chapter 4. In the 1972 cohort there are no ethnic distinctions among whites; the categories are white, black, and Hispanic.[15]

The variables pertaining to aspirations and attitudes are these:

1. *Degree aspirations*. Students were asked whether they aspired to no degree, an associate degree, a bachelor's degree, a master's degree, a Ph.D., M.D., LL.B., and the like.

2. *Academic self-rating.* In the 1970 survey students were asked how they would rate their academic preparation relative to that of other students at their college (better than average, about average, poorer than average). In the 1971 and 1972 surveys they were asked how "bright" they were compared to other students in their college class.

3. *Need to work while in college.* In the 1970 survey students were asked to estimate the chances that they would have to work at an outside job while in college. The 1971 and 1972 cohorts were asked the number of hours per week they worked at an outside job if they had such a job.

4. *Job plans after college.* The 1970 freshmen were asked to select their probable careers from a list of occupations. Those who did not know could check "undecided." In 1971 and 1972 students were simply asked whether they had decided on a postcollege occupation.

5. *Reasons for attending college.* Students rated the importance of various reasons for attending college. A factor analysis of the items revealed two main orientations: vocational reasons and reasons of personal growth. Two scales were constructed composed of the items defining these orientations. The vocational scale included two items: "to get a better job" and "to make more money." The personal growth scale was defined by three items: "to gain a general education and appreciation of ideas," "to make me a more cultured person," and "to learn more about things that interest me."[16]

6. *Perceptions and attitudes toward open admissions.* There were two aspects to student perceptions of open admissions. The first stemmed from a single question (asked only in 1970) about their perceptions of personal benefit from the policy (such as, "it made college possible," "it encouraged me," or "it nearly discouraged me from coming"). The second, asked in all three surveys, involved judgments about the policy. Students indicated agreement or disagreement with statements such as "the reputation of this college will suffer because of open admissions," "open admissions will probably lower the academic standards of this college," and "open admissions has discouraged many of the city's outstanding high school graduates from attending this college." An index composed of these items was created, ordering students according to their support of the policy.

These survey data have been combined with the academic performance files so that the record of each student who responded to the questionnaire also contains information on educational background, Open-Admissions Test results, application and admissions data, and academic performance data at CUNY. Records for some of the students in the survey sample are incomplete. That is, some students did not respond to every item in the questionnaire, and/or data were missing for them in the educational background section of the file. For each of the major independent variables used in our analyses, the percentage of missing cases is indicated in table 3.1,

TABLE 3.1. Percentage of Missing Cases for Sample Survey Questionnaire Items and Educational Background Variables

| | 1970 | | 1971 | | 1972 | |
| | | | LEVEL OF COLLEGE[a] | | | |
	S	C	S	C	S	C
Age	0.3	0.7	1.8	1.5	1.7	2.0
Gender	0.0	0.0	3.9	1.6	0.5	0.2
Father's education	2.4	4.2	8.9	10.6	4.5	4.4
Mother's education	1.5	3.0	5.4	6.6	4.4	4.8
Income	10.9	17.3	14.2	14.5	20.2	12.4
Ethnicity	1.2	1.2	4.9	5.9	3.6	3.2
Degree aspirations	2.9	5.9	1.7	2.0	1.3	5.1
Academic self-rating	2.0	5.7	5.2	24.6	8.8	36.9
Need to work	2.1	5.9	6.4	5.4	4.6	14.1
Job plans	7.2	16.1	3.7	23.5	1.7	12.4
Reasons for college						
Personal growth	3.4	9.5	14.7	36.3	12.2	35.8
Vocational	2.5	7.7	4.7	24.7	3.7	17.2
Open-admissions						
attitudes	5.0	9.8	7.3	27.3	8.0	26.3
Open-admissions test	16.1	24.4	23.5	45.9	_[b]	_[b]
High school average	1.7	6.7	1.2	6.0	2.0	9.5
Rank in high school class	11.4	20.6	16.8	31.0	11.7	32.9
College preparatory						
courses	2.7	9.3	1.3	6.5	2.0	9.5
Total cases	9,110	4,415	3,105	5,422	3,610	9,115

[a]S = senior college; C = community college.
[b]The Open-Admissions Test was not administered to this cohort.

with senior-college students shown separately from community-college students. Among the principal social origins variables (age, gender, parents' education, income, and ethnicity), overall response rates were very high, usually well over 90 percent, except in the case of income, where nonresponse varied from 10 to 20 percent. For the attitudinal and aspiration variables (such as academic self-rating, personal growth as a reason for college, and attitudes toward open admissions), response rates were very high for the 1970 entrants but fell off in the 1971 and 1972 cohorts, especially among community-college students.[17] For the educational background variables (high school average, rank, and college preparatory units), there was little missing data except in the case of high school rank, where information was missing for about 20–30 percent of community-college students. On the Open-Admissions Test the percentage of missing scores was higher than for any other variable. It was particularly high among the 1971 community-college entrants as a result of difficulties in following up students who did not report for the initial testing.[18]

These merged files are used to analyze a variety of open-admissions results for students of different backgrounds. Since we are generalizing from samples, albeit large ones, of the three cohort populations, it is necessary to determine whether the samples are representative by comparing them with the total populations. The details of this comparison are presented in appendix A. The overall pattern is clear. The samples contain greater proportions of able students and the academic performance of these students was in some respects better than that of the corresponding populations. In almost all cases, however, the superiority of the samples is only slight. Of course, we do not have population measures for every variable measured in our samples, but as far as we have been able to compare samples and populations, there seems little reason to suspect that findings from the samples are invalid. We will point out, however, the few instances in which findings need qualification because of possible sample bias.

In using the population files and the sample survey data, our primary purpose is to assess the results of the open-admissions policy. Given the nonrandomness of each sample, we need the data from all three cohorts to strengthen our conclusions. In a sense each cohort gives us an opportunity to replicate our results. Insofar as the patterns observed in one cohort are consistent with those observed in the others, this bolsters the validity of our findings.

However, as we have formulated our analyses of these data sets, they do not furnish a basis for intercohort comparisons and thus the analysis of trends. Inferences about trends are not warranted for several reasons. One is that by June 1975 (the end point of our data), each cohort had been in college for a different length of time and thus differences among cohorts in academic outcomes are partly a result of the varying duration of the students' collegiate careers.[19] Intercohort comparisons are also tenuous because the colleges represented in each sample vary somewhat from cohort to cohort. Limiting our analyses to the same period of time for each cohort and to a common set of colleges would run counter to our primary purpose, to describe fully the academic outcomes of open admissions. And while we could have formulated additional analyses in ways that would have allowed for the consideration of trends, we chose not to do this because it would have added greatly to the complexity of our already very detailed presentations.[20]

Types of Data Analysis

Throughout this volume two kinds of data analysis are used. The basic academic outcomes of the open-admissions policy are described in tabular form. These tables were prepared from all three data sources. To describe the effects of open admissions upon the ethnic composition of the University, we use the CUNY census and the ethnicity data from the sample survey. Frequently, and especially in chapter 6, our interest is in comparing open-admissions with regular students. In these instances we use the academic performance files for the three populations, that is, the entire cohorts of 1970, 1971, and 1972 entering freshmen. Where results are tabulated by important social origins variables, especially ethnicity, we use the combined sample survey–academic performance file. For each table presented in subsequent chapters, we shall specify the data source.

In using the samples for our tabular presentations of results, we have been cavalier about significance tests for differences. In part this is because we had a large number of cases, and therefore almost any sizable difference is likely to be significant.[21] Also, almost always we have paid attention mainly to patterns consistent across the three cohorts. Such consistency adds to our confidence in the results.

Our analyses go well beyond the simple description of results. We also attempt to provide a clearer understanding of the major determinants of those results. In doing this we have used the techniques of multiple regression analysis. The merged sample survey–academic performance files constitute the data source for these analyses. We have tried to present the results of these regression analyses so that the reader unfamiliar with the technique can understand the essential findings simply by reading the text. However, for these readers, a basic, nontechnical description of regression analysis and how to interpret its results is presented, together with examples, in appendix B.

A few comments are in order for those who are knowledgeable about regression analysis. Certain of our key variables occur in the form of categories —sometimes ordered, sometimes not—to which numerical values cannot plausibly be assigned. Ethnicity is an obvious case in point; family income is a less obvious one. In the case of income, we resorted to categories rather than an income scale because we were reluctant to assume anything about the functional form of the relationship between income and academic outcome. Following standard practice, we represent categorical variables in our regression equations by sets of dummy variables. Their standardized coefficients are the so-called sheaf coefficients described by Heise.[22]

It was necessary deliberately to choose a method for coping with missing data, especially because the regression equations potentially could include many variables. There is disagreement in the literature over the most appropriate strategy. In one widely advocated strategy—sometimes called "listwise deletion"—regression equations are based on only those cases that contain complete information for all relevant variables. In another widely advocated approach—frequently referred to as "pairwise deletion"—each correlation in the matrix from which an equation is estimated is derived from all cases with valid information for the two relevant variables. Thus, each correlation may be derived from a somewhat different set of cases.

At the outset, the listwise procedure seemed inappropriate. Because we wished to consider a number of variables as potential influences on academic outcomes, the set of cases that contained complete information for all the variables would have been far smaller than the original sample,[23] which would have raised serious questions about the representativeness of the resulting regression equations. Moreover, as table 3.1 shows, this drastic reduction would have been brought about by only a few variables, such as the scores on the Open-Admissions Test; most variables have little missing data. Therefore, we elected to use pairwise deletion in all of our analyses. Subsequently, however, we have replicated some of the key analyses in chapter 7, using listwise deletion; the results were gratifyingly similar to those we have reported.

Notes

1. For the initial year of open admissions, CUNY contracted with an outside agency, the American Council on Education (ACE), to conduct an evaluation. The results of that one-year study are presented in Jack E. Rossman, Helen S. Astin, Alexander W. Astin, and Elaine H. El-Khawas, *Open Admissions at City University of New York: An Analysis of the First Year* (Englewood Cliffs: Prentice-Hall, 1975). The University realized that a long-term research effort would be needed in order to assess many of the important questions surrounding the open-admissions policy. Initially, however, it had no capability for such a project. While the ACE study was under way, CUNY began to develop a centralized student data system that would allow routine monitoring of student academic performance. With support from Exxon Education Foundation, detailed data were collected on remedial and other support services, and social background information was collected from samples of students entering in 1971 and 1972. These activities were carried out under Lavin's direction.

2. The actual instruments used were selected from the Stanford achievement test battery. The reading test was the *High School Reading Test, Form W* (New York: Harcourt, 1965). The test of numerical competence was the arithmetic computation section of the *Advanced Arithmetic Tests, Form X* (New York: Harcourt, 1964). In 1970 the tests were administered in the high schools, and the testing was directed by Max Weiner, a member of CUNY's doctoral faculty in educational psychology. In 1971 prospective students were asked to report to testing centers set up on several CUNY campuses. The 1971 testing was directed by Lavin.

3. The number of credits a student was taking was not necessarily equal to the number for which he or she had registered at the beginning of a term. Students sometimes officially withdrew from courses. These official withdrawals were (as a matter of CUNY policy at that time) not counted in the total number of credits that students attempted.

4. Not all grades at CUNY were on the A through F scale. Pass-fail grades were also given. These grades were not calculated in students' grade point averages.
5. Two colleges required somewhat fewer than 128 credits for graduation. So as to provide a more precise estimate of credit underreporting, we excluded them from these calculations.
6. Some of the community-college career programs, such as nursing, required more than sixty-four credits.
7. Our assessments disclosed other problems of a minor nature. For example, there were a few students shown as graduating for whom the college granting the degree was missing. In other cases the types of degree (B.A., A.A., etc.) was not listed in the record. These instances were infrequent and have no substantive effect upon our analyses.
8. The 1970 questionnaire was the ACE student information form, administered every fall at campuses throughout the nation. Appended to that questionnaire was a special supplement designed to elicit information related to the open-admissions program.
9. For each freshman cohort, the missing institutions are the following: 1970, Kingsborough and Hostos community colleges; 1971, City, Baruch, Hunter, and Brooklyn colleges; 1972, City, Brooklyn, John Jay, and Hostos.
10. As a result, students who dropped out early may be underrepresented in our samples. Bias in our samples is discussed in appendix A.
11. There was considerable variation in response rate at the colleges that administered the questionnaires. The percentages of freshmen responding at the senior colleges in each year were as follows. For 1970, Baruch, 83; Brooklyn, 74; CCNY, 60; Hunter, 10; John Jay, 30; Lehman, 37; Queens, 58; and York, 85. For 1971, Medgar Evers, 22; John Jay, 19; Lehman, 62; Queens, 41; and York, 35. For 1972, Baruch, 14; Hunter, 32; Medgar Evers, 23; Lehman, 46; Queens, 56; and York, 29. In the community colleges the percentages of freshmen responding in each year were as follows. For 1970, Manhattan, 26; Bronx, 32; New York City, 33; Queensborough, 76; and Staten Island, 26. For 1971, Manhattan, 74; Bronx, 30; Hostos, 25; Kingsborough, 30; LaGuardia, 49; New York City, 15; Queensborough, 45; and Staten Island, 27. For 1972, Manhattan, 54; Bronx, 30; Kingsborough, 73; LaGuardia, 82; New York City, 53; Queensborough, 85; and Staten Island, 38.
12. The questionnaires included more variables than are listed in the following discussion. Almost all of the major variables that played a statistically significant role in explaining various academic outcomes or that had some intrinsic significance (for example, attitudes toward open admissions) are listed. A few variables that were used in only one or two analyses are not listed. For example, the 1970 questionnaire elicited information about students' high school programs and about the type of high school attended (e.g., public or parochial). These data are described where they are used (see chapters 5 and 7).
13. Response categories differed slightly in each of the three questionnaires. It should be noted that occupation of the head of household is typically used in constructing indices of socioeconomic status. Unfortunately, the 1970 questionnaire did not provide occupational data appropriate to the CUNY student body (it did not list enough occupations typical of the parents of CUNY stu-

dents). The 1971 and 1972 questionnaires contained open-ended items on parents' occupations, but insufficient resources were available to code these.

14. Our assignment of respondents to the Catholic and Jewish categories was based upon responses to three items. Students were asked to indicate the religious background of father, mother, and self. If the same response was given for at least two of the three reference individuals, the respondent was classified in that religious category. The assignment of individuals to the Hispanic category in 1970 was based on an item that asked what languages other than English were spoken at home. Respondents who indicated that Spanish was spoken were classified as Hispanic. In 1971 the Hispanic category was composed of those who were born in Puerto Rico and/or whose parents were born there, as well as those who identified themselves as being from other Latin countries.

15. After the 1971 questionnaire was administered, controversy developed regarding the collection of data on religion and national origin. The result was the deletion from the 1972 questionnaire of the relevant ethnic items. In that year Hispanics were those who identified themselves as Puerto Rican or Latin.

16. These are the items from the 1970 questionnaire. They varied in a minor way from those in the later questionnaires, but they are representative of the type used in all three surveys.

17. In 1971 Manhattan Community College used its own questionnaire for the collection of social background data. In 1972 both Manhattan and LaGuardia community colleges used their own questionnaires. These contained social origins items that were very similar to those in ours, and these data were included in our files. The attitudinal items with high percentages of missing cases were ones not included in these colleges' questionnaires.

18. The implications of these lower response rates on the Open-Admissions Test are discussed in chapter 9, where the characteristics of takers and nontakers of the tests are compared.

19. For example, the 1970 cohort obviously had more time to earn credits and to graduate than did the later cohorts. As we have designed our analyses, even the comparison of cohorts over a standardized time period does not always allow trend interpretations. Thus, dropout rates after one year (see chapter 6) are not entirely comparable because students in the 1970 cohort had more semesters in which to return to college than did students in subsequent cohorts.

20. Contributing to this decision were the results of some preliminary analyses that provided a basis for trend interpretation. Comparisons of the 1970, 1971, and 1972 cohorts failed to reveal any clear trends in academic outcomes.

21. To simplify the data presentations, we do not report for every table the number of cases on which percentages are computed. Thus, in chapter 5, which uses sample survey data, table 5.1 presents the maximum possible bases for percentages calculated in the other tables of that chapter. The actual number of cases for any specific table is somewhat reduced by the missing cases for the variable in question.

22. David R. Heise, "Employing Nominal Variables, Induced Variables, and Block Variables in Path Analyses," *Sociological Methods and Research* 1 (November 1972): 147–173.

23. For example, tables 7.6 and 7.11 in chapter 7 regress several academic out-

comes variables on a large number of independent variables. Had we used list-wise regression, the number of senior-college students in the 1970 sample would have been reduced from 9,110 to 4,939. Among community-college students the number would have been reduced from 4,415 to 1,504.

4. Access to Educational Opportunity under Open Admissions

THE OPEN-ADMISSIONS experiment built on an important tradition of the City University of New York. The University, and particularly City College, had provided a broad avenue for the social mobility of the children and grandchildren of European immigrants, especially for Jews coming from eastern Europe at the end of the nineteenth century and the beginning of the twentieth. Nonetheless, what the University had done for earlier groups coming from Europe it had failed to do by the late 1960s for the newly arriving groups from the American South and the Caribbean. Blacks and Puerto Ricans were virtually excluded from the University's four-year colleges because of increasingly stringent entrance requirements. Since the explicit intent of the open-admissions policy was to aid minority students who were thought to be disadvantaged in the competition for educational credentials, any evaluation of the policy must start with an assessment of the extent to which it gave them—and others—access to educational opportunity. In this chapter, we will provide such an assessment, considering two basic questions: who came to the University as a result of its open-admissions policy and how were they placed?

These questions are more complex than they seem. We have already noted that the policy allowed not only minority students to enter the University but also many whites—both working- and middle-class, both Jewish and Catholic. The consequences of the open-admissions policy for the ethnic composition of the University require careful examination, as does the placement of students within the University.

Placement has two separate aspects. The more important involves the allocation of students to various levels of the University, such as its two- and four-year colleges, which are linked to specific educational opportunities. It need hardly be said that placement at a four-year as against a two-year institution affects the degree that a student is likely to earn and the benefits he or she is likely to derive from college. Placement in these terms concerns the internal stratification of the University and raises a critical question: to what extent did placement coincide with social origin?[1] The other aspect of placement involves the assignment of students to specific campuses and thus the effect of the open-admissions policy on the ethnic integration of the University. Even though many minority students came to CUNY during the era of open admissions, it is possible that its colleges remained largely segregated. Indeed, since CUNY is a system of commuter colleges, the high degree of residential segregation in New York City[2] would suggest some segregation at CUNY. The quality of educational opportunity afforded minority students under open admissions may have been affected by their attendance at segregated schools.

Our examination in this chapter will seek to determine not only the degrees of segregation and stratification by ethnicity but also, if they existed, the processes from which these features arose.

Ethnicity at CUNY: Data

Which are the principal ethnic groups[3] at CUNY for an evaluation of the open-admissions program? The importance of minority groups, specifically blacks and Hispanics, is obviously implied by the rationale for the policy. But we think that ethnic distinctions among whites are important, too. The significance of white ethnicity in the city from which the University draws its students cannot be disputed. Ethnic groups in New York City, a primary port of entry for many European immigrants, both white and nonwhite, can be seen as communities of collective experience, with distinctive and evolving patterns of entry and participation in key institutional areas of city life, the City University not the least among these.[4]

From the perspective of past participation in the City University, it is valid to distinguish Jews, whose use of the University was the most notable, from other whites—mostly Catholics (there are few white Protestants in New York City and those few rarely attend the City University). Catholic students in the city had attended the University in the past but they also had availed themselves of the numerous Catholic colleges and universities in the metropolitan area. Within the Catholic group, nationality distinctions, especially between Irish and Italian Catholics, remain important outside the walls of the University. We suggest that they are less important within those walls, however.[5] The key distinction among whites for an evaluation of open admissions appears to be religion.

The three types of data described in chapter 3 provide us with different parts of the answers to questions about ethnic access to educational opportunity under open admissions. To begin with, the ethnic census data allow us to distinguish white from minority students, although they do not permit ethnic distinctions among whites. Nonetheless, these census data provide the basis for a very important set of trend analyses dealing with the impact of open admissions on the enrollment of black and Hispanic students at CUNY.

Such analyses meet with one significant problem. Open admissions was not the only vehicle for increasing access to CUNY for minority students. Both the senior-college program known as SEEK and the community-college program called College Discovery added minority students as well. In fact, these programs consisted almost entirely of black and Hispanic students during the years under examination. In assessing the impact of open admissions on minority enrollments, these special program students must be separated from other minority students. We have done this by using the University's annual fall enrollment reports, which provide headcount data for each CUNY college and separate enumerations for the special program students. By relying on both the ethnic census and the enrollment reports, we have been able to make those estimates necessary for the trend analyses of the effects of open admissions on the minority composition of the University.

The survey questionnaires administered to the first three freshman classes entering after open admissions began (i.e., the 1970, 1971, and 1972 freshmen) constitute our most important means of assessing ethnicity's relation to access. Using the data collected from these questionnaires, which include information about the student's racial and religious background, we have derived the following ethnic categories for the 1970 and 1971 freshmen: blacks, Hispanics,[6] Jews, and non-Hispanic Catholics.[7] (For simplicity, the non-Hispanic Catholics will be called Catholics throughout.) For the 1972 freshmen, religious data are not available and we cannot distinguish the Catholic and Jewish groups; our analyses will be presented for whites, blacks, and Hispanics. It should be noted that the groups we have omitted, such as white Protestants and Asians, are numerically small (our ethnic categories include over 85 percent of the freshmen in 1970, for example).

In discussing ethnicity, we will make use of a terminological convention to avoid clumsy formulations, referring to blacks and Hispanics collectively as minorities and to Jews and Catholics collectively as white ethnics. By implication, and with some imprecision in the case of Hispanics, the minority groups are nonwhites.[8]

Ethnic Stratification at CUNY

Those who have highlighted the role of education in maintaining inequality have seen the two- and four-year colleges as constituting very different tracks, with different curricula implying widely divergent occupational and economic outcomes. CUNY is formally such a two-tier system (in contrast to the California three-tier model), but it can also be viewed as a three-tier system by distinguishing between two groups of senior colleges: elite and nonelite. The schools we are calling elite are older than the other CUNY senior colleges and have, for that reason, stronger public reputations.[9] Our examination of the distribution of students across levels will use both the two- and three-tier views of the CUNY system. The CUNY colleges and their classification are shown in table 4.1.[10]

Open admissions produced a sizable increase in the number of students entering CUNY: the first freshman class entering under the new policy in 1970 was about 75 percent larger than that of the previous year. The students entering under the new admissions criteria were admitted in large

TABLE 4.1. The Colleges of CUNY

	FRESHMAN ENROLLMENT IN FALL 1970[a]
Elite Senior Colleges	
Brooklyn	4,278
City	3,234
Hunter	3,156
Queens	3,672
Nonelite Senior Colleges	
Baruch	1,582
Medgar Evers (founded in 1971)	654[b]
John Jay	1,071
Herbert H. Lehman	2,593
Richmond	0[c]
York	878
Community Colleges	
Borough of Manhattan	1,556
Bronx	1,681
Hostos	623
Kingsborough	2,610
LaGuardia (founded in 1971)	669[b]
New York City	3,052
Queensborough	3,324
Staten Island	2,205

[a]The freshman enrollments included students in the special programs, SEEK and College Discovery, and were taken with minor modifications from the enrollment reports.
[b]These enrollments were from fall 1971, when these colleges opened their doors.
[c]This college is an upper-division college only.

numbers to all levels of the University, as is seen in table 4.2, which shows the proportions of open-admissions students at different levels of the University for the 1970, 1971, and 1972 freshmen.[11] As a percentage of the entering class, open-admissions students were most numerous at the nonelite senior colleges and the community colleges. Two-thirds of the students entering these schools were open-admissions students, making it apparent that the new policy did not simply channel students into terminal programs in the community colleges. Open-admissions students were, however, least numerous at the elite four-year schools, accounting for less than a third of the freshmen entering these schools and thereby lending credence to the distinction between the two groups of senior colleges.

The number of minority students attending CUNY also leapt upward as soon as the program began. Blacks and Hispanics increased their representation from 20 percent of the 1969 class to 27 percent of the 1970 class. Taking into account the increased size of the 1970 freshman class, we can see that the number of freshman blacks and Hispanics more than doubled between 1969 and 1970 (and more than tripled if SEEK and College Discovery students are discounted).

How were these increased numbers of minority students distributed across the levels of CUNY? Table 4.3 presents the proportions of minority freshman enrollment, in which blacks and Hispanics are combined, at the different levels of CUNY for the years 1969 through 1975. The table makes dramatically clear the changes that took place. From 1969 (the last year before open admissions) through 1975, the proportions of black and Hispanic students among all entering students more than doubled at CUNY as well as at most of its levels.

As we said earlier, in order fully to understand the distribution of ethnic groups in CUNY, it is necessary to consider the consequences for minority enrollment of the special programs, SEEK and College Discovery. Both

TABLE 4.2. Percentages of Open-Admissions Students at Different Levels of CUNY

Cohort	Elite Senior[a]	Other Senior[a]	All Senior[a]	Community[b]	All of CUNY[c]
1970	27	69	39	66	37
1971	30	66	42	67	41
1972	32	68	45	65	41

Source: Population data.
[a]At the senior-college level, open-admissions students are defined as those with high school averages below 80.
[b]At the community-college level, open-admissions students are defined as those with high school averages below 75.
[c]For all of CUNY, open-admissions students are defined as those who would not have been admitted to any level of the University by traditional criteria—in other words, those with high school averages below 75.

TABLE 4.3. Representation of Minority Students among Students Entering Different Levels of CUNY from 1969 to 1975

Cohort	Elite Senior	Other Senior	All Senior	Community	All of CUNY	Size of Cohort
	% of Minority Students among All Entering Students					
1969	15.2	14.8	15.1	26.3	20.0	19,948
1970	22.1	23.0	22.3	33.3	27.0	35,515
1971	24.0	28.6	25.5	37.3	31.2	38,829
1972	23.0	34.1	27.0	43.8	34.8	37,912
1973	30.1	36.9	32.6	49.2	40.3	37,342
1974	30.9	41.8	35.1	49.7	42.0	40,014
1975[a]	33.8	48.4	40.0	46.9	43.3	38,114
	% of Minority Students among Non-Special Program Students					
1969	4.5	2.3	4.1	16.6	9.5	17,645
1970	10.4	13.5	11.4	26.5	17.9	31,596
1971	15.7	22.6	18.1	32.5	25.0	35,639
1972	12.8	27.3	18.1	39.8	28.5	35,545
1973	21.1	29.2	24.0	44.1	33.5	33,529
1974	18.6	30.1	23.0	44.2	33.4	34,846
1975[a]	26.1	42.6	33.1	41.7	37.3	34,352

Source: CUNY annual censuses.
[a]Hunter is excluded from the 1975 calculations because of its low response rate to the census.

programs provided access to CUNY and before open admissions SEEK was virtually the only mechanism by which black and Hispanic students could attend CUNY's senior colleges. In the last year before open admissions, about 75 percent of minority students enrolled in the senior colleges were in the SEEK program, and about 45 percent of all minority students in the community colleges were in College Discovery. SEEK and College Discovery continued to provide large shares of minority enrollment after open admissions, and it is therefore necessary to take them into account since the students they contribute are not beneficiaries of open admissions as a distinct program. When we exclude special program students, the increases in minority enrollment under open admissions look even more stunning. At the senior-college level, in particular, the representation of blacks and Hispanics more than quintupled from 1969 to 1975.

To what extent were minority students underrepresented or overrepresented at specific levels of CUNY? To assess the degree to which ethnicity was an important stratifying principle, we calculated the ratio of the percentage of blacks and Hispanics at any level of CUNY for a given year to their percentage among the entering students for that year. These ratios appear in table 4.4: a ratio below 1 indicates that minority students were underrepresented at that level by comparison with their overall proportion in the freshman class, while a ratio above 1 indicates their overrepresentation.

TABLE 4.4. Stratification of Entering Minority Students across the Levels of CUNY from 1969 to 1975[a]

| COHORT | ALL ENTERING STUDENTS | | | |
	Elite Senior	Other Senior	All Senior	Community
1969	.76	.74	.76	1.32
1970	.82	.85	.83	1.23
1971	.77	.92	.82	1.20
1972	.66	.98	.78	1.26
1973	.75	.92	.81	1.22
1974	.74	1.00	.84	1.18
1975	.78	1.12	.92	1.08
COHORT	NON–SPECIAL PROGRAM STUDENTS ONLY			
	Elite Senior	Other Senior	All Senior	Community
1969	.47	.24	.43	1.75
1970	.58	.75	.64	1.48
1971	.63	.90	.72	1.30
1972	.45	.96	.64	1.40
1973	.63	.87	.72	1.32
1974	.56	.90	.69	1.32
1975	.70	1.14	.89	1.12

Source: Table 4.3.
[a]Ratios of actual proportions to those expected if minority students were uniformly distributed across the levels of CUNY.

Considerable inequality existed in the distribution of minority students before open admissions, as shown by the ratios for 1969. Omitting the special program students, we see that minority students were greatly underrepresented at the senior colleges, particularly at the nonelite senior colleges. Including the special program students reduces the inequality to some degree, but it nevertheless remains substantial. This simple comparison demonstrates the importance of SEEK in gaining representation for minority students at the senior-college level.

But, as table 4.4 shows, considerable change occurred in the distribution of minority students during the years of open admissions, generally in the direction of greater equality. The more important shifts occurred between the senior and the community colleges. Whether we include or exclude special program students, the overrepresentation of minority students at the community-college level had sharply declined by 1975 and, with it, their underrepresentation at the senior-college level. Their increasing representation at the senior-college level resulted for the most part from changes in their representation at the nonelite senior colleges, where blacks and Hispanics had become slightly overrepresented among the entering students by 1975. Their underrepresentation at the elite senior colleges was little changed during open admissions. It should be noted, however, that when we examine only students admitted outside SEEK, then the representation of minority students at the elite senior colleges did increase. The lack of change in their representation when all students are considered probably indicates a decline in the importance of SEEK at the elite senior colleges during the early years of open admissions.

Although the representation of minority students increased throughout CUNY, some inequality in their distribution existed even as late as 1975, and it is not clear so far how to assess that inequality. Given the unequal high school backgrounds of minority and white students and their different social class origins, it was probably inevitable that in the 1970s there would continue to be differences between them in access to educational resources, even under an open-admissions system. One preliminary way to assess the degree to which racial stratification existed at CUNY under open admissions is to look at other open-admissions systems. The older California system provides a clear contrast. Data presented by Jaffe and Adams[12] demonstrate that the University of California was far more racially stratified than CUNY. For example, the proportion of blacks and Hispanics was ten times as great in the California community colleges than at its university centers in the late 1960s, while the minority proportion in the community colleges was not even twice as large as that in the elite senior colleges of CUNY. CUNY under open admissions appears far more equitable in this comparison.

But minority students were not the sole beneficiaries of open admissions. Large numbers of whites were also admitted under the new program, as can be seen from table 4.5. First, table 4.5 presents the percentages of each ethnic group's members who were admitted as a result of open admissions. Second, it presents each group's percentage of the total number of beneficiaries. These two kinds of percentages are presented for each level of CUNY and for CUNY as a whole.[13] Four groups are considered: blacks, Hispanics, Jews, and Catholics.

As the changes in the racial composition of CUNY imply, larger proportions of blacks and Hispanics than of Jews and Catholics were admitted to CUNY and to its senior-college system under open admissions. The differences between minority groups and the traditional beneficiaries of CUNY education were largest at the elite senior colleges, where over half of the black students in each cohort were admitted under the new criteria as compared with 20 percent or fewer of Jews and Catholics. The disparity is much smaller at the other senior colleges, where large percentages of every group were admitted under open admissions. Finally, the disparity disappears at the community colleges, where—in great contrast to the senior colleges—the proportion of Jews admitted by the new criteria was one of the two largest.

When we look at the percentage each group forms among all beneficiaries—or, to put it another way, when we compare groups in terms of their

TABLE 4.5. How Ethnic Groups Benefited from Open Admissions

Ethnic Group	Elite Senior	Other Senior	All Senior	Community	All of CUNY	Number in Sample

% of Group[a] Benefiting from Open Admissions

Ethnic Group	Elite Senior	Other Senior	All Senior	Community	All of CUNY	Number in Sample
---------------- 1970 ----------------						
Jews	15	69	27	70	19	(4,378)
Catholics[c]	20	61	36	53	26	(4,723)
Blacks	66	91	78	70	59	(1,098)
Hispanics	40	71	51	56	36	(1,026)
---------------- 1971 ----------------						
Jews	6	46	26	65	30	(1,551)
Catholics[c]	12	45	35	51	32	(2,567)
Blacks	54	76	73	76	72	(1,220)
Hispanics	33	63	60	63	53	(784)
---------------- 1972 ----------------						
Whites	9	59	27	60	42	(7,666)
Blacks	55	84	72	77	70	(2,141)
Hispanics	46	69	58	59	51	(1,258)

% of All Beneficiaries[b] Belonging to Group

Ethnic Group	Elite Senior	Other Senior	All Senior	Community	All of CUNY
---------------- 1970 ----------------					
Jews	33	30	31	21	23
Catholics[c]	26	38	33	39	35
Blacks	14	13	13	16	18
Hispanics	11	8	10	10	10
Other[d]	15	11	13	13.	14
---------------- 1971 ----------------					
Jews	25	23	23	16[e]	16[e]
Catholics[c]	36	38	38	29[e]	28[e]
Blacks	13	15	15	25	26
Hispanics	5	10	10	13	12
Other[d]	21	14	15	18	18
---------------- 1972 ----------------					
Whites	45	65	60	59	57
Blacks	29	20	23	27	28
Hispanics	21	11	14	11	12
Other[d]	4	3	3	3	3

Source: Sample data.

[a]The base for each percentage is the number of students from a given ethnic group at a specific level of CUNY.

[b]The base for each percentage is the number of open-admissions students at a given level of CUNY. Percentages are rounded, and columns may not total 100 percent.

[c]We remind the reader that throughout the book the term "Catholics" refers to non-Hispanic Catholics.

[d]The "other" row indicates the percentages of open-admissions students who do not belong to the distinguished groups. In 1970 and 1971, these students may be Protestant whites, whites of some other or no religion, whites of unknown religion, Asian-Americans, or other nonwhites. In 1972, these other students may be Asian-Americans or other non-whites. None of these categories consistently contributed more than a few percentage points to the ranks of open-admissions students.

[e]These percentages are adjusted to compensate for the absence of religious data at one community college.

numbers rather than the percentages admitted under open admissions—a very different impression of benefit results. As table 4.5 shows, open-admissions Jewish and Catholic students generally outnumbered open-admissions blacks and Hispanics throughout the CUNY system. One aspect of the extent to which white ethnics benefited is especially striking. Many have previously recognized that whites have been important beneficiaries, but they have—with considerable unanimity—pointed to Catholic ethnics as the white beneficiaries. But table 4.5 makes clear that Jews were also major beneficiaries of open admissions, even at the senior-college level. Roughly a quarter or more of the students at the senior colleges who would not have been admitted under the old requirements were Jewish.

Of course, not all of the students who were open-admissions students according to the traditional criteria for entry to CUNY owe their college educations to the open-admissions program. Some undoubtedly would have gone to college even if they had been denied entry to CUNY. Hence, it is possible that classifying students in terms of the traditional admissions criteria overstates the benefits of the program to white students, who were more likely than minority students to possess the financial resources necessary to attend less selective private or state colleges.

It is difficult to quantify the benefits of the policy in terms of the numbers of students who went to college only because of the program, but one question asked of the 1970 freshmen suggests some rough proportions. They were asked how the open-admissions policy had affected their plans for college: "it made college possible for me" and "it encouraged me to go, but I probably would have gone anyway" were possible responses. We will analyze the responses to this question in greater detail in the next chapter, but we make some use of them here in order to pin down further the ethnic benefits of the policy.

Probably not all students knew how much they had benefited from the policy; certainly not everyone would have known his or her high school average in the special form used in the admissions process. For this reason, as well as the fact that some students would have gone to college no matter what, there is only a modest relation between the perception of benefit from the policy and formal admissions status. Moreover, senior-college students were less likely than community-college students to perceive themselves as beneficiaries. Only 7 percent of the senior-college students said that open admissions had "made college possible"; another quarter felt encouraged by the policy. It should be recognized that some of the other senior-college students probably felt that they would not have been able to go to a four-year school but for the policy; however, the question did not ask about that aspect of benefit. Among community-college students, a fifth felt that the policy had made college possible and another two-fifths felt encouraged to go because of it.

White ethnic students were less likely than minority students to perceive themselves as benefiting from the program even when formal admissions status is controlled. However, at both the senior and the community colleges, a majority of those who felt that open admissions had made college possible for them were Jewish or Catholic, while only a third were black or Hispanic; the remainder were mostly other white students. Also at both the senior and the community colleges, almost two-thirds of those who felt encouraged by the policy to go to college were Jewish or Catholic, while a quarter or less were black or Hispanic. Again, the remainder were mostly other whites.

In sum, these analyses of formal admissions status and perceived benefit reveal two different but ultimately consistent aspects of the consequences of open admissions. Since so few blacks and Hispanics qualified for CUNY and its senior colleges under the older criteria, open admissions had a powerful impact on the racial composition of the University. But *more* whites than minority students benefited from open admissions, at least from 1970 through 1972. Moreover, all of our analyses probably neglect some of the policy's benefits. Many in the regular admissions category were still beneficiaries of open admissions because it enabled them to attend colleges such as City and Queens, which had very selective entrance requirements before open admissions. The sudden opening of the elite schools at CUNY probably accounts for the drop in the number of freshmen attending some private colleges in New York City during the first year of the policy.[14] Given the very few minority students in the senior-college regular admissions category, these unidentified beneficiaries were undoubtedly white ethnics for the most part. Thus, in this way as in others, it is clear that when the doors of the prestigious senior-college system were opened to students who did not meet the traditional criteria for admission, it was not only the apparent objects of the open-admissions policy, minority students, who crowded in but also students from the groups that historically have benefited most from CUNY education, white Catholics and Jews.

Integration on the Campuses

That minority students not only increased their representation at CUNY but also became more equally distributed over its levels during the first five years of open admissions does not speak directly to the issue of integration on CUNY's seventeen campuses. Despite the declining ethnic stratification at CUNY—or perhaps as a response by whites to it—it is possible that individual colleges either remained predominantly white or became predominantly minority as the number of minority students increased.

Issues related to integration have aroused passions over the last few decades, both among the general public and among scholars, as the controversy over busing and white flight indicates.[15] Yet, astonishingly, uncontested evidence of important benefits to blacks, or whites, as a result of integration is lacking. The many studies of integration have yielded contradictory results: just as some have found benefits in the form of improvements in academic achievement or reduction in prejudice and discrimination, others have not. And even when benefits have been found, they frequently have been small in magnitude,[16] as in the case of the greater academic achievement of black students in integrated schools discussed in the Coleman Report, long used in support of integration efforts.[17] The issue of integration at CUNY remains important, however, even if the demonstrable effects of integration generally are small or nonexistent. Segregation at CUNY's colleges allows for at least the possibility that largely minority colleges provided an education inferior to that provided by largely white colleges.

To measure segregation, we will use the so-called Index of Dissimilarity, which often has been used in studies of residential segregation and of segregation in educational systems.[18] Simply stated, the index compares the distributions of two groups over some set of units—CUNY's colleges in our case. The index is higher as the dissimilarity between those distributions, or segregation, is greater, and, in fact, its precise value can be interpreted as the proportion of either group that must be redistributed to make the two distributions equal.

Table 4.6 reports indices of dissimilarity for the college distributions of entering white and minority students in the years 1969 through 1975. Be-

TABLE 4.6. Indices of Dissimilarity for CUNY and Its Levels from 1969 to 1975

Cohort	Elite Senior	Other Senior	All Senior	Community	All of CUNY
		All Entering Students			
1969	.147	.256	.170	.298	.264
1970	.219	.101	.183	.430	.305
1971	.171	.268	.201	.406	.351
1972	.236	.175	.228	.434	.359
1973	.258	.175	.224	.470	.384
1974	.358	.264	.319	.518	.435
1975	—[a]	.259	.302	.529	.421
		Non-Special Program Students Only			
1969	.411	.541	.426	.355	.424
1970	.240	.164	.203	.503	.413
1971	.312	.331	.299	.431	.415
1972	.322	.250	.324	.473	.458
1973	.317	.174	.278	.505	.439
1974	.481	.326	.403	.574	.545
1975	—[a]	.276	.342	.571	.469

Source: CUNY annual censuses.
[a]Not calculated because the lack of data for Hunter in that year leaves only three elite senior colleges.

cause we already know that the distribution of minority students between the community and the senior colleges changed over these years, we have computed indices separately for the community and the senior colleges, for the elite and nonelite senior colleges, and for the whole CUNY system to disentangle the segregation at individual colleges from the ethnic stratification across the levels of the City University.

If we look at all entering students, without distinguishing those in special programs from the others, it seems that segregation increased at CUNY's colleges during the first five years of open admissions. Segregation increased overall for the system, as well as separately within the community and within the senior colleges. Only at the nonelite senior colleges did segregation remain both modest and stable. Interestingly, segregation seems to have been rather insubstantial at the senior colleges before open admissions —highest at the nonelite schools, where there were proportionately few students before the new policy. During the policy's first two years, segregation increased only modestly at the elite senior colleges and at the senior colleges overall, but thereafter its pace accelerated. The picture is rather different for the community colleges, where segregation was consistently higher than at the senior schools throughout the period under discussion. The community colleges were not only more segregated to begin with, but community-college segregation increased substantially as soon as open admissions began.

The increasing segregation at CUNY does not mean that whites became rare in some schools and nonwhites rare in others. To the contrary, as the numbers of nonwhites grew at CUNY there was, in an absolute sense, undoubtedly more ethnic mixing in classes and colleges. But, as open admissions wore on, the concentrations of whites and nonwhites grew more disparate. Some colleges remained largely white despite the increasing numbers of blacks and Hispanics attending other colleges in the same tier, while others became largely nonwhite.

One reason for the increasing segregation under open admissions was the declining relative contribution of the special programs to the representation of minority students, particularly at the senior colleges. The mechanism for creating SEEK and College Discovery places at the various colleges and the virtual exclusion of whites from these programs guaranteed that they would contribute to the integration of the colleges.[19] Thus, the indices of dissimilarity calculated with special program students excluded are nearly always higher than those calculated with these students included, indicating that the special program students were more equally distributed than were minority students admitted outside these programs. But open admissions brought in large numbers of minority students outside SEEK and College Discovery, and as the numbers of these students increased, their distribution became the primary factor in CUNY's growing segregation.

The establishment of two colleges, Hostos in the community-college system and Medgar Evers in the senior system, also added to the segregation of CUNY's colleges. These colleges, which opened their doors to incoming freshmen early in the open-admissions era, were intended to appeal to minority students through their locations, names, and special programs. As a consequence, they were overwhelmingly segregated during the period under discussion. By 1973, whites made up less than 5 percent of the freshmen entering these schools.

Elsewhere, stability of ethnic enrollments in some schools along with dramatic shifts in others helps to account for the increasing segregation. Brooklyn and Queens among the senior colleges and Kingsborough, Queensborough, and Staten Island among the community colleges remained heavily white in the open-admissions era, experiencing at best modest increases in minority enrollment. In 1975, the percentages of whites among entering freshmen at Brooklyn (62 percent), Queens (69 percent), and Queensborough (76 percent) were reduced somewhat from 1969 levels (79 percent, 88 percent, and 86 percent, respectively). However, the percentages of whites among entering students in 1975 at Kingsborough and Staten Island (81 percent and 82 percent, respectively) were unchanged from 1969 percentages. The contribution of these five schools to segregation was especially important because they accounted for substantial proportions of white enrollments in CUNY's community and senior colleges. In 1975, the two senior colleges welcomed over 50 percent of whites entering the senior colleges, compared to less than 30 percent of entering minority students (including those in SEEK). In the same year, the three community colleges accounted for over two-thirds of whites entering the community colleges, compared to less than 15 percent of entering minority students (including those in College Discovery).

In contrast to these five schools, others experienced sharp changes in ethnic composition. Among the senior colleges, City College, Lehman, and York went from predominantly white to predominantly minority over the period under discussion. In the case of City College, 78 percent of the freshmen entering in 1969 were whites; by 1975, only 30 percent were. A change of equal magnitude took place at York. Among the community colleges, the same process occurred at Bronx and New York City community colleges; and although the Borough of Manhattan Community College was never predominantly white, it was heavily minority by 1975. The three community colleges contributed very substantially to the increasing segregation at CUNY. In 1975, over two-thirds of minority students entering community colleges enrolled in one of the three, compared to less than a quarter of entering whites.

So far we have discussed changes in segregation at CUNY's senior and community colleges over the open-admissions years without actually examining how open-admissions students from the different ethnic groups were distributed. But such an examination is important because our finding of increasing segregation throughout the open-admissions years raises the possibility that open-admissions students, even more than regular students, were allocated to largely segregated colleges. Unfortunately, our sample data do not extend to the entering cohorts of 1974–1975, when segregation apparently reached its peak. But even an analysis of the earlier open-admissions cohorts may offer significant traces of the processes leading to the substantial segregation visible in later years.

Using our samples, we have examined the segregation in senior and community colleges separately, taking into account the distinction between regular and open-admissions students at the two levels. Even without distinguishing between the elite and nonelite senior colleges, interpretations require caution because the indices of dissimilarity are based on the numbers in each group at individual campuses and the campuses represented in our samples vary somewhat from year to year.[20] Also, since the sample data contain four major ethnic groups, each of which contributes students to the two admissions categories, the index yields matrices in each year that are too large to interpret easily. Therefore, we have chosen to illustrate the patterns of segregation by summarizing visually the 1970 dissimilarity matrices for the community and senior colleges. Mappings of segregation among the regular and open-admissions students from the four ethnic groups are shown in figure 4.1.[21] In both parts of this figure, the distance between any pair of points gives a fair idea of the degree of segregation between the corresponding categories of students: the further apart, the more segregated from each other.

Figure 4.1 suggests an important difference between the senior and the community colleges in the pattern of segregation. In the senior colleges, the open-admissions students from the different groups were generally less segregated from each other than were the regular students from each other. It would seem from this fact that the distribution of minority open-admissions students ought to have contributed to some desegregation of the senior colleges, but this was not the case. The open-admissions students from each group were quite segregated from the regular admissions students, including those of the same ethnic background, because they were especially likely to attend the nonelite senior colleges. In consequence, the ethnic segregation among regular students was little changed by the addition of open-admissions students to the senior-college system.

In the senior colleges, there is also an interesting contrast in the significance of ethnic differences within the minority and white groups. Regardless of admissions category, blacks and Hispanics were not very segregated from each other, but *regular* Jewish and Catholic students tended to go to different schools to a surprising degree and also differed in their segregation from minority students. In fact, regular Catholic students in the senior col-

Segregation at the Senior Colleges, 1970 Cohort
stress = .009

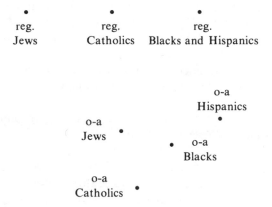

Segregation at the Community Colleges, 1970 Cohort
stress = .007

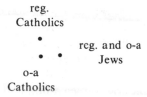

reg. Blacks • • o-a Blacks
reg. Hispanics • • o-a Hispanics

Figure 4.1. Multidimensional scaling of indexes of dissimilarity for the 1970 cohort.

leges in 1970 were as segregated from Jewish students as they were from blacks and Hispanics, and the regular Jewish students were extremely segregated from their minority peers.

In contrast to the senior colleges, the community colleges in 1970 showed little segregation by admissions status. The distribution of open-admissions students from each group was quite close to that of regular students from the same group. But there was considerable segregation by ethnic background, with ethnic distinctions within the white and minority pools of little consequence. Jews and Catholics were not very segregated from each other; nor were blacks and Hispanics from each other. There was, however, considerable segregation between white and minority students. Indeed, the spatial arrangement of the community-college groups in figure 4.1 offers a stark portrayal of segregation between whites and non-whites, which the addition of open-admissions students could do little to mollify.

In sum, as the numbers of minority students increased at CUNY, so did the segregation of the campuses, even though open admissions helped to bring about a more equal sorting of minority students between CUNY's tiers. It appears from an inspection of the ethnic enrollments at individual campuses that, as the years of open admissions wore on, some of the largest colleges either remained or became ethnic enclaves—in the midst of a higher educational system containing unusual and growing ethnic diversity. It deserves note that the ethnic colorations of these schools are, in the main, consistent with their geographical locations and the spatial arrangement of New York City's ethnic groups, but the additional processes bringing about this segregation are worth further study, as are its consequences.

Determinants of College Placement

The increasing segregation of students at CUNY under open admissions raises some obvious questions for us. Most immediately, the question of how it came about—or more precisely, how students were placed at CUNY's colleges—begs for an answer. The same question is raised by our finding that some stratification in the distribution of minority students continued to exist in the era of open admissions.

In the great majority of cases, the immediate cause of the student's placement was his or her own preferred college, indicated in the application for admission to CUNY. When we compare preferences with placements for the years 1970, 1971, and 1972, we find that most students in all ethnic groups were placed at their preferred college, and many others enrolled in their second-choice college. In 1970, 77 percent of all entering students had been placed in their preferred college, as was true for 69 percent in 1971 and 73 percent in 1972. Of course, some others enrolled at a college in the same level as their preferred college (in terms of the three tiers used earlier). More than 80 percent of students were placed at their preferred level in the three cohorts under examination.

As one might guess, then, from the stratification of minority students in these three years (see table 4.4), substantial differences in college preference existed among groups. Table 4.7 shows the college preferences of ethnic

TABLE 4.7. College Preference and Rate of Admission to Preferred Level, by Ethnic Group

Ethnic Group	COLLEGE PREFERENCE			RATE OF ADMISSION ACCORDING TO PREFERRED LEVEL[a]		
	Elite Senior	Other Senior	Com-munity	Elite Senior	Other Senior	Com-munity
			1970			
Jews	74%	13%	13%	88%	96%	100%
Catholics	51	19	30	73	94	100
Blacks	37	16	47	63	86	100
Hispanics	44	16	40	81	94	100
			1971			
Jews	54	25	21	65	86	100
Catholics	29	33	39	54	84	100
Blacks	15	17	68	16	59	100
Hispanics	11	21	69	22	77	100
			1972			
Whites	42	13	45	51	69	100
Blacks	22	11	67	32	60	100
Hispanics	21	12	67	49	75	100

Source: Sample data.
[a]In calculating rates of admission, we counted those few students placed at higher levels than they had preferred as placed at their preferred level.

groups in each of these years according to level. Because the representation of community and senior colleges in our samples varies from year to year, it is especially important in examining this table—one of only two tables in which level of college is not controlled—to pay attention to the pattern of ethnic differences rather than the magnitudes of individual percentages. And, as is easily seen, a consistent pattern exists. Jewish students aimed the highest in the two years for which religious data are available, with the largest percentages preferring an elite senior college and the smallest choosing a community college. Blacks and Hispanics fell equally far behind Catholics and Jews in preference for an elite senior college or, indeed, any senior college.[22]

It appears also from table 4.7 that in the aggregate there were major discrepancies in white and minority rates of admission to the senior colleges. Without taking high school average and rank into account, we see that blacks were the worst off in each cohort, least likely by far to be admitted to a senior college if they wanted to be. Hispanics also lagged far behind whites in rates of admission in 1971, although not in the other years. Overall, this seems to suggest that minority students were treated unfairly in the admissions process.

But a very different picture of the admissions process is revealed when we take into account high school average and rank, the two main formal admissions criteria under open admissions. It should be noted that according to our analysis of rates of admission to senior colleges, a high school average above 80 or rank in the top half of the student's high school class did not always result in admission to a senior college, nor did their absence result in rejection. The particular senior college the student chose had an important effect on the level of placement. Entry to some senior colleges was easier because fewer students wanted admission. In 1970, for example, nearly everyone with an average of 75 or better who preferred admission to a nonelite senior college was admitted to one, while a substantial number of students with equivalent averages who preferred an elite senior college were placed at a community college. Another element affecting the student's placement was the number of senior colleges named among his or her preferences. The more senior colleges named, the greater the likelihood of admittance to at least one. This worked to the advantage of some minority students since students applying for SEEK usually listed only senior colleges among their preferences, thereby increasing their chances of gaining admission to one even if they were denied a place in the SEEK program.[23]

Among students with equal high school credentials, blacks and Hispanics were not disadvantaged relative to Jews and Catholics. In 1972, in fact, they were distinctly advantaged by comparison with whites in senior-college admissions. In that year, among those with high school averages between 75 and 79.9 and in the top half of their class, over two-thirds of blacks and Hispanics who preferred admission to an elite senior college were placed at one, compared with less than one-third of similarly qualified whites. Furthermore, less than 20 percent of these same blacks and Hispanics were placed at a community college, while over 40 percent of the same whites were. Other differences in favor of minority admission are found among open-admissions students desiring senior-college placement in 1972. Given the limitations of our data, we cannot definitively say that the source of minority advantage in that year lies in the number of SEEK applications, a possibility raised above. But, whatever the source, the admissions process clearly did *not* work against minority students in any simple discriminatory way.

Generally similar findings emerge from an evaluation of the role of the admissions process in producing ethnic segregation. It is immediately apparent from an examination of college preferences that groups differed substantially in terms of the colleges their members preferred within CUNY's tiers. But students from the different groups apparently were not disadvantaged in gaining entry to those colleges in which their group had been poorly represented. Once their high school records are taken into account, blacks and Hispanics are seen to have had no more difficulty getting into Queens, to take an example of a school that remained disproportionately white through the years in question, than Jews and Catholics did.

To understand both the stratification and the segregation of minority students, then, we must turn to events prior to CUNY, particularly to those that influenced the student's college preference. To be sure, ethnic groups also differed substantially in their academic credentials at the time of application to CUNY in ways important for understanding the placement of students. Nonetheless, open enrollment was clearly designed to encourage minority admissions, particularly among those who lacked the traditional criteria. Why, then, were blacks and Hispanics so much less likely than whites to apply to a senior college? And why, even when they did apply for admission to a senior college, were they less likely to apply to a school like Queens?

High school curriculum tracking looms large in many discussions of education as a mechanism for reproducing social inequality. Black and Hispanic students are more likely to be placed in nonacademic high school tracks, and this has major consequences, especially for subsequent education. Tracking seems to affect aspiration and self-esteem. And, in the New York situation, its classroom effects are reinforced by high school guidance counselors. They possess considerable knowledge of the CUNY admissions process, extended to them in part by the University, and usually provide crucial advice to the student filling out the application, particularly regarding the colleges from which he or she can expect acceptance. The role of the counselors partly explains the strong congruence between college preference and placement because many students are probably discouraged by counselors from applying to schools where they cannot get in.

There are of course other ways of interpreting ethnic differences in college preference. It might be imagined that the generally lower high school achievement of minority students would curb their educational aspirations and hence their college preferences or that students from lower-class families would be more vocationally oriented than other students and hence more likely to prefer admission to a community college. Finally, peer and family networks might play the role some ascribe to the guidance counselor. Indeed other research suggests that peers and family are very important.[24]

We have examined some possible determinants of college preference, distinguishing preference for a senior college from that for a community college. Since we assume that many students make their choice based on a realistic assessment of their admissions chances, our regression analyses include as possible determinants the two aspects of high school achievement formally used as criteria in the admissions process—high school average and rank in high school class. Our analyses also include two indicators of curriculum track in high school—the student's identification of his or her high school program (available only for the 1970 cohort) and number of college preparatory courses. Finally, we include several measures of family background such as family income, mother's and father's education, and, of course, ethnicity. The standardized regression coefficients[25] of these variables are presented in table 4.8. These coefficients can be interpreted as indicating the strengths of the effects of the independent variables on level of preference.[26]

Our analysis reveals that characteristics of high school background more strongly affected level of college preference than did characteristics of social background. In each cohort, high school average and curriculum track had the largest impact. The magnitude of the effect of high school average is not surprising, given its role in the admissions process. More surprising is the effect of high school curriculum track. In the 1971 and 1972 cohorts, in fact, one of its measures—number of college preparatory courses—has the largest standardized coefficient. Its effect appears weaker in the 1970 cohort because that effect is spread over two measures. When the coefficients of both are taken into account, it is clear that there, too, high school curriculum track was the most powerful determinant of level of preference.

The aspect of the student's social or family background that had the strongest effect on level of preference is ethnicity. In the 1970 and 1971 cohorts, it was the most important of all the social background variables. In the 1972 cohort, where it appears not preeminent, its apparent effect is reduced by the unavailability of the religious distinction among whites; were

TABLE 4.8. Standardized Regression Coefficients[a] Associated with Determinants of Preference for a Senior, as Opposed to a Community, College

	COHORT					
	1970		1971		1972	
High school average	.209	p<.001	.178	p<.001	.096	p<.001
Rank in high school class	.076	p<.001	.002	N.S.	.068	p<.001
College preparatory courses	.186	p<.001	.270	p<.001	.251	p<.001
Academic high school program	.174	p<.001	—[b]		—[b]	
Family income[c]	.023	p<.05	.059	p<.001	.044	p<.001
Father's education	−.008	N.S.	.010	N.S.	.037	p<.01
Mother's education	.024	p<.001	.049	p<.01	.057	p<.001
Ethnicity[d]	.083	p<.001	.140	p<.001	.052	p<.001
R^2	.295		.262		.168	

Source: Sample data.

[a]The standardized regression coefficient of a categorical variable (e.g., ethnicity) is the so-called sheaf coefficient.

[b]Unavailable for the 1971 and 1972 cohorts.

[c]Family income has been divided into four categories in each cohort: $0–3,699 ($0–3,999 in the 1970 cohort); $3,700–7,499 ($4,000–7,999 in the 1970 cohort); $7,500–14,999 ($8,000–14,999 in the 1970 cohort); $15,000 and above. These categories are represented by dummy variables in each equation.

[d]In 1970 and 1971, ethnicity is divided into the following categories: Jewish, Catholic, other white, black, Hispanic, and other nonwhite. In 1972, ethnicity is divided into white, black, Hispanic, and other nonwhite.

that distinction available, ethnicity probably would appear most important in that cohort, too. The measures of the student's social class origins, family income and parents' education, have generally small effects on level of preference.

Despite the effect of ethnicity on level of preference, the bulk of the overall ethnic differences in preference for a senior college are due to differences in high school background. This can be seen in the degree to which the impact of ethnicity in table 4.8 is reduced from the impact it appears to have when no controls exist for relevant educational differences among groups. When level of preference is regressed on ethnicity alone, the standardized coefficients of ethnicity are .248, .340, and .202 in the 1970, 1971, and 1972 cohorts, respectively. The magnitude of this reduction is conveyed also by an example from the 1970 cohort: without taking account of high school background, black students were 34 percent less likely than Jewish students to prefer a senior college and Hispanic students were 27 percent less likely (see table 4.7); among students with similar high school backgrounds, black students were only 6 percent less likely and Hispanic students only 7 percent.

Given the importance of the measures of high school track, even by comparison to high school average, a formal criterion in the admissions process, these results underline the role of high school tracking in explaining group differences in college preference. Surely, nonacademic high school programs (and, of course, vocational high schools) have a general atmosphere that is less conducive to high educational aspirations. And even students from such programs with high educational aspirations are likely to approach college with a diffidence about their academic preparation that makes them choose community colleges as a first step. We think the role of guidance counselors takes on added importance within nonacademic programs, especially since their impact on lower-class students is greater than that upon middle-class pupils.[27] It seems likely to us that guidance counselors, who play such a crucial role in helping students apply to CUNY, more easily think of those in nonacademic programs as poor material for higher education and counsel them accordingly.[28] However, guidance counselors cannot explain all of the differences between white and minority students in preference for a senior college. As we will see in the next chapter, some of the minority students, especially in the community colleges, came to CUNY after having been out of school. The preferences of these returning students probably were not directly affected by the advice of guidance counselors.

Once the level of a student's preference was determined, the college he or she listed first on the application for admission depended probably on a number of factors, such as the specific programs offered at each college. Undoubtedly important among these was the student's place of residence. It must be remembered that CUNY is a commuter rather than a residential university and that its colleges are scattered throughout New York City's five boroughs. Where a student lives and ease of travel are factors that influence the colleges to which he or she might apply and that must be considered along with institutional advantages and disadvantages.

The relation between residence and college preference demands some attention because it may have contributed substantially to the segregation visible at CUNY during open admissions. Ethnicity is a force that powerfully shapes the city's neighborhoods, which include large nonwhite ghettoes such as Harlem, the South Bronx, and Bedford-Stuyvesant and large white enclaves such as Manhattan's East Side and the Bronx's Riverdale. One study of New York's residential segregation as revealed by the 1960 census found that a dissimilarity index of about .80 described the separation of blacks and whites, indicating that 80 percent of either group would have to be moved to achieve parity in residential distribution.[29] In such a residentially segregated city, any relation between residence and college preference must lead to segregation in the City University.

Analysis of a separate file containing student addresses and college preferences strengthens this assumption. Using zip code to place each student into one of twenty-six neighborhoods, we find a strong relation between neighborhood and college preference within both the community and the senior level. In every neighborhood, a majority of first preferences were given to one or two colleges within each level. The influence of propinquity was strong, so that given knowledge of both the level of college preference and where the student lived, one can predict much of the time the specific college a student would prefer.[30]

It is unclear, however, just how much of the *increase* in segregation at CUNY during open admissions we can attribute to residential segregation. Obviously, it is very unlikely that residential segregation changed much over the years we are discussing. But it may be that the relation between neighborhood and college preference became stronger among minority students as larger numbers of them entered levels of CUNY in which few had been before. That is, college preference may have been more and more determined by a desire to remain part of cliques and crowds that had been formed in high school and before. The influence of friendship, then, may have reinforced the influence of neighborhood.

Nonetheless, it is unlikely that residential segregation per se produced all of the segregation at CUNY under open admissions. Although we can only speculate about the reasons for change in ethnic composition at some schools, the pattern does suggest that whites became increasingly unwilling to attend schools that might become predominantly nonwhite. The already mentioned changes at City College offer an ironic example, given that school's symbolic importance to the open-admissions policy. At CUNY, some white flight appears to have occurred within the boundaries of the University.

In summary, responsibility for inequality in the initial placement of students from different ethnic groups, and hence for ethnic stratification and segregation at CUNY, does not appear to lie primarily with policies and procedures under the control of the CUNY administration. To be sure, there are other conceivable policies, such as awarding seats by lottery, that would have reduced further ethnic stratification, but these policies would not have been politically acceptable and, even if they could have been implemented, they probably would not have retained for CUNY the allegiance of white groups in the city. In this sense, the responsibility for inequality in placement appears to rest with inequalities outside CUNY. Although we have not been able to analyze fully the determinants of college preference once its level is given, it is noteworthy that the colleges that became highly segregated under open admissions were generally located in segregated neighborhoods. Also, from the evidence we have been able to analyze, we cannot reject some of the mechanisms, such as the link between guidance counselors and college preferences, posited by those who see a new form of tracking in open admissions. Our analyses testify to the limitations inherent in policy changes at any one level of the educational system in order to generate equality of educational opportunity. While CUNY open-admissions policies had substantial effects, impacts of residential segregation and of stratification at preceding levels of the educational system, in high schools and elementary schools, continued to be felt.

Curriculum Placement in the Community Colleges

Enrollment in a senior or a community college has important consequences, but so does curriculum placement, especially for those who begin at the community-college level. Although the CUNY open-admissions policy guaranteed entry to the senior colleges upon completion of a community-college degree, it does not follow that all curricular paths were equally likely to lead to the senior colleges. Community colleges offer essentially two curricula, the liberal arts and the technical-vocational. The former provides the coursework necessary to prepare students for the junior year in a four-year college. The latter is generally considered terminal, although at CUNY, to a greater extent than in other university systems, several of the community-college technical-vocational programs are designed to dovetail with similar programs in the four-year institutions. Nevertheless, a clear distinction is made between the two: the liberal arts students are expected to transfer; for those in the technical-vocational programs transferring is simply an option. In addition to differences in course content, then, there are undoubtedly differences in atmosphere. Liberal arts students are assumed to be destined for baccalaureates.

At CUNY under open admissions, minority students in the community colleges were more likely to be found in the vocational curricula than were white ethnic students. The relation of ethnicity to curriculum placement in the community colleges for students in the two admissions categories is shown in table 4.9. As the table indicates, there were consistent differences among the ethnic groups in the three cohorts. In general, the curriculum placement of Jewish and Catholic students did not depend on their admissions status, and usually over half of the white ethnic students in either admissions category were found in the liberal arts curriculum. By contrast, the curriculum placement of minority students did depend on their admissions status, and open-admissions students were—somewhat surprisingly—more likely to be placed in liberal arts. Among minority students, generally a quarter or fewer of regular students entered that curriculum, while about 40 percent of open-admissions students did so. In sum, the differences between white and minority students were often substantial, and they appear to have been larger for regular students than for open-admissions students.

The explanation for these ethnic differences in curriculum placement lies with the curriculum preferences of students entering the community colleges. Our examination of the match between preference and placement shows that over 90 percent of the community-college students in each cohort were placed in their preferred curriculum. Undoubtedly, then, many students do not drift into vocational curricula but choose them consciously in accordance with occupational goals. Some of the career programs, par-

TABLE 4.9. **Percentage Placed in the Liberal Arts Curriculum,[a] by Ethnic Group and Admissions Status in the Community Colleges.**

ETHNIC GROUP	REGULAR	OPEN
------------- 1970 -----------		
Jews	58	56
Catholics	53	52
Blacks	19	38
Hispanics	25	38
------------- 1971 -----------		
Jews	60	60
Catholics	52	44
Blacks	31	40
Hispanics	21	41
------------- 1972 -----------		
Whites	43	55
Blacks	21	40
Hispanics	20	34

Source: Sample data.
[a]Preengineering curricula are also included in the liberal arts category.

ticularly those in the health professions, were viewed as attractive by students and were, in fact, harder to get into than were the liberal arts and other curricula. The desirability of some of these programs is suggested by the fact that academically stronger students were more likely to prefer the career programs than were those with weaker high school records.[31] The fit between curriculum preference and occupational goals can also be seen in the relationship between preference and degree aspirations: our analysis shows that those who wanted to terminate their education with an associate degree were far more likely to choose a vocational curriculum than were those who intended to go on.

Oddly, the liberal arts curriculum apparently was the residual one for many students. Better students are more likely to be well informed about the career implications of different curricula. Thus, the greater preference for the liberal arts curriculum among academically weaker students at CUNY suggests that it may have been a last resort, chosen in the absence of any clear academic career goals. Or perhaps since the possibility of attending college was not apparent to the weaker students in the early open-admissions cohorts until late in high school or even after high school, they were more likely to approach this sudden possibility with unlimited aspirations.

The curriculum preferences of community-college students also were a function of the curriculum tracks in high school from which students came. Paralleling the pattern we found in college preference, students coming from nonacademic high school programs were far less likely to prefer the liberal arts curriculum than were students from academic programs. It appears that within nonacademic curriculum tracks in high school a positive value is attached to career-oriented education, channeling better students toward such programs in the community colleges.

When their high school backgrounds are taken into account, the greater preference of minority students for technical-vocational curricula appears to a substantial degree to be an outcome of the nonacademic curriculum tracks from which they frequently came. We have conducted regression analyses of curriculum preference employing the same indicators of high school achievement and of high school program used in our analysis of college preference. Although curriculum preference was not as determined by high school background as was college preference, disparities in high school background and especially curriculum track do explain a large part of the relation of ethnicity to preference.

Our comments about the impact of guidance counselors on college preference may apply to the issue of curriculum preference, but here especially one should avoid a simplistic interpretation of the role of guidance counselors. Since the strongest students from nonacademic high school tracks were generally more willing than the weakest students to enter the technical-vocational curricula in the community colleges, it seems clear that the process of curriculum choice by community-college students was not simply one of im-

posing terminal vocational curricula on unwilling students, as it is sometimes painted in critical analyses of higher education. Nonetheless, minority
students were more likely than whites to be found in the technical-vocational curricula—a fact of some consequence for the educational opportunities
they obtained.

Conclusion

Probably the most significant changes brought about by the open-admissions policy related to ethnicity. Almost overnight, the policy inspired
important shifts in the ethnic composition of the University, as large numbers of blacks and Hispanics were able to enroll under the changed admissions criteria. In the program's first year, for example, over half the blacks
and more than a third of the Hispanics would not have qualified for any level of CUNY by the traditional admissions standards, and these fractions do
not include those students who met the traditional academic criteria but
came to college only because open admissions encouraged them to believe
that CUNY was open to them. Of course, the open-admissions policy was
designed to bring about just such results, but in so doing it also brought
substantial benefits to whites, who in fact comprised the majority of open-
admissions students.

Further evidence for the egalitarian impact of the policy lies in the distribution of minority students across the community- and senior-college levels. Not only was access to CUNY increased absolutely, but over time minority students at the University came to attend its four-year colleges with
almost the same frequency as whites. Indeed, the ethnic imbalance existing
at CUNY in the period before open admissions was greater than it ever was
subsequently. The CUNY situation therefore does not provide support for
those who have asserted that increased access to higher education is offset
by increasing internal stratification of the system.

But ethnic inequality in access to educational opportunity remained at
CUNY in the era of open admissions. Six years after open admissions began, black and Hispanic students were still more likely—albeit only slightly
—to be found in the community colleges, and minority students at the senior-college level were distinctly less likely to be found in the elite schools (the
result, we should note, of their great underrepresentation at Brooklyn and
Queens colleges). Minority students in the community colleges were distinctly more likely than whites to be found in the vocational curricula,
which are less likely to lead onward to the four-year schools. And ethnic
segregation apparently increased at CUNY's campuses during the open-admissions period.

Despite the intent of the policy to lower the barriers created by the unequal high school educations of white and minority students, open admis-

sions could not eliminate them. Inequality in access to opportunity under the policy was to a large degree a function of the tracking of students in high schools. The tracks from which students came affected their college and curriculum preferences, with the result that minority students were more likely than whites to be channeled into community colleges and their vocational programs. Also, the segregation at CUNY's campuses resulted in great part from the residential segregation of students' families. That ethnicity continued to be so salient at CUNY even as the University became more open is, in many ways a reflection of New York City's ethnic profile: great diversity along with considerable demarcation of life chances and experiences along ethnic lines.

Notes

1. This question has been raised by Ellen Kay Trimberger, "Open Admissions: A New Form of Tracking?" *Insurgent Sociologist* 4 (Fall 1973): 29–43.
2. Nathan Kantrowitz, *Ethnic and Racial Segregation in the New York Metropolis* (New York: Praeger, 1973).
3. For convenience, we use the term "ethnic group" to refer to any group based on common racial, religious, or national ancestry. Although this usage is not universal, it is very common in the literature on ethnicity. See, for example, Milton M. Gordon, *Assimilation in American Life* (New York: Oxford University Press, 1964).
4. The classic statement of this position is provided by Nathan Glazer and Daniel P. Moynihan, *Beyond the Melting Pot*, 2d ed. (Cambridge: M.I.T. Press, 1970).
5. The significance of ethnic distinctions among Catholics has been discussed by Andrew Greeley in many of his numerous works on ethnicity in America. See, in particular, *Ethnicity in the United States: A Preliminary Reconnaissance* (New York: Wiley, 1974) and *The American Catholic: A Social Portrait* (New York: Basic Books, 1977). Also of value is Harold Abramson, *Ethnic Diversity in Catholic America* (New York: Wiley, 1973). Our conclusions about the weakness of nationality differences within religious groups are drawn from analyses involving data about languages spoken at home (from the 1970 cohort). Surprisingly, over a quarter of the Jewish students reported Yiddish as spoken at home, and over a fifth of non-Hispanic Catholics claimed Italian. Clearly, these data do not identify all Jews of eastern European origin and all Catholics of Italian background. But, since they do identify students from families whose ethnic ties are strong, it is reasonable to expect these students to be different from those in whose families only English is spoken, if nationality differences are important. But our analyses of a wide variety of measures show students from Yiddish or Italian-speaking families to be little different from their co-religionists, suggesting that nationality differences are weak.
6. The Hispanic category is probably composed largely of individuals of Puerto Rican origin or ancestry, who form the bulk of New York City's Spanish-speaking population.

7. Some of our analyses contain two other categories: whites who are neither Jewish nor Catholic ("other whites") and nonwhites who are neither black nor Hispanic ("other nonwhites").

8. The characterization of Puerto Ricans, the bulk of the Hispanic category, as nonwhite is common but inaccurate. Most Puerto Ricans are classified as white in the U.S. census, although as a group they are physically quite diverse. For a discussion of the social significance of color among Puerto Ricans see Joseph Fitzpatrick, *Puerto Rican Americans* (Englewood Cliffs: Prentice-Hall, 1971), chap. 7.

9. We borrowed the three-tier view of CUNY from Trimberger. However, she classified only three colleges, Brooklyn, Hunter, and Queens, as elite, omitting City, which seems to be classified as elite in the public perception. We placed all four in the elite category. It should be noted that although there was a meaningful distinction between elite and nonelite colleges, this distinction existed mainly in the public mind and had no administrative legitimacy within CUNY during the period covered by this research.

10. Because our focus is upon those who began as full-time students, the enrollment figures in table 4.1 excluded those registered in evening sessions since these latter students were far more likely to be part-timers. As a result of this exclusion, the yearly freshman enrollments shown in table 4.3 are generally lower than those shown for corresponding years in official CUNY ethnic censuses.

11. We remind the reader that beneficiaries of open admissions are defined as those students who would not have been admitted to a particular level by the criteria prevailing before open admissions. Thus, benefit is defined in terms of high school average. In senior colleges, the beneficiaries consist of all students who enrolled with averages lower than 80. In community colleges, they consist of those who enrolled with averages less than 75. Regular students were those who would have qualified without open admissions. These official definitions offer useful ways of comprehending the policy's impact but they are also somewhat hypothetical. Just before open admissions, high school averages in the middle and upper eighties were required to enter some senior colleges, such as City and Queens, but students with averages in the low eighties who could enter these schools after open admissions are classified as regular students.

12. Abraham Jaffe and Walter Adams, "Two Models of Open Enrollment" *Universal Higher Education: Costs and Benefits* (Washington: American Council on Education, 1971).

13. With these analyses, we commence our use of the samples of the first three entering cohorts since the ethnic census does not record the students' high school averages.

14. Jaffe and Adams, pp. 161–163.

15. A storm was aroused by the contentions of James Coleman and his co-workers that an indirect consequence of desegregation efforts in many large cities was the departure of whites from those cities and their public school systems. See James Coleman, Sara Kelly, and John Moore, *Trends in School Segregation, 1968–73* (Washington: Urban Institute, 1975). The response of many was severe. See, in particular, Thomas Pettigrew and Robert Green, "School Desegregation in Large Cities: A Critique of the Coleman 'White Flight' Thesis," *Harvard Educational Review* 46 (February 1976): 1–53; Christine Rossell,

"School Desegregation and White Flight," *Political Science Quarterly* 90 (Winter 1975): 675–695.

16. A comprehensive overview of research about desegregation has been provided by Nancy Holt St. John, *School Desegregation: Outcomes for Children* (New York: Wiley, 1975). A concise overview is found in Christopher Jencks, Marshall Smith, Henry Acland, Mary Jo Bane, David Cohen, Herbert Gintis, Barbara Heyns, and Stephan Michelson, *Inequality: A Reassessment of Family and Schooling in America* (New York: Basic Books, 1972).

17. James S. Coleman, Ernest Q. Campbell, Carol J. Hobson, James McPartland, Alexander M. Mood, Frederic D. Weinfeld, and Robert L. York, *Equality of Educational Opportunity* (Washington: U.S. Department of Health, Education, and Welfare, 1966), pp. 330–331.

18. The computation of the measure is described by Otis D. Duncan and Beverly Duncan, "A Methodological Analysis of Segregation Indices," *American Sociological Review* 20 (April 1955): 210–217. Some well-known examples of its use in analyzing residential patterns are Stanley Lieberson, *Ethnic Patterns in American Cities* (New York: Free Press, 1963), and Karl E. Taeuber and Alma F. Taeuber, *Negroes in Cities* (Chicago: Aldine, 1965).

19. This is true because the number of special program places at a college was roughly proportional to the size of its entering class. However, one qualification must be noted. We have assumed that all special-program students were minority. A few were not, and these few probably were found at predominantly white campuses. For this reason, table 4.6 may slightly overstate the contribution made by the special programs to the integration of the colleges.

20. For each year, we eliminated any campus represented by fewer than 100 students in our sample. In addition, we eliminated the Borough of Manhattan and Hostos community colleges from the 1971 sample because religious information was lacking for whites at those campuses in that year.

21. Nonmetric multidimensional scaling, as embodied in J. B. Kruskal's program MDSCAL, version 4M, was used to produce the mappings shown in figure 4.1. A useful overview of multidimensional scaling, including a description of the method in Kruskal's program, is Roger N. Shepard, "A Taxonomy of Some Principal Types of Data and Multidimensional Methods for Their Analysis," in Roger N. Shepard, A. Kimball Romney, and Sara Beth Nerlove (eds.), *Multidimensional Scaling: Theory and Applications in the Behavioral Sciences*, vol. 1 (New York: Seminar, 1972). The stress values in figure 4.1 show the degree of fit between the segregation indices and interpoint distances. These values are unusually low and indicate an excellent fit.

22. It should be noted, however, that the differences between whites and nonwhites may be exaggerated in the samples since these lack special program students, who were more senior- than community-college oriented. We have made an attempt to adjust the samples for the omission of special-program students, using the known distribution of the latter and assuming that they are placed at the level they prefer. Although the adjusted differences in preference between minority and white students are somewhat smaller than the raw differences in the samples, they are still large.

23. This description of the admissions process is based upon a discussion with J. Joseph Meng, former CUNY vice-chancellor.

24. This has been reviewed in David E. Lavin, "Selection Processes for Higher Ed-

ucation," *Encyclopedia of Education* (New York: Macmillan and Free Press, 1971), pp. 181–188.

25. For the reader unfamiliar with regression analysis, a brief guide is provided in appendix B. Other technical details are discussed in chapter 3.

26. As in the case of table 4.7, considerable care must be exercised in interpreting table 4.8 because year-to-year fluctuations in the colleges represented in the samples have considerable impact on analyses in which level of college is not controlled. These fluctuations undoubtedly account for a large part of the year-to-year inconsistencies observable in the effects of the independent variables. In addition, one key variable, high school program as identified by the student, is present for only one sample, adding to the inconsistencies across the samples.

27. This is reported in David J. Armor, *The American School Counselor* (New York: Russell Sage, 1969).

28. We should point out that although guidance counselors used admissions information provided by CUNY in advising students, nothing said by the University should have made them think that students from nonacademic programs would have had a more difficult time gaining admission to a senior college. To the contrary, a feature of the open-admissions policy was that the type of high school diploma, whether academic or not, was to be ignored in the admissions process.

29. Kantrowitz, p. 25.

30. One way of measuring this predictability is the lambda measure of association. Lambda is a so-called proportional reduction in error statistic, meaning that it describes the improvement in our ability to predict the value of a dependent variable (college preference in this case) brought by knowledge of the independent variable (neighborhood). To take an example, the value .38, found for the match between neighborhood and college preference for those applying to senior colleges in 1970, indicates that we will make 38 percent fewer errors in predicting the senior college any student preferred if we simply guess the modal college preferred by others from the same neighborhood than if we guess at random.

    The values of lambda for students applying to senior colleges are .38, .40, and .38 in the 1970, 1971, and 1972 cohorts, respectively. The corresponding values for students applying to community colleges are .53, .50, and .41. These values suggest that neighborhood was a more important influence on choice of a community college than on choice of a senior college. This difference accords with one of the major aspects of segregation at CUNY's colleges; namely, segregation was stronger in the community colleges than it was in the senior colleges.

31. This was not only true of minority students. As we noted, minority open-admissions students were more likely than minority regular students to prefer the career programs. Although a similar difference is not found among Jews and Catholics, the very top Jewish and Catholic students—those with above 80 high school averages—were usually less likely to opt for liberal arts than were their academically weaker counterparts.

5.   Who Were the Open-Admission Students?

WHO WERE THE open-admission students? Were they a "new" kind of student, previously unknown to higher education? Or, rather, were they like the students who had traditionally attended the nation's colleges but with lower high school grades?

Answers seem implied by the responses of many to the new policy. Many commentators, as well as CUNY faculty and alumni, envisioned the University's colleges as flooded by students who were not "college material" and who would both hinder the University's attempt to provide a college education to those who were prepared and damage the University's image within higher education. Some even had apocalyptic visions, characterizing open admissions as the "death of the University" and perhaps symbolic of a decline in American civilization under the pressure of liberal ideologies. According to these views, the expectations of the students entering higher education via the open-admissions policy were fundamentally different from the expectations of traditional students. Lacking standard cultural equipment, unacquainted with Shakespeare or Charlemagne, the new students appeared to demand that education be remade to suit their needs. Relevance and ethnic studies became the new shibboleths, and the changes implied by these slogans appeared to be aimed at the belly of what many saw as the role of higher education: to transmit the historic culture of educated Western man.

Although not sharing these pessimistic visions, others also saw the open-admissions student as a new kind of student. In an influential book, *Beyond the Open Door*, Cross[1] attempted to develop a portrait of the new students who would enter college in an approaching egalitarian era. A key to understanding these students, she argued, is their comparatively unsuccessful high school experiences. Characterizing them as possessing "failure-threatened personalities," Cross interpreted their educational aspirations and behavior as conditioned by their anxieties about failure. Their aspirations are rarely realistic, but either extravagant or too modest, since failure to achieve an excessively difficult goal does not reflect on the individual who fails and accomplishment of an overly easy one is still an accomplishment; goals that offer realistic challenges, however, are anxiety inducing and usually avoided. Uncomfortable with many academic activities, the new students do not fit into the traditional academic model of college. Preferring television watching to reading and fearing the challenge of intellectual puzzles and abstract reasoning, they prefer directed instruction over that which leaves questions open for students to answer for themselves. And by contrast with the orientations of traditional students to higher education, the orientations of new students are essentially vocational. Cross thus concluded that open access policies require a new model of higher education.

The apparent conclusion that open admissions brought a new kind of student into the City University should not be allowed to go unexamined. Just as the apparent ethnic consequences of the policy are modified by close scrutiny, so it is possible that the new students were not as different from traditional students as many have concluded. Were this to be so, gloomy prophesies about the state of the University may stand in need of correction. But so, too, may our assessment of the opportunities open admissions offered.

The Social Backgrounds of Students

We begin with an examination of the social backgrounds from which open-admissions students came. Clearly among the explicit goals of the policy was interruption of the cycle of poverty that characterized the lives of many New Yorkers. Although this goal was often translated into ethnic terms, it also could be viewed as an attempt to provide educational opportunities to students of lower-class origins, who were disadvantaged in the struggle for educational credentials. Supporting this intent was the recognition that lower-class families (and, to be sure, working-class ones also) face numerous hurdles in attempting to provide their children with adequate educations. By the time they are teenagers, many children from lower-class families are already so academically ill-prepared and discouraged that they have little hope of attending college.

We can gauge the class origins of open-admissions students in part by examining their family incomes,[2] but in doing so it is useful to control for their ethnic origins, as we will do throughout this chapter. We have already established that open-admissions students were drawn disproportionately from minority groups. Since ethnicity in New York is correlated with other important characteristics, such as income, the ethnic consequences of open admissions could be expected to give rise to other differences between new and regular students.

Table 5.1 shows the median family incomes of regular and open-admissions students in the senior and community colleges by ethnic group. The table clearly demonstrates that most CUNY students, whatever their admissions status, were not drawn from affluent families, but it makes clear also that there were important and consistent ethnic differences in income levels. Jewish students had the highest median family incomes and Catholics had the second highest. The median family incomes of blacks and Hispanics were sharply lower than those of whites. These differences are accentuated when family size is taken into account. Over 60 percent of Jewish students in the 1970 cohort, for example, came from families with only one or two children; among no other ethnic group were family sizes typically so small.[3] Catholic students came from the second smallest families, although these were considerably larger in general than those of Jewish students. And minority students were especially likely to come from very large families: about a third of black students in the 1970 cohort were from families with

TABLE 5.1. Median Family Income (in Thousands of Dollars), by Ethnicity and Admissions Status

ETHNIC GROUP	SENIOR COLLEGES				COMMUNITY COLLEGES			
	Regular		Open		Regular		Open	
				1970				
Jews	12.0	(2,650)[a]	12.1	(987)	11.9	(223)	12.8	(518)
Catholics	10.3	(1,864)	10.4	(1,044)	10.4	(859)	10.7	(956)
Blacks	8.2	(117)	6.7	(420)	5.7	(166)	7.0	(395)
Hispanics	7.8	(291)	6.5	(340)	5.9	(188)	5.8	(243)
				1971				
Jews	12.7	(703)	12.4	(242)	12.4	(212)	11.6	(394)
Catholics	10.8	(758)	10.6	(400)	10.8	(685)	10.7	(724)
Blacks	8.4	(56)	6.8	(153)	6.1	(239)	6.1	(772)
Hispanics	7.2	(68)	7.1	(103)	4.9	(227)	5.0	(386)
				1972				
Whites	12.2	(1,912)	11.4	(724)	11.1	(2,033)	10.8	(2,997)
Blacks	8.1	(108)	6.8	(275)	6.6	(411)	6.3	(1,347)
Hispanics	8.5	(120)	5.7	(165)	5.8	(402)	5.6	(571)

Source: Sample data.

[a]These numbers give the maximum possible bases for statistics throughout the chapter. The actual bases for any specific table may be somewhat reduced by the missing values of the variable in question (see table 3.1).

five or more children.[4] Obviously, many black and Hispanic students came from impoverished circumstances.

Also relevant to an assessment of open admissions is a comparison of the family incomes of regular and open-admission students within each ethnic group: were open-admissions students different from those who could have been admitted under the old criteria? Among Jews and Catholics, family income bore little relation to admissions status at either the senior or the community level. In 1970, open-admissions students from the white ethnic groups had, if anything, somewhat higher family incomes than did regular students at the same colleges. In subsequent years, the pattern became the more expected one: open-admissions students had somewhat lower incomes, but the differences remained rather small. Among blacks and Hispanics, however, family income was related to admissions status in the senior colleges (except among Hispanics in 1971). In the community colleges, the family incomes of minority students did not vary by admissions status and were much like those of open-admissions minority students in the senior colleges.

Family income is important because it determines the financial resources available to the student and thus the degree to which his or her energies must be divided between school and an outside job. But, curiously, family income did not play the only role in determining the student's need to work; it appears that cultural prescriptions about the young person's economic responsibility to the family played a role also. This can be seen from table 5.2, which shows the student's anticipated need to hold a job while attending college, by ethnicity and admissions status (i.e., open-admissions versus regular admissions students in community and senior colleges).

There is no evident relation between the need to work and admissions status consistent for the four ethnic groups. But there is a clear pattern of anticipated need among the four groups, which is partly consistent with their average income levels and partly not. Jewish students, who came from the most affluent families, were the least likely to anticipate having to work. Black and Hispanic students, far more likely to come from impoverished families, were more likely to need to work. However, Catholics, despite

TABLE 5.2. **Percentage of 1970 Cohort Very Likely to Need to Work while Attending College, by Ethnicity and Admissions Status**

ETHNIC GROUP	SENIOR COLLEGES		COMMUNITY COLLEGES	
	Regular	Open	Regular	Open
Jewish	20	24	28	32
Catholic	44	45	52	49
Black	50	32	44	43
Hispanic	39	47	38	46

Source: Sample data.

their comparatively high family incomes, were as or more likely than minority students to need to work. It appears likely to us that the exceptional position of the Catholic students was a result of cultural norms prevailing among some Catholic nationality groups. The Italians, in particular, coming from underdeveloped rural areas in southern Italy, were at the time of their immigration a group that expected children to make an economic contribution as soon as they were able. Immigrant parents, in fact, frequently withdrew their children from American schools as early as possible so that they might take full-time jobs.[5] While immigrant expectations are no longer the rule, it is quite possible that young persons are still expected to make some contribution, if only to pay part of their own expenses while they are attending school.

Another way in which open-admissions students might be expected to differ from regular students is in the educational backgrounds of their parents. In the formulation of the policy, the students for whom the doors to higher education would be opened were presumed to come frequently from families whose older members had limited educations. Such families do not provide the role models that make high educational attainment likely and they are unlikely to instill in their children the values and attitudes that lead to aspirations for college. This vision of who the open-admissions students would be was strengthened by the assumption that they would come primarily from lower- and working-class families whose chief wage earner would be a blue-collar worker with at best a high school diploma. In sum, the open-admissions policy was expected to open CUNY's doors to students who would constitute the first college-going generation in their families.

The correctness of this view of the open-admissions students can be assessed from table 5.3, which shows the percentage of first-generation college attenders by admissions and ethnic group. A first-generation college attender is one whose parents have had no exposure to college. What is most striking about this table is the extent to which CUNY students in general belong to this first generation. Only among the Jewish group are there any categories of students in which more than 50 percent came from families with at least one college attending parent. Large majorities of all the remaining groups came from families in which neither parent had attended college.

In general, the pattern evident in table 5.3 only weakly conforms to the expectation that open-admissions students would be more likely than regular students to represent a first generation in college. Only among Jews and Hispanics in the senior colleges were open-admissions students consistently more likely than regular students to have parents who did not go to college, and these differences between admissions categories are small. (The greater proportion of first-generation students among open-admissions whites in 1972 is at least partly a function of the absence of any ethnic distinction among whites in that year, since we know from other years that Catholics, who were more likely than Jews to belong to the first generation, were also

TABLE 5.3. Percentage of First-generation College Attenders,[a] by Ethnicity and Admissions Status

ETHNIC GROUP	SENIOR COLLEGES		COMMUNITY COLLEGES	
	Regular	Open	Regular	Open
------------- 1970 -------------				
Jews	49	56	50	56
Catholics	74	76	78	76
Blacks	73	66	78	72
Hispanics	73	78	83	87
------------- 1971 -------------				
Jews	46	50	55	56
Catholics	73	71	76	75
Blacks	57	61	82	75
Hispanics	79	84	87	87
------------- 1972 -------------				
Whites	54	66	71	69
Blacks	61	70	84	76
Hispanics	77	81	88	89

Source: Sample data.
[a] A first-generation college attender is a student whose parents never attended college.

disproportionately represented among the open-admissions students in the senior colleges.) In the community colleges, there was generally little difference between regular and open-admissions students in the education of their parents, but community-college students were somewhat more likely than senior-college students to belong to the first college-going generation.

Another assumption about the new policy was that, in a city that has served as a port of entry for so many migrants from the Old and New Worlds, open admissions would extend opportunity to students from families in strong ethnic subcultures who consequently had difficulty competing on an equal footing in a school system characterized by a single cultural standard. Of course, the fact that large proportions of blacks and Hispanics were open-admissions students indicates that the policy did provide such an opportunity. But one might also expect that within each major ethnic grouping the policy would provide a special avenue of access for those more rooted in an ethnic culture.

Nevertheless, our evidence does not support this expectation. The 1970 sample, for example, contains data about languages other than English spoken at home. This measure of immersion in an ethnic subculture does not vary in the expected way by admissions status and level of college among Jews, Catholics, and blacks.[6] Among Jews and Catholics, in fact, the highest percentages of students claiming that languages other than English are spoken at home are found among regular admissions to the senior colleges. In addition, measures of recency of migration—such as citizenship, nativity, and parents' nativities—show little or no intraethnic variation by admissions status, and what little exists is often inconsistent with the anticipated opportunities under open admissions for more ethnically rooted students. Among blacks and Hispanics in 1970, for example, the highest percentages of non–U.S. citizens are found among regular senior-college students (although intraethnic variations are small).

But, as was the case with students whose parents had not attended college, many students of recent ethnic origins were able to attend CUNY under the older admissions criteria. Thus, in 1970, over a third of the Jewish students in every admissions category but one (that of regular students in the community colleges) claimed that languages other than English were spoken at home, as is also true for over a quarter of the Catholic students in each admissions category in the same year. And, except for Hispanic students, generally on the order of a fifth of Jewish, Catholic, and black students in each admissions category indicated mothers or fathers born outside the United States. In the case of Hispanic students, the percentages indicating foreign-born mothers or fathers rose to great heights. In 1972, over 75 percent of Hispanic students in every admissions category indicated foreign-born parents.[7]

In summary, open admissions apparently was limited in the extent to which it broke down special barriers for students from families disadvantaged in their ability to provide educational opportunities for their children. In the main, this appears to have happened because large numbers of students from such families were able to attend CUNY under the regular admissions criteria. Only in terms of family income and then only among minority students in the senior colleges did open admissions give entrance to students who were clearly different from those who could have gained admission under the older criteria.

The Personal Characteristics of Students

One way in which open-admissions and regular students were indisputably different was in terms of gender, as shown in table 5.4. In all cohorts and for all ethnic groups, open-admissions students at both the senior and the community colleges were more likely than regular students to be males.

There is a lengthy literature on gender differences in academic performance and their relation to sex-role socialization.[8] By and large, that literature shows that girls academically outperform boys in the early years but that boys surpass girls in eventual educational attainment. Thus, although the high school records of girls are more often superior, boys are somewhat more likely to take college attendance for granted. The gender differences

TABLE 5.4. Percentage Female, by Ethnicity and Admissions Status

ETHNIC GROUP	SENIOR COLLEGES		COMMUNITY COLLEGES	
	Regular	Open	Regular	Open
			1970		
Jews	48	35	60	39
Catholics	48	29	61	30
Blacks	69	61	80	55
Hispanics	48	39	70	50
			1971		
Jews	53	43	67	46
Catholics	58	46	63	37
Blacks	72	57	71	62
Hispanics	79	55	78	55
			1972		
Whites	58	42	67	37
Blacks	81	68	76	60
Hispanics	78	61	74	52

Source: Sample data.

associated with admissions status among the white groups seem not quite consistent with these generalizations. Females did have superior records: with the exception of the 1970 cohort, they formed majorities among the regular students at both the senior and the community colleges, and males predominated among the open-admissions students. But, except in the 1970 cohort, males did not form overall majorities among those attending CUNY, and they would have constituted even smaller minorities without open admissions. One possible explanation for the predominance of females among the white groups is that academically stronger white males were sent to more prestigious colleges than CUNY since their educations were assumed to be the basic determinants of the financial status of their future families.

Among minority groups, the relationship of gender to admissions status suggests that minority disadvantages especially hindered males. With the exception of Hispanics at senior colleges in 1970, females were clear majorities of both regular and open-admissions students even though they formed a smaller proportion of the open-admissions group than of the regular one. Since frequently three-quarters or more of the regular students were female, open admissions had great importance in providing access to higher education for minority males. Overall, this situation conforms to the portrait some have drawn of the special burdens borne by young minority males, stemming from the disruptive effects of discrimination in the job market on the family.[9] Also, the number of minority males in the pool of high school graduates in New York City probably was reduced by discrimination in the city's high schools.[10]

Age is another personal characteristic by which to assess open admissions. For each ethnic group, table 5.5 presents the percentage of students who were nineteen or more years old[11] and thus past the modal age of freshmen.

To a startling degree, the minority groups were composed of older students. In 1971 and 1972, over half the minority students entering the community colleges were older than the usual freshman. Many of these older students had graduated later than usual from high school. Others, especially among blacks, were entering CUNY after a period out of school, presumably in the work force. Moreover, for all ethnic groups, open-admissions students at the senior colleges were more likely to be nineteen or older than were regular students; however, the magnitude of this age gap was larger among the minority groups. Community-college students were, in general, older than senior-college students and, with the exception of blacks, open-admissions students in the community colleges were again older than regular students. The exception of blacks to the general pattern reflected in part the large number of older students among black regular students in these colleges.

The extent to which older minority students came to CUNY as open-admissions students suggests that the open-admissions policy encouraged many who had previously felt excluded to believe that the door to a college

TABLE 5.5. Percentage Aged Nineteen or Older, by Ethnicity and Admissions Status

ETHNIC GROUP	SENIOR COLLEGES		COMMUNITY COLLEGES	
	Regular	Open	Regular	Open
		1970		
Jews	1	5	8	14
Catholics	4	11	8	20
Blacks	18	28	48	39
Hispanics	24	38	43	56
		1971		
Jews	2	6	10	18
Catholics	7	16	14	24
Blacks	25	45	55	55
Hispanics	21	41	48	60
		1972		
Whites	4	13	11	25
Blacks	24	32	59	54
Hispanics	28	40	48	68

Source: Sample data.

education was finally open to them. This interpretation is reinforced by the numbers of minority students who were returning to school after an interruption in their school careers. According to one item in the 1970 questionnaire,[12] very few whites entered CUNY after such an interruption. But, among open-admissions students in the senior colleges, 16 percent of the blacks and 9 percent of the Hispanics did so, and these percentages were larger among open-admissions students in the community colleges. Interestingly, the largest percentage of returning students was found among blacks entering as regular community-college students—nearly 30 percent had interrupted their school careers. Undoubtedly, some who could satisfy the traditional criteria for admission came only because the new policy encouraged them to believe that CUNY was truly prepared to meet their needs.

In sum, the relations of gender and age to ethnicity and admissions status affirm the special meaning of the open-admissions policy for minority groups. The large proportions of older students among the minority groups indicate that the encouragement of the policy was felt especially among these groups. The importance of open admissions to blacks and Hispanics is also visible in the relationship between admissions status and gender, which makes it apparent that minority men would have had little chance of gaining admission to CUNY's senior colleges outside the SEEK program but for the open-admissions policy.

The Educational Backgrounds of Students

By definition, open-admissions students had weaker high school grades than did regular students. But an important question concerning the significance of the open-admissions policy is whether the educational experiences of open-admissions students were different in kind rather than in degree from those of regular students.

This may well have been true in terms of high school curriculum track. We have already seen the effects of prior tracking in the patterns of college preference, which led to some ethnic stratification even under open admissions. Also, we have noted the research that shows that race and social class appear to play some independent role in the assignment of students to tracks. Thus, a policy that aimed to remedy ethnic inequality and to open doors to lower-class students would have to reach students in nonacademic tracks and high schools in order to be successful. In part it is a matter of encouraging these students to apply since a primary effect of such tracks is to lower students' self-esteem and aspirations and thereby to reduce their likelihood of applying for college. But, in general, students from nonacademic tracks also would require changed admissions criteria to gain entry since their preparation is poorer and grades in these tracks are on average lower than they are in academic tracks.

Evidence that open-admissions students were different in this way from regular students is found in table 5.6, which shows the average number of college preparatory courses in high school[13] by ethnicity and admissions status. This index of the curriculum tracks from which students came reveals a pattern remarkably strong and consistent in the three cohorts. To begin with, there were differences in preparation among students from different ethnic groups who were in the same admissions category. Jewish students were generally the best prepared, but they were followed closely by Catholics. Black and Hispanic students were less prepared than the white students, and the differences between white and minority students were generally larger outside the regular senior-college category.

Within each group, there were consistent differences between regular and open-admissions students, both at the community and the senior colleges, with open-admissions students less prepared. Since there were also consistent differences in preparation between senior- and community-college students, there was a monotonic decline in the average number of college preparatory courses from regular senior-college students to open-admissions community-college students (i.e., from left to right in table 5.6). Open-admissions community-college students had on the order of four fewer courses in preparation for college than did regular senior-college students from the same ethnic group. That open-admissions students came more frequently from nonacademic curriculum tracks and that minority students did also is demonstrated anew by students' identifications of their

TABLE 5.6. **Average Number of College Preparatory Courses, by Ethnicity and Admissions Status**

ETHNIC GROUP	SENIOR COLLEGES		COMMUNITY COLLEGES	
	Regular	Open	Regular	Open
--- 1970 ---				
Jews	15.2	13.4	13.2	11.1
Catholics	14.6	13.2	13.1	11.3
Blacks	13.8	11.6	10.5	9.6
Hispanics	14.0	12.3	10.8	9.9
--- 1971 ---				
Jews	15.0	13.7	13.3	11.4
Catholics	14.5	13.4	12.9	11.1
Blacks	14.1	11.3	11.1	9.6
Hispanics	13.8	12.5	10.7	9.4
--- 1972 ---				
Whites	14.6	12.9	12.8	10.6
Blacks	13.1	11.1	10.4	8.9
Hispanics	13.0	10.9	10.1	8.7

Source: Sample data.

high school programs, which we have analyzed but do not present here. Thus, open admissions clearly created opportunities for those who had been placed in nonacademic tracks in high school, students who otherwise would probably not have gone to college.

This difference in the school backgrounds of regular and open-admissions students and also of white and minority students may provide a key to understanding the dire reactions of many to the CUNY policy and to the students they presumed it was bringing into the University. Indeed, this fundamental difference suggests that we ought to look for more specific differences in the educational behavior or cultural interests to which different high school backgrounds might have given rise and which might have seemed salient in the minds of many who were profoundly disturbed by the policy.

The disparity in high school background is implicated in the images students held of themselves. Students were asked to rate themselves in comparison to others entering the same college. Those in the 1970 cohort were asked to rate their academic preparation, and those in the other two cohorts were asked to rate their brightness. At both the senior and the community colleges, regular students were more likely than open-admissions students to rate themselves above average, and in assessing their academic preparation, senior-college students were somewhat more likely than community-college students in the same admissions category to rate themselves highly. Academic self-image varied also by ethnic group. Comparing students only in the same category of admission, we found that white ethnic students were more likely to rate their academic preparation as better than average, but Jewish students were more likely than others, including Catholics, to rate themselves as brighter than average. Catholic and black students were about equally likely to see themselves as brighter than average, and Hispanic students were less likely than the others to hold such favorable images of themselves.

Two sets of questions in the 1970 survey allow us to go further. One probed the student's achievements in high school—whether he or she "edited the school paper, yearbook, or other literary journal," for example. The other asked the student to indicate the frequency of various experiences, such as chess playing or coming late to class, in the past school year. To be sure, these questions do not touch all areas in which differences among students seem to have identified some as "aliens" within the world of higher education, but they do offer a way to test otherwise vague assumptions about these differences and their meaning.

Despite widespread negative characterizations of open-admissions students, there was little variation in high school achievement by either admissions status[14] or ethnic background. Open-admissions students were as likely as regular students to have been presidents of student organizations, to have had major parts in plays, and to have won varsity letters and also art awards. In the senior colleges, open-admissions students were generally only slightly less likely than regular students to have edited school publications or to have published in them. In the community colleges, open-admissions students were not usually different from regular students in these ways. Within the same category of admissions status, there were only occasional differences between ethnic groups, and there was no clear tendency for these differences to be in favor of a particular group.

Differences between admissions categories were strong only in relation to strictly academic achievements. Both in the senior and the community colleges, regular students were much more likely to have been members of honor societies and to have received certificates of merit or letters of commendation from the National Merit program. These differences were not found between students from different ethnic groups in the same category of admission, however, with the one exception that minority students entering the community colleges in the regular admissions category were unusually likely to have been members of high school honor societies.

Turning away from achievements to patterns of behavior in and out of the classroom that are related to the student role, there were a few differences that may provide some basis for the negative reactions to the new students. At both community and senior colleges, open-admissions students were more likely than regular students to report having been late to class or having been late in completing a homework assignment during the past year in school. If carried over into college, these may have been very important deviations from the behavior faculty expected of their students. Open-admissions students were also less likely, at least in one way, to report a behavior that indicates confidence in one's knowledge of a subject: they were less likely than regular students, and especially so at the senior colleges, to have tutored other students.

But, in other ways, open-admissions students do not appear very different from regular students in performance of the student role. Regular students were only slightly more likely to report having done extra reading. There were only very minor differences between these categories of students, when there were differences at all, in reports of studying in the library, taking books out of the library, typing homework assignments, and arguing with teachers in class.

In terms of outside activities that might have some bearing on the classroom, there were also surprisingly few differences between regular and open-admissions students. For example, there were fairly equal proportions of chess players and musicians in the two admissions categories. Among the men at least, open-admissions students were somewhat more likely to visit art museums and galleries. However, they may have been a little less likely to discuss topics that usually involve some intellectual analysis. At both senior and community colleges, open-admissions students were less likely to report discussing religion. At the senior colleges, open-admissions students were also less likely to report discussing politics.

There were some ethnic differences in these behaviors that may have influenced reactions to the open-admissions policy since open admissions and minority students were equated in the minds of many. Even controlling for admissions status, black students were considerably more likely than others to report coming late to class frequently or occasionally during their last year in school. Among open-admissions men entering the senior colleges, for example, over 75 percent of black students reported coming late to class, by comparison with under 60 percent of other students. Minority students may also have felt less confidence in the classroom. Again controlling for admissions status, we found that black and Hispanic students were less likely to have argued with the teacher in class than were white students. Among open-admissions men entering the senior colleges, to take the same example as before, 57 percent of black students and 59 percent of Hispanic students reported having argued with teachers "not at all," by comparison with 44 percent of Jewish and 46 percent of Catholic students.

But these comparisons are not all one-sided. In other ways, minority students apparently were more likely to participate in or to show enthusiasm for events in school. Black men, and to some extent Hispanic men, were more likely to have tutored other students. Among open-admissions students entering the senior colleges, 57 percent of black men and 49 percent of Hispanic men had tutored other students, by comparison with 45 percent of Jewish and 39 percent of Catholic men. Regardless of admissions status, black men were also unusually likely to have read extra poetry, and minority students appear to have been somewhat more likely to ask their teachers for advice. Finally, they were more likely than whites to study in the library, but this finding may not reflect more attentiveness to schoolwork on the part of minority students but rather the different socioeconomic circumstances of minority and white students and thus differences between them in the availability of books and a study place at home.

One final difference of significance for the policy is the school system from which students came. New York City contains numerous nonpublic primary and secondary schools; the most important of these for the City University are those that are religiously affiliated, especially Catholic schools. Large proportions of the non-Hispanic Catholic students came from the Catholic school system, as did significant proportions of Hispanic and black students. Jewish students were the most likely to come from the public school system. But beyond these ethnic differences, as responses to one question asked of the 1970 cohort indicate, the policy eased the way for students from the city's own public school system. At the senior colleges, in particular, open-admissions students in each ethnic group were more likely to come from public high schools than were regular students, with this difference between the two categories smallest in the case of Jewish students. A similar pattern is not consistently found at the community colleges, although Catholic open-admissions students in the two-year schools were far more likely to come from public high schools than were Catholic regular students.

In conclusion, open-admissions students were not simply students with lower high school averages but differed more fundamentally in their educational backgrounds from regular students. Less likely than regular students to have been enrolled in academic high school programs, with fewer college preparatory courses, and more likely to have attended public high schools, open-admissions students were accordingly less likely to go to college until the new policy tore down barriers. Despite these basic differences in educational background, differences between the two admissions categories in the specifics of education related behavior that we have reviewed here were modest. Open-admissions students did hold less favorable images of themselves, but except for strictly academic achievements, they were not very different from regular students in their accomplishments during the high school years. Also, with a few important exceptions, such as coming late to class or handing in assignments late, open-admissions students do not appear to have been very different from regular students either in their behavior in the classroom or in their behavior out of it. Noteworthy also is that ethnic differences in the main do not seem profound, although we must acknowledge that there were major ethnic differences in the need for remedial coursework (see chapter 9). But overall this portrait does not provide a compelling basis for the pessimistic visions many had of the fate of the University in the open-admissions era.

What Did the New Students Want?

The gloomy reactions of many observers to the open-admissions experiment sprang in part from a belief that the students who were being admitted as a result of the policy possessed a conception of higher education that was inappropriate in important ways. By contrast with traditional college students, the new students were seen as demanding that education be made relevant for their lives. Because of the impoverished backgrounds from which they were believed to come, they were seen as looking to education for vocational training rather than personal growth through broad exposure to the liberal arts. Reactions to the new students were not totally one-sided, however. For some, particularly those sympathetic with the goals of the policy, the new students were more open to a variety of influences than were traditional students and were also skeptical of mere authority. They appeared thereby to be more in tune with the deeper, critical values a college education is intended to impart.

What, in fact, did the new students want? Certainly one way to assess the motivations of students and their orientations toward a college education is in terms of the degrees they ultimately intend to receive. Table 5.7 presents the percentages of students who intended to continue their education beyond the colleges they had entered. Students who intended to continue their educations were of two kinds: those who aspired to postbaccalaureate degrees, regardless of their level of entry, and community-college students who aspired to the baccalaureate. (Percentages are lower in the 1971 and 1972 cohorts because a response of "don't know" was available to students in those years but not in 1970.)

Many students in all cohorts wanted to continue their education beyond the colleges they had entered. Indeed, in the 1970 cohort, such students were a majority of every group in each admissions category. Nonetheless, there were substantial and unsurprising differences in degree intentions between senior- and community-college students, with the former more likely than the latter to aspire to a postbaccalaureate degree (table 5.7 does not show this because of its construction). In addition, the relation of admissions status to degree intentions varied between the two types of colleges. In the senior colleges, regular students were more likely than open-admissions students to want a postgraduate degree, while in the community colleges the open-admissions students were, if anything, more likely to intend to go on. The higher aspirations of open-admissions students in the community col-

TABLE 5.7. Percentage Intending to Attain Further Degrees,[a] by Ethnicity and Admissions Status

ETHNIC GROUP	SENIOR COLLEGES		COMMUNITY COLLEGES	
	Regular	Open	Regular	Open
		1970		
Jews	74	58	66	73
Catholics	63	51	67	69
Blacks	63	56	64	74
Hispanics	62	55	55	67
		1971		
Jews	54	46	45	46
Catholics	40	36	44	48
Blacks	56	43	52	50
Hispanics	42	32	29	41
		1972		
Whites	47	37	36	37
Blacks	49	43	45	48
Hispanics	44	35	34	35

Source: Sample data.
[a]Postbaccalaureate in the case of senior-college students and postassociate in the case of community-college students.

leges are related to a fact uncovered in the preceding chapter: regular students were more oriented toward the career programs offered by the two-year schools and their associated terminal degrees.

Ethnic variations in degree intentions were weak and inconsistent but suggest some ethnic differences in educational aspirations. In the senior colleges, Jewish and black students had somewhat higher aspirations than did others; in the community colleges, black students overall had slightly higher aspirations and Hispanics somewhat lower aspirations than did others. But the weakness of these differences must be emphasized.

Students from the various ethnic groups emphasized somewhat different reasons for attending college. In the questionnaires, students were asked about the importance of a better job and of more money in a list of possible reasons for attending college. Broadly, the more important differences in response to these questions were ethnic ones—between Jews and Catholics, on the one hand, and blacks and Hispanics, on the other—although there also were fairly consistent differences between regular and open-admissions students in the senior colleges. In general, minority students viewed these reasons for college attendance as more important than did white students and, by and large, the differences in white and minority evaluations were largest at the community colleges. In 1970, for example, two-thirds or more of blacks and Hispanics in the community colleges felt that a better job and more money were very important reasons for going to college, while only half of Jews and Catholics did. Interestingly, white community-college students do not seem to have been much more likely than white senior-college students to rate these reasons highly even though vocational curricula play much more of a role in the community colleges.

Yet another indication of the extent to which occupational goals were salient for minority students comes from students' assessments of their post-college job plans. In both 1971 and 1972, students were asked how definite their future job plans were. There were not consistent differences in response between regular and open-admissions students at either the community or the senior colleges. But minority students, especially blacks, were usually more likely to feel decided about their job plans than were white students, and generally the largest differences between white and minority students were found in the senior colleges. Given the duration of senior-college programs, minority students in the four-year schools seemed unusually certain of their job plans. In the 1972 cohort, for example, about a third of black students in these schools and over a quarter of Hispanic students said that their postcollege job plans were definite, in contrast to only 15 percent of whites.

However, minority students were not only more likely to see college as critical for their subsequent occupational lives; they were also more likely to see it as critical in other ways (e.g., self-development). In evaluating their reasons for attending, students were asked the importance of such reasons as getting "a broad, general education," learning "more about myself," becoming "a more cultured person," and learning "more about things that interest me." Obviously, in contrast to vocational motives for attending college, these reasons involve the extent to which a student sees college as a broadening experience, furthering personal growth, and minority students were often more likely than white students to see these as very important reasons for attending college.

In addition, minority students tended to link their own development and that of their community or group. "To be able to contribute more to my community" (asked of the 1970 cohort) and "to learn things that would enable me to help others" (asked of the 1971 and 1972 cohorts) are reasons for attending college that were evaluated quite differently by minority and white students. In each category of admissions status, black and Hispanic students were distinctly more likely than either Jewish or Catholic students to see these as very important reasons for attending college. Indeed, white students did not see the greater contribution a college educated person can make to his or her community as much of a reason for attending college. By contrast, minority students were quite sensitive to the significance of college trained men and women for their groups.

It might be thought that these ethnic differences in evaluations of reasons for college attendance reflect not so much distinctive orientations on the part of minority and white students but rather, and more simply, a greater tendency on the part of minority students to embrace any and all positive benefits of college. But the lack of substantial ethnic differences in evaluation of another reason, "meeting new and interesting people," undermines this alternative explanation. Although about half of all students thought this a very important reason for attending college, student evaluations of it did not vary consistently by ethnicity (or by admissions status, for that matter). In no way were minority students more likely than others to affirm this positive reason for attending college.

Were open-admissions students that different from regular students in their orientations toward college education? It does not appear so on the basis of evidence about their educational aspirations and reasons for college-going. True, in the senior colleges, open-admissions students were somewhat less likely to desire a postbaccalaureate degree and somewhat more likely to evaluate the vocational benefits of college highly. But, except for differences in degree intentions, differences between regular and open-admissions students are neither strong nor consistent. In the community colleges, the comparisons between the two admissions categories are very mixed.

Probably more important in understanding reactions to open admissions are the differences between minority and white students. Broadly speaking, minority students, regardless of admissions status, appear to have been less likely to take college attendance for granted and consequently more likely to see it as crucial for their future development. Since minority students came from distinctly less comfortable circumstances than did white students, they were more likely to see college as consequential for their future socioeconomic circumstances in the widest sense. As a result, they were more likely than whites to emphasize vocational reasons for attending college. But they were also more likely to espouse idealistic reasons for going to college and to see their attendance as contributing to the welfare of others as well as themselves.

Perception of the Open-Admissions Policy

That the open-admissions policy was controversial is clear, but of course many of those who objected most stridently to it or were its most ardent supporters spoke from outside the walls of the University. So far, we have not considered how the students who benefited from the policy felt about it, nor have we seen whether those who did not need the new criteria for admission resented it. CUNY students in the era of open admissions may have differed in terms of their attitudes toward the policy, and, given the controversy surrounding open admissions, this may have been a very visible way.

Let us begin by reexamining student perceptions of their own personal benefit from the policy, briefly discussed earlier. Remember that the dividing line between admissions categories was undoubtedly less clear to students than it appears to us. Many students were probably fuzzy about the exact details of the policy. Also, many may not have known their high school average, at least not in the form used in the admissions process, which took account only of grades in college preparatory courses. Such ambiguities partly account for the lack of a one-to-one correspondence between the perception of benefit—the belief that open admissions "made college possible for me" or "encouraged me to go"—and formal admissions status. Nonetheless, 11 percent of the students in our 1970 sample said that the open-admissions policy had made college possible for them, and another 28 percent said that it had encouraged them. The perception of such benefit is shown by ethnicity and admissions status in table 5.8.

As the table indicates, some regular students in both the senior and the community colleges said that open admissions had made college possible or at least had encouraged them, although such students were far more numerous in the community than in the senior colleges, and some open-admissions students did not see themselves as benefiting from the policy. Nonetheless, formal admissions status was clearly related to the student's perception of benefit: open-admissions students at both the senior and the community colleges were usually much more likely to see themselves as beneficiaries than were regular students. Also, ethnicity was related to self-perception as an open-admissions student. Within each admissions category at both the senior and the community colleges, black and Hispanic students were most

TABLE 5.8. Perception of Personal Benefit from Open Admissions,[a] by Ethnicity and Admissions Status, 1970 Cohort

ETHNIC GROUP	SENIOR COLLEGES		COMMUNITY COLLEGES	
	Regular	Open	Regular	Open
Jews	12	48	39	64
Catholics	20	53	43	69
Blacks	32	61	59	72
Hispanics	36	69	62	79

Source: Sample data.
[a]Measured by the responses that the policy "made college possible" or "encouraged me."

likely to have perceived themselves as benefiting from open admissions and Jewish students were least likely.

It is worth analyzing further the sources of this perception since they are likely to provide important clues about the view of the open-admissions policy more generally, especially in light of the correlation between ethnicity and the perception of benefit. That correlation raises the possibility that the personal impact of the policy was identified to some degree according to the ethnic lines that stood out in the policy's public image. Therefore, we have conducted a regression analysis of students' perception of personal benefit from open admissions,[15] considering a number of variables as possible determinants, including high school average, level of college entered, number of college preparatory courses, type of high school program, parental education, family income, sex, age, and ethnicity.[16] With all these variables in the equation, nearly a quarter of the variation in perceived benefit is explained, but only some of the independent variables have significant and substantial effects. The unstandardized and standardized regression coefficients of these variables are shown in table 5.9.[17]

One cluster of variables, that associated with formal admissions status, dominates in the explanation of the student's perception of the personal impact of open admissions. It follows from the standardized coefficient of that cluster that over 13 percent of the variance of the perception can be attributed to high school average in relation to the level of college entry. Thus, this cluster accounts for more than half of the total explained variance. But curriculum track in high school, indexed by number of college preparatory courses and high school program, also had an important effect on the perception of personal benefit from open admissions. Even so, its effect was decidedly minor by comparison with that of formal admissions status.

By contrast with high school background, social origin had little effect on the student's perception of the policy. In addition to ethnicity, mother's education and family income affected the perception of personal benefit,

TABLE 5.9. Determinants of Perception of Personal Benefit from Open Admissions[a], 1970 Cohort.

	UNSTANDARDIZED COEFFICIENTS	STANDARDIZED COEFFICIENTS	
Formal admissions status		.367	
High school average	−.018		$p < .001$
Level of entry[b]	−.038		$p < .01$
Interaction[c]	−.008		$p < .001$
High school curriculum track		.146	
College preparatory courses	−.020		$p < .001$
Academic high school program	−.067		$p < .001$
Mother's education	−.016	−.034	$p < .001$
Family income[d]		.051	$p < .001$
$4,000–7,999	.020		
$8,000–14,999	−.008		
$15,000 and over	−.056		
Ethnicity[e]		.063	$p < .001$
Jewish	−.017		
Catholic	.017		
Black	−.000		
Hispanic	.100		
R^2		.247	

Source: Sample data.

[a]The student's perception of personal benefit was a dummy variable scored as 1 if the student said that open admissions "made college possible" or "encouraged me"; otherwise it was scored 0.

[b]A dummy variable: 1 for a student entering a senior college and 0 for a student entering a community college.

[c]The interaction between high school average and level of entry allowed the relationship of high school average to perceived benefit to differ between the community and senior colleges.

[d]The omitted category contained students from families with incomes under $4,000.

[e]The omitted category contained other white students. The regression equation contained an additional category, "other nonwhites," which has not been reported.

but the effects of these indicators of social class origin were quite weak, as was the effect of ethnicity. Controlling for disparities in high school background, we found little difference among Jews, Catholics, and blacks. Only Hispanics stood out as unusually likely to have perceived themselves as beneficiaries of open admissions, but even the largest difference among ethnic groups was small by comparison with the differences associated with high school background.

In brief, although perceptions of the personal impact of open admissions did not coincide perfectly with the objective definition of admissions status, the student's high school average and the level of the college to which he or she gained admittance were the major determinants of these perceptions. So, perceptions of open admissions' personal impact reflected not so much social origins, and a sense of systematic disadvantage stemming from them, but a relatively objective assessment of individual chances for college attendance on the basis of high school performance.

Nearly 40 percent of students in the 1970 cohort believed they were helped to some degree by the policy. What did students think of a policy so widely perceived as creating personal opportunities? The best measure of attitudes toward open admissions is a scale composed of responses to four statements: "the reputation of this college will suffer because of open admissions"; "open admissions will probably lower the academic standards of this college"; "open admissions is okay, but the students who have high school deficiencies or poor marks should attend separate colleges"; and "open admissions has discouraged many of the city's outstanding high school graduates from attending this college." The mean scores of students on an index created from the combined responses to these items are shown in table 5.10. We developed the index by summing the responses to the items; it ranges from 0 to 12, with 0 the score of those students least favorably disposed toward the policy and 12 the score assigned to those most fa-

TABLE 5.10. Attitudes Toward Open Admissions,[a] by Ethnicity and Admissions Status

ETHNIC GROUP	SENIOR COLLEGES		COMMUNITY COLLEGES	
	Regular	Open	Regular	Open
---------------- 1970 ----------------				
Jews	4.8	6.4	6.5	7.1
Catholics	5.8	6.7	6.6	7.0
Blacks	8.4	9.3	8.9	8.9
Hispanics	6.8	8.4	8.1	8.7
---------------- 1971 ----------------				
Jews	5.4	6.1	6.5	7.1
Catholics	5.4	6.2	6.4	7.4
Blacks	8.5	8.9	8.6	8.9
Hispanics	7.0	8.5	8.1	8.5
---------------- 1972 ----------------				
Whites	5.9	6.9	6.7	7.2
Blacks	8.3	8.8	8.7	9.0
Hispanics	8.1	8.5	8.4	8.4

Source: Sample data.
[a]Measured by an index combining responses to four questionnaire items. The index runs from 0, marking responses most unfavorable to open admissions, to 12, marking the most favorable responses.

vorably disposed. In the scale of the index, each unit represents a shift of one category in response to one of the statements.

Profound ethnic differences are visible in the table. To be sure, whatever their ethnic origins, open-admissions students appear to have been more favorably disposed toward the policy than were regular students at the same schools. And among the white groups, community-college students were consistently more favorably inclined toward the policy than were senior-college students in the same admissions category. But the most profound variations in attitude were associated with ethnicity. Not only were minority students consistently more supportive of the policy, but the magnitudes of the differences between white and minority students were often startlingly large—larger in general than the differences between regular and open-admissions students. Overall, blacks were the most favorably disposed toward the policy, and, in each cohort, black *regular* senior-college students, the least supportive category of blacks, were more generously disposed than were Jewish and Catholic (or white) *open-admissions* community-college students, the most supportive white students. Not only had the white students in this comparison objectively benefited from the policy, whereas the blacks had not, but, paradoxically, these same white students were also more likely to perceive themselves as beneficiaries than were black regular senior-college students (see table 5.8).

To pursue the importance of ethnicity for attitudes toward the open-admissions policy, we have regressed the index of attitudes on the same set of variables considered as possible determinants of perceived personal benefit, but in doing so we have made one important addition to that set: perceived personal benefit. Since this last variable is available for the 1970 cohort only, we have restricted our analysis to it. As before, only some of the possible determinants had significant effects; table 5.11 shows the standardized and unstandardized coefficients of these.

Even when other disparities are taken into account, ethnicity had a substantial influence on attitudes toward open admissions. By the measure of its standardized coefficient, ethnicity was among the most powerful determinants of those attitudes, although it does not dominate among the independent variables as formal admissions status did in the case of perceived personal benefit. When other relevant variables are controlled, the attitudes of the members of different ethnic groups still rank in the same way as in table 5.10: blacks and Hispanics were distinctly more supportive than Jews and Catholics, with black students the most supportive and Jewish students the least. The ethnic differences in attitudes among students—even when they were similar in other ways, including perception of personal benefit from the policy—were quite substantial. Thus, the difference between comparable Jews and blacks was over two points, about equal to a shift of one category in response to two of the four items. The difference may not seem large when stated this way, but a very different impression is conveyed by its equivalence with the attitudinal change produced by a difference of twenty-two points in high school average between otherwise comparable senior-college students and with the change produced by a larger difference than empirically exists, seventy-four points in high school average, between comparable community-college students.

Still, attitudes toward open admissions were also substantially associated with formal admissions status, as indicated by the standardized coefficient of that cluster of variables. The effects of other variables were weak, however. Noteworthy is that the one significant measure of social class origin, family income, accounts for only a very small part of the variation in open-admissions attitudes. Most surprising of all, the student's own perception of personal benefit from open admissions only modestly accounts for attitudes toward the policy.

This analysis implies that student attitudes toward the policy were shaped to a considerable degree by the general image of open admissions as

TABLE 5.11. Determinants of Attitudes Toward Open Admissions, 1970 Cohort.

	UNSTANDARDIZED COEFFICIENTS	STANDARDIZED COEFFICIENTS	
Formal admissions status		.198	
High school average	−.03		p < .001
Level of entry[a]	−.19		p < .01
Interaction[b]	−.07		p < .001
Perceived benefit	.68	.114	p < .001
College preparatory courses	−.07	−.060	p < .001
Male	−.37	−.062	p < .001
Family income[c]		.035	p < .001
$4,000–7,999	−.24		
$8,000–14,999	−.32		
$15,000 and over	−.44		
Ethnicity[d]		.218	p < .001
Jewish	−.57		
Catholic	−.09		
Black	1.57		
Hispanic	.93		
R^2		.202	

Source: Sample data.
[a]A dummy variable: 1 for a student entering a senior college and 0 for a student entering a community college.
[b]The interaction between high school average and level of entry allows the relationship of high school average to attitudes to differ between the community and the senior colleges.
[c]The omitted category contains students from families with incomes under $4,000.
[d]The omitted category contains other white students. The regression equation contained an additional category, "other nonwhites," which has not been reported.

primarily for the benefit of minority students. This implication in turn suggests that the many white students who believed they personally benefited were probably unaware of how general their condition was: their attitudes toward the policy may have been founded to some degree on a state of "pluralistic ignorance," a belief that they were rare exceptions to a general rule.[18] The substantial association between ethnicity and attitudes toward this controversial policy, which undoubtedly provoked many heated discussions in classrooms and corridors, probably contributed to the popular equation between open-admissions and minority students and thereby helped to shape further the reactions to the open-admissions students.

Conclusion

The findings reported in this chapter lend credence to the notion that despite the large number of whites who benefited from open admissions, the true significance of the policy lay in the opportunities it created for minority students. What stands out as a fundamental pattern amidst the many and somewhat diverse findings we have presented is that white open-admissions students were not much different, in the main, from white students who were regularly admitted. White open-admissions students did not generally come from family situations that in and of themselves would have drastically limited the students' chances to attend CUNY without open admissions. This was true when we looked at their social class origins, as measured by family income or parents' education, and when we looked within each group to the variation in ethnic strength among its members, as indicated by citizenship, recency of migration, and use of a language other than English at home.

But minority students were frequently and importantly different from whites. It was the minority students who generally came from impoverished backgrounds. Open admissions therefore changed the social class composition of the CUNY student body, at both the senior and the community level, through its addition of many minority students. The significance of the opportunities created for blacks and Hispanics is also visible in the relationship of admissions status to gender. Without the new policy, few minority men could have entered CUNY and especially its senior colleges. The depth of the response to the opportunities is evidenced by the surprising number of minority students who were older than the typical freshman; some of these students were coming back to school, presumably encouraged by the new policy.

Minority students, especially those outside the regular senior-college category, were also far more likely than whites to come from nonacademic high school programs. Other research suggests that race and class play roles that are somewhat independent of ability in the assignment of students to educational tracks and that this assignment has enduring effects on subsequent educational and occupational attainment. Open admissions, then, opened a door for many minority students who appeared destined by their prior educational channeling for terminal high school degrees. This ethnic significance of the policy was registered in attitudes toward open admissions: minority students were distinctly more likely than whites to support it, and it appears that these attitudes reflected perceptions of the policy's benefit for groups more than perceptions of its benefit for individuals.

Were the open-admissions students, and especially the minority students among them, so different from regular students in ways that would explain the reactions many had to them and to the policy that brought them into CUNY? Speaking of behavior that we were able to measure, we found only a few substantial differences (lateness to class, for example) that might have been salient to others. Overall, our comparisons showed only modest differences between open-admissions and regular students or between white and minority. Of course, minority students were more likely to come from nonacademic high school programs, and this difference between them and white students in educational background may have given rise to other, unmeasured differences in school related behavior that perhaps accounted for these reactions. We will show in chapter 9 that both open-admissions students and minority students were more likely than others to need remedial work to compensate for deficiencies in their academic preparation. As we noted in this chapter, minority students were more likely to emphasize the vocational benefits of college education, but they were also more likely to emphasize other benefits, such as self-development, that mesh well with traditional conceptions of higher education.

We think it likely that the intense controversy surrounding open admissions can be explained only partially by reference to educationally relevant differences between categories of students. It seems to us that the ethnic change induced by the policy is a necessary part of any explanation. Given the public's perception of the policy as primarily for the benefit of minority groups, it is difficult not to believe that many were responding to the sudden presence of large numbers of blacks and Hispanics at CUNY and especially at its senior colleges. This response was probably strengthened by an ambiguity inherent in admissions status: even though many students may have been aware of their admissions category, they did not wear it on their foreheads like an identifying brand. Consequently, the temptation to equate admissions status with skin color must have been strong. And it was probably encouraged by the more enthusiastic support of minority students for the program and by general differences between white and minority students. Not only were the minority students frequently from impoverished families, older, more often women, and more likely to be from high schools or high school tracks that previously had sent few students to college, but they were unquestionably different in terms of dress, manner, language style, and musical taste,[19] which are only incidental to the educational process but nonetheless helped to characterize them as strangers in a strange land. In this respect, the open admissions experience at CUNY resembles many other situations of ethnic mobility: when sudden shifts in the structure of opportunity bring large numbers of "strangers" into realms that only "natives" had entered before, characteristically the natives seek to restore and protect their prior advantage by defining the strangers as unworthy of this new privilege.[20]

Notes

1. K. Patricia Cross, *Beyond the Open Door* (San Francisco: Jossey-Bass, 1971).
2. The occupation of the head of household is the index of socioeconomic standing most usually employed by sociologists. We have no disagreement with this index, but none of the questionnaires provided adequate occupational data for the parents of CUNY students. We are forced to use family income and parental education instead.
3. The small size of the typical Jewish family is well known; see, for example, Marshall Sklare, *America's Jews* (New York: Random House, 1971), pp. 79–85.
4. One qualification must be noted. Minority students were slightly less likely than whites to live with their parents. For this and other reasons, the number of siblings noted in the text exaggerates the number of persons in black and Hispanic households supported by the family incomes reported in table 5.1. In fact, it may be that the size of minority households was no different from that of Catholic students. Nonetheless, the conclusion that minority students generally came from impoverished circumstances clearly holds.
5. Of special value in documenting this is the classic work, published long after it was originally written, by Leonard Covello, *The Social Background of the Italo-American School Child* (Leiden: Brill, 1967), pp. 223–237, 296–311. For a recent discussion of Italian-American cultural values in relation to education see Richard Gambino, *Blood of My Blood* (New York: Doubleday, 1974), chap. 8.
6. This measure has no meaning for Hispanics since the 1970 questionnaire items on ethnic identity lacked a Hispanic category and the language item had to be used to identify Hispanics in that cohort.
7. It is interesting to note that even though most of the students in the Hispanic category were probably of Puerto Rican origin, the percentages reporting foreign-born parents were very high.
8. This literature has been conveniently summarized by Sarane S. Boocock, *An Introduction to the Sociology of Learning* (Boston: Houghton Mifflin, 1972).
9. This is a classic issue in the sociology of American minority groups and has been widely discussed in the case of American blacks. Although the pathological character attributed to the black family in some of these discussions has generated intense controversy, there is general agreement that the weak labor market position of the black man is at the root of his frequent absence from the

black household. For evidence of this connection see Elliot Liebow, *Tally's Corner* (Boston: Little, Brown, 1967), and Lee Rainwater, *Behind Ghetto Walls* (Chicago: Aldine, 1970). For some evidence that similar patterns are found among New York City's Puerto Ricans see *The New York Puerto Rican: Patterns of Work Experience* (Washington: U.S. Department of Labor, 1971).

10. That minority students are more likely to be suspended from New York City schools is well known. In a letter to Irving Anker, chancellor of the New York City Board of Education, dated October 4, 1977, William Valentine, then an acting regional director of the Office for Civil Rights, wrote: "Black and Hispanic students are suspended more often than their white counterparts for the same offenses." It is plausible that minority men form the bulk of the suspended students.

11. Age is defined as the student's age in years on December 31 of the year he or she entered the City University. This definition was used throughout for the sake of consistency with the wording of the 1970 questionnaire; it results in percentages that slightly overstate the proportions of students entering college later than usual.

12. The item inquired whether the student had graduated from high school in the class of 1970. Presumably, those who had not had graduated earlier.

13. In contrast to the semester-long courses at CUNY, a college preparatory course taken in high school occupied a full year. Students who took only half a year in a college preparatory subject were credited with half a course.

14. Gender has been controlled throughout the remainder of the discussion in this section since many of the achievements and behaviors are sex-linked.

15. The perception of benefit is treated as a dichotomy. Students who said that open admissions made college possible or encouraged them are given a score of 1; others are given a score of 0.

16. We also created an interaction term between high school average and level of entry to allow for the possibility of different relationships between high school average and perceived benefit in the senior and community colleges.

17. Insignificant variables were excluded from the final version of the equation.

18. For a discussion of the concept of pluralistic ignorance see Robert K. Merton, *Social Theory and Social Structure*, enlarged ed. (New York: Free Press, 1968), p. 431.

19. We personally observed that differences in musical taste generated intense disputes among students that divided them along ethnic lines. These disputes were salient for students because much of the little money that student governments have to spend goes for bands to play at student functions. At CUNY, whether the band should play white rock, soul, or salsa was a decision with numerous partisans on every side.

20. One illustration of how this process works is provided by discussion of the "Jewish problem" in higher education during the 1920s, described by Stephen Steinberg in *The Academic Melting Pot* (New York: McGraw-Hill, 1974), chap. 1.

6. Academic Progress, Dropout, and Graduation I: What Happened

OUR ANALYSES THUS FAR show that the CUNY open-admissions policy increased opportunity for higher education in very substantial ways. Not only was the sheer number of minority students increased, but their distribution between senior and community colleges was more equal than in other open access systems. Of no less importance, white students were also major beneficiaries of the new opportunities. Indeed, the benefits to them were in some ways even greater than those to minority group students.

That all groups benefited substantially from CUNY's relatively unstratified system of access was not the only distinctive characteristic of the University's open-admissions policy. In other open access systems, the academic events occurring after entry have been largely the responsibility of the student. Generally, the faculties in colleges with unselective admissions criteria tend to be hostile toward freshmen, with a substantial rate of dropout by the end of the first year the consequence.[1] At CUNY, not only were students to be given the chance for a college education, but the institution accepted a share of the responsibility for their academic success. In its decision to implement open-admissions, the CUNY board stated that it did not want to "provide the illusion of an open door to higher education which in reality is only a revolving door, admitting everyone but leading to a high proportion of failure after one semester."[2] The primary means for slowing the revolving door was the introduction of remedial programs, supportive counseling, and a policy that no student be dismissed for academic reasons during the grace period of the freshman year. Since the University had made a commitment to affect students' entire college careers, to the extent that they did

119

poorly or dropped out, CUNY failed to achieve one of its major open-admissions goals.

A consideration of student academic achievement under open admissions takes on added significance because it bears upon the controversy over academic standards. To many within the University community and on the outside, the prospects seemed dim that the expected deluge of open-admissions students would result in anything more than a trickle of graduates. Given the precedents set in other places, there was ample reason to be skeptical that CUNY would do better, considering that large numbers of open-admissions students were underprepared by traditional college entrance criteria. On the other hand, some anticipated that open admissions would seriously compromise standards—that underlying the apparent academic success of open-admissions students would be a deterioration of academic rigor. It was feared that in the effort to equalize not only educational opportunity but also educational results, CUNY would lapse into "social promotion" (allowing students to progress through the system even if they were not academically prepared), a charge often leveled at the city's primary and secondary schools. These conflicting expectations—between those who thought open-admissions students were destined to failure and those who saw their academic success as signaling the erosion of academic standards—seem irreconcilable. Our data can help to clarify whether either view reflected the realities at CUNY although we cannot resolve definitively the standards question because we lack an objective yardstick to measure the worth of academic achievements under open admissions.

In assessing the fate of students under open admissions, we shall focus on two major aspects of academic success: first, how far students went in terms of dropout, graduation, and credit accumulation; and second, how they performed academically, as measured by their grades.

Dropout and graduation are frequently viewed by colleges and students as the bottom line of educational accounting.[3] A college degree carries with it the likelihood of greater earnings and occupational attainment, although there is disagreement about the precise level of socioeconomic benefits.[4] But the many studies of status attainment and social mobility suggest strongly that even a partial exposure, when no degree is earned, brings some socioeconomic benefits to the student; the extent of these benefits appears to be determined by the number of years of college the student completes, which we shall measure more finely by the number of credits a CUNY student accumulated.[5] Because we observed academic progress for no more than five years, during which time not all persisting students were able to complete the requirements for graduation, credit accumulation also indicates something about the rate at which CUNY students progressed toward a degree.

As indicators of academic success, grades are important not only because they reflect upon the attainment of CUNY's open-admissions goals but also because the quality of academic achievement has important implications for students' life chances. Strong academic performance increases the prospects for acceptance to graduate school and the consequent opportunity for reaching the higher level professions. And in community colleges strong performance increases the likelihood of attaining a baccalaureate degree among those who aspire to this goal.

In addition to these socioeconomic outcomes, there are a variety of other probable consequences of a college education.[6] For example, college graduates show higher information levels about public affairs and current events than do high school graduates,[7] and cognitive characteristics such as open-mindedness, objectivity, and flexibility of thinking are more developed among college graduates.[8] It is reasonable to think that these benefits of college are, like the socioeconomic ones, a function of how far students go and the quality of their academic work.

Academic Achievement in the Freshman Year

The academic events occurring in the first year of college are thought to hold great significance for students' subsequent college careers. Good grades in the first semester are believed to be very effective reinforcers that strengthen later performance and increase the chances of remaining in college, while initially unsuccessful students may develop a "failure identity," which will increase the likelihood of dropping out.[9] The initial academic success of the many weak students admitted under the open-admissions policy would seem especially important. Few of these students embarked on their college careers with a strong sense of confidence in their academic capacities, and a poor beginning might have led to early discouragement and dropout.

Just how well did students do in their freshman year of college? Table 6.1 shows the results for one measure of that performance, grade point average, with those who did not complete the freshman year separated from those who were present both terms; open-admissions students are distinguished from regular students. The numbers reported in the top panel of the table are means based upon a numerical scoring of letter grades ranging from 0 for an F to 4 for an A.[10]

Among students present for both terms, the regular students earned higher grades than did their open-admissions peers. In the senior colleges their superiority was on the order of two-thirds of a point or more. In absolute terms, regular students had, on the average, achieved at around the B − level, compared with a C for open-admissions students. In the community colleges, the differences—not as large as in the senior colleges—were on the order of half a point. Regular students earned roughly a C + average compared with below a straight C for open-admissions students.

Many students finished the freshman year needing to improve: table 6.1 shows the percentages of each group completing the freshman year with less than a 2.00 grade point, or C average, the minimum level necessary for graduation.[11] Among senior-college students completing both terms, slightly more than 10 percent of the regulars but more than 40 percent of the open-admissions group needed to improve. In the community colleges, as many as a quarter of the regulars and about 40 percent of the open-admissions students (almost 50 percent in the case of the 1970 cohort) needed to raise their averages.

As the table also makes clear, substantial proportions of regular students completed the first year with strong records (i.e., a 3.00, or solid B, average). A third or more of those in senior colleges and a quarter or more in two-year schools compiled such records. Among the open-admissions students, in the neighborhood of 10 percent were able to capitalize on the opportunity for college in such strong fashion.

The grades of students who did not complete the freshman year were in all cases sharply lower than those of the persisters, and in most instances

TABLE 6.1. One-Year Cumulative Grade Point Averages for Entering Freshmen, by Admissions Status[a]

	SENIOR COLLEGES							
MEANS								
	Regular				Open			
Cohort	*Not Present*	*N*	*Present*	*N*	*Not Present*	*N*	*Present*	*N*
1970	1.75	518	2.65	9,331	0.93	563	1.99	5,584
1971	1.58	471	2.69	8,968	1.04	678	2.00	5,974
1972	1.38	396	2.75	8,248	0.96	664	2.00	6,068
DISTRIBU-TIONS	%	*N*	%	*N*	%	*N*	%	*N*
1970 cohort								
No average[b]	32		0		43		1	
< 2.00	30		13		42		42	
2.00–2.99	23		54		10		48	
≥ 3.00	15	764	32	9,360	5	991	9	5,639
1971 cohort								
No average[b]	39		0		38		1	
< 2.00	31		13		42		43	
2.00–2.99	15		50		14		46	
≥ 3.00	15	770	37	8,980	6	1,091	11	6,022
1972 cohort								
No average[b]	48		0		45		1	
< 2.00	31		12		40		43	
2.00–2.99	10		46		9		44	
≥ 3.00	11	762	42	8,284	6	1,214	11	6,135

TABLE 6.1.   Continued

	COMMUNITY COLLEGES							
MEANS								
	Regular				Open			
Cohort	Not Present	N	Present	N	Not Present	N	Present	N
1970	1.43	449	2.40	3,343	1.19	916	1.91	6,082
1971	1.05	461	2.50	3,708	0.77	1,094	1.92	6,772
1972	1.16	351	2.59	3,728	0.91	932	2.04	6,363
DISTRIBU- TIONS	%	N	%	N	%	N	%	N
1970 cohort								
No average[c]	43		1		52		3	
< 2.00	32		25		32		48	
2.00-2.99	16		49		11		42	
⩾ 3.00	9	792	25	3,370	6	1,891	8	6,245
1971 cohort								
No average[c]	44		6		49		8	
< 2.00	39		22		41		44	
2.00-2.99	11		44		7		37	
⩾ 3.00	7	827	29	3,923	4	2,142	10	7,360
1972 cohort								
No average[c]	50		7		50		9	
< 2.00	35		17		37		38	
2.00-2.99	7		44		9		40	
⩾ 3.00	8	699	32	4,020	5	1,878	13	7,017

Source: Population data.
[a]Those present both terms are separated from those not present both terms.
[b]Some students earned no grade point average because they officially withdrew from courses or took only pass-fail or noncredit remedial courses. These students were not included in calculating the mean cumulative grade point average.
[c]Some students earned no grade point average because they officially withdrew from courses, took only pass-fail or noncredit remedial courses, or attended colleges that used nontraditional grading. These students were not included in calculating the mean cumulative grade point average.

they were not even close to the minimum 2.00 grade point average required for graduation. A large proportion compiled no academic average at all.[12] In the senior colleges this was true for at least a third and sometimes almost half of students, and in the community colleges it was true for no less than 40 percent and often closer to 50 percent. This suggests that many experienced initial difficulty, became discouraged, and withdrew of their own accord before the end of the first semester. Nonetheless, CUNY's effort to encourage slow starters was at least partly successful since substantial minorities of open-admissions students with initially weak averages did complete the freshman year.

Not all students who failed to complete both semesters were dropping out for good. As table 6.1 shows, some of them performed satisfactorily.

Further analyses indicate that some of the students with satisfactory grade point averages later returned to the University; they were stopouts.[13] Others may have been transferring to colleges outside the CUNY system (we will discuss transferring at a later point).

The number of credits students earned during the freshman year is another significant index of their academic progress. For one, it gives an indication of the length of time they would require to earn a degree. For another, like grades, it affected the probability that students would continue beyond the freshman year. Those who earned few credits and thus made little progress toward a degree were probably unlikely to persist for long. The record of students in earning credits during the first year is presented in table 6.2.

In the senior colleges, regular students earned, on the average, six to seven more credits than did open-admissions students. At CUNY full-time students had to register for at least twelve hours of coursework per term.[14] Accordingly, a fully productive student should have earned at least twenty-four credits in the freshman year. About 75 percent of regular students but only about one-third of open admissions students earned this many credits (among the 1970 open-admissions students about 40 percent reached this level). At the low end, only about 5 percent of regular students finished the

TABLE 6.2. One-Year Cumulative Credits Earned by Entering Freshmen, by Admissions Status

| | MEAN CREDITS[a] | | | | | | | |
| | Senior Colleges | | | | Community Colleges | | | |
Cohort	Regular	N	Open	N	Regular	N	Open	N
1970	25.6	9,360	20.0	5,639	22.7	3,370	17.1	6,245
1971	25.4	8,980	18.3	6,022	21.1	3,923	16.1	7,360
1972	25.0	8,284	18.0	6,135	21.8	4,020	16.7	7,017

	CREDIT DISTRIBUTIONS			
1970 cohort				
24+	75%	42%	55%	29%
12–23.9	21	41	31	40
<12	4	17	15	31
1971 cohort				
24+	74	33	47	25
12–23.9	20	45	37	42
<12	6	23	16	33
1972 cohort				
24+	71	31	49	28
12–23.9	22	45	35	40
<12	7	24	16	32

Source: Population data.
[a]Calculations were made only for those present both terms of the freshman year.

first year with under twelve credits, compared with about 20 percent of open-admissions students. All in all, these early results indicate that open-admissions students would require longer than regular students to attain a degree and that many students in both groups would need more than the traditional four years to earn the 128 credits required for a bachelor's degree.[15]

Community-college students earned credits at a slightly lower rate than did senior-college students. But, again, regular students earned more credits on the average than did the open-admissions group. As one might imagine, they were also more likely to earn credits at the rate expected of a full-time student (i.e., at least twenty-four credits over the course of a year). Close to half earned this many, compared with less than one-third of the open-admissions students. About 15 percent of regular students finished the freshman year with under twelve credits, compared with about a third of the open-admissions students.[16] Just as in the senior colleges, the initial results indicate that many open-admissions and regular students in community colleges would need more than the standard time (two years) to earn the credits required for an associate degree.

So far these early student performances hardly suggest a collapse of academic standards under open admissions. Many students made only slow progress in earning credits, and while quite a few open-admissions students did well, many started poorly and dropped out. Typically, the grades of open-admissions students who completed the first year were satisfactory but not outstanding, and their averages were lower than those earned by the better prepared regular students.

To complete this portrait of student achievements in the early academic career, it is important to consider dropout rates over the first year.[17] These are shown in table 6.3, which presents the rates both after one semester and after one year. In the senior colleges, the rates of early dropout were low. Overall, only about 6 percent of entering freshmen left after the first semester, and about 15 percent did not return for the second year (shown in the table as one-year dropout rates).[18] Dropout rates for open-admissions students were always higher than for regular students. For example, among 1970 entrants 9 percent of regular and 19 percent of open-admissions students did not return for the second year. On their face, these rates do not seem high; the CUNY board had shown concern that open admissions might result in an early exodus of students but this did not happen.

At the community colleges, rates of early dropout were slightly higher. Between 12 and 15 percent (depending on the cohort) left CUNY after one semester, and about 25 percent did not return for the second year. Open-admissions students were slightly more likely to drop out than were regular students: a quarter or more of the former dropped out after one year compared with about a fifth of the regulars. While these figures exceed those for the senior colleges, they hardly suggest a mass exodus in the early stages.

TABLE 6.3. Early Dropout Rates among CUNY Students, by Admissions Status, and National Dropout Rates

Period	SENIOR COLLEGES			COMMUNITY COLLEGES		
	Regular	Open	Total	Regular	Open	Total
1970 cohort						
One semester	4%	9%	6%	11%	13%	12%
One year	9	19	13	21	25	23
1971 cohort						
One semester	5	10	7	13	16	15
One year	11	19	14	23	29	27
1972 cohort						
One semester	6	13	9	12	17	15
One year	13	24	18	22	30	28
National data						
One year	18	33	22	33	37	34

Source: Population data. National data computed from Alexander W. Astin, *College Dropouts: A National Profile* (Washington: American Council on Education, 1972).

The conclusion that the rates of early dropout were low receives added confirmation when they are compared with national data,[19] shown at the bottom of table 6.3: the one-year CUNY rates are lower than the national rates, both for open-admissions and for regular students at the senior and at the community colleges.[20]

In summary, differences in high school performance that separated open-admissions from regular students continued to be seen in these students' initial achievements at CUNY. Regular students earned better grades and more credits than did open-admissions students, and though dropout rates were low, the latter were still more likely to leave CUNY than the former. Nonetheless, a substantial proportion of the open-admissions students did use the opportunity provided by the policy to good advantage: about half (and sometimes more) earned satisfactory grades, some 10 percent completed the first year having compiled at least a B average, and the overwhelming majority returned for a second year of college.

Academic Performance over the College Career

By the end of the first year, both open-admissions and regular students had progressed slowly—the former more slowly than the latter. We now shall consider whether these early achievements were forerunners of how long it would take to finish and of the quality of academic performance over the course. With the passage of time, open admissions students might have developed a greater academic momentum, which would narrow the initial gap in grades and credits that separated them from the more traditional CUNY students. On the other hand, initial differences might have remained or become more pronounced as time went by. To assess these possibilities, we look at students' cumulative academic standing as of June 1975, the end point of our records, but—we remind the reader—not necessarily the completion date of these students' academic careers.

Senior-College Results

The cumulative academic achievements of senior-college students are shown in table 6.4, which presents grade point averages and credits earned as of June 1975. All students are considered, but those who either had graduated or were still enrolled (shown in the table as persisters) are separated from those who had dropped out along the way.

Among those who had graduated or were still enrolled, regular students showed a rather solid performance. Their mean cumulative grade point average was close to a straight B. The record of open-admissions students was not as strong: typically, these students had a C+ average.[21] The academic distance between these two groups was also evident in the fact that few regular students—only 3 percent for the 1970 cohort—had averages below the minimum 2.00 required for graduation. In contrast, among open-admissions students, 17 percent of the 1970 cohort and 25 percent of the 1971 group were still enrolled with averages of less than 2.00.[22]

Nonetheless, the great majority of persisting open-admissions students did satisfactory work—75 percent or more in the first two cohorts earned at least a 2.00 average, including almost 15 percent who compiled records of 3.00 or higher, strong enough to have a reasonable chance for graduate or professional training. Regular students were even more likely to turn in a strong performance: almost half earned at least 3.00 averages.

Table 6.4 indicates that regular students also earned more credits, but neither group had, on average, accumulated enough credits to graduate within four years (shown by the results for the 1971 entrants). However, the regular students were far closer to graduation, with an average of twenty-one credits (about six or seven courses) more than open-admissions students had completed. From the average credits for the 1971 cohort, it appears that after an additional semester, many more of the regulars would have been at —or very close to—the number of credits needed to graduate, while many open-admissions students would have required two or three additional semesters. If four years was not the typical period of time for students to earn enough credits to graduate, the great majority of persisting students were nevertheless productive. For example, in the 1970 cohort, whose data files covered a period of five years, 90 percent of regular students and about 75 percent of open-admissions students had earned more than ninety credits.

TABLE 6.4. Senior-College Cumulative Grade Point Averages and Credits Earned, by Admissions Status[a]

	REGULAR				OPEN			
Cohort[a]	Drop-outs	N	Per-sisters	N	Drop-outs	N	Per-sisters	N
Cumulative Grade Point Averages								
1970 cohort								
Mean GPA	2.34	3,899	2.94	6,059	1.54	3,486	2.44	2,815
No average[b]	4%		0%		9%		0%	
< 2.00	28		3		62		17	
2.00–2.99	44		49		25		69	
≥ 3.00	24		48		5		14	
1971 cohort								
Mean GPA	2.28	3,239	2.90	6,287	1.46	3,609	2.34	3,178
No average[b]	6%		0%		8%		0%	
< 2.00	32		6		65		25	
2.00–2.99	36		46		23		62	
≥ 3.00	26		48		4		13	
1972 cohort								
Mean GPA	2.23	2,459	2.85	6,289	1.44	3,135	2.24	3,718
No average[b]	11%		0%		13%		0%	
< 2.00	30		7		60		33	
2.00–2.99	36		48		21		56	
≥ 3.00	23		45		6		11	
Cumulative Credits Earned								
1970 cohort								
Mean credits	55	4,065	117	6,059	32	3,813	106	2,817
0–30	37%		1%		61%		3%	
30.01–60	25		3		23		7	
60.01–90	15		7		10		13	
>90	24		90		7		77	
1971 cohort								
Mean credits	38	3,460	107	6,290	23	3,932	86	3,181
0–30	51%		2%		70%		8%	
30.01–60	28		5		23		16	
60.01–90	13		14		6		25	
>90	8		79		1		51	
1972 cohort								
Mean credits	26	2,757	80	6,289	16	3,624	62	3,725
0–30	62%		3%		83%		12%	
30.01–60	29		13		16		31	
60.01–90	9		49		1		46	
>90	0		35		0		11	

Source: Population data.

[a]Results cover five years for the 1970 cohort, four years for the 1971, and three years for the 1972.

[b]Some students earned no grade point average because they officially withdrew from courses or took only pass-fail or noncredit remedial courses. These students were not included in calculating the mean cumulative grade point average.

128

That CUNY students took longer than the standard four years to graduate is shown dramatically by table 6.5, which presents graduation, retention, and dropout rates after two, three, four, and five years.[23] Only about 25 percent of all students graduated four years after entry. However, as the figures for the 1970 cohort reveal, after five years there was a sharp increase to about 40 percent. Rates for regular students were considerably above those for open-admissions students: in the 1970 cohort almost half of the regulars earned diplomas after five years, compared with 26 percent for the open-admissions group.

Almost half of all senior-college students ultimately dropped out,[24] but most left with something to show for their college work. Dropout rates were always higher among open-admissions students. In the 1970 cohort 40 percent of regulars but almost 60 percent of open-admissions students dropped out. Though most of the latter left with low grades—about 70 percent had less than a C average at the time they left—many had nevertheless completed a fair amount of college work. In fact, 40 percent had completed more than a year of higher education, i.e., more than thirty credits (see table 6.4).

Among regular students who appear to have dropped out, a strong majority in the 1970 cohort left not only with more than a year's worth of credits but also with satisfactory averages. Indeed, about 25 percent had solid B averages. This suggests that many who left CUNY were not dropping out of

TABLE 6.5. Graduation, Retention, and Dropout Rates for Senior-College Students and National Sample

Period	REGULAR			OPEN			ALL STUDENTS		
	Grad.[a]	Ret.	Drop.	Grad.	Ret.	Drop.	Grad.	Ret.	Drop.
1970 cohort									
Two years	0	83	17	0	68	32	0	77	23
Three years	0	74	26	0	57	43	0	67	33
Four years	32	33	35	13	34	53	25	33	42
Five years	48	12	40	26	16	58	39	14	47
1971 cohort									
Two years	0	77	23	0	63	37	0	71	29
Three years	1	68	31	1	49	50	1	60	39
Four years	30	35	35	10	35	55	22	34	44
1972 cohort									
Two years	0	75	25	0	57	43	0	67	33
Three years	1	68	31	1	50	49	1	60	39
National data									
Four years[b]	49	9	42	21	14	65	42	11	47

Source: Population data.

[a]Grad. = graduated; Ret. = retained; Drop. = dropout.

[b]National data are from special tabulations provided by Alexander W. Astin.

college but rather were transferring outside the CUNY system.[25] Open-admissions students who left CUNY appeared far less likely to be transferring since a minority had satisfactory averages and only about 5 percent left with solid B averages.

Overall, how do these graduation and dropout rates reflect on the CUNY goal of stopping the revolving door? On their face, graduation rates seem low and dropout rates seem high, especially among the open-admissions students. To evaluate better the CUNY record we have compared the senior-college graduation and dropout rates with national data,[26] shown at the bottom of table 6.5. Among regular students, the five-year graduation rate of 48 percent is close to the national four-year rate of 49 percent. Although it may seem inappropriate to compare a national graduation rate, measured after four years, with a CUNY rate measured after five, this is in some ways the most appropriate comparison. First, CUNY students (including regular students) were often registered for remedial work offering little or no credit. Moreover, stopping out was a very common occurrence at CUNY, both before and after open admissions,[27] and many students anticipated that they would have to work while attending college (see chapter 5). These factors would be expected to delay the time of graduation. Indeed, when the four-year national rates are compared with the four-year CUNY rates for regular students, the national graduation rate of 49 percent is substantially higher than the CUNY rate of about 30 percent. However, this difference in graduation rates is more than complemented by a difference in the percentage of students still in school (shown as retention rates in the table). Nationally, only 9 percent of students comparable to the CUNY regular students were still in school after four years, while at CUNY this was true for a third. It follows that the national graduation rate could not increase much after four years, while the CUNY rate in fact rose substantially between the fourth and the fifth year.

Open-admissions students appear especially successful compared with their peers nationwide. After four years the graduation rate of these students was well below the national rate—among 1970 entrants only 13 percent had graduated. But 34 percent were still enrolled—far higher than the nationwide total of 14 percent. As this might lead one to expect, after five years the graduation rate of 26 percent for the CUNY open-admissions students exceeded the national rate of 21 percent for students with comparable high school averages.

Community-College Results

The cumulative academic record of community-college students is summarized in table 6.6. For students who transferred to senior colleges, only that portion of their records compiled at community colleges is included

TABLE 6.6. Community-College Cumulative Grade Point Averages and Credits Earned, by Admissions Status[a]

	REGULAR				OPEN			
	Drop-outs	N	Per-sisters	N	Drop-outs	N	Per-sisters	N
Cumulative Grade Point Averages								
1970 cohort								
Mean GPA	1.85	1,806	2.70	2,058	1.45	4,332	2.28	2,896
No average[b]	12%		2%		15%		5%	
< 2.00	45		8		61		22	
2.00–2.99	32		58		21		64	
≥ 3.00	10		32		3		10	
1971 cohort								
Mean GPA	1.90	1,954	2.74	2,274	1.42	4,905	2.30	3,188
No average[b]	15%		7%		18%		9%	
< 2.00	40		8		59		23	
2.00–2.99	31		50		19		54	
≥ 3.00	14		35		4		13	
1972 cohort								
Mean GPA	2.00	1,662	2.74	2,468	1.50	3,908	2.26	3,576
No average[b]	19%		7%		23%		7%	
< 2.00	36		9		50		29	
2.00–2.99	29		49		21		52	
≥ 3.00	16		34		6		13	
Cumulative Credits Earned								
1970 cohort								
Mean credits	24	2,060	58	2,102	29	5,103	55	3,033
0–15	44%		5%		55%		8%	
15.01–30	23		5		21		7	
30.01–45	14		6		12		8	
>45	19		85		13		77	
1971 cohort								
Mean credits	22	2,304	57	2,446	17	5,981	52	3,521
0–15	49%		5%		59%		10%	
15.01–30	21		6		19		8	
30.01–45	12		7		10		10	
>45	18		81		11		71	
1972 cohort								
Mean credits	20	2,054	56	2,665	14	5,048	48	3,847
0–15	52%		4%		65%		10%	
15.01–30	23		7		20		12	
30.01–45	13		10		9		15	
>45	13		79		7		63	

Source: Population data.
[a]Results cover five years for the 1970 cohort, four years for the 1971, and three years for the 1972.
[b]Some students earned no grade point average because they officially withdrew from courses, took only pass-fail or noncredit remedial courses, or attended colleges that used nontraditional grading. These students were not included in calculating the mean cumulative grade point average.

(the senior-college achievement of those who transferred from two-year schools is considered in chapter 8).

As in the senior colleges, the community-college regular students who persisted outperformed the open-admissions group. They earned around a B− average, or about half a letter grade above that of open-admissions students. The overwhelming proportion of the regular students (roughly 85–90 percent) earned at least satisfactory grades, and about 35 percent demonstrated strong performance (a 3.00 average or better). Among open-admissions students about two-thirds earned satisfactory grades and about 10 percent compiled solid B averages. Only a small proportion of regular students had done unsatisfactory work—about 10 percent, compared to about a quarter of open-admissions students.[28]

Persisting regular students accumulated more credits than did the open admissions group, but since both groups had considerable time to earn the credits for what is normally a two-year program, the differences between them were much smaller than the gap observed in the senior colleges. The great majority of regular students who persisted either had earned the required number of credits for graduation (most community-college programs require sixty-four credits) or were near that number. Open-admissions students accumulated credits at a slower pace: after three years (shown by the 1972 cohort) they were eight credits, or about three courses, behind regulars. But after five years their credit totals almost matched those of the regulars. All in all, relatively few persisting students had only a small number of credits to show for the time spent.

The graduation, retention, and dropout rates of community-college students are summarized in table 6.7. Before considering these results, it is important to note a significant career contingency of community-college students: transfer to senior colleges. For many, a community-college diploma represents an important step in the pursuit of a bachelor's degree. However, at CUNY some students bypassed this route and transferred to a senior college without attaining the associate degree. These students are shown separately in the table.[29]

Rates of graduation from community college after two years were extremely low—less than 10 percent. However, after three years the graduation rate jumped substantially to about 20 percent, and it continued to rise until, after five years, it exceeded 25 percent. Moreover, an additional 10 percent of students had moved directly to a senior college without attaining an associate degree, so that more than a third of community-college students must be reckoned as successful in terms of graduation or transfer. Graduation rates for regular students were always higher than for open-admissions students. After five years 35 percent of regulars had graduated from community college (and 12 percent had transferred to a senior college without earning an associate degree). Among the open-admissions group about 20 percent graduated (and 11 percent had transferred to senior colleges without the two-year degree).

TABLE 6.7. Graduation, Retention, and Dropout Rates for Community-College Students and National Sample

Period	REGULAR				OPEN				ALL STUDENTS			
	Grad.[a]	Ret.	Drop.	Trans.	Grad.	Ret.	Drop.	Trans.	Grad.	Ret.	Drop.	Trans.
1970 cohort												
Two years	15	44	38	2	5	50	44	1	8	48	42	1
Three years	31	16	45	8	16	23	55	7	21	21	52	7
Four years	33	7	49	12	19	10	61	10	25	9	57	10
Five years	35	3	50	12	21	5	63	11	26	4	59	11
1971 cohort												
Two years	13	45	40	3	5	46	48	2	7	46	45	2
Three years	30	14	47	9	15	19	60	6	20	17	56	7
Four years	34	7	49	11	18	10	63	10	23	9	58	10
1972 cohort												
Two years	11	46	41	3	4	43	51	2	6	44	48	2
Three years	32	17	44	7	16	22	57	6	22	20	52	6
National data												
Four years	32	2	66	–	20	3	77	–	29	2	69	–

Source: Population data. National data are from special tabulations provided by Alexander W. Astin.

[a]Grad. = graduated from community college; Ret. = retained at community college; Drop. = dropout from community college; Trans. = transferred from community college prior to attaining associate degree.

In the community colleges dropout rates were higher than in the senior colleges. After four years almost 60 percent of all community-college students had dropped out. Open-admissions students showed higher rates (over 60 percent) than did regular students (about 50 percent). Although most of these dropouts left with low grades, a fair number still had something to show for their efforts: among 1970 entrants, a third of regular dropouts and a quarter of the open-admissions group took with them more than a year's worth of credits (see table 6.6). However, compared with the senior-college figures, smaller proportions in the two-year schools left with records strong enough to suggest transferring out of the City University.

In absolute terms, the graduation rates of CUNY community-college students seem strikingly low, but they were almost identical to the graduation rates of community-college students nationwide, also shown in table 6.7. Nationwide only about three in ten comparable to regular CUNY students had graduated from two-year colleges four years after entry, and among those comparable to open-admissions students only two in ten had graduated. However, a significant proportion of CUNY students were transferring to senior colleges prior to earning a community-college degree —perhaps more were doing so there than nationally, if only because CUNY is a single university structure.[30]

Critical theorists such as Karabel and Bowles and Gintis have identified the community colleges as contributing to the maintenance of class and ethnic inequalities in American education.[31] In their view, even though such colleges have played a major role in expanding access to higher education, they function to cool students out, reducing educational and occupational aspirations. As a result, many become discouraged, and according to Bowles and Gintis fewer than half of community-college students earn even an associate degree. Both the national and the CUNY results we have presented so far seem compatible with the critical viewpoint.

Summary of Findings

The patterns of academic achievement, dropout, and graduation that we have reviewed bear out some of the central interpretations in the literature. High school average has been found to be one of the best predictors of success in college, and this was certainly evident in CUNY's senior and community colleges. Correspondingly, regular students established a superiority during the freshman year, achieving better grades and earning credits at a faster rate than did open-admissions students. These initial advantages in grades and credits were still visible in students' cumulative records. As a result, regular students were more likely to graduate and less likely to drop out than were open-admissions students.

Notwithstanding these inequalities of results, CUNY open-admissions students did well by comparison to a national yardstick. If we take into account their somewhat slower progress toward a degree, CUNY senior-college open-admissions students outdid their national counterparts, and in the community colleges open-admissions students did about as well as their national peers. By these criteria of graduation and dropout, open admissions was no revolving door. It gave opportunity to students that they would not have had otherwise, and many used the opportunity well. Even among the dropouts, many did not leave empty-handed: a substantial minority (40 percent of 1970 entrants in senior colleges and 25 percent in community colleges) had compiled more than a year of college credit at the time they left.

Despite these positive results, open admissions clearly did not eradicate differences in the success rates of open-admissions and regular students. Indeed, we have reason to think that some regular students who appear to have dropped out may have actually transferred and earned degrees at colleges outside CUNY, and thus differences may have been larger than our data revealed. Moreover, even though open-admissions students did well relative to a national standard, an optimistic judgment of their success must be tempered by the fact that most did not graduate.

How do these results square with the concerns that many expressed before open admissions began? As we noted earlier, some worried that because of weak preparation, open-admissions students would meet with academic disaster. Yet many open-admissions students earned satisfactory grades and graduated, so this clearly did not happen. Other observers feared that the success of these students would conceal an underlying collapse of academic standards. While it is impossible in the absence of any independent yardstick to say anything definitive about grade inflation under open admissions, the patterns we have described do not suggest a collapse of standards: many students did poorly and dropped out, and success at CUNY was clearly related to high school performance.

Educational Background, Social Origins, and Academic Success

To this point we have considered the academic success of students under the open-admissions policy in the broadest terms, comparing the achievements of those whose enrollment was made possible only by the policy with those of regular students. But our assessment has not yet addressed the fact that open admissions was designed to bring into the mainstream of higher education economically marginal and minority students who had not been served to any substantial extent by City University in the 1960s. It is essential to survey the achievements of class and ethnic groups in any evaluation of open admissions. While the policy had egalitarian effects in the access it provided and in the distribution of ethnic groups across the levels of CUNY, it does not follow that this greater equalization of opportunity was accompanied by academic outcomes equally propitious for all groups.

In examining academic performance, we have used our samples, which include data on ethnicity and income. As noted in appendix A, these sam-

ples contain greater proportions of able students whose academic performance was in some respects better than that of the corresponding populations. In almost all instances, however, the superiority of the samples is only
slight. This bias does not affect comparisons among the groups at CUNY,
but it does affect comparisons of CUNY results, as indicated by these samples, to a national baseline. We will point out the few instances in which
findings need qualification because of possible sample bias.

The Academic Fate of Ethnic Groups

Because of the central role that ethnicity played in the emergence of
open admissions, let us begin with an examination of the academic fate of
the major ethnic constituencies: Jewish, Catholic, black, and Hispanic students. We compare these groups on four major outcomes: grades, credits,
dropout, and graduation.

For senior colleges, table 6.8 summarizes the cumulative grade point averages and credits earned by each ethnic group, with open-admissions students separated from regulars and dropouts separated from persisters.[32]
Among regular students who persisted in college, a clear rank order is present in the grades earned by the different groups. Jewish students earned
higher grades than Catholics, who in turn performed more strongly than
both blacks and Hispanics. In the 1972 cohort, where Jewish and Catholic
students cannot be distinguished, whites outdistanced the minority groups.
On average, differences between white and minority regular students ranged
from about a third to a half letter grade. Among persisting open-admissions
students, there was little difference between Jews and Catholics, but both of
these groups earned better grades than did the minorities. Differences between the highest and the lowest groups were smaller than they were for regular students, the maximum being about a third of a letter grade.

Looked at as a whole, these grade differences between ethnic groups
within the same category of admissions status were generally moderate.
However, Jews and Catholics were more likely to be regular students, while
minority students were more likely to be in the open-admissions category.
Thus, the combined effects of admissions status and ethnicity were often
quite substantial: the difference between the "typical" white student and
the "typical" minority student sometimes approached a full letter grade.

White ethnics also outdistanced minority students in credits. Among
both open-admissions and regular students who persisted, minorities were
usually about two to three courses behind Catholics and three to four
courses behind Jews. In one instance the gap was larger than this: among
open-admissions students in the 1971 cohort, blacks were five to six courses
behind Jews and Catholics. In 1972 whites were about three to four courses
ahead of minorities. Without doubt, then, minority students would have required more time to graduate than would have whites of the same admissions category: given the rates at which they were accumulating credits,
minority students were often running about a semester behind whites, espe-

TABLE 6.8. Senior-College Cumulative Grade Point Averages and Credits Earned, by Ethnicity and Admissions Status[a]

	REGULAR		OPEN	
	Dropouts	Persisters	Dropouts	Persisters
	Cumulative Grade Point Averages			
1970 cohort				
Jewish	2.71	3.03	1.85	2.50
Catholic	2.18	2.89	1.50	2.48
Black	1.90	2.71	1.33	2.24
Hispanic	2.01	2.72	1.50	2.34
1971 cohort				
Jewish	2.74	3.08	1.90	2.53
Catholic	2.16	2.92	1.63	2.57
Black	2.12	2.63	1.24	2.20
Hispanic	1.84	2.60	1.56	2.40
1972 cohort				
White	2.53	2.95	1.48	2.31
Black	1.78	2.56	1.25	2.00
Hispanic	1.83	2.48	1.37	2.13
	Cumulative Credits Earned			
1970 cohort				
Jewish	75.0	121.5	52.5	113.6
Catholic	55.0	118.6	34.4	111.8
Black	52.6	116.8	33.7	103.0
Hispanic	49.2	114.2	37.7	104.0
1971 cohort				
Jewish	45.6	110.3	37.1	100.1
Catholic	36.4	106.2	31.6	98.9
Black	30.8	99.7	26.6	82.5
Hispanic	33.8	98.0	27.0	91.4
1972 cohort				
White	31.6	81.4	20.8	68.2
Black	28.1	72.9	17.1	57.4
Hispanic	28.5	70.3	16.6	57.6

Source: Sample data.
[a]Results cover five years for the 1970 cohort, four years for the 1971, and three years for the 1972.

cially Jews (and for open-admissions blacks in 1971 the lag between them and white ethnics was closer to two semesters).

Just as we noted in the case of grades, the combined effects of admissions status and ethnicity were more substantial. Taking the 1971 cohort as an example, the most productive group of regular admissions status, Jews, were almost twenty-eight credits, or nine courses, ahead of open-admissions blacks and nineteen credits, or more than six courses, ahead of open-admissions Hispanics. Even in the 1970 cohort (which had an additional year to accumulate credits), open-admission minority students were five to six courses behind regular admissions Jews and Catholics.

These ethnic differences in academic performance translated into differences in rates of graduation, retention, and dropout, as shown in table 6.9. There is a broadly consistent ethnic pattern in these rates. Jewish students were generally the group least likely to drop out. Indeed, their persistence in higher education was probably greater than the table indicates since among those shown dropping out of CUNY regular Jewish students had the highest grade point averages of any group (see table 6.8) and thus were the most likely to have transferred out of the City University system. At the other end, Hispanics were the most likely to drop out. Blacks and Catholics fell in the middle, though judging by their grade point averages, regular Catholics were perhaps a bit more likely to transfer than were blacks. Ethnic differences in graduation were usually greater than differences in dropout. As one might expect, Jewish students were most likely to graduate, followed in descending order by Catholics, blacks, and Hispanics. In most cases, the Hispanic rate was sharply lower than those of the other groups.

Notwithstanding these differences, all groups but Hispanics were about as successful as comparable students nationwide. The five-year graduation rates of regular senior-college ethnic groups (that is, the rates of the 1970 cohort) were not far from the national rate for three of the four CUNY groups, even allowing for some bias in our samples (for both regular and open-admissions students, the figures shown in the table for the 1970 cohort are probably inflated by about 4 percent).[33] Among open-admissions students, the graduation rates of Jews and Catholics exceeded the national rate, while the rate of blacks was about the same. Only the Hispanic rate

TABLE 6.9. **Senior-College Graduation, Retention, and Dropout Rates: CUNY Ethnic Groups and National Data**

	REGULAR			OPEN		
	Grad.[a]	Ret.	Drop.	Grad.	Ret.	Drop.
1970 cohort[b]						
Jewish	57	9	34	37	15	48
Catholic	49	11	40	29	11	60
Black	48	12	40	23	19	59
Hispanic	34	15	51	19	16	65
1971 cohort[c]						
Jewish	43	33	24	23	38	39
Catholic	37	33	30	21	35	44
Black	31	43	27	14	52	34
Hispanic	20	39	41	5	27	68
Four-year						
national data	49	9	42	21	14	65

Sample: Sample data. National data are from table 6.5.
[a]Abbreviations are as in table 6.5.
[b]Rates after five years.
[c]Rates after four years.

was clearly lower. However, the percentages of minority students who remained in school even after five years were slightly higher at CUNY than the four-year national retention rates. Thus, it is likely that the graduation rate of blacks came still closer to the national rate in the sixth and subsequent years. But with the possible exception of open-admissions students in the 1970 cohort, Hispanics appear certain to have lagged behind since their graduation rates in both cohorts were well below national rates and their dropout rates were already at or above national dropout rates.

TABLE 6.10. Community-College Cumulative Grade Point Averages and Credits Earned, by Ethnicity and Admissions Status[a]

	REGULAR		OPEN	
	Dropouts	Persisters	Dropouts	Persisters
	Cumulative Grade Point Averages			
1970 cohort				
Jewish	1.91	2.64	1.44	2.24
Catholic	1.72	2.75	1.28	2.30
Black	1.64	2.54	1.32	2.07
Hispanic	1.94	2.70	1.44	2.25
1971 cohort				
Jewish	2.44	2.86	1.70	2.40
Catholic	2.26	2.85	1.65	2.37
Black	1.94	2.59	1.53	2.09
Hispanic	1.99	2.65	1.65	2.17
1972 cohort				
White	2.05	2.82	1.53	2.38
Black	1.78	2.48	1.41	2.05
Hispanic	1.85	2.61	1.55	2.15
	Cumulative Credits Earned			
1970 cohort				
Jewish	27.4	56.9	22.6	54.3
Catholic	24.0	59.1	19.6	56.9
Black	26.9	60.4	22.2	55.1
Hispanic	29.3	59.4	21.8	60.7
1971 cohort				
Jewish	33.3	58.4	27.4	57.2
Catholic	31.6	60.1	26.4	57.9
Black	28.3	60.3	21.7	51.8
Hispanic	24.2	59.7	20.2	49.7
1972 cohort				
White	20.8	58.4	16.0	51.7
Black	20.8	55.8	15.1	46.9
Hispanic	18.3	56.2	14.4	45.6

Source: Sample data.
[a]Results cover five years for the 1970 cohort, four years for the 1971, and three years for the 1972.

The academic performance of ethnic groups in the community colleges is summarized in table 6.10. Students' cumulative grade point averages show a somewhat different picture from that seen for the senior colleges. Ethnic differences within each category of admissions status were neither as large nor as consistent as they were in the four-year schools. Among persisters, both Jews and Catholics earned higher averages than did blacks. The position of Hispanics varied: in 1970 they performed about as well as the two white groups, but among 1971 and 1972 entrants grades were somewhat lower than those of the whites.

The credit picture in the community colleges is somewhat muddy. Among persisting regular students differences are small, and there is no consistent rank order of groups. As for open-admissions students, Hispanics in the 1970 cohort earned slightly more credits than did the other groups, among whom there were no differences. However, in the 1971 and 1972 cohorts the pattern is the more familiar one: whites earned more credits than did minorities, but the gap was not as large as that in the senior colleges, amounting to about six credits. The generally smaller differences among groups in the community colleges can be explained largely by the fact that all three cohorts had more than two years to complete their studies, as well as by the fact that Jewish students (and Catholics to a lesser extent) were more likely to transfer to CUNY's senior colleges without obtaining an associate degree, thus depressing the number of credits they earned as community-college students.

Community-college graduation, retention, and dropout rates are presented in table 6.11. Among regular students, Jews consistently had the lowest dropout rates, followed by Catholics. Blacks and Hispanics had the highest rates. However, the record of dropouts in the community colleges, unlike that in the senior colleges, generally does not suggest that they were transferring out of CUNY since in most cases their grades were below the minimum necessary for graduation.[34] In the open-admissions category, Jewish students were also least likely to drop out, but differences among the other groups were small. With regard to graduation, the rates of Jews and Catholics (and whites in 1972) were higher than those of blacks and Hispanics. The magnitude of these differences was smaller than that observed in the senior colleges, but the full range of ethnic differences is probably understated in the table since the graduation rates do not take into account that Jewish students, and to a lesser extent Catholics, were more likely than minority students to transfer to CUNY's senior colleges without earning an associate degree.

In terms of their graduation rates, white community-college students at CUNY did better than their national peers, but the rates of blacks and Hispanics are below the national rates when sampling bias is taken into account.[35] In the case of open-admissions minority students, the disparity in favor of the national rates is only partly counterbalanced by the higher percentages of CUNY students still enrolled after four years (as shown by the

TABLE 6.11. Community-College Graduation, Retention, and Dropout Rates: CUNY Ethnic Groups and National Data

	REGULAR				OPEN			
	Grad.[a]	Ret.	Drop.	Trans.[b]	Grad.	Ret.	Drop.	Trans.
1970 cohort[c]								
Jewish	39	2	40	19	25	4	54	16
Catholic	42	2	44	12	24	3	62	11
Black	30	4	60	7	18	8	64	10
Hispanic	30	6	54	9	19	5	70	7
1971 cohort[d]								
Jewish	49	3	32	17	33	6	48	13
Catholic	45	5	39	12	27	8	58	8
Black	36	8	49	8	18	14	60	6
Hispanic	36	5	54	5	19	12	62	8
1972 cohort[e]								
White	41	13	39	7	20	17	55	7
Black	29	26	40	5	15	29	53	5
Hispanic	30	22	45	4	15	26	55	5
Four-year national data	32	2	66	–	20	3	77	–

Source: Sample data. National data are from table 6.7.
[a]Abbreviations are as in table 6.7.
[b]Included are students who moved from community to senior colleges without first earning an associate degree. Those who obtained the associate degree and then transferred are shown only once in the table under the column "Grad."
[c]Rates after five years.
[d]Rates after four years.
[e]Rates after three years.

1971 cohort).[36] Thus, the ultimate graduation rates for minority students might well have approximated the national rates, but it seems unlikely that they would have exceeded them.

In sum, open admissions clearly did not eradicate ethnic differences in educational attainment. CUNY's white groups in senior colleges were superior to the national baseline for graduation, and blacks were about even when measured against the national yardstick, with Hispanics lower. In community colleges white groups were above the national baseline and minority students were below. Broadly speaking, relatively consistent and sometimes large differences were visible in each group's overall academic success. In the senior colleges Jewish students were most successful and Hispanics were least, and in the community colleges the white groups were more successful than were blacks and Hispanics.

Income and Academic Achievement

To provide educational opportunity for low-income groups has been a traditional mission of CUNY, one that it reaffirmed through the open-admissions policy. If we define a low-income family in New York City as one earning less than $7,500,[37] then a third and more of the first three freshmen classes under the policy came from families below this level. Many of these low-income students were in the open-admissions category. Indeed, in the community colleges between 60 and 70 percent came from low-income families, while at senior colleges half or more of open-admissions students were of low income. It goes almost without saying that for these low-income students with weak records in high school, a college education would simply have been unavailable except through the open-admissions policy.

We have examined the academic performance of students from various income groups, looking at grades, credits, and rates of graduation, retention, and dropout. Overall, these analyses yield a surprising result: differences in favor of higher income groups were usually small when we controlled for admissions status. Some sense of the differences among income groups is given by a consideration of graduation rates. The largest difference occurs for senior-college open-admissions students in the 1970 cohort. Low-income students had a graduation rate of 25 percent, compared with 32 percent for students above the $7,500 level. Among community-college open-admissions students, no difference in graduation rates exceeds 4 percent. Among regular students, differences by income category were even smaller.

One of our analyses focused upon a particularly critical target group: welfare students. Data pertaining to welfare were collected for the 1971 freshmen. Most welfare students were enrolled in community colleges, and at some of these schools they represented about 20 percent of the freshman class. Among the open-admissions students from welfare families, 18 percent had graduated after four years and another 20 percent were still enrolled in CUNY. For nonwelfare open-admissions students the graduation rate was 26 percent, with another 17 percent still enrolled. In short, the success rates of welfare students were not very far below those of other open-admissions students in community colleges. Given the extreme economic disadvantage of these students, their relative success is striking. In a nutshell, when the doors of CUNY were opened wide, students' chances for success were not greatly affected by their economic background.

A Summary Model of the Effects of High School Background and Social Origin

In our analyses thus far, two findings stand out: open-admissions students did less well than did regular students and whites generally met with greater academic success than did minority students. But these analyses did not take account of other aspects of students' high school background and social origin. For example, we saw in chapter 5 that open-admissions students in general, and minority students in particular, took fewer college preparatory courses in high school. Students who took fewer such courses were more likely to have been in vocational high schools or, if they graduated from academic high schools, were more likely to have been in the slower, somewhat diluted academic tracks. To this point it is not clear just how much high school tracking may have contributed to differences in achievement at CUNY. Moreover, we do not know the extent to which differences between ethnic groups in academic performance might be explained by other social origins factors such as parents' education and family economic status.

To provide a more complete picture of the role of educational background and social origin in students' academic achievement at CUNY, we have conducted a set of regression analyses that allow us to consider simultaneously the effects of a larger number of background variables, including educational factors such as high school average, number of college preparatory courses taken, and rank in high school graduating class, as well as such social origin variables as father's education, mother's education, family income, and ethnicity. By considering all of these factors together, we are able better to assess the effects of high school background and social origin and to determine the relative importance of each for the academic fate of students. The results of these analyses (which include both dropouts and persisters) are presented for the senior colleges in table 6.12, which examines for each cohort the relationships of the background factors to the following achievement variables: cumulative grade point average, cumulative credits earned, persistence, and graduation.

One main finding emerging from these analyses is that high school background is generally a stronger predictor of academic outcomes than is social origin, although this is more true for students' college grade point averages, the number of credits they earned, and their graduation status than for their persistence. Within the set of high school factors, the one with the greatest influence is high school average. Indeed, for the outcomes other than persistence, it was the single most important predictor. Thus, there was a degree of consistency between how well a student did in high school and how well he or she did at CUNY.

Nonetheless, the other high school factors were not so important. A student's rank in the high school graduating class played only a minor role in success at CUNY. For example, among 1970 entrants, a student in the eightieth percentile of the graduating class would have earned a cumulative grade point average only .04 points above that of a student comparable in other respects who ranked in the sixtieth percentile. Our measure of high school track, the number of college preparatory courses taken, had more consistent and slightly stronger effects, but its influence was still weak compared to that of high school average. Again using the 1970 freshmen as an example, a difference of six points in high school average resulted in a difference

TABLE 6.12. Senior-College Academic Outcomes as a Function of High School Background and Social Origin

	1970 Cohort		1971 Cohort		1972 Cohort	
	b	beta	b	beta	b	beta
Cumulative Grade Point Average						
High school average	.056	.435	.057	.419	.073	.519
	p<.001		p<.001		p<.001	
Rank in high school class	.002	.051	.001	.035	.000	−.003
	p<.01		N.S.		N.S.	
College preparatory courses	.029	.070	.037	.089	.034	.091
	p<.01		p<.01		p<.01	
Father's education	.023	.036	.016	.026	.022	.038
	p<.01		N.S.		N.S.	
Mother's education	.024	.030	.028	.037	−.005	−.007
	p<.01		N.S.		N.S.	
Family income[a]		.011		.026		.035
$4,000–7,999	.011		−.093		.089	
$8,000–14,999	.022		−.051		.037	
$15,000 or more	.034		−.041		.098	
	N.S.		N.S.		N.S.	
Ethnicity[b]		.137		.146		.102
Jewish	.074		.073		—	
Catholic	−.138		−.098		—	
Black	−.214		−.171		−.170	
Hispanic	−.243		−.370		−.277	
	p<.001		p<.01		p<.01	
Constant	−2.751		−2.730		−4.132	
R^2		.339		.314		.387
Cumulative Credits Earned						
High school average	1.464	.209	1.170	.169	1.650	.330
	p<.001		p<.001		p<.001	
Rank in high school class	.119	.054	.170	.088	−.006	−.004
	p<.01		p<.01		N.S.	
College preparatory courses	2.500	.108	1.873	.088	1.635	.123
	p<.001		p<.01		p<.001	
Father's education	.823	.023	1.157	.037	.656	.032
	N.S.		N.S.		N.S.	
Mother's education	.115	.003	−.010	.000	.202	.008
	N.S.		N.S.		N.S.	
Family income[a]		.020		.021		.028
$4,000–7,999	2.807		−3.330		3.826	
$8,000–14,999	2.462		−2.979		4.054	
$15,000 or more	.584		−1.459		3.468	
	N.S.		N.S.		N.S.	
Ethnicity[b]		.146		.124		.085
Jewish	8.242		4.192		—	
Catholic	−3.465		−.672		—	
Black	−3.256		−2.315		−3.285	
Hispanic	−9.918		−17.803		−8.976	
	p<.001		p<.01		p<.01	
Constant	−81.293		−54.150		−103.965	
R^2		.146		.119		.203

Source: Sample data.
[a]The omitted category contains those with family incomes under $4,000. For the 1971 and 1972 cohorts the intervals are slightly different: the omitted category consists of students

TABLE 6.12. Continued

	1970 Cohort		1971 Cohort		1972 Cohort	
	b	beta	b	beta	b	beta

Persistence

High school average	.006	.083	.004	.052	.013	.172
	p<.01		N.S.		p<.001	
Rank in high school class	.001	.054	.002	.101	.000	−.018
	p<.01		p<.01		N.S.	
College preparatory courses	.017	.065	.018	.072	.018	.091
	p<.01		p<.05		p<.001	
Father's education	.007	.018	.014	.038	.006	.018
	N.S.		N.S.		N.S.	
Mother's education	−.003	−.007	−.005	−.011	.014	.039
	N.S.		N.S.		N.S.	
Family income[a]		.029		.016		.035
$4,000–7,999	.058		−.006		.036	
$8,000–14,999	.047		−.017		.035	
$15,000 or more	.027		.000		−.002	
	N.S.		N.S.		N.S.	
Ethnicity[b]		.106		.112		.057
Jewish	.038		.045		—	
Catholic	−.028		.023		—	
Black	−.014		.091		.011	
Hispanic	−.076		−.177		−.091	
	p<.01		p<.01		p<.01	
Constant	−.328		−.143		−.697	
R^2		.041		.051		.063

Graduation

High school average	.012	.158	.016	.200		
	p<.001		p<.001			
Rank in high school class	.001	.045	.001	.025		
	p<.01		N.S.			
College preparatory courses	.019	.074	.013	.053		
	p<.001		p<.05			
Father's education	.005	.012	.017	.046		
	N.S.		N.S.			
Mother's education	.004	.008	.003	.007		
	N.S.		N.S.			
Family income[a]		.034		.021		
$4,000–7,999	.066		−.031			
$8,000–14,999	.054		−.044			
$15,000 or more	.029		−.043			
	p<.05		N.S.			
Ethnicity[b]		.094		.086		
Jewish	.073		.069			
Catholic	.003		.047			
Black	−.011		.025			
Hispanic	−.091		−.087			
	p<.01		p<.01			
Constant	−.998		−1.275			
R^2		.080		.082		

with family incomes under $3,700, and the first category shown in the table is $3,700–7,499; the second category is $7,500–14,999.
[b]In 1970 and 1971 the omitted category contains "other whites." In 1972 "whites" form the omitted category. The regression equations contained another category, "other non-whites," which has not been reported.

of over a third of a letter grade in CUNY performance, while a difference of two college preparatory courses—a sizable one in terms of the distribution of this variable—resulted in a gap of less than a tenth of a letter grade.[38] This suggests, therefore, that high school tracking was not a profound source of advantage or disadvantage in the academic achievement of senior-college students.

For one outcome, persistence, high school background had weak effects compared not only to the weight it showed for the other outcomes but also relative to social factors. However, this small association with persistence may not have accurately reflected its importance. Earlier in the chapter we noted that some students shown in our data as dropouts were doing quite well at the time they left. We surmised that quite a few of these students were not dropping out of higher education but were simply transferring from CUNY. Such transferring would have diminished the influence of high school average on persistence as we were able to measure it.

While high school background had a primary influence on the ultimate academic success of senior-college students, social origin also played a role —one that was unexpected in some ways. In the first place, the two measures of social class, parental education and family income were, for all practical purposes, unrelated to achievement at CUNY. Though much has been made of the transmission of class cultures through the family and of the conversion of such cultural capital into educational advantages and disadvantages, at CUNY differences in parental educational attainment (a reasonable index of the cultural atmosphere of the family) and in income (a resource facilitating educational attainment), were for the most part unrelated to the performance of the offspring.

In contrast, ethnicity played quite a different role. We noted earlier that there were ethnic differences in academic performance and that, generally speaking, whites outperformed minority students. Our regression analyses make clear that these ethnic differences can be explained only partly by differences in high school or social class background. For example, among those entering CUNY in 1970, the regression results show that even with these background differences controlled, Jewish students stood almost a third of a letter grade above Hispanics and more than a quarter of a letter grade higher than blacks. These differences did not result from the generally higher educational attainment of Jewish parents, or the generally higher income of Jewish families, or the generally stronger high school records of Jewish students. The observed differences in grades would hold even if the Jewish and minority students were alike in all other respects measured in this analysis. To be sure, the ordering of groups is not entirely consistent across all of the major academic outcomes. Sometimes the two white groups outperformed the two minority groups. In other cases, the records of Catholic and black students seem indistinguishable or blacks outperformed Catholics. But what is clear is, first, that Jewish students consistently outperformed all others and that Hispanics were weakest and, second, that these differences were to some extent independent of other ways in which the groups differed. These analyses thus confirm that in CUNY's senior colleges, ethnic group membership was an independent source of advantage and disadvantage. Indeed, in some ways our data probably underestimate the extent of ethnic differences: because Jewish students (and, to a lesser extent, Catholics) seemed more likely to transfer from CUNY, our data overstate their dropout and understate their graduation rates from higher education.

We have conducted a parallel set of analyses for the community colleges (see table 6.13). High school background again emerges as a stronger predictor of academic outcome than social origin. However, this relationship is more complex than it was for the senior colleges. At the latter the role of high school average was overwhelmingly important. In the community colleges high school average was important, but high school track (indexed by the number of college preparatory courses taken) and rank also carried considerable weight in explaining academic achievement. To give an idea of the various effects, consider the following example. In the 1970 cohort a difference of six points in high school average yielded a difference of more than a fifth of a letter grade in cumulative grade point average; a difference of twenty percentile points in high school rank resulted in a gap of a tenth of a point in cumulative grade point average; and a difference of three college preparatory courses led to a difference of about .15 points in the cumulative average. In absolute terms, the effects of rank and track were somewhat larger than those observed in the senior colleges, but these variables carried still more weight in explaining grades because the proportion of students from nonacademic tracks and from lower high school ranks was considerably greater than in the senior colleges. For other academic outcomes such as persistence and graduation, the effects of rank and track were also larger in the community colleges. With regard to credits, senior-college students from nonacademic high school tracks showed slightly larger deficits than did the community-college students. This is probably caused by the greater range of credits involved in senior colleges, as well as by the fact that more time was available for the accumulation of credits in the two-year schools, somewhat masking the effects of track there.

The role of social background factors was less important in the two-year schools than in the senior colleges. Parental education was not associated with any of the academic outcomes for any cohort. Family income did have some effects, but these occurred inconsistently and varied as to direction. Sometimes the lowest income students did more poorly than more affluent students, and sometimes they did better. Overall, we conclude that these social class factors had no effect upon academic success in CUNY's community colleges.

As in the senior colleges ethnicity emerges in the community colleges as having some independent effects upon academic performance. But these net ethnic differences were generally not as large as the ones we observed in the

TABLE 6.13. Community-College Academic Outcomes as a Function of High School Background and Social Origin

	1970 Cohort		1971 Cohort		1972 Cohort	
	b	beta	b	beta	b	beta
Cumulative Grade Point Average						
High school average	.036	.219	.040	.283	.038	.259
	p<.001		p<.001		p<.001	
Rank in high school class	.005	.129	.003	.077	.003	.063
	p<.01		p<.01		p<.01	
College preparatory courses	.057	.175	.043	.156	.043	.142
	p<.001		p<.001		p<.001	
Father's education	.018	.023	.016	.022	.005	.008
	N.S.		N.S.		N.S.	
Mother's education	.001	−.001	−.019	−.024	−.020	−.030
	N.S.		N.S.		N.S.	
Family income[a]		.059		.044		.028
$4,000–7,999	−.104		.038		.027	
$8,000–14,999	−.096		.056		.049	
$15,000 or more	−.216		−.059		.027	
	p<.01		p<.05		N.S.	
Ethnicity[b]		.069		.151		.052
Jewish	.048		−.055		—	
Catholic	−.084		−.175		—	
Black	−.131		−.322		−.109	
Hispanic	−.029		−.319		−.073	
	p<.01		p<.01		p<.01	
Constant	−1.462		−1.170		−1.158	
R^2		.173		.217		.165
Cumulative Credits Earned						
High school average	.226	.049	.554	.136	.491	.126
	N.S.		p<.01		p<.001	
Rank in high school class	.161	.137	.082	.078	.095	.089
	p<.001		p<.01		p<.01	
College preparatory courses	1.608	.171	.966	.120	1.210	.150
	p<.001		p<.001		p<.001	
Father's education	.626	.028	.262	.013	.224	.014
	N.S.		N.S.		N.S.	
Mother's education	−.194	−.007	−.088	−.004	−.010	−.005
	N.S.		N.S.		N.S.	
Family income[a]		.050		.053		.026
$4,000–7,999	−3.369		2.241		−.212	
$8,000–14,999	−3.074		2.152		.719	
$15,000 or more	−5.495		−1.463		1.830	
	p<.05		p<.05		N.S.	
Ethnicity[b]		.087		.127		.038
Jewish	2.701		5.875		—	
Catholic	−.506		2.922		—	
Black	1.177		−.879		1.299	
Hispanic	.021		−4.113		−.795	
	p<.01		p<.01		p<.05	
Constant	−1.823		−17.299		−18.961	
R^2		.076		.094		.084

Source: Sample data.
[a]The omitted category contains those with family incomes under $4,000. For the 1971 and 1972 cohorts the intervals are slightly different: the omitted category consists of students

TABLE 6.13. Continued

	1970 Cohort		1971 Cohort		1972 Cohort	
	b	beta	b	beta	b	beta
Persistence						
High school average	.006	.073	.013	.157	.005	.068
	p<.01		p<.01		p<.01	
Rank in high school class	.001	.056	−.001	−.026	.001	.056
	p<.05		N.S.		p<.01	
College preparatory courses	.029	.165	.016	.100	.021	.133
	p<.001		p<.01		p<.001	
Father's education	.007	.017	−.002	−.006	.003	.008
	N.S.		N.S.		N.S.	
Mother's education	.002	.004	−.007	−.014	.000	.001
	N.S.		N.S.		N.S.	
Family income[a]		.048		.045		.016
$4,000–7,999	−.018		.002		.019	
$8,000–14,999	−.003		.005		.026	
$15,000 or more	−.069		−.067		.022	
	p<.05		N.S.		N.S.	
Ethnicity[b]		.087		.083		.057
Jewish	.072		.080		—	
Catholic	.001		−.017		—	
Black	−.005		−.021		.063	
Hispanic	−.027		−.078		.031	
	p<.01		p<.01		p<.01	
Constant	−.414		−.588		−.201	
R^2		.061		.050		.039
Graduation						
High school average	.007	.089	.013	.175	.005	.077
	p<.01		p<.001		p<.01	
Rank in high school class	.002	.103	.000	.017	.002	.127
	p<.01		N.S.		p<.01	
College preparatory courses	.016	.102	.010	.066	.015	.111
	p<.01		p<.01		p<.001	
Father's education	−.002	−.006	−.011	−.029	.003	.010
	N.S.		N.S.		N.S.	
Mother's education	.006	.013	−.007	−.015	−.002	−.005
	N.S.		N.S.		N.S.	
Family income[a]		.029		.067		.017
$4,000–7,999	.002		.002		.003	
$8,000–14,999	.002		.017		.018	
$15,000 or more	−.033		−.084		.009	
	N.S.		p<.01		N.S.	
Ethnicity[b]		.089		.102		.052
Jewish	.044		.112		—	
Catholic	.045		.040		—	
Black	−.009		−.020		−.043	
Hispanic	−.019		−.043		−.053	
	p<.01		p<.01		p<.01	
Constant	−.529		−.773		−.384	
R^2		.060		.067		.069

with family incomes under $3,700, and the first category shown in the table is $3,700–7,499; the second category is $7,500–14,999.
[b]In 1970 and 1971 the omitted category contains "other whites." In 1972 "whites" form the omitted category. The regression equations contain another category, "other nonwhites," which has not been reported.

four-year schools. For example, in the 1971 senior-college cohort, the largest ethnic difference in cumulative grade point average approached half a letter grade, while for that class in the community colleges it was only a quarter of a letter grade. With regard to number of credits earned, differences between whites and minorities were also smaller than in senior colleges. However, since whites were more likely to transfer to senior colleges without attaining the associate degree, our data probably understate the ethnic gap in credit productivity. There were also ethnic differences in persistence and graduation independent of other educational and social factors; as in the senior colleges, the largest were between Jewish and Hispanic students.

In summary, high school background was an important determinant of success in community college: students whose records were stronger in high school were likely to do better in college, and the nonacademic high school tracks did somewhat hinder students in their community-college careers. But above and beyond these effects of prior education, ethnic membership made a difference. Broadly speaking, white students, especially Jews, were likely to do better than blacks and Hispanics even when the white and minority students were comparable in other respects.

One of the aims of the open-admissions policy was to provide a second chance to those students who had not done very well in high school or who had been in those tracks that traditionally do not lead to college. Clearly, the idea of a second chance implies that those who had not met with much success in high school and who were disadvantaged in other ways (such as having low-income and/or minority status) should be able to change the educational trajectories that had been set before college. Since our regression analyses assess how well students' educational histories and social origins predict their success at CUNY, we can use them to evaluate the extent to which open admissions did indeed offer a second chance. Put another way, our regression models provide a means of summarizing the extent to which success at CUNY was, or was not, foreclosed by educational and social background. If predictability is high, one would have to conclude that success or failure at CUNY was in a real sense predestined by individuals' histories. If predictability is low, this would suggest that individuals' educational trajectories could indeed be altered by the opportunities that open admissions provided. Predictability is revealed by one of the most important statistics provided by regression analysis, the R^2.

In senior colleges the most predictable aspect of academic performance was the cumulative grade point average. Approximately a third of the variation in grades was accounted for by our background measures. As prediction goes in social science, especially prediction of academic achievement, this is a fairly high figure, but it is a far cry from any doctrine of predestination. Some students who did poorly in high school were able to do satisfactory work at CUNY's senior colleges, and others whose high school records were strong compiled only mediocre averages in college. Our other outcome measures—credits earned, persistence, and graduation—were far less predictable than grades. Only about 15 percent of the variation in credits (but 20 percent for the 1972 freshmen), 5 percent of persistence, and 8 percent of graduation could be accounted for from knowledge of students' high school backgrounds and social origins. That background factors were only weakly associated with persistence and graduation, and not very strongly with credits, may not, however, be a true reflection of their relationship to these outcomes; as noted earlier, many students shown in our data as dropouts were doing quite well at the time they left, and we have concluded that most of these students were probably transferring to colleges outside CUNY. If we had had a direct measure of persistence and graduation in the higher education system, rather than only at CUNY, fewer students would have been classified as dropouts, more would have been listed as graduates, and they would have earned more credits. Nevertheless, it is doubtful that the predictability of these outcomes would have increased much.[39] Thus, even though educational history and social origin continued to affect students' chances for success at CUNY, under open admissions the link between students' histories and college performance was only a very loose one.

In the community colleges, students' grades and credits were less predictable than in the four-year schools. Whereas in the senior colleges, a third of the variation in grades was accounted for by background, only about 20 percent was explained in the two-year schools. In part this difference reflected the apparent variability in grading standards in the community colleges (the effects of attendance at different CUNY colleges will be examined in some detail in chapter 7). While 15–20 percent of the variation in credits was predictable from background in the senior colleges, only about 8 percent could be accounted for in the community colleges. Again, our data underestimate the predictability of credits since some students transferred to senior colleges without attaining the associate degree, thus lowering their credit accumulation in the community colleges. The association of background with persistence and graduation was quite weak. The rather low predictability of graduation was partly a result of the effects of early transfer to senior colleges. Again, even if adjustments were made to correct for this factor, predictability would not have increased much.

Conclusion

Our analyses necessarily lead to a mixed judgment about the academic fate of CUNY students in the era of open admissions. In important ways the achievements of open-admissions students provide ground for optimism about the success of the policy. A great many earned at least satisfactory grades and some (more than 10 percent) compiled solid B averages. Against a baseline of national rates, CUNY's senior-college open-admissions students were more likely to graduate and less likely to drop out than were students with comparable high school records in public colleges around the nation. And open-admissions students in the community colleges were about as likely to graduate and less likely to drop out. By this yardstick, it is fair to say that the dire predictions of an open-admissions revolving door never materialized at CUNY.

Despite these positive results, it must be recognized that the achievements of open-admissions students did not equal those of regular students at either the four-year or the two-year colleges. Compared to these students, the open-admissions students earned lower grades, accumulated fewer credits at a slower pace, took longer to graduate and at a lower rate, and were more likely to drop out. Particularly with regard to graduation and dropout, any judgment of their success is a relative one: they did well, measured against the national rates, but it must be remembered that the majority did not graduate. In short, while open admissions took a large step toward equalizing opportunity for higher education, it did not erase inequalities of results.

In some ways these outcomes correspond to what is generally known about the determinants of academic achievement. That high school performance is one of the most, if not the most, important determinants of college performance is one of the literature's best documented findings.[40] The CUNY data certainly fit this picture. It is difficult to reconcile these results with the furor over academic standards under open admissions. The University does not appear to have been a deviant institution. Many did poorly and left the system, though to be sure most dropouts probably were not expelled but became discouraged and left of their own accord.

In our assessment of the success of particular groups toward which open admissions was targeted, low-income and minority students, there were some surprises. First, economic status bore almost no relationship to success at CUNY. Low-income students stood almost the same chance of doing well (or poorly) as did more affluent students. Second, ethnic membership was clearly associated with students' educational life chances. While open admissions substantially benefited every group, broadly speaking, white ethnics did better than both blacks and Hispanics, and white open-admissions students were more successful than their minority peers. They earned higher grades, were less likely to drop out, and were more likely to graduate. Even though ethnic inequalities in academic success were to an important degree a result of past educational disadvantages of minority students, the ethnic differences we have described are partly independent of students' school histories.

While high school background and social origin did make a difference for students' chances of success in the University, it would certainly be an overstatement to say that their chances of doing well were set inevitably by their backgrounds. It is true that grades could be predicted fairly well from a knowledge of background and therefore that a student whose high school record was weak was not very likely to become an academic star at CUNY. On the other hand, the number of credits earned could be predicted only moderately, and the probabilities of dropping out and of graduating were affected to an even smaller degree by students' background characteristics. Thus, in terms of staying in school and earning a degree, often thought of as the bottomline outcomes of college, neither high school background nor social origin destined students to either success or failure. In this sense it is fair to say that when CUNY's doors were opened wide, the University did indeed offer a second chance—one that a great many used to good advantage.

Notes

1. Christopher Jencks and David Riesman, *The Academic Revolution* (New York: Doubleday, 1968).
2. Board of Higher Education, "Statement of Policy" July 9, 1969, item 4.
3. For broad reviews of the dropout phenomenon see Frank Newman, *Report on Higher Education* (Washington: U.S. Government Printing Office, 1971); Robert G. Cope and William Hannah, *Revolving College Doors: The Causes and Consequences of Dropping Out, Stopping Out, and Transferring* (New York: Wiley, 1975); William G. Spady, "Dropouts from Higher Education: An Interdisciplinary Review and Synthesis," *Interchange* 1, (1970): 64–85; Vincent Tinto, "Dropout from Higher Education: A Theoretical Synthesis of Recent Research," *Review of Educational Research* 45 (Winter 1975): 89–125; Timothy J. Pantages and Carol F. Creedon, "Studies of College Attrition, 1950–1975," *Review of Educational Research* 48 (Winter 1978): 49–101.
4. Some of the major studies were cited in chapter 2. Detailed consideration of the economic impacts of higher education may be found also in Lewis C. Solmon and Paul J. Taubman (eds.), *Does College Matter? Some Evidence on the Impacts of Higher Education* (New York: Academic, 1973). There has been increased concern that the expansion of college-going may have outdistanced the demand of the labor market for college educated persons. This is discussed in Richard Freeman, *The Overeducated American* (New York: Academic, 1977).
5. That each year of college yields benefits for subsequent earnings and occupational status is pointed out in Christopher Jencks, Susan Bartlett, Mary Corcoran, James Crouse, David Eaglesfield, Gregory Jackson, Kent McClelland, Peter Mueser, Michael Olneck, Joseph Schwartz, Sherry Ward, and Jill Williams, *Who Gets Ahead?* (New York: Basic Books, 1979), chap. 6.
6. These are most extensively reviewed in Kenneth A. Feldman and Theodore M. Newcomb, *The Impact of College on Students* (San Francisco: Jossey-Bass, 1969). Technical problems sometimes make it difficult to attribute these consequences directly to the college experience. For a methodological discussion see Feldman and Newcomb. Such difficulties are also surveyed in Kenneth Keniston and Mark Gerzon, "Human and Social Benefits," in Logan Wilson and O.

Mills (eds.), *Universal Higher Education: Costs and Benefits* (Washington: American Council on Education, 1972). The latter also contains a good discussion of some important college effects.

7. Herbert H. Hyman, Charles R. Wright, and John Shelton Reed, *The Enduring Effects of Education* (Chicago: University of Chicago Press, 1975).

8. James W. Trent and Leland Medsker, *Beyond High School: A Psychosociological Study of 10,000 High School Graduates* (San Francisco: Jossey-Bass, 1968).

9. The importance of the initial semester for later performance was noted in Pantages and Creedon.

10. A substantial number of students earned no grade point average in the freshman year and were excluded from these calculations. The overwhelming majority were students who did not complete both terms. Students who took only remedial courses for zero credit, or who registered for courses with credit–no credit options, and/or who withdrew from courses would not have a grade point average.

11. At all CUNY campuses the minimum grade point average required for graduation was 2.00. However, the minimum average necessary for good academic standing in the freshman year was usually slightly lower than this. This minimum then increased each year. Typically, a 2.00 average was required for good standing on entry to the junior year.

12. In the community colleges, 6–10 percent of persisting students in the 1971 and 1972 cohorts had no averages. This occurred largely because two of these colleges did not use a standard A through F grading system. Rather, they used a pass–no credit system in which grade point averages were not calculated. Thus, many students at these schools may have been doing well even though they showed no averages.

13. A substantial minority of those who did not complete both semesters later returned. As an example, among open-admissions students in the senior colleges in the 1970 cohort, 38 percent of those who did not complete the freshman year subsequently returned to CUNY.

14. The number of credits for a course is, as a rule, equal to the number of hours that course meets during the week. However, for many remedial courses, the number of weekly classroom hours exceeded the number of credits. Thus, some students taking remedial courses were registered for fewer than twelve credits, but they were counted as full-time students if their classes met for at least twelve hours per week.

15. The conclusion is not modified when credit underreporting is taken into account. As we noted in chapter 3, the underreporting is quite small, amounting to an average of one to two credits per academic year—in the case of senior colleges, about four to eight credits over four years.

16. It may seem surprising that in some cases close to 30 percent of students who attended for an entire academic year earned fewer than twelve credits. There appear to be two main reasons for this. Some students took remedial courses offering little or no credit. More important, students who were in danger of failing a course or courses often were able to withdraw even fairly late in a semester. Although our data do not directly indicate such withdrawals, we know

from our inspection of original records that these occurrences were not infrequent, especially among weaker students.

17. The term "dropout" has considerably less finality than it appears to have. Over a limited period a student who has interrupted his or her attendance in college may look like a dropout, but over a longer interval this same student may reenroll, thus becoming a "stopout." As Astin put it, "It should be recognized that there can never be a wholly satisfactory definition of the term *dropout* until all students either obtain their degrees or die without obtaining a degree; any former student can, in theory, go back to school at any time to complete his degree" (Alexander W. Astin, *College Dropouts: A National Profile* [Washington: American Council on Education, 1972], p. 6).

18. The fact that dropout rates appear to increase slightly in each successive cohort should not be interpreted as showing that students in the later cohorts were doing less well. These intercohort differences result largely because stopouts in succeeding cohorts had less time to return.

19. A full report of the national findings is presented by Astin. The one-year rates are for all colleges and universities. In the national data we considered students with high school averages of less than B− as comparable to senior-college open-admissions students and those with averages of less than C+ as comparable to community-college open-admissions students. That there are students in the national sample comparable to CUNY's open-admissions students does little to vitiate our assertions in chapter 1 about the uniqueness of the CUNY experiment. Open-admissions students form a far larger proportion of CUNY's student body. Nationally, 24 percent of all four-year college students had high school averages comparable to those of CUNY's open-admissions students; in two-year schools the figure was 29 percent. The corresponding figures for CUNY are 40 percent and 65 percent.

20. A difference between the CUNY and the national data in the method of calculating one-year dropout rates should be noted. In the national data, students who did not return for the second year were counted as dropouts. However, the one-year CUNY dropout rates were calculated retrospectively; that is, students were counted as one-year dropouts only if they failed to enroll in the fall term of the second year *and* never again enrolled at CUNY. Students who did not enroll for the second year but who did enroll at some later time are not counted as dropouts. Therefore, this difference in method accentuates the CUNY superiority. However, when the CUNY data are calculated in exactly the same way as the national data, CUNY students still had lower dropout rates than the national sample. For example, table 6.3 shows a one-year dropout rate of 19 percent for open-admissions students in the 1970 cohort. Calculated by the method used for the national data, the rate for these students is 25 percent, compared with the national rate of 33 percent. And in community colleges the one-year rate of 25 percent for open-admissions students in the 1970 cohort becomes 32 percent when computed in the same way as the national data, still lower than the national rate of 37 percent.

21. It is important to note that intercohort comparisons cannot be interpreted as indicating a trend in performance from one cohort to the next. That each succeeding cohort shows a lower grade point average results mainly because the

later the cohort, the less the opportunity students had to drop out. Some of those who would have dropped out had there been more time available for that class to compile its record are shown as persisters in the table. Thus, those shown as persisters in the 1970 cohort are a stronger group because marginal students had more time to drop out.

22. That these students remained in school can be ascribed to two factors. First, some had interrupted their attendance and had actually been enrolled for only a few semesters. Second, CUNY schools allowed some students to continue into the later years of their careers with below par grades.

23. The 1972 entrants had not been in college long enough to have accumulated graduates. The small percentage of graduates shown after three years for this cohort and also for the 1971 cohort consists of students who were early graduates as a result of attendance during summer sessions, as well as a small number of students at two senior colleges that also offered associate degrees.

24. However, it should be noted that table 6.5 probably overestimates dropout rates in the later (fourth and fifth) years. Some who left CUNY in that period were undoubtedly stopouts who returned to the University subsequent to the end point of our records.

25. As noted in chapter 3, CUNY keeps track of students who transfer within the University but not of those who leave CUNY to continue their education outside that system.

26. So as to obtain greater comparability between the national sample and the CUNY data, we asked Astin to recompute his national data to provide four-year graduation, retention, and dropout rates for his subset of public colleges and universities.

27. That many CUNY students take more than the normal four years to graduate is not a recent development. A study done in the 1960s, focusing on an academically strong sample, found that after four years the graduation rate was less than 50 percent. However, over 70 percent graduated after seven years. Pearl Max, *How Many Graduated?* (New York: City University of New York, 1968).

28. These figures do not include students having no grade point average, as explained in note 12 above. Because two of the community colleges did not use a traditional grading system, many of the students with no average could have been doing quite well, but their achievements were reflected in credit attainment rather than in grades.

29. It should be understood that table 6.7 does not portray the *total* rates of transfer from community to senior colleges because students who received the associate degree and *then* went on to a senior college are shown in the table as community-college graduates. A full analysis of transfer from community to senior college is presented in chapter 8.

30. A direct comparison of community-senior college transfer rates is not possible since the national data contain no transfer measure comparable to ours.

31. Jerome Karabel, "Community Colleges and Social Stratification," *Harvard Educational Review* 42 (November 1972): 521–562; Samuel Bowles and Herbert Gintis, *Schooling in Capitalist America* (New York: Basic Books, 1972), pp. 211–212.

32. One senior college, Medgar Evers (founded in 1971), was removed from the analyses for the 1971 and 1972 cohorts, which are presented in tables 6.8, 6.9,

and 6.12. This college offered both baccalaureate and associate degree programs. A substantial number of students at this almost all-black institution were enrolled in the latter. Our data files do not provide any direct way of separating two-year and four-year students. The presence of the two-year students could sharply distort the academic performance results for black students (for example, by giving underestimates of cumulative credits earned and by overestimating graduation rates).

33. Sample-population differences in graduation rates are mirrored in sample-population differences in dropout rates. In the case of dropout, of course, sample rates are lower than population rates. Since sample-population differences in graduation and dropout offset each other, there is little difference between sample and population in rates of retention. For a more detailed discussion see appendix A.

34. Jewish and Catholic students in the 1971 cohort seem an exception: table 6.10 shows that many had satisfactory averages. However, these grade point averages may be inflated by about a quarter of a letter grade (.28) as a result of sampling bias. Thus, their likelihood of transferring out of CUNY is less than it appears to be.

35. The apparent superiority of regular black and Hispanic students in the 1971 cohort should be discounted since these rates are inflated by about 7 percent through sampling bias. Thus, the graduation rates for these groups are probably slightly below the national rates.

36. The percentage of minority students still enrolled after three years (shown by the 1972 cohort) seems quite high, suggesting that the ultimate graduation rates for these students would have exceeded national rates. However, our data indicate that the great majority of students who graduate from community college do so within three years. Subsequent years add only slightly to the percentage of graduates (see table 6.7). Thus, allowing for the possibility that the three-year graduation rates shown for the 1972 cohort are slightly inflated in table 6.11, it seems unlikely that the four- or five-year rates for minority students in this cohort would have exceeded national rates.

37. This definition of a low-income family approximates but does not correspond exactly to various definitions of low income used by public agencies. For example, the Department of Labor defined the annual costs for a "lower budget" in a family of four in New York in spring 1970 as $7,183. See Bureau of Labor Statistics, U.S. Department of Labor, *Handbook of Labor Statistics, 1971* (Washington: U.S. Government Printing Office, 1971), table 126, p. 390. A lower budget is one in which the family would perform most services by itself, rather than purchase them, and in which use is made of free recreational facilities rather than private facilities. In New York City it was highly unlikely in the early 1970s that a family with an income of less than $7,500 could send a son or daughter with a weak high school record to any college other than an open-admissions institution with free tuition (i.e., CUNY or no college at all).

38. In comparing the effects of different background variables in this chapter, we chose intervals approximately equal to the standard deviations of the variables; thereby, in effect, we have standardized our comparisons.

39. To assess this assumption, we regressed persistence upon the high school background and social origins variables, defining as persisters those who were still

enrolled or had graduated *and* those who left CUNY with grade point averages of 2.50 or higher. The results showed an increase in the explained variance. The R^2's increased from about .05 to .12. This increase is not large enough to change our conclusion that educational background and social origin are only weakly associated with persistence and graduation.

40. David E. Lavin, *The Prediction of Academic Performance* (New York: Wiley, 1967).

7.　Academic Progress, Dropout, and Graduation II: How It Happened

WHAT ACCOUNTS FOR academic success? The ethnic variations in academic performance among regular and open-admissions students and the generally lower success of minority students raise serious concerns in any assessment of open admissions. The program was intended for minority students, but it also attracted many white ethnic students, who seemingly were somewhat more successful in taking advantage of the opportunities the policy offered. The record of white ethnic students at CUNY can be explained only in part by their high school backgrounds; hence it deserves further examination.

The relationship of social class and ethnicity to educational attainment has been the subject of controversy for years.[1] It is clear that students from more affluent white families do better and go further in school, but it is not clear why. One explanation, part of folklore and a long tradition in social science, links educational achievement to the characteristics of students. In this view, students bring to school from their families and larger social milieus many characteristics, frequently rooted in class and ethnic subcultures, that determine how well they are able to do in school, how committed they are to educational goals, and what benefits they draw out of the school experience. Thus, their values and aspirations affect important choices they must make, as well as their responses to academic pressure. One of the older explanations for educational achievement points to such cultural residues as ability to defer gratification as critical to students' ability to invest themselves in education.[2] In addition, their life-cycle status and the economic resources of their families determine whether they must work while attending school and thus how fully they can concentrate their efforts on schoolwork. Their images of themselves as students, the product of past interactions with family members, teachers, and peers, affect their confidence in their ability to survive and do well in school.

Characteristics such as these may explain some of the ethnic variation in success we found among CUNY's students, but so may other characteristics that are intrinsically less related to education. Recently many have pointed out that academic success is not the result of student characteristics alone but the way in which these interact with the expectations of teachers and the organization of schools. Schools promote success on the part of students with some characteristics and failure on the part of students with others. Some of the most important scholarship of the 1970s argued that the characteristics schools favor are frequently devices, like class- and ethnic-related modes of language use, that foster success on the part of students with advantaged class and ethnic origins and hence preserve class and ethnic privilege in each new generation.[3] In an extreme form of this argument, schools are seen as imposing success and failure on students in accordance with their social origins through such means as stereotypes held by teachers.

We cannot examine these last arguments as directly as we would like. In essence, the arguments that schools create success require one to look within them to observe the acts by teachers and administrators that favor students from privileged groups.[4] This we cannot do. What we can do is to assess the extent to which success and failure are explained by the characteristics of students, like their skills or their reasons for attending college, that seem intrinsically related to educational achievement. Then we can infer the extent to which measured ethnic variations in success were the result of ethnic privilege from the extent to which they are not explained by these student characteristics.

To relate the characteristics of students to academic success, we must chart more exactly students' careers. Such a career can be seen as a series of contingencies; events at one moment in time, such as grades received in a given semester, not only result from preceding events, such as preparation for college during high school, but also exert an independent influence on subsequent events. The student who earns high grades in any semester not only gains confidence but also may affect faculty perceptions of himself or herself; both consequences are likely to facilitate high grades thereafter.

In this chapter, we will analyze the temporal process of academic attainment by decomposing a student's career into a sequence of one-year stages. Decomposing a student's career in this way will allow us both to map its course of development and also to see how influences on academic performance may change from one stage to another.[5] In general, we will view performance in any year as dependent on prior performance as well as on high school background and characteristics of the student's social and cultural situation. Performance in any year will be seen as having certain consequences—altering the probability that the student will return for the next year and affecting that year's performance if he or she does return. By tracking student performance from year to year in this way, we will be able to see a student's career unfold in a fashion that will allow us to account to a substantial degree for ultimate success or failure as indicated by dropout or graduation.

One aspect of this strategy deserves some attention before we proceed. Analyzing student achievement on a yearly basis implies that our population will change from year to year. Obviously we can include in the analysis for any year only students who were present for at least some part of it. Consequently, as the number of students who have permanently dropped out increases with each year, the number of students who could be included in our analyses declines.[6] Of course, not only do students drop out; they also return. Hence, our data include students present in one year who were not present in some preceding years. It is obvious from this fact that the students present in any one year aside from the first may not all be at the same stage according to the designations "sophomore, junior, senior". It probably makes sense nonetheless to group students, as we do in this chapter, by the length of time elapsed since entry rather than by formal standing with respect to graduation. Students inevitably must evaluate their own progress by calendar time. The student who has sophomore standing after five years is not equivalent to the student who has sophomore standing after one. Both schools and students recognize this.

The Senior Colleges

We shall look first at student careers in the senior colleges, analyzing student performance in the first, second, third, and fourth years after entry to CUNY. Here, as later in the chapter, we shall focus on three major academic variables for each year. Two measure performance: the student's grade point average for courses taken during the fall and spring semesters and the average number of credits earned in each of these semesters.[7] With respect to the latter, the shift from accumulated credits, analyzed in the last chapter, to the rate at which credits were earned will reveal important differences between groups of students in the speed of their progress. The third major variable is whether or not the student returned for the fall semester of the next year. For students present in the fourth year in the senior colleges and in the second year in the community colleges, we add one more variable: whether or not they graduated.

Year-by-Year Achievement in Terms of High School Background and Ethnicity

In our preliminary analyses we track year-by-year performance in terms of high school background and ethnicity. These preliminary analyses give a baseline indication of how the effects of these student characteristics varied over the course of a career at CUNY. As we saw in the preceding chapter, high school background, particularly grades, and ethnicity were related (and sometimes strongly so) to academic outcomes. What we seek to determine is whether those relations diminished or remained constant over time. Were the latter the case, we could conclude that an open-admissions program could not make up for the inequalities students brought with them. But were those relations to diminish over time, we might be able to conclude that academically and ethnically disadvantaged students who survived the competition of the early years drew near to those who were more advantaged at entry. Such a result would be important to the evaluation of open admissions as an egalitarian policy.

Table 7.1 presents this preliminary analysis for year-by-year grade point average in the 1970 cohort. Each year's grade point average has been regressed on ethnicity and the three components of high school background. We will limit our presentation of statistics to one cohort throughout this chapter because the number of statistical analyses is overwhelming. Needless to say, we have conducted parallel analyses for the 1971 and 1972 cohorts, and will indicate in the text where these analyses differ from that for the 1970 cohort.

As we found for cumulative grades, high school average (and hence admissions status) was by far the most important determinant of grades earned during each year in the senior colleges. During the first three years for the 1970 cohort, a difference of ten points in high school average corresponded to a difference of over half a letter in grades among otherwise equivalent students; differences of roughly the same magnitude are found in the 1971 and 1972 cohorts. Other aspects of high school background were much less important. Preparation for college, a result of track placement in high school, modestly but inconsistently affected senior-college grades. Visible in some years but not in all, this effect was never strong. Rank in high school class did not have an important relation to grades.

Ethnicity was a second major influence on grades, but the pattern of ethnic differences varied somewhat between the early and the late years for a cohort. That is to say, minority students were not consistently behind whites. Although Jewish students earned the highest grades in all years for the 1970 and 1971 cohorts,[8] Catholic students generally earned low grades in the early years. But the grades of these two groups grew more similar, as did the grades of blacks and Hispanics. In the third and fourth years, the grades of black and Hispanic students were below those of Catholic and Jewish students. In the end, then, a pattern of minority-white differences prevailed.

Although ethnic differences were clearly important, they had generally modest effects by comparison with those of high school average. In most years, the range of ethnic difference among students with similar high

TABLE 7.1. Year-by-Year Grade Point Average in the Senior Colleges as a Function of High School Background and Ethnicity, 1970 Cohort

	First Year		Second Year		Third Year		Fourth Year	
	b	beta	b	beta	b	beta	b	beta
High school average	.056	.426	.060	.433	.058	.377	.046	.296
	$p<.001$		$p<.001$		$p<.001$		$p<.001$	
Rank in high school class	.001	.032	-.001	-.013	-.001	-.026	.001	.030
	$p<.05$		N.S.		N.S.		N.S.	
College preparatory courses	.028	.064	.017	.037	.014	.027	.027	.049
	$p<.001$		$p<.01$		N.S.		$p<.01$	
Ethnicity[a]		.129		.137		.100		.094
Jewish	.039		.086		.087		.121	
Catholic	-.197		-.133		-.063		.033	
Black	-.111		-.152		-.204		-.115	
Hispanic	-.205		-.287		-.204		-.144	
	$p<.001$		$p<.001$		$p<.001$		$p<.001$	
Constant	-2.629		-2.692		-2.332		-1.543	
R^2		.276		.246		.171		.143

[a]The omitted category contains "other whites"; the regression equation contained another category, "other non-whites," which has not been reported. The construction and presentation of the ethnicity variable is the same in this chapter as in others.

school backgrounds, the grade difference between similar students in the highest and lowest earning ethnic groups, was roughly on the order of the difference to be expected between students whose high school averages were five points apart. In some years, like the freshman year for the 1970 cohort, the range of ethnic difference was smaller than this, and only rarely was it much larger. The largest range occurred in the second year of the 1971 cohort: comparable Jewish and Hispanic students differed by half a letter grade, a difference to be expected between students with high school averages ten points apart. But, generally speaking, the differences in high school average corresponding to ethnic differences in grades were not very large. Ethnic differences were not great by this measure.

Did high school background and ethnicity wane in significance over the course of student careers? An affirmative answer is suggested by the decline in the overall R^2's from year to year, with the result that high school background and ethnicity explain only half as much of fourth-year grades as they do of first-year grades. This fading of the imprint of high school and ethnicity was more apparent than real, however. Not only did the number of students in the senior colleges decline from year to year, but those who left were disproportionately the weakest and strongest students, those at the extremes of the distribution of high school grades. As a result, high school background and ethnicity explain less of individual grade differences at the end than at the beginning in part because the group of students who persisted was more homogeneous than the group that entered.

To put matters another way, the difference in college grades corresponding to a given difference in high school average changed little over the first three years for each cohort.[9] Only in the fourth year did high school grades produce smaller differences in CUNY grades. Only for the fourth year, then, could we conclude that grade differences between regular and open-admissions students shrank. But ethnic differences did not decrease from year to year: in both the 1970 and 1971 cohorts, their range was about as large in the fourth year as in the first.

In addition to grades, the rate at which students earn credits is a very important measure of academic performance: it is *the* measure of their progress toward a degree. For the 1970 cohort, table 7.2 presents year by year the average number of credits earned in each semester as a function of high school background and ethnicity. There are some important similarities between the patterns in table 7.2 and those in table 7.1. As before, high school average and ethnicity consistently affected the rate of credit accumulation, but they were joined by the number of college preparatory courses taken in high school, reflecting curriculum track. The effect of track was most pronounced in the first year, when it exceeded that of ethnicity in the 1970 and 1972 cohorts. But its effect declined sharply in the second, third, and fourth years, during which high school average and ethnicity appear to have been the two most important influences on credits.

TABLE 7.2. Year-by-Year Credits per Semester in the Senior Colleges as a Function of High School Background and Ethnicity, 1970 Cohort

	First Year		Second Year		Third Year		Fourth Year	
	b	beta	b	beta	b	beta	b	beta
High school average	.205	.318	.189	.272	.190	.246	.092	.122
	p<.001		p<.001		p<.001		p<.001	
Rank in high school class	-.001	-.005	-.001	-.002	-.008	-.031	.012	.051
	N.S.		N.S.		N.S.		p<.01	
College preparatory courses	.322	.151	.216	.092	.109	.041	.120	.046
	p<.001		p<.001		p<.01		p<.01	
Ethnicity		.138		.127		.107		.097
Jewish	.558		.652		.899		.702	
Catholic	-.440		-.008		.392		.447	
Black	-.904		-.573		-.479		-.711	
Hispanic	-1.157		-1.391		-.857		-.660	
	p<.001		p<.001		p<.001		p<.001	
Constant	-9.533		-6.699		-5.180		1.367	
R^2		.229		.149		.089		.054

165

The relation of ethnicity to the rate of credit accumulation deserves attention. That rate reveals a consistency of ethnic differences that was not visible in credit totals. In all years of all cohorts, white students earned credits at faster rates than did minority students. These ethnic differences were perhaps not so visible in accumulated credits because, at least in the 1970 cohort, slower students had some additional time to catch up with faster ones and also because some of the faster white students appear to have transferred out of CUNY with limited credit totals.

Ethnicity appears important in another way as well. Even though high school average was still the most important determinant of the rate of credit accumulation, ethnic differences in credits were large in relation to differences associated with high school average. Generally, the largest credit differences occurred between Jewish and Hispanic students. In the first year of the 1970 cohort, for example, Hispanic students accumulated 1.7 fewer credits per semester than did comparable Jewish students; in other words, Hispanic students fell behind by more than a course during the freshman year. This credit difference was of the same order of magnitude as that between students who differed by more than eight points in high school average. In the second year, the credit difference between Jewish and Hispanic students was even larger.[10] In the second year of the 1971 cohort, in fact, the difference between them was nearly a course a semester, approximately equivalent to the difference between students whose high school averages were twenty points apart. Clearly, this was a substantial difference, as were many of the differences between black and white ethnic students.

As in the case of grades, the predictability of credits from high school background and ethnicity declined from year to year. More so than in the case of grades, however, this decline was a result of a waning of the influence of high school background. The impact of high school track on credits faded throughout the four years, and the effect of high school average on credits declined sharply in the fourth year.[11] The fourth year was somewhat of an anomaly because some students, needing less than a full year's work to graduate, slowed down their accumulation of credits. Even so, the significant effect of high school average on credit accumulation in the fourth year indicates that open-admissions students did not achieve credit equality during that year, nor, it might be added, did minority students. In fact, ethnic differences were usually as large in the later years as they had been in the earlier ones.

Finally, we present in table 7.3 analyses of persistence from year to year as a function of high school background and ethnicity. For those present during some part of any year, persistence is defined as return to a senior college for the fall semester of the next year. Since many students graduated by the end of the fourth year, persistence on the part of students present during the fourth year is defined as graduation or return for the fifth year. In addition, for these students present during the fourth year, the table shows an

TABLE 7.3. Persistence[a] in and Graduation from the Senior Colleges as a Function of High School Background and Ethnicity, 1970 Cohort

	First Year		Second Year		Third Year		Fourth Year[b]		Graduation[c]	
	b	beta	b	beta	b	beta	b	beta	b	beta
High school average	.004	.078	.004	.071	.002	.029	.002	.028	.011	.133
	$p<.001$		$p<.001$		N.S.		N.S.		$p<.001$	
Rank in high school class	.001	.058	.001	.057	.001	.050	.001	.065	.001	.030
	$p<.001$		$p<.01$		$p<.01$		$p<.01$		N.S.	
College preparatory courses	.013	.071	.006	.030	.011	.055	.003	.016	.016	.058
	$p<.001$		$p<.05$		$p<.001$		N.S.		$p<.001$	
Ethnicity		.090		.072		.065		.047		.087
Jewish	.040		.015		.021		.013		.063	
Catholic	-.033		-.023		-.003		.012		.059	
Black	.023		-.034		-.052		-.053		-.028	
Hispanic	.002		-.078		-.053		-.025		-.093	
	$p<.001$		$p<.001$		$p<.001$		N.S.		$p<.001$	
Constant	.236		.370		.475		.577		-.586	
R^2	.041		.028		.019		.013		.051	

[a]For those present in a given year, persistence is defined as return to a senior college for the fall semester of the next year.
[b]The persistence of fourth-year students was defined as graduation or return for the fall semester of the fifth year.
[c]This column reports graduation by the end of the fifth year for students present during the fourth.

analysis of graduation by the end of the fifth year, also the end of our academic records.

As was true of ultimate dropout and persistence, analyzed in the last chapter, neither high school background nor ethnicity explains very much of persistence from year to year, even for students present during the early years, when these variables explain a considerable part of grades and credits. The R^2 for each equation in each cohort is small, and the effects of the variables usually are weak and inconsistent—even high school average was not consistently related to return. Of course, it should be noted that in each equation at least one high school variable is related to return, and in each case students with stronger high school records were more likely to return. This paucity of important effects requires care in its interpretation, as described in the last chapter. In a literal reading of the equations, there was hardly any difference in dropout between open-admissions and regular students, but this was so partly because some of the students with strong high school records who appear to have dropped out actually transferred out of the CUNY system. Such transferring is indicated by the high grade point averages of some who failed to return, as described in chapter 6, and the relation of this outcome to high school background will be made clearer in the next section.

Ethnicity generally did have significant effects on persistence, but they were usually small and the ordering of groups was inconsistent. In the first year of the 1970 cohort, the largest ethnic difference in dropout rates lay between Jewish and Catholic students, with Catholics 7 percent less likely to return for the fall semester of the second year than were comparable Jewish students. In the first year of the 1971 cohort, by contrast, the largest difference lay between black and Hispanic students, with the latter nearly 10 percent less likely to return than the former. The largest ethnic differences occurred in the 1971 cohort. Hispanic students, with low grades and few credits, were much less likely than others to return—15 percent less likely to return for the third year, to take the worst instance.

The contrast between the persistence of students present in the fourth year and their graduation by the end of the fifth year provides significant insight into the progress of senior-college students. Dropout among fourth-year students was almost unrelated to high school background and ethnicity. It appears that once students lasted that long, systematic advantages and disadvantages almost vanished in their effects on subsequent persistence and, we suspect, ultimate graduation. Transferring as the explanation for the weak effect of high school average on persistence does not apply well here, for students with academic records strong enough to transfer were less likely to do so if they persisted into the fourth year, since graduation was imminent for many of them.

But, among those present during the fourth year, graduation by the end of the fifth year did depend more strongly on high school background and ethnicity. Although the overall R^2 of the equation is not large, some of the effects are noteworthy. Thus, the probability of graduation increased by 1 percent for each additional point in high school average and by well over 1 percent for each additional college preparatory course taken in high school. There were also substantial differences among students from different ethnic groups, with Jewish and Catholic students equally more likely to graduate than were comparable minority students. White ethnic students were, in fact, 15 percent more likely to do so than were comparable Hispanic students. These same basic patterns are visible in graduation at the end of the fourth year on the part of students in the 1971 cohort. Although high school track did not have a significant impact on graduation chances among fourth-year students in that cohort, the effect of high school average was greater: the probability of graduation increased by nearly 2 percent for each additional point in high school average. Ethnic differences were also large: Jewish and Catholic students were 17 percent more likely than Hispanic students to graduate. Black students, however, were only 5 percent behind white ethnics.

So far, we have noted that high school average and ethnicity left enduring marks on the academic performance of students who entered CUNY's senior colleges; to a lesser extent, track placement in high school did so also. These marks were most pronounced during the early years, when students were establishing themselves in college. Although the effects diminished in later years, especially the fourth, our analyses exaggerate their weakening because each year's winnowing of students left behind a more homogeneous group. Of course, the generally weaker performance of open-admissions and minority students in the early years affected their whole careers, as it was necessarily reflected in their cumulative grade point averages and credits and slowed their progress toward graduation. Even so, with the exception of Hispanic students in the 1971 cohort, these students were not dramatically less likely to persist at CUNY.

A Longitudinal Model of a Senior-College Student's Career

In order to understand better student careers in CUNY's senior colleges, we need to do more than track year-by-year performance in terms of high school background and ethnicity. A college career undoubtedly develops in a cumulative fashion. The influence of a student's high school record on performance in later years in college is modified by performance during the early years. Whatever his or her high school record, a student who does well in any one year becomes more likely to do well in subsequent years. Not only does academic success in any one year imply that the student has mastered necessary skills, but success also bolsters the student's confidence and self-image. Probably a successful record in any year affects faculty perceptions in a way that facilitates subsequent success. In an obvious way, the policy of open admissions was founded on these assumptions and on the hope that, aided by intensive counseling and remediation, enough students with unpromising high school records would find the wherewithal for success during the early years to justify the policy.

We have constructed a model of academic performance in the senior colleges which conforms to this cumulative notion of student careers. In this model, the grades and credits earned by a student present in any one year are viewed as a function not only of high school background and ethnicity but also of grades and credits earned in prior years. So, too, the probability of return for the fall of the next year is assumed to be a function of academic performance at CUNY, including that of the current year, as well as of high school background and ethnicity. We have also added a new independent variable to the model, intended to represent the effects of stopping out; it is defined as the number of semesters the student was out of school prior to appearing in the year under analysis.

This model is presented for the 1970 cohort in the quite complicated table 7.4. It should be noted that since there is no prior record of performance at CUNY for first-year students, their grades and credits per semester can be regressed only on high school background and ethnicity. These are the same regressions as those presented in parts of tables 7.1 and 7.2, but they are reported here also in order to aid the reader in seeing the development of student careers. We have constructed the model for the 1971 and 1972 cohorts as well, and our discussion will indicate where student careers diverged in these two cohorts from those in the 1970 cohort. In general, the models are remarkably similar across the three cohorts.

Succinctly, the model establishes that college careers at CUNY were distinctive from high school careers, despite the continuing impact of high school on college performance. Student careers in the senior colleges developed rapidly, so that after two years academic performance was fairly predictable from events that had happened since entry and far more predictable from them than from high school background. Except for the anomaly of fourth-year credits, to be explained shortly, typically a third or more of the individual variation in grades and credits during the last two years is explained by each equation, with nearly all of the explanation resting on past performance at CUNY. Thus, although grade and credit performance in any year was not completely determined by past performance, there was a fair amount of consistency from year to year. High school background was quite important to career beginnings, but many students began considerably better or worse than one would have expected from their high school records and their later performance frequently represented a continuation of their college career beginnings. Consequently, high school background adds little beyond prior CUNY record to our ability to predict performance during the late part of student careers.

The chief exception to this general pattern is persistence, which was conditional in each year on high school background. This was as it should have been since a student's ability to transfer to another college or university was dependent on his or her total record, including that of high school. Although we have not made this clear yet, the model allows us to distinguish the pattern of transferring from that of dropping out, with the result that far more of failure to return is explained here than in previous tables.

Turning to its details, the model highlights important aspects of the academic processes at CUNY—for example, in the earning of grades and credits. Grades in each year after the first were most predictable from prior grades but prior credits also contributed. The predictablity of current grades from past credits probably is explained by the past withdrawal of some students from courses they were in danger of failing, thereby preserving their grades at the cost of reducing their credits. Consequently, the combination of grades and credits was a much better index of the quality of academic performance than were grades alone. By contrast, credits in each year after the first were very dependent on prior credits; prior grades played only a limited role, one that declined, moreover, through the years. Credit accumulation appears to have proceeded at a characteristic rate for each student from early on.

Aside from past grades and credits, the two major features of a student's record at CUNY, other academic variables had only a limited effect on grades and credits from the second year on. In some years, students who had stopped out earned higher grades and fewer credits than one would have expected from their records. A reduction in credits could have been anticipated as a consequence of the shock of renewed academic pressure, but the reason for their higher grades is not so clear. Perhaps they were more cautious after returning to school and concentrated their efforts on fewer or easier courses, often improving their grades but limiting their credits.

From the second year on, high school background contributes only modestly to the predictability of grades and credits. In any year after the first, then, students with similar records at CUNY were likely to achieve similar grades and credits regardless of disparities in their high school backgrounds. One exception is the relation of high school average to second-year grades. Evidently, the freshman year was not an adequate test of how well students could do in college: among students with equal freshman records there were sizable second-year grade differences corresponding to differences in their high school averages. Except for the 1971 cohort, where these second-year differences were smaller, a ten-point difference in high school average among students with equal freshman records corresponded to a difference of a quarter of a letter in second-year grades. But the relation

TABLE 7.4. A Longitudinal Model of a Senior-College Student's Career, 1970 Cohort

	Grade Point Average		Credits Per Semester		Return for Fall	
	b	beta	b	beta	b	beta
	First Year					
High school average	.056	.426	.205	.318	-.006	-.106
	p<.001		p<.001		p<.001	
Rank in high school class	.001	.032	-.001	-.005	.001	.056
	p<.05		N.S.		p<.001	
College preparatory courses	.028	.064	.322	.151	-.000	-.002
	p<.001		p<.001		N.S.	
Grade point average in past years	—	—	—	—	—	—
Credits per semester in past years	—	—	—	—	—	—
Grade point average in current year	—	—	—	—	.045	.107
					p<.001	
Credits per semester in current year	—	—	—	—	.037	.436
					p<.001	
Semesters out of school	—	—	—	—	—	—
Ethnicity		.129		.138		.061
Jewish	.039		.558		.017	
Catholic	-.197		-.440		-.008	
Black	-.111		-.904		.062	
Hispanic	-.205		-1.157		.054	
	p<.001		p<.001		p<.001	
Constant	-2.629		-9.533		.709	
R^2	.276		.229		.241	

Second Year

	b	β	p	b	β	p	b	β	p
High school average	.026	.189	p<.001	.032	.047	p<.001	-.007	-.121	p<.001
Rank in high school class	-.000	-.003	N.S.	.003	.015	N.S.	.001	.062	p<.001
College preparatory courses	.000	.001	N.S.	.077	.033	p<.01	-.003	-.014	N.S.
Grade point average in past years	.438	.351	p<.001	.808	.130	p<.001	.021	.040	p<.01
Credits per semester in past years	.052	.199	p<.001	.581	.444	p<.001	.006	.055	p<.001
Grade point average in current year	—	—		—	—		.058	.142	p<.001
Credits per semester in current year	—	—		—	—		.027	.334	p<.001
Semesters out of school	.158	.039	p<.001	-.323	-.016	N.S.	.012	.007	N.S.
Ethnicity	.085			.066			.012		
Jewish	.066			.403			-.010		
Catholic	-.077			.079			-.013		
Black	-.040			.164			-.001		
Hispanic	-.167		p<.001	-.732		p<.001	-.014		N.S.
Constant	-1.451			-1.384			.788		
R^2	.406			.359			.223		

TABLE 7.4. Continued

Third Year

	Grade Point Average		Credits Per Semester		Return for Fall	
	b	beta	b	beta	b	beta
High school average	.016	.103	.011	.014	−.007	−.113
	p<.001		N.S.		p<.001	
Rank in high school class	−.000	−.003	−.002	−.007	.001	.061
	N.S.		N.S.		p<.001	
College preparatory courses	−.008	−.015	−.060	−.023	.007	.035
	N.S.		N.S.		p<.05	
Grade point average in past years	.540	.328	.778	.095	−.043	−.069
	p<.001		p<.001		p<.001	
Credits per semester in past years	.089	.267	.840	.503	.002	.014
	p<.001		p<.001		N.S.	
Grade point average in current year	—	—	—	—	.093	.246
					p<.001	
Credits per semester in current year	—	—	—	—	.025	.331
					p<.001	
Semesters out of school	.079	.035	−.328	−.029	−.045	−.053
	p<.01		p<.01		p<.001	
Ethnicity		.042		.051		.018
Jewish	.057		.605		−.001	
Catholic	−.010		.387		−.013	
Black	−.058		.372		−.023	
Hispanic	−.050		−.007		−.016	
	p<.05		p<.001		N.S.	
Constant	−1.165		−1.056		.768	
R^2	.349		.335		.269	

174

			Fourth Year							Graduation		
	b	beta		b	beta		b	beta		b	beta	
High school average	.000	.003	N.S.	−.039	−.052	p<.05	−.003	−.056	p<.05	−.005	−.067	p<.001
Rank in high school class	.002	.048	p<.01	.014	.060	p<.001	.001	.037	p<.05	.000	.019	N.S.
College preparatory courses	.008	.015	N.S.	.007	.003	N.S.	−.002	−.010	N.S.	.003	.012	N.S.
Grade point average in past years	.675	.401	p<.001	.362	.045	p<.01	−.038	−.059	p<.01	.086	.099	p<.001
Credits per semester in past years	.083	.244	p<.001	.771	.468	p<.001	.006	.050	p<.01	.051	.290	p<.001
Grade point average in current year	—	—		—	—		.093	.246	p<.001	.025	.049	p<.001
Credits per semester in current year	—	—		—	—		.018	.233	p<.001	.034	.321	p<.001
Semesters out of school	−.000	−.000	N.S.	−.629	−.099	p<.001	−.044	−.088	p<.001	−.041	−.060	p<.001
Ethnicity	.040			.025			.027			.032		
Jewish	.066			.275			−.016			.006		
Catholic	.057			.208			−.005			.032		
Black	.028			−.095			−.025			.048		
Hispanic	.018		p<.05	.079		N.S.	.006		N.S.	−.009		N.S.
Constant	−.431			3.083			.667			−.387		
R^2	.372			.295			.210			.404		

[a]Students who graduated at the end of the fourth year are counted as returning.

of high school average to grade differences among students with similar CUNY records declined in the third year and disappeared in the fourth.

After the first year, high school background had only a very minor relation to credits earned by students with similar CUNY records, although fourth-year credits in the 1970 cohort (but not in the 1971) represented a puzzling exception. High school average and rank were both related to credit differences among students with similar records, but the relation of average was negative while that of rank was positive. This seemingly contorted pattern suggests that some students with very high past credit rates slowed down their credit accumulation in the fourth year because they needed less than a full year's course load to graduate. This interpretation is made plausible by the kind of student who appears to have slowed down. According to the equation, students who decelerated their credit acquisition had relatively good high school grades but relatively low high school rank—that is, they were strong students from competitive high schools. As a result of this deceleration, fourth-year credits were not as characteristic of student past performance as were credits earned in the second or third years, with the consequence that the R^2 of the fourth-year equation was lower.

Return for the fall semester of a new year is the one aspect of student careers that shows a continuing direct influence of high school background, but persistence was still largely a function of events at CUNY. The most important determinant of return for a new year was performance during the current year: as one would expect, students who did well were more likely to return. Interestingly, freshman credits were far more important than freshman grades in determining return for the second year. Evidently, freshman students were encouraged more by signs of tangible progress toward a degree than by judgments about the quality of their work.[12] Grades did grow in importance from year to year, however, so that toward the end of student careers return for a new year was as determined by the preceding year's grades as by its credits.

The continuing influence of high school background on persistence from year to year was related to the transfer of some students outside the CUNY system and helps explain the seemingly weak effects of high school background on dropout and graduation when CUNY performance is not controlled. That such transferring occurred was indicated in chapter 6 by the high grade point averages of some students who were shown as not persisting. The ability of a student to transfer is clearly a function of his or her total academic record, including that from high school. Consequently, with academic performance at CUNY controlled, students with stronger high school records were somewhat less likely to return. This is indicated in the 1970 and 1971 cohorts by the modestly negative effects of high school average and the slightly positive effects of rank in high school class on return. As in the analysis of fourth-year credits, this configuration of variables suggests that students with good high school averages who did not rank high in their graduating class because they came from strong high schools were somewhat less likely to return. Although a similar configuration does not appear in the 1972 cohort, return for each year in that cohort was affected negatively by high school average and, in one year, by number of college preparatory courses in high school. This interpretation of the student's past record in relation to return is strengthened by the occasionally negative effects of grades in years prior to the current one on the return of students present during the current year. These negative effects of past grade performance are consistent with an interpretation that among students with comparable satisfactory records during the current year, those with weaker past records were more likely to return for the next year. Presumably, many of those with stronger records must have been transferring, not dropping out.

Finally, graduation by the end of the fifth year in the 1970 cohort (and by the end of the fourth year in the 1971 cohort) was chiefly a function of the rate at which students earned credits during semesters when they were attending school. Stopping out of school for a semester or two does not appear to have strongly affected graduation chances.

This model of student careers sheds more light on the significance of ethnicity in the senior colleges. It makes clear that the persisting grade and credit differences among students from diverse ethnic backgrounds were part of career patterns established during the first two years. Thus, there were only modest ethnic differences in the third year and none in the fourth year among students with similar records at CUNY—in contrast to the substantial ethnic differences in these years when only high school background is controlled. In fact, the 1970 cohort is the only one to show ethnic differences in the later years. The largest ethnic difference in third-year grades among students with similar CUNY records in that cohort was quite trivial, with Jewish students ahead of comparable black students by little more than a tenth of a letter grade. The ethnic difference in third-year credits was a bit more substantial, but even the largest difference, between Jewish and Hispanic students, was less than a credit per semester.

There were also some ethnic differences in return for a new year among students with similar records at CUNY. These generally were most pronounced among freshman students, but even in this instance they were modest. In all cohorts, minority freshmen were slightly more likely than white ethnic freshmen with comparable records to return for the second year. Undoubtedly, the white students, who came from more affluent families (see chapter 5), were more likely to transfer to other colleges. This transferring by some white students with strong academic records raises a question: was it a form of white flight, a response to open admissions? We do not believe that it generally was. We infer this from evidence we do not present here: attitudes toward the open-admissions program were generally unrelated to return, once the academic characteristics of students were taken into account, and students from Brooklyn and Queens colleges, largely white schools, were more likely than others to leave with high grade point averages. We suspect that some students came to the City University to take advantage of its free tuition and to reduce expenses further by living at home for a few years and then went to more prestigious colleges to complete their degrees.

To conclude, this longitudinal analysis of careers in the senior colleges has clarified some of the processes leading to unequal chances for success experienced by different groups of students. Most important, the model demonstrates that student careers were well established by the end of the second year, after which high school background and ethnicity add little to our ability to predict academic performance from student records at CUNY. This model also clarifies the weak relation of high school background and ethnicity to dropout and graduation. Failure to persist and thus failure to graduate must be explained differently for different groups of students. Those with weak high school backgrounds who disappeared from CUNY's rolls without graduating, and thus most minority dropouts, were usually dropping out of higher education. Those with strong high school backgrounds who left CUNY, and thus some white ethnic students who appear to have dropped out, actually were transferring out of the system. As we argued in the last chapter, high school background and ethnicity had a somewhat stronger relation to persistence within higher education than can be demonstrated directly from our data.

Finally, the importance of career beginnings as revealed by the model allows us to narrow our search for the determinants of academic success to the early years, and other analyses we have conducted lead us to a common wisdom: the freshman year is critical. Including many possible determinants of academic performance within our focus, we next examine influences on freshman grades and credits and then compare our results for freshman performance to those for cumulative outcomes.

Other Determinants of Senior-College Achievement

In assessing the extent to which student characteristics can explain individual variations in academic success or failure, we have examined a wide range of possible influences on freshman grades and credits. Several are the kind of culturally engendered orientations to the college experience that have been identified by others as explaining ethnic differences in educational attainment: student degree aspirations and reasons for attending college are examples.[13] Some add further detail to students' educational backgrounds, such as attendance at public versus private high school. Still others characterize their social persons—gender and age—and the families from which they came. Even though the socioeconomic positions of student families seem to have been little related to cumulative outcomes (in chapter 6), we have allowed for the possibility that they influenced freshman performance. Finally, we have examined a different sort of aspect of student careers, not what students bring to college but the academic contexts in which they are placed—namely, the colleges themselves.[14] They are rather broad contexts, each containing considerable internal variation, but they are possibly important ones, especially since they were fairly segregated during open admissions (see chapter 4).

We have added these possible influences to the equations for freshman grades and credits reported in table 7.4. Table 7.5 reports the new, augmented equations, in which only those additional variables that make significant contributions beyond that of high school background have been retained. Generally, the additional variables do not contribute very substantially to the explanation of performance. Thus, they raise the explained variance of freshman grades by 6 percent and that of freshman credits by only 4 percent.

Nonetheless, they illuminate aspects of the academic processes at CUNY. For one, the new equations add detail to the differences among students based on high school preparation and perhaps also on ability. Many of the students who entered in 1970 and 1971 took tests that were intended to measure their preparation for college work and to form a basis for their assignment to remediation courses (a subject discussed further in chapter 9). These tests, one in mathematics and one in reading, are useful gauges of student skills.[15] Even with high school background controlled, the scores of students on the reading test were related to their freshman grades, and their scores on both tests were related to freshman credits. Both of these results imply that the academic skills of students were not fully indexed by their high school records. Nonetheless, these test scores clearly were overshadowed in importance by formal aspects of high school education, average in relation to grades and average and curriculum track in relation to credits.

There were also differences among students corresponding to the type of high school they attended—public, Catholic, or other non-public high school. Students from Catholic schools earned distinctly lower grades than did other students with formally similar records, and students from public schools earned more credits. Probably these grade and credit differences at CUNY testify as much to differences in grading standards among high school systems as to anything else, implying that the low grades received by Catholic students in the early years were partly an artifact of the lack of exact comparability between high school records from Catholic and non-Catholic systems.

In addition to educational background, several personal characteristics of students exerted noteworthy influence on the beginnings of their college careers. One of these was gender. The open-admissions group contained greater proportions of men than did the regular one (see chapter 5), and it appears that men did more poorly than one would predict on the basis of

TABLE 7.5. Determinants of Freshman Performance in the Senior Colleges, 1970 Cohort

	Grade Point Average		Credits Per Semester	
	b	beta	b	beta
High school average	.050	.384	.180	.278
	p<.001		p<.001	
Rank in high school class	.001	.016	−.004	−.019
	N.S.		N.S.	
College preparatory courses	.020	.046	.200	.093
	p<.001		p<.001	
Open-admissions reading test score	.009	.103	.015	.034
	p<.001		p<.01	
Open-admissions math test score	—a	—a	.027	.047
			p<.001	
Academic high school program	—a	—a	.714	.050
			p<.001	
High school type[b]		.091		.046
Catholic	−.170		−.401	
Other nonpublic	.081		−.517	
	p<.001		p<.01	
College attended[c]		.168		.109
Brooklyn	−.181		.143	
City	−.135		−.153	
Hunter	.235		−.529	
Queens	.129		−.597	
Baruch	−.039		−.649	
John Jay	.342		.317	
Lehman	−.106		.917	
	p<.001		p<.001	
Academic self-rating[d]	.075	.045	.367	.045
	p<.001		p<.001	

their comparatively weak high school records. The reasons for this pattern at CUNY are not clear, although some have noted that women outperform men at other colleges.[16] But we suspect that some of the most talented males were sent to more prestigious colleges since their occupational futures were assumed to be more critical than those of their sisters. Whatever the reasons, the differences between men and women were sharp and undiminishing over time. In the 1970 cohort, men earned 1.4 fewer credits than did comparable women during the freshman year and had slightly lower grades. Despite their poorer performance, they were not more likely than women to drop out, but they remained behind women throughout their college careers.

Even though we found in the previous chapter that social class was only occasionally related to academic success at CUNY, a student's need to work while going to school was a considerable hindrance to such success. It should be remembered that the need to work was not strictly a function of

TABLE 7.5.   Continued

	Grade Point Average		Credits Per Semester	
	b	beta	b	beta
Degree aspirations[e]		.037		.054
Baccalaureate	−.051		−.349	
Less than baccalaureate	−.146		−1.123	
	p<.001		p<.001	
Personal growth as reason	.036	.057	.132	.042
for college[f]	p<.001		p<.001	
Male	−.142	−.083	−.679	−.081
	p<.001		p<.001	
Need to work[g]	−.075	−.070	−.479	−.090
	p<.001		p<.001	
Ethnicity		.067		.093
Jewish	.050		.368	
Catholic	−.069		−.163	
Black	−.047		−.821	
Hispanic	−.080		−.822	
	p<.001		p<.001	
R^2		.337		.270

[a]This variable did not contribute significantly to this equation.
[b]The omitted category contains public high schools.
[c]The omitted college is York.
[d]A scale of integer values from 0 to 2; the positive direction indicates a positive evaluation.
[e]The omitted category contains those who aspired to postgraduate degrees.
[f]A scale of integer values from 0 to 6; the positive direction indicates increasing emphasis on personal growth as a reason for attending college.
[g]A scale of integer values from 0 to 2; the positive direction indicates increasing need to work.

family income but rather a result of family income refracted through culturally prescribed expectations about the young person's contribution to the family and, as such, this tendency was as prevalent among Catholics as it was among minority groups. Students who needed to work earned fewer credits and lower grades during the freshman year. And, although our table does not show it, they were also more likely to stop out, further slowing their progress toward a degree.

Career beginnings were also greatly affected by the student's academic self-image, although this does not show up well in the 1970 cohort because of the wording in that year's questionnaire. Students in 1970 were asked to rate their academic preparation in comparison to that of other students in the same college; in 1971 and 1972, they were asked how bright they were in comparison to other students in the same college. The two wordings produced somewhat different responses from students, with white students rating their academic preparation more highly and Jewish students rating themselves as brighter (see chapter 5). Although both kinds of self-image were related to freshman achievement, the student's conception of his or her brightness was related more strongly. In the 1971 cohort, it appears to have been responsible for considerable variation in freshman grades and, somewhat less so, in credits.

Finally with respect to student characteristics, what students wanted from a college education determined in part how well they did. The higher their degree aspirations, the better the grades and the more credits they earned. Likewise, students who emphasized personal growth as an important reason for college earned better grades and more credits than others.

In addition to these characteristics of students and their educational backgrounds, the college contexts in which they were placed affected their chances for success, although not in ways that seem to account for group differences in important outcomes. College differences in freshman grades provide a clearer test of the impact of the college context than do college differences in freshman credits since these may be affected by the credit underreporting noted in chapter 3, which apparently was a function of variations in administrative procedures at some of the colleges. Yet, it is difficult to see larger than local patterns in the college effects on freshman grades. Probably, these patterns reflected college variations in grading standards as much as anything else. Even so, they certainly were real in their consequences for dropout and ultimate graduation. But, the grade (and credit) differences among schools do not correspond in any visible way to either the social compositions of schools or their places in the CUNY system. The so-called elite schools did not award one set of grades in comparison to those awarded by the nonelite schools: students at Queens and Hunter received relatively high grades, while those at Brooklyn and City received relatively low ones. Brooklyn and Queens, at opposite ends of the grade spectrum, were schools with predominantly white student bodies; Hunter and City, also at opposite ends, were schools with substantial numbers of minority students.

By and large, the social and educational characteristics of students that affected their career beginnings left enduring marks, as did the colleges they entered. As a way of summarizing the effects of a range of influences on college performance, table 7.6 presents regression analyses of the cumulative credits and grades earned by students in the 1970 cohort, as well as their enrollment status at the end of their fifth year. As in our analyses of freshman performance, we considered a number of potential influences on cumulative performance but retained only those that contributed significantly beyond high school background.

There is a fairly close correspondence between the determinants of freshman grades and credits and those of cumulative grades and credits. Nearly all of the influences on freshman grades and credits were influences as well on cumulative grades and credits, and generally their importance, indicated by their standardized coefficients, was similar in both freshman and cumulative records. Among the most notable differences between the freshman and cumulative equations is the absence of college from the equation for cumulative credits, suggesting perhaps that reporting variations largely balanced out over the years. Also absent from the equation for cumulative credits are scores on the Open-Admissions Test, suggesting that initial skill differences among students narrowed over college careers.

We have already described at some length the difficulties in interpreting dropout and, to a lesser extent, graduation with data taken from a bounded educational system. In order to gain insight from the equations for persistence and graduation that are presented in table 7.6, one must keep the possibility of transfer out of CUNY in mind. For example, students from private, non-Catholic high schools were less likely to persist and less likely to graduate but many of them probably were transferring. Similarly, students from Queens and Brooklyn colleges were less likely to persist and to graduate, but many of them left with satisfactory grade point averages; they, too, were transferring in all likelihood. It follows that the range of college variation in dropout and graduation was not as large as it appears in the table. What the table does elucidate are the importance of vocational goals to graduation and the detrimental effects of working while attending school. Students who emphasized vocational reasons for attending college and had definite job aspirations at entry were more likely to graduate. Students who needed to work were less likely to persist and to graduate.

What does this discussion of the determinants of first-year and cumulative performance tell us about the differences in success associated with ethnicity? In brief, it tells us something, but by no means everything.

Ethnic differences during the freshman year, especially in grades, appear to be better explained than are cumulative differences by the determinants of academic success we have discussed in this section. When we take these into account along with high school background, the remaining ethnic differences in freshman grades, on the order of a tenth of a letter grade according to table 7.5, seem trivial. Ethnic differences in first-year credits— Jewish students were 2.4 credits ahead of black and Hispanic students at the end of the year—seem more substantial but are still reduced from their magnitude in table 7.2. Cumulative differences in grades and credits appear still more substantial and are scarcely changed from their magnitudes in chapter 6 (see table 6.12). Moreover, when we take many more student characteristics into account, the advantages to white ethnic students generally—not simply Jewish students—appear more clearly defined than they were in the last chapter. Thus, the span of ethnic differences in grades was nearly a third of a letter grade, with black and Hispanic students equally behind Jewish students and Catholic students falling in the middle. The span of ethnic differences in credits amounted to fifteen credits separating Jewish from Hispanic students, with Catholic and black students falling at inter-

TABLE 7.6. Determinants of Cumulative Performance in the Senior Colleges, 1970 Cohort

	Grade Point Average		Cumulative Credits		Graduation		Persistence	
	b	beta	b	beta	b	beta	b	beta
High school average	.050	.392	1.660	.237	.016	.204	.009	.114
	p<.001		p<.001		p<.001		p<.001	
Rank in high school class	.001	.031	.005	.002	.000	.005	.001	.029
	p<.05		N.S.		N.S.		N.S.	
College preparatory courses	.024	.057	1.964	.085	.019	.075	.015	.061
	p<.001		p<.001		p<.001		p<.001	
Open-admissions reading test score	.006	.069	_a	_a	_a	_a	_a	_a
	p<.001							
Academic high school program	_a	_a	5.569	.036	_a	_a	_a	_a
High school type[b]		.070		.048		.048		.035
Catholic	-.118		-3.667		-.020		.004	
Other nonpublic	.097		-7.399		-.100		-.072	
	p<.001		p<.001		p<.001		p<.05	
College attended[c]		.125	_a	_a		.111		.089
Brooklyn	-.015				-.078		-.073	
City	.047				.011		.038	
Hunter	.240				.016		.026	
Queens	.159				-.037		-.007	
Baruch	.017				.033		-.005	
John Jay	.490				.032		-.012	
Lehman	.054				.106		.052	
	p<.001		_a	_a	p<.001		p<.001	
Academic self-rating[d]	.054	.033	_a	_a	_a	_a	_a	_a
	p<.001							

Variable	Eq1 (b)	Eq1 (β)	Eq2 (b)	Eq2 (β)	Eq3 (b)	Eq3 (β)	Eq4 (b)	Eq4 (β)
Degree aspirations[e]								
Baccalaureate	-.074	.052	-7.387	.088	-.062	.066	-.068	.065
Less than baccalaureate	-.190	.118	-15.350	.102	-.117	.095	-.060	.075
	$p<.001$		$p<.001$		$p<.001$		$p<.001$	
Personal growth as reason for college[f]	.023	.038	—a		.023	.052	—a	
	$p<.001$				$p<.001$			
Vocational reason for college[g]	—a		2.354	.059	—a		—a	
			$p<.001$					
Job plans after college	—a		—a		.033	.025	—a	
					$p<.05$			
Male	-.230	-.139	-4.401	-.048	-.099	-.099	-.046	-.073
	$p<.001$		$p<.001$		$p<.001$			
Need to work[h]	-.065	-.062	-6.262	-.109	-.059	-.093	—a	
	$p<.001$		$p<.001$		$p<.001$			
Father's education	.018	.028	—a		—a		—a	
	$p<.01$							
Ethnicity								
Jewish	.091		5.939		.070		.045	
Catholic	-.046		-1.243		.011		-.021	
Black	-.209		-4.425		-.033		-.004	
Hispanic	-.190		-9.072		-.098		-.074	
	$p<.001$		$p<.001$		$p<.001$		$p<.001$	
R^2	.390		.172		.113		.057	

a This variable did not contribute significantly to this equation.
b The omitted category contains public high schools.
c The omitted college is York.
d A scale of integer values from 0 to 2; the positive direction indicates a positive evaluation.
e The omitted category contained students who aspired to postgraduate degrees.
f A scale of integer values from 0 to 6; the positive direction indicates increasing emphasis on personal growth as a reason for attending college.
g A scale of integer values from 0 to 4; the positive direction indicates increasing emphasis on vocational reasons for attending college.
h A scale for integer values from 0 to 2; the positive direction indicates increasing need to work.

185

vals in between. The differences in the table are those found five years after entry to CUNY and thus one year after many had graduated, giving others a chance to catch up. These credit differences, based on an analysis of *all* students in our 1970 sample who entered the senior colleges, do not result simply from the fact that students from some groups were more likely to drop out or to transfer and hence to accumulate fewer credits than those who persisted. An analogous analysis of only persisting students shows white ethnic students still about seven credits ahead of minority students.

Needless to say, these ethnic differences in grades and credits gave rise to ethnic differences in persistence and graduation. In all cohorts, there was a consistent ethnic pattern in dropout: Hispanic students were distinctly less likely to stay in school, but there were not great differences between white ethnic and black students. Of course, some of the white ethnic students who appear to have dropped out had transferred to other colleges, so that their persistence within higher education was undoubtedly greater than that of black students. In both the 1970 and 1971 cohorts, for which graduation data are available, there was also a consistent ethnic pattern in graduation chances: Jewish students were most likely to have graduated, followed in order by Catholics, blacks, and Hispanics. The magnitudes of ethnic differences among students who otherwise were similar in ways that affected graduation were large. As the table shows, for example, Jewish students in the 1970 cohort were over 10 percent more likely than blacks and over 16 percent more likely than Hispanics to have graduated by the end of five years.

In sum, there appears to have been a crude order to the life chances of students from different ethnic groups at CUNY's senior colleges even when they were similar in other ways. Jewish students were most successful, followed by Catholics, followed in turn by blacks, with Hispanic students at the rear. These ethnic differences are hardly explained by the additional influences on academic performance we have analyzed in this section. We have considered a number of possible influences, not all of which made significant contributions to our analysis. These included reading and mathematics skills as measured by standardized tests, educational aspirations, as well as attitudes toward college education, and the colleges in which students were placed. Yet, when all is said and done, important ethnic differences stand out.

The Community Colleges

We turn now to our analysis of student careers in the community colleges. The year-by-year analysis will prove particularly useful in the two-year schools with respect to the rate of progress of students as indexed by their credits per semester. In the previous chapter, we found only small group differences in the cumulative credits earned by community-college students, but this equality is less striking than it seems. In all cohorts, students had a considerable period of time to acquire the credits needed for graduation from what is considered normally a two-year program. Thus, their fairly equal cumulative credit totals may obscure differences in their rates of progress.

As in the senior colleges, our analysis will focus on three major academic variables in each year: grade point average, credits per semester, and return for the fall of the next year. Since a substantial proportion of students in each cohort had advanced out of the community colleges by the third year, through either graduation or transfer to a senior college, we restrict our analysis to the first two years of their careers.

Year-by-Year Achievement in Terms of High School Background and Ethnicity

The year-by-year analyses corroborate the cumulative analyses of the preceding chapter as well as supplement them. Some corroboration emerges from table 7.7, which presents year-by-year grade point averages for students in the 1970 cohort. A comparison of this table to table 7.1, for the senior colleges, demonstrates anew a finding from the previous chapter: the relation of high school background to grades was different in the community colleges and in the senior colleges.

TABLE 7.7. Year-by-Year Grade Point Average in the Community Colleges as a Function of High School Background and Ethnicity, 1970 Cohort

	First Year		Second Year	
	b	beta	b	beta
High school average	.031	.184	.037	.200
	p<.001		p<.001	
Rank in high school class	.006	.138	.006	.119
	p<.001		p<.001	
College preparatory courses	.046	.132	.058	.153
	p<.001		p<.001	
Ethnicity		.079		.080
Jewish	−.030		−.017	
Catholic	−.178		−.026	
Black	−.140		−.228	
Hispanic	−.080		−.127	
	p<.001		p<.01	
Constant	−1.059		−1.553	
R^2		.129		.149

To begin with, the correspondence between high school background and college grades was less strong in the two-year than in the four-year schools. In other words, high school records were a less accurate guide to how well students would do in the community colleges, and this was true even for the freshman year. Moreover, although high school average was the single most important determinant of grades in both types of schools, it was less important in the community colleges; other aspects of high school background, particularly curriculum track, were more important. For example, in the first year in the community colleges for the 1970 cohort, a difference of ten points in high school average corresponded to a difference of approximately a third of a letter grade, while a similar difference in high school average made over half a letter grade difference in the senior colleges. On the other hand, a college preparatory course taken in high school produced nearly twice as large a difference in freshman community-college grades as it did in freshman senior-college grades.

Ethnic differences in grades seem to have been less sharp in the community colleges, both in magnitude and in consistency from cohort to cohort. Except for the 1971 cohort, in the first year such differences were small and white groups were not consistently favored. In the second year, they were somewhat larger, with white ethnic students receiving higher grades than minority students. In the second year of the 1970 cohort, for example, the grades of Jewish and Catholic students were about a fifth of a letter higher than those of black students. In the somewhat exceptional 1971 cohort, grade differences between white and minority students were large in both years, ranging as high as a third of a letter grade among students with similar high school backgrounds.

The credits earned during each semester in the community colleges are shown year by year as a function of high school background and ethnicity in table 7.8. As in the case of grades, the distinctiveness of the two-year schools is visible in the weak relation between high school background and credit performance and in the comparative importance of high school track. However, the career course of credits in the community colleges was different from that of grades. The influence of high school background on grades was stable for the first two years, but its influence on credits became weaker in the second year. This decline was especially noticeable in the case of high school track. Students from nonacademic high school tracks were not as far behind in the number of courses they completed in the second year as they had been in the first, even though their second-year grades did not improve relative to those earned by students from academic tracks.

Minority students earned credits at lower rates than did white ethnic students with similar high school backgrounds, despite their apparent equality with whites in total credits earned in the community colleges. In the first year of the 1970 cohort, for example, the number of credits earned in each semester declined in rather even steps from Jewish to Catholic to black and

TABLE 7.8. Year-by-Year Credits per Semester in the Community Colleges as a Function of High School Background and Ethnicity, 1970 Cohort

	First Year		Second Year	
	b	beta	b	beta
High school average	.126	.133	.119	.116
	p<.001		p<.001	
Rank in high school class	.036	.148	.034	.128
	p<.001		p<.001	
College preparatory courses	.432	.225	.271	.128
	p<.001		p<.001	
Ethnicity		.089		.087
Jewish	.530		.681	
Catholic	−.211		.375	
Black	−.638		.055	
Hispanic	−1.030		.306	
	p<.001		p<.001	
Constant	−6.834		−4.472	
R^2		.155		.088

finally to Hispanic students. The credit gap between Jewish and Hispanic students amounted to over 1.5 credits per semester, or more than a course during the freshman year. A similar ethnic order was present during the freshman year of the 1971 cohort (and, ignoring the religious distinction, in the 1972 cohort, too), but the credit gap was larger—nearly 2.5 credits per semester. In the second year of the 1970 cohort, credit differences among the four major groups were much smaller; the magnitude of ethnicity's relation to credits as indicated by its standardized coefficient is largely caused by the unusually high credit accumulation of Asian-Americans (not shown in the table). But this attenuation of ethnic credit differences in the second year is not found in other cohorts. There were substantial ethnic differences in the second year of the 1971 cohort—nearly two credits a semester between Jewish and black students—and ethnic differences were larger in the second year of the 1972 cohort than they were in the first year. Generally speaking, then, the credit differences between white and minority students did not decline in the second year.

Table 7.9 shows return for the fall semester of a new year[17] as a function of high school background and ethnicity in the 1970 cohort. It also presents an analysis of graduation from a community college by the end of our records (the fifth year) for students who were present during the second.

Although a sizable proportion of community-college students dropped out quickly—about a quarter during the freshman year in each cohort—departure from the community colleges was only minimally related to high school background. Ethnicity also had an only slight relation to persistence;

TABLE 7.9. Persistence[a] in and Graduation from the Community Colleges as a Function of High School Background and Ethnicity, 1970 Cohort

	First Year		Second Year[b]		Graduation[c]	
	b	beta	b	beta	b	beta
High school average	−.003	−.035	.006	.080	.010	.126
	N.S.		p<.01		p<.001	
Rank in high school	.002	.085	.000	.021	.002	.089
class	p<.001		N.S.		p<.001	
College preparatory	.017	.109	.010	˙.059	.015	.089
courses	p<.001		p<.05		p<.001	
Ethnicity		.090		.048		.101
Jewish	.043		.002		.036	
Catholic	−.032		.004		.072	
Black	.050		.015		−.025	
Hispanic	−.007		.042		−.021	
	p<.001		N.S.		p<.001	
Constant	.670		.111		−.688	
R²		.021		.018		.072

[a]For those present in a given year, persistence is defined as return to either a senior or a community college for the fall semester of the next year.
[b]Students who graduated at the end of the second year are defined as persisters for the analysis reported in this column.
[c]This column reports graduation from a community college by the end of the fifth year for students present during the second.

even the lower return by Catholic students for a second year in the 1970 cohort was not duplicated in the 1971 cohort.

Graduation was another story. Even among students who persisted into the second of what is traditionally a two-year program of study, graduation by the end of the fourth or fifth year was no certainty. Graduation chances depended heavily on high school background and varied between white ethnic and minority students even when they had similar high school backgrounds. These ethnic differences were not uniformly large but they are surprising given the length of time students had to complete their degrees. Such differences were largest in the 1971 cohort, where Jewish students were 15 percent more likely than black students and 17 percent more likely than Hispanic students to have graduated by the end of the fourth year.

To sum up, although student careers in the community colleges were less uniformly a function of high school background than they were in the senior colleges, grade and credit differences among students corresponding to their tracks in high school were more salient in the two-year schools. Differentiation by high school track is an appropriate feature since community-college students vary so much in the high school tracks from which they come. Ethnicity also corresponded to important grade and credit differences among students, although these were sometimes less sharp and less consistent than were ethnic differences in the senior colleges. In general, white ethnic students were better off in comparison to minority students.

Other Determinants of Community-College Achievement

As we did for senior-college students, we have developed longitudinal models that unravel the careers of community-college students in each cohort. We will not present such a model, however, because its details add little that is distinctive about the community colleges to our discussion of similar models in the senior colleges. To tick off a few similarities, second-year grades were dependent on freshman grades and credits, indicating that some students preserved their freshman grade point averages by withdrawing from courses in which they were not doing well; second-year credits were most dependent on freshman credits. There was one difference between the two types of models: high school background was not consistently related to dropout from the community colleges among students with similar records at CUNY. Thus, the considerable exodus of students from the community colleges was not as much the result of transferring as was the outflow from the senior colleges. Of course, this was also indicated by the low grade point averages of dropouts, revealed in the last chapter.

The most important feature of the community-college models is that student careers took predictable courses once students had established themselves in the community colleges. Although freshman grades and credits were not very predictable from high school background, second-year grades and credits were quite predictable from those of the first year. So predictable were they, in fact, that ethnic differences during the second year largely mirrored differences that began in the first year. Thus, the lack of uniformity in community-college academic processes appears evident only in the transition from high school to college.

To examine this transition more carefully, we have conducted analyses similar to those for the senior colleges, regressing freshman grades and credits on a wide range of possible determinants. We have added one variable of great theoretical significance for the community colleges to those we used in analyzing freshman performance in the four-year schools: the curriculum in which the student was placed.[18] Table 7.10 reports the resulting equations for the 1970 cohort, retaining only those variables that make significant contributions to the freshman equations of tables 7.7 and 7.8.

Two points stand out. The first is the absence of curriculum from the equations. Placement in the liberal arts curriculum rather than in one of the vocational curricula did not affect freshman grades and credits in the 1970 cohort; however, it had a modest effect on freshman grades in both other cohorts and a slight effect on freshman credits in the 1971 cohort. Appar-

TABLE 7.10. Determinants of Freshman Performance in the Community Colleges, 1970 Cohort

	Grade Point Average		Credits Per Semester	
	b	beta	b	beta
High school average	.020	.119	.067	.071
	p<.001		p<.001	
Rank in high school class	.005	.122	.025	.104
	p<.001		p<.001	
College preparatory courses	.023	.066	.336	.175
	p<.001		p<.001	
Open-admissions reading test score	.009	.099	.034	.064
	p<.001		p<.001	
Open-admissions math test score	.015	.135	.064	.105
	p<.001		p<.001	
College attended[a]		.272		.315
Bronx	.131		−1.162	
Manhattan	.706		2.391	
New York City	.282		2.065	
Queensborough	−.195		−1.948	
	p<.001		p<.001	
Academic self-rating[b]	.124	.055	.780	.062
	p<.001		p<.001	
Degree aspirations[c]		.041		.070
baccalaureate	−.034		−.409	
less than baccalaureate	−.098		−.937	
	p<.05		p<.001	
Personal growth as reason for college[e]	.047	.066	−[d]	−[d]
	p<.001			
Male	−.182	−.092	−1.448	−.131
	p<.001		p<.001	
Nineteen years old	.140	.061	−[d]	−[d]
	p<.001			
Need to work[f]	−.058	−.047	−.467	−.067
	p<.01		p<.001	
Ethnicity		.086		.103
Jewish	.026		.745	
Catholic	−.141		−.012	
Black	−.216		−.939	
Hispanic	−.159		−.925	
	p<.001		p<.001	
R^2		.234		.280

[a]The omitted college is Staten Island Community College.
[b]A scale of integer values from 0 to 2; the positive direction indicates a positive evaluation.
[c]The omitted category contains students who aspired to postbaccalaureate degrees.
[d]This variable did not contribute significantly to this equation.
[e]A scale of integer values from 0 to 6; the positive direction indicates increasing emphasis on personal growth as a reason for attending college.
[f]A scale of integer values from 0 to 2; the positive direction indicates increasing need to work.

ently, then, the vocational curricula did not create severe additional handicaps for students attempting to earn a college degree. This finding takes on considerable significance given the concentration of minority students in these curricula. Second, the colleges in which students were placed, frequently on the basis of their preferences, had a dramatic impact on their freshman grades and credits. The college-to-college variation in grades and credits awarded to similar students was much larger in the two-year schools than in the four year schools; in the case of credits, it was much larger than differences that might stem plausibly from reporting variations. In the 1970 cohort, the freshman grades of students attending the Borough of Manhattan Community College were nearly a full letter higher than those received by similar students at Queensborough Community College. Borough of Manhattan students also received over four credits more *a semester* than did Queensborough students. Credit differences, but not grade differences, were of similar magnitudes in the 1971 and 1972 cohorts, and there was some rough consistency in the relative positions of different colleges. Students attending Bronx, Queensborough, and Staten Island community colleges generally received lower grades and fewer credits than did students attending Borough of Manhattan, Kingsborough (not present in the 1970 sample), and New York City community colleges.[19]

Since the grades and credits awarded to similar students varied so much by college, even in the first year, academic standards undoubtedly differed greatly from one community college to another.[20] Indeed, the academic standards at one community college, Borough of Manhattan, became a matter of public controversy during the period under study.[21] This variation in academic standards at the community colleges did not exclusively benefit either white or minority groups. Thus, grades and credits were relatively low at one largely minority school, Bronx Community College, but high at another, Borough of Manhattan. Likewise, grades and credits were low at one largely white school, Queensborough Community College, but high at another, Kingsborough. Nonetheless, in each cohort, even allowing for some reporting variation, the colleges appear to have been the most important determinant of the credits earned by individual students during the first year; they were also an important determinant of first-year grades. There was, in other words, a very arbitrary element to the academic rigors students confronted in the community colleges.

Generally speaking, student characteristics had similar effects on grades and credits in the community and senior colleges. Men did more poorly than women, and students who needed to work did not do as well as those who could devote themselves fully to their schoolwork. Community-college grades and credits were also influenced by the self-images and self-confidence of students as well as by their educational aspirations and reasons for attending college. However, at the community colleges, unlike the senior-

TABLE 7.11. Determinants of Cumulative Performance in the Community Colleges, 1970 Cohort

	Grade Point Average		Persistence[a]		Graduation[b]	
	b	beta	b	beta	b	beta
High school average	.023	.140	.006	.065	.005	.063
	p<.001		p<.05		p<.05	
Rank in high school class	.004	.106	.001	.048	.002	.078
	p<.001		p<.05		p<.001	
College preparatory courses	.033	.101	.026	.148	.017	.111
	p<.001		p<.001		p<.001	
Open-admissions reading test score	.013	.142	—c	—c	—c	—c
	p<.001					
Open-admissions math test score	.014	.134	—c	—c	.004	.070
	p<.001				p<.001	
College attended[d]		.295		.101		.124
Bronx	.147		.095		.105	
Manhattan	.613		.156		.199	
New York City	.211		.079		.179	
Queensborough	−.281		.001		.078	
	p<.001		p<.001		p<.001	
Academic self-rating[e]	.112	.053	.048	.042	—c	—c
	p<.001		p<.05			
Degree aspirations[f]	—c	—c		.098	—c	—c
Baccalaureate			−.010			
less than baccalaureate			−.109			
			p<.001			
Personal growth as reason for college[g]	.048	.071	.022	.061	.014	.044
	p<.001		p<.001		p<.01	
Vocational reason for college[h]	—c	—c	—c	—c	.016	.038
					p<.05	
Job plans after college	—c	—c	—c	—c	.057	.043
					p<.01	

college pattern, students who were older earned somewhat higher grades than did younger students, perhaps because their experiences in the job market gave them greater incentive to do well in school and improve their labor market position.

Academic processes in the community colleges were distinctive in one other way: student scores on the Open-Admissions Test were related more strongly to performance in these schools. Since their students came from more varied high school backgrounds, including many from vocational high schools and nonacademic tracks within general high schools, there were wide disparities in their preparation for college. Thus, stratification of students by their skills—including, appropriately for many vocational curricula, their mathematics skills—was a more important feature of the community colleges than of the senior colleges, where minimal skill levels usually could be assumed.

TABLE 7.11. Continued

	Grade Point Average		Persistence[a]		Graduation[b]	
	b	*beta*	*b*	*beta*	*b*	*beta*
Male	−.229	−.121	−.059	−.060	−.083	−.092
	p<.001		p<.001		p<.001	
Nineteen years of age	.124	.056	−c	−c	−c	−c
	p<.001					
Need to work[i]	−.042	−.036	−.031	−.049	−.027	−.048
	p<.05		p<.01		p<.01	
Ethnicity		.094		.103		.101
Jewish	.104		.059		.022	
Catholic	−.058		.011		.046	
Black	−.189		−.059		−.048	
Hispanic	−.094		−.084		−.053	
	p<.001		p<.001		p<.001	
R^2		.295		.089		.091

[a]Only students who dropped out of community colleges are defined as not persisting. Those who transferred to senior colleges and then dropped out are defined as persisting.
[b]Graduation from community college only.
[c]This variable did not contribute significantly to this equation.
[d]The omitted college is Staten Island Community College.
[e]A scale of integer values from 0 to 2; the positive direction indicates a positive evaluation.
[f]The omitted category contains students who aspired to postbaccalaureate degrees.
[g]A scale of integer values from 0 to 6; the positive direction indicates increasing emphasis on personal growth as a reason for attending college.
[h]A scale of integer values from 0 to 4; the positive direction indicates increasing emphasis on vocational reasons for attending college.
[i]A scale of integer values from 0 to 2; the positive direction indicates increasing need to work.

Even more so than in the senior colleges, these additional influences on freshman grades and credits in the community colleges do not explain ethnic disparities. The range of ethnic differences remains on the same order of magnitude as in previous tables, although the apparent order of the ethnic groups is changed somewhat. In particular, the position of black students now appears worse than it did before, perhaps partly because the influence of college is controlled and black students benefited from their disproportionate attendance at Borough of Manhattan Community College. According to the new equations, Jewish students received grades roughly a quarter of a letter higher than those received by similar black students and outpaced black and Hispanic students by 1.7 credits per semester.

As in the senior colleges, the influences on freshman performance generally were enduring and are visible in the cumulative performance of students and their chances for persistence and eventual graduation. Thus, they can be seen in table 7.11, which presents analyses of cumulative grades, retention, and graduation for the 1970 cohort. We ignore cumulative credits because in the community colleges the long period of time students had to accumulate sixty-four credits and the fact that some students transferred to the senior colleges without completing the associate degree makes the comparison of cumulative and freshman credits confusing at this point.

The effects of the colleges on the cumulative records of students and on their chances for persistence and graduation loom large in the table. Even in their cumulative records, students attending Borough of Manhattan remained nearly a full letter grade ahead of similar students attending Queensborough. Students at the Manhattan school were also nearly 16 percent less likely than those at State Island Community College to drop out and nearly 20 percent more likely to graduate. These are extraordinary differences for entry to one college rather than another within the same university system to make.

Ethnic differences in cumulative grades and in dropout and graduation chances are not explained in these augmented equations. In fact, they seem larger than the ethnic differences among students with similar high school backgrounds presented in the previous chapter. In the case of the 1970 cohort, they seem also to mirror more clearly a division between white and minority chances for success, although this was not true with respect to dropout and graduation for students in the 1971 and 1972 cohorts. In the other two cohorts, however, grade differences between white and minority students appeared more sharply defined than in the 1970 group.

The previous chapter appeared to show the community colleges as places where ethnic advantages and disadvantages did not loom so large. Our analyses of student careers reveal greater ethnic disparities, especially in the rate of student progress, than can be found in the cumulative records, which obscure differences between faster and slower students. These differences are not simply a matter of the rate at which students proceeded toward a goal at which all eventually arrived. For instance, they affected chances of transfer to the senior colleges, as we will show in the next chapter. Still, ethnic differences in the community colleges do not seem either as consistent or as large in magnitude as those in the senior colleges.

Conclusion

There was a consistency to student careers at the University. After the first year in college, student performance was fairly predictable from previous performance at CUNY. Student careers frequently can be seen as individual trajectories fixed in the early years, especially the first. Our longitudinal analysis of student careers thus has led us to a common wisdom: the freshman year is a critical period of adjustment to college. Following the implicit advice, we analyzed first-year performance, thereby revealing a number of influences on career beginnings and subsequent academic success.

Yet the ethnic disparities to which we called attention in the last chapter remain unexplained. In fact, our longitudinal model has added to their magnitude in the community colleges: obscured in cumulative credit totals were important ethnic differences in the rate of credit accumulation. And our year-by-year analyses revealed more sharply than the analyses of the last chapter that advantages lay generally with white ethnic students. Fairly consistently, Jewish students were most successful and Catholic students were next most successful; the minority students usually trailed the white groups. We have taken into account a number of potential influences on academic performance without being able to explain the sources of these systematic ethnic advantages and disadvantages. For example, we have taken account of mathematics and reading skills, measured by standardized tests taken by many students at entry; values and attitudes that may be relevant to college achievement, such as reasons for attending college; and the need to work while attending school. Some of these influences appear to have been less important than one would have predicted. Unquestionably, not all of our measures of student characteristics were as satisfactory as we would have liked, and there are other student characteristics related to educational attainment that we did not measure. But, even given the general weakness of our measures in explaining individual variations in academic success generally and ethnic differences specifically, we are skeptical that ethnic differences in principle could be explained by student characteristics.

One could argue in accordance with the conventions of statistical interpretation that ethnic differences were small when students' characteristics, colleges, and high school backgrounds are all taken into account. Certainly, they were generally small in relation to differences associated with high school background and frequently not a great deal larger than the performance differences associated with the student characteristics we have described as not very influential. But, since the open-admissions policy was conceived to aid minority students, ethnic differences are of great concern to any evaluation of it. Minority students were disadvantaged at the outset by their weaker high school backgrounds, the result of both racial segregation in grammar and high schools and the concentration of minority students in vocational and other non-college preparatory programs in high school. Our analysis makes clear that they did even less well than one could have expected from their weak high school backgrounds and suggests that the relatively better performance of whites is not explained by other student characteristics that seem intrinsically related to educational attainment. It appears, then, that the CUNY system did not make up for the initial academic disadvantages of minority students but added to them.

Notes

1. An excellent review of perspectives on education and inequality is provided by Christopher J. Hurn, *The Limits and Possibilities of Schooling: An Introduction to the Sociology of Education* (Boston: Allyn & Bacon, 1978).
2. Two famous articles that utilize this and related cultural traits as explanations for ethnic differences in mobility are Bernard Rosen, "Race, Ethnicity, and the Achievement Syndrome," *American Sociological Review* 24 (February 1959): 47–60; and Fred Strodtbeck, "Family Interaction, Values, and Achievement," in David McClelland, Alfred Baldwin, Urie Bronfenbrenner, and Fred Strodtbeck (eds.), *Talent and Society* (Princeton: Van Nostrand, 1958). A recent example of this tradition is by Carmi Schooler, "Serfdom's Legacy: An Ethnic Continuum," *American Journal of Sociology* 81 (May 1976): 1265–1286.
3. A persuasive review of educational research that argues for this position is found in Caroline Persell, *Education and Inequality* (New York: Free Press, 1977). The educational significance of class related modes of language use has been stressed by Basil Bernstein in *Class, Codes, and Control*, vol. 1 (London: Routledge & Kegan Paul, 1973).
4. For example, Ray Rist, "Social Class and Teacher Expectations: The Self-fulfilling Prophecy in Ghetto Education," *Harvard Educational Review* 40 (August 1970): 411–451.
5. That these influences may change from one stage to another is not always appreciated in educational research. See Larry Griffin and Karl Alexander, "Schooling and Socioeconomic Attainments: High School and College Influences," *American Journal of Sociology* 84 (September 1978): 319–347; Andrew Kohen, Gilbert Nestel, and Constantine Karmas, "Factors Affecting Individual Persistence Rates in Undergraduate College Programs," *American Educational Research Journal* 15 (Spring 1978): 233–252.
6. Consequently, even though our analyses have some formal resemblance to the kind of causal modeling called path analysis, they are also different from it because here the same population is not present throughout the model.
7. Only semesters in which the student was present are counted. By focusing on the average number of credits earned during semesters of attendance, rather than the total number of credits for each year, our analyses gracefully handle the considerable number of students who were present for one semester in a year but not for the other. Also, we did not include summer sessions in our analysis of student careers. This decision was made not because summer sessions are unimportant but because their inclusion would have complicated an analysis that was already complex. The relation of summer session achievements to student careers will be the subject of a doctoral dissertation by Richard Silberstein.
8. We remind the reader that the religious distinction is not available for students in the 1972 cohort, and hence we have ignored that cohort in this part of the discussion.
9. In statistical terms, the declining explanatory power of high school average, indicated by the decline of its standardized coefficient, is caused at least partly by its shrinking variance. We therefore have resorted to comparisons involving unstandardized coefficients, as is frequently done in comparing populations

where variables have different variances. See Jae-On Kim and Charles W. Mueller, "Standardized and Unstandardized Coefficients in Causal Analysis: An Expository Note," *Sociological Methods and Research* 4 (May 1976): 423–438.

10. The size of the second-year difference demonstrates that ethnic differences in credits did not result simply from the fact that minority students were more likely to take remediation courses, which carried few or no credits, since these usually were taken during the first year.

11. In fact, the impact of high school average on credits declined over the first three years as well. We have not indicated this in the text because its discussion would introduce a new technical consideration. Over the first three years, the variation of credits among individuals increased so that even though given differences in high school average corresponded to stable differences in credits during this period, this correspondence counted for less and less in terms of the credit variation among individuals.

12. The very strong relation of credits to persistence is an artifact to some degree, however. Some students enrolled for a semester but withdrew from all or most of their courses before the semester's end and did not return for the next year. Thus, these students earned few credits during the year because they effectively had withdrawn. Our model reverses the causal ordering, positing that they dropped out because they earned few credits.

13. Two scales emerged from the questionnaire items pertaining to reasons for college. The scale indicating the importance of personal growth as a reason for college combines a student's evaluations of the following in a list of reasons: "to gain a general education and appreciation for ideas"; "to make me a more cultured person"; and "to learn more about things that interest me." The scale of the importance of vocational reasons for college combines evaluations of these reasons: "to be able to get a better job," and "to be able to make more money."

14. It should be noted at this point that the colleges in which students were placed, usually on the basis of their own preferences, were for the overwhelming majority the colleges in which they spent their careers. Only students who transferred from the community to the senior colleges, to be discussed further in chapter 8, formed a sizable exception.

15. We have not made student scores on these tests part of our basic models because substantial proportions of students did not take them, giving rise to considerable missing data.

16. The academic superiority of women at CUNY is also noted by Jack E. Rossman, Helen S. Astin, Alexander W. Astin, and Elaine H. El-Khawas, *Open Admissions at City University of New York: An Analysis of the First Year* (Englewood Cliffs: Prentice-Hall, 1975), chap. 4. In addition, that women do slightly better than men in colleges generally is asserted by Alexander W. Astin, *Four Critical Years* (San Francisco: Jossey-Bass, 1978), pp. 214–216.

17. Community-college students are defined as returning if they appeared in either the senior or the community colleges for the fall of a new year. In addition, second-year students who graduated at the end of that year are counted as returning.

18. The curricula are divided into two categories: liberal arts and vocational (or ca-

reer). These curricula are the ones to which students were assigned at entry. We have no data about curriculum changes over the course of community-college careers.

19. Because they used nontraditional academic schedules or did not award traditional letter grades, Hostos and LaGuardia community colleges were not included in this analysis.

20. To a limited degree, these grade and credit variations among the colleges perhaps testify to the beneficial academic climates or programs at some schools; we think that this was partly the case at Kingsborough Community College, but we are less certain about other schools. Relying upon several visits and detailed interviews with key administrators and faculty at each community college, we were struck more at Kingsborough than at other schools by what appeared to be a high level of faculty and staff morale and a pervasive sense of commitment to open admissions.

21. Gene I. Maeroff, "Kibbee Urges Board to Ask a College Head to Resign," *New York Times*, April 19, 1975.

8.   Community Colleges and Stratification in Higher Education

SOME WRITERS have viewed community colleges and their vocational programs as crucial to the paradoxical compatibility of increasing access to higher education with the persistence of ethnic and class disadvantage. Karabel and others have argued that these schools are central to educational inflation, whereby increasing access to higher education results in a raising of the educational credentials required for desirable middle-class occupations, keeping them out of the reach of the majority of educationally mobile working- and lower-class men and women.[1]

According to this view, community colleges constitute a social buffer. One of their primary roles in the era of mass higher education is to protect four-year colleges, and hence the sanctity of the baccalaureate, from the crowds of working-class and minority students clamoring for educational credentials. In this sense, the two-year schools and especially their vocational programs function as dead ends for upwardly aspiring students of low social origins.[2] As evidence that elites have well understood this function, Karabel and others cite remarks like that of Amitai Etzioni (also quoted approvingly by then Vice-President Spiro Agnew): "If we can no longer keep the floodgates closed at the admissions office, it at least seems wise to channel the general flow away from the four-year colleges and toward two-year extensions of high school in the junior and community colleges."[3]

This buffering is accomplished largely by what Clark has described as the cooling out process.[4] Clark identified a number of mechanisms by which community colleges discourage and ultimately block upward movement on the part of many students who enroll in a community-college liberal arts

201

program, seeking the chance to attain a baccalaureate or even a postbacca-laureate degree. These mechanisms include counseling such students to en-roll in terminal vocational curricula and harder hitting tactics such as "need for improvement" notices and probation. In Clark's view, these mecha-nisms are central to the role of the community colleges, which is to convince "latent terminal students," whose talents do not permit them to rise higher, to harness their educational ambitions to more realistic goals. That, in the end, it is the students who make the decision to drop out or to stop their ed-ucation with an associate degree serves to legitimate a system structured so that many fail to achieve their ambitions.

Building in part on Clark's analysis, Karabel gives further depth to the portrait of community colleges as social buffers in his interpretive survey of research about higher education.[5] He marshalls considerable evidence to show a coincidence between the prestige hierarchy of American colleges and universities, on the one hand, and the social origins of their students, on the other. Community colleges are the bottom rung of the higher educational system in terms of the family incomes and parental occupations and educa-tions of their students. There is even a correlation between social origin and type of curriculum within community colleges. Working-class students are more likely to be enrolled in vocational curricula, which typically do not lead onward to enrollment in a four-year school. Noting the high attrition rates and the corresponding low mobility to four-year colleges on the part of community-college students, Karabel espies a "class-based tracking sys-tem" in which community-college vocational programs constitute the low-est track. And, remarking upon the sudden growth of those programs, par-alleling increases in access to higher education, he fears the emergence of a rigid tracking system in which "the community college . . . is likely to ab-sorb the vast majority of students who are the first generation of their fami-lies to enter higher education."[6]

Of course, we know already that first-generation college students were well represented at CUNY's four-year colleges, even in the regular admis-sions category (see chapter 5). Nonetheless, this view of the community col-leges as constituting a track of limited potential for students of lower status social origins holds obvious significance for the understanding of open ad-missions. Indeed, some expected that access would be expanded by the poli-cy primarily at the community-college level.[7] And despite the evidence that ethnic stratification diminished under the policy, inequalities remained in the distribution of ethnic groups across the levels of the University, and our analyses have shown a substantial relationship between ethnicity and type of curriculum in CUNY's community colleges. That these inequalities re-sulted largely from student preferences does not diminish their potential in-fluence on subsequent inequalities in the attainment of educational cre-dentials.

In order to understand the role of the CUNY community colleges under open admissions, we must look to the extent of transfer from community to senior colleges and the academic success of transfer students. Most students who entered the community colleges intended to go on for the baccalaureate —about two-thirds of the students from each ethnic group in the 1970 cohort, for example.[8] The open-admissions policy guaranteed a place in a senior college to every student who completed a community-college program. The encouragement offered by this guarantee was reinforced by another aspect of CUNY's transfer policy: senior colleges were required to accept all of the credits that students earned in community college. Thus, the liberal arts transfer could view himself or herself as halfway toward the baccalaureate at the time of transfer.[9] In short, even though inequalities remained in the initial placement of students, the principle of guaranteed transfer was designed to provide yet another avenue of opportunity for the baccalaureate.

In examining transfer to the four-year colleges, we have chosen to consider all students who entered the community colleges, regardless of their announced degree intentions. It may seem thereby as though we were prescribing a baccalaureate for some students who were well served by vocational curricula and an associate degree. One can readily imagine that from the point of view of a student who grew up on welfare or whose parents could obtain only marginal and unsteady sorts of jobs, an associate degree in medical technology or another desirable vocational concentration might represent a distinct step up in the world. Nonetheless, it still makes sense to consider all community-college students in the analysis of transfer. Even though the bachelor's degree is not always preferable to the associate degree, it is probably the case that the four-year degree is associated with higher socioeconomic benefits. Thus, to exclude from view those students who intended to obtain only an associate degree is to accept a certain amount of inequality in educational attainment as inevitable and as not requiring explanation. Moreover, it is to accept these degree intentions as immutable even in the face of positive educational experiences. This, we think, makes little sense in the analysis of an open-admissions program intended to offer encouragement to disadvantaged students. In any event, most community-college students did desire to go on.

Basic Aspects of Community-Senior Transfer at CUNY

One obvious implication of the view of the community college as a track of limited potential would be low overall rates of community to senior transfer. If a primary function of the two-year colleges is to absorb the overflow of upwardly aspiring students of low social origins entering colleges in an era of mass access to higher education, then it follows that few ought to be allowed through into the higher prestige, four-year schools. How, then, did community-college students fare at CUNY? Table 8.1 presents rates of transfer for the 1970 and 1971 cohorts, overall and broken down by admissions status, community-college curriculum, and whether or not the associate degree was earned.[10] Examined in the aggregate, rates of transfer at CUNY were not impressive. Approximately 26 percent of the students entering the community colleges in 1970 and 21 percent of those entering in 1971 had moved to the senior colleges by spring 1975, five years after entry in the case of the 1970 group and four years after entry in the case of the 1971 cohort. Rates of transfer among open-admissions students were even lower than these overall rates. In the 1970 cohort, 24 percent of the open-admissions students, compared to 29 percent of the regular students, had moved to a senior college by the end of the fifth year. Likewise, in the 1971 cohort, 18 percent of the open-admissions students, compared to 27 percent of the regular students, had made such a move by the end of their fourth year.

Some of the pathways students took to the senior colleges can be examined from table 8.1. In striking contrast to the low overall rates of transfer is the frequency with which students coming to the end of the most likely

TABLE 8.1. Community to Senior College Transfer Rates by Curriculum, Degree, and Admissions Status

	REGULAR			OPEN			
Curriculum	Associate Degree	No Degree	Total	Associate Degree	No Degree	Total	Grand Total
			1970 Cohort				
Liberal Arts	67 (550)	30 (1,049)	43	75 (705)	21 (2,608)	33	36
Career	34 (855)	11 (1,490)	20	44 (912)	10 (3,461)	17	18
Total	47	19	29	58	15	24	26
			1971 Cohort				
Liberal Arts	65 (695)	25 (1,458)	38	64 (851)	15 (3,429)	25	29
Career	32 (895)	9 (1,659)	17	41 (885)	7 (4,224)	13	14
Total	47	17	27	52	11	18	21

Source: Population data.

transfer path took the next step into the senior colleges. About two-thirds of those who graduated from the liberal arts curriculum, the one generally seen as preparing the student for transfer, ended up in the senior colleges. Open-admissions graduates were at least as likely to transfer as regular graduates; in the 1970 cohort, in fact, they were more likely. Even the graduates of the vocational programs, which are often viewed as terminal, seem to have been reasonably mobile, with a third or more of them in both admissions categories moving into the four-year colleges. In this case, open-admissions students in both cohorts were more likely than regular students to transfer.

A surprising number of liberal arts students managed to transfer without the associate degree. In the 1970 cohort, about a quarter of the liberal arts students without degrees ultimately enrolled in the senior colleges, with regular students more likely than open-admissions students to accomplish a move in this way. Not surprisingly, transfer without the benefit of an associate degree was very unlikely for students in the vocational programs.

Despite the frequency of transfer without an associate degree, at least among those enrolled in liberal arts programs, the vast majority of transfers spent at least two years in the community colleges before entering the senior schools. Almost no students moved during the first year, and few—nearly all, of course, without an associate degree—moved during the second. In the 1970 cohort, about 18 percent of moves without a degree were accomplished by the spring semester of the second year. The third year was the earliest time for large numbers of moves: in the 1970 cohort, over 40 percent of the moves without a degree and over 60 percent of those with a degree occurred during that year. The fourth year added considerably to the number of transfers, with a quarter of the moves in the 1970 cohort, on the part of both degree holders and those without degrees, taking place at that time. Movement slackened appreciably during the fifth year. Somewhat more than 10 percent of the moves in the 1970 cohort, with similar proportions drawn from degree holders and those without degrees, happened then. From this pattern of growth and decline, it seems likely that few moves occurred in the sixth year, for which we have no data. Thus, the transfer rate of the 1970 cohort, for which we have five years of data, is underrepresented probably only slightly by our data, while that for the 1971 cohort is more substantially so.[11]

High School Background, Social Origin, and Community-Senior Transfer

The possibility that CUNY's community colleges served to limit the educational mobility of those from lower-class or minority backgrounds while permitting those of more advantaged origins to pass onward seems on the surface compatible with the infrequency of transfer. This possibility makes the examination of the relationship between social origins and community-senior transfer of some interest. Because ethnicity is the aspect of social origins most strongly related to success at CUNY, we focus our analysis on it. Thus, for students in the 1970 and 1971 cohorts, table 8.2 presents the relationship of transfer to ethnic background, with open-admissions students distinguished from regular ones.[12]

The table demonstrates that minority students were considerably less likely than whites to transfer. In both cohorts, Jewish students were the most likely to transfer and Catholics were the next most likely. Blacks and Hispanics were distinctly less likely than either white group to transfer, but they had no clear ordering relative to each other. Transfer differences among ethnic groups were substantial in magnitude. Within the same category of admissions status, Jewish students were about 20 percent more likely to transfer than were students from the least mobile group in three out of the four comparisons in the table. Across the admissions categories, regular Jewish students were over 20 percent more likely than open-admission Hispanics to transfer in the 1970 cohort and over 30 percent more likely in the 1971 cohort.

These ethnic differences possibly derived from disparities in educational background. Because minority students came more frequently than whites from nonacademic high school tracks, they were more likely to enroll in the career programs, thus reducing their transfer chances. Also in part because of their weaker high school backgrounds, minority students were less likely to earn the associate degree, further reducing their chances. To clarify transfer differences, we regressed transfer on high school background and social origin, including parental education and family income in the equations. The results for both cohorts are presented in table 8.3.[13] Like the graduation and return variables in the previous two chapters, the transfer

TABLE 8.2. **Community to Senior College Transfer Rates by Ethnicity and Admissions Status**

ETHNIC GROUP	1970 COHORT		1971 COHORT[a]	
	Regular	Open	Regular	Open
Jewish	38	33	46	31
	(223)	(518)	(207)	(376)
Catholic	31	24	31	21
	(859)	(956)	(642)	(665)
Black	17	20	23	16
	(166)	(395)	(225)	(701)
Hispanic	26	16	17	12
	(188)	(243)	(195)	(350)

Source: Sample data.
[a]Hostos and Laguardia community colleges were eliminated from analyses of the 1971 sample because their nonstandard grading practices were not compatible with the construction of the academic variables used to explain transfer.

TABLE 8.3. Community to Senior College Transfer as a Function of High School Background and Social Origin

	1970 Cohort		1971 Cohort	
	b	beta	b	beta
High school average[a]	.000	.006	.011	.152
	N.S.		p<.001	
Rank in high school class	−.000	−.007	−.002	−.113
	N.S.		p<.001	
College preparatory courses	.029	.190	.017	.122
	p<.001		p<.001	
Father's education	.001	.002	−.000	−.000
	N.S.		N.S.	
Mother's education	.004	.008	−.006	−.015
	N.S.		N.S.	
Family income[b]		.040		.018
$4,000-7,999	−.014		−.013	
$8,000-14,999	−.001		−.005	
$15,000 or more	−.050		−.027	
	N.S.		N.S.	
Ethnicity[c]		.080		.120
Jewish	.055		.050	
Catholic	−.031		−.076	
Black	−.032		−.076	
Hispanic	−.023		−.118	
	p<.05		p<.001	
Constant	−.051		.240	
R²		.045		.058

Source: Sample data.

[a]Throughout this chapter, the zero point of high school average has been moved to 75 (see note 13).

[b]The stated category limits apply to the 1970 cohort. In the 1971 cohort, they are: $3,700-$7,499; $7,500-14,999; and $15,000 or more. The omitted category for the 1970 cohort contains students from families with under $4,000 in income; for the 1971 cohort, it contains students from families with under $3,700 in income.

[c]The omitted category contains "other whites"; the regression equation contained another category, "other nonwhites," which has not been reported.

variable is constructed so that the unstandardized coefficients of the independent variables are interpretable in terms of differences in the probability of transfer.

The results of these analyses are somewhat inconsistent for the two cohorts, so we will discuss them separately, taking the 1970 cohort first. For that cohort, the only element in the student's educational background that affected transfer chances was the number of college preparatory courses taken in high school—in other words, the student's high school track. The only element in the student's social origin that affected transfer was his or her ethnicity, but the effect of ethnicity appears different now that high school background has been controlled more carefully. Of the four major groups, Jewish students appear as before to have been the most likely to transfer, but there are no discernible differences among Catholics, blacks, and Hispanics. Ethnic differences in transfer among students with similar high school backgrounds were not as strong as they appear in the previous table. Jewish students were about 9 percent more likely to transfer than were comparable students in the other groups.

In the 1971 cohort, the student's high school track again had an effect on probability of transfer but so, too, did the student's high school grades and quality of high school. The higher were his or her grades, the greater was the probability of transfer. The negative effect of high school rank indicates additionally that students from better high schools were more likely to transfer. That is, among students with similar high school grades, those with lower rank in their graduating class, i.e., those coming from more competitive high schools, were more likely to transfer.

As in the 1970 cohort, ethnicity was the only social background element that had a bearing on transfer chances, but the effect of ethnicity appears to have been stronger for the 1971 cohort than for the 1970 group. As before, the largest differences lay between Jewish students and others, and they were substantial. The difference in probability of transfer between comparable Jewish and Hispanic students, to take the biggest, was 17 percentage points. Nonetheless, controlling for high school background reduces ethnic differences from their magnitude in table 8.2.

These regressions give a fairly clear picture of how high school background and social origin affected a student's chances to make the leap from a community to a senior college. Specifically, they highlight the consequences of high school track, and they indicate that ethnic differences in transfer among students with similar high school backgrounds were not simply between white ethnic and minority students, despite the large differences between those groups in table 8.2. But they do not indicate the mechanisms by which differences among students entering CUNY were translated into different outcomes. We turn now to that explication.

A Basic Academic Model of Community-Senior Mobility

To examine the academic processes at the community colleges that brought about differences in transfer chances, we have constructed a basic academic model of transfer that is reasonably consistent across the two cohorts. Separately within each, we have considered a number of potential influences on transfer chances, including attainment of an associate degree, community-college curriculum, grade point average and credits per semester, number of semesters out of school during the community-college career, degree intention, and the usual indicators of high school background.

Also, since transfer was guaranteed by the associate degree and since the liberal arts curriculum was oriented toward transfer but the vocational curricula were not, we have allowed for the possibilities that the determinants of transfer were different for degree holders and non-degree holders and also that they were different for those in the liberal arts curriculum and for those in the vocational.[14] The resulting equations, in which only significant influences were retained, are shown in table 8.4.

As table 8.1 also indicated, attaining an associate degree usually gave a powerful lift to the student's transfer chances. This lift was particularly great for students with *low* high school grades. According to the equation for the 1970 cohort, a student with a 75 high school average who intended to obtain a postgraduate degree was 28 percent more likely to transfer with an associate degree than was a student without one. A similar student with an 85 high school average was only 20 percent more likely to transfer with an associate degree. The benefits brought by an associate degree to open-ad-

TABLE 8.4. Basic Academic Model of Transfer, Unstandardized Coefficients Only[a]

	1970 Cohort		1971 Cohort	
High school average[b]	−.001	N.S.	.000	N.S.
Degree aspirations[c]		p<.001		p<.001
Baccalaureate	−.028		−.067	
Associate	−.099		−.093	
Curriculum[d]	−.057	p<.05	−.094	p<.001
Credits per semester	.013	p<.001	.021	p<.001
Semesters out	−.031	p<.001	−.026	p<.01
Associate degree	.284	p<.001	.225	p<.001
Interaction effects				
Curriculum × credits per semester	.023	p<.001	.025	p<.001
Degree × degree aspirations		p<.001		p<.001
Baccalaureate	−.033		.015	
Associate	−.199		−.106	
Degree × high school average	−.009	p<.001	−.009	p<.001
Degree × semesters out	−[e]		−.168	p<.001
Constant	.088		.033	
R^2	.293		.311	

Source: Sample data.

[a]Standardized coefficients are not reported because of the confounding presence of interaction effects.

[b]The zero point of high school average has been moved to 75. Despite this variable's lack of significance in both equations, it is retained because it is a component of an interaction term.

[c]The omitted category contains students who aspired to postgraduate degrees.

[d]This is a dummy variable with a score of 1 assigned to liberal arts students.

[e]This interaction term did not appear in the equation for the 1970 cohort.

missions students are an indication that the guarantee of transfer to degree holders was a useful one and gave opportunities to students whose high school grades would not have qualified them otherwise for the four-year colleges.

Among those with the associate degree, ultimate degree aspirations were clearly related to transfer chances. Students with low degree aspirations were not impelled to transfer merely by graduation. In the 1970 cohort, for example, graduates not aspiring beyond the associate degree were 24 percent less likely to transfer than others aspiring to the baccalaureate[15] and 30 percent less likely than others aspiring to a postgraduate degree. This relation between degree aspirations and transfer appears somewhat weaker in the 1971 cohort, probably a result of the shorter time period in which to observe transfer in this cohort, since some graduates did not have time to transfer by the end of the fourth year. In any event, the link between aspirations and transfer is evidence against a simple interpretation of community colleges as dead-end institutions.

Another major influence on transfer chances was the student's rate of progress in the community colleges as reflected in the average number of credits he or she earned in each regular-year semester, but the magnitude of this influence varied greatly between the liberal arts and the vocational curricula. In both cohorts, students in the vocational curricula gained between 1 and 2 percent in probability of transfer for each additional credit added to their semester average. Students in the liberal arts curriculum gained considerably more for each additional credit—over 3.5 percent in the 1970 cohort and over 4.5 in the 1971.[16] Clearly, curriculum did exert a major effect on probability of transfer. Moreover, since degree aspirations are controlled in both equations, this effect of curriculum suggests that equally aspiring students interpreted the same signals of progress differently depending on their curriculum. Thus, the two major curriculum types apparently are characterized by distinctive subcultures with respect to ultimate transfer to a four-year school.

Once we take these academic processes into account, few other characteristics of students appear to have affected their transfer chances.[17] Those who stopped out were less likely to transfer, but this is hardly surprising. More important, the number of college preparatory courses failed to enter the equations and thus the relation of high school curriculum track to transfer has now been explained. And so, for the most part, has the relation of ethnicity to transfer. Ethnic differences in transfer among students equivalent in terms of the model were nonexistent in the 1970 cohort, although some small differences remain in the 1971 cohort. When we take the model into account, Catholics appear to have been least likely to transfer; they were about 5 percent less likely to transfer than were academically similar Jewish and black students.

There was one other important determinant of transfer—the community college the student attended. Its importance is to be expected in light of the profound community-college variation in academic success revealed in the last chapter. Table 8.5 shows overall rates of transfer from CUNY's colleges as well as the "net" effects of the colleges, i.e., their effects on the mobility of academically similar students.[18] A close inspection of the table reveals two important facts about the effects of community colleges on the transfer of their students. First, the overall rates of the colleges do not parallel precisely their net effects. In both cohorts, for example, Bronx Community College ranked low in overall transfer rate, but when academically similar students are compared, students from this school were next most likely to transfer. Second, the college effects were quite consistent across the two cohorts. For example, in both cohorts, students from Kingsborough Community College were near the top in transfer overall and those from New York City Community College were near the bottom. In both cohorts also, students from Borough of Manhattan and Bronx community colleges were most likely to transfer in comparison to academically similar students from other colleges.

The reasons for these effects of the community colleges, even on students who were similar in degree intentions, curriculum, rate of progress,

TABLE 8.5. Rates of Transfer from the Community Colleges, with and without Controls for the Academic Model

COMMUNITY COLLEGE	1970 COHORT		1971 COHORT	
	Without Controls[a]	With Controls[b]	Without Controls[a]	With Controls[b]
Borough of Manhattan	32	7	26	8
Bronx	23	5	16	6
Hostos	25	—[c]	19	—[d]
Kingsborough	30	—[c]	29	1
LaGuardia	—[e]	—[e]	32	—[d]
New York City	18	–6	17	–0
Queensborough	23	–1	19	–0
Staten Island	27	0[f]	22	0[f]

Source: Population and sample data.
[a]This column reports the overall transfer rate from each college. Figures were compiled from the population data.
[b]This column reports the net effect of attending each college, with the academic model controlled. Each college's effect, which represents a net difference between its students and those from Staten Island Community College, was multiplied by 100 to make it comparable to the percentages reported in adjacent columns.
[c]These colleges are not represented in the 1970 sample.
[d]These schools have been eliminated from the regressions for the 1971 cohort because of their nontraditional grading.
[e]LaGuardia Community College did not exist in 1970.
[f]Students from Staten Island Community College form the omitted category.

and degree status, are not obvious. The effects were substantial, however. In 1970, the net effect of attending one college as opposed to another could be a difference of 13 percent in a student's transfer chances, and in the 1971 cohort it could make a difference of nearly 8 percent. Undoubtedly, the colleges differed somewhat in general "atmosphere"—in the extent to which their students were viewed as likely to go on to four-year schools. This may have resulted in part from the extent to which a school was dedicated to vocational as opposed to liberal arts curricula. New York City Community College, which had one of the lowest rates of transfer, was also a school dominated by vocational programs. Even students in the liberal arts curriculum in such a school may have been unlikely to transfer by comparison with similar students in other schools. By contrast, the atmosphere in schools dominated by the liberal arts curriculum may have encouraged even vocational students to transfer.

No matter what their origin, the effects of the colleges on transfer did not strengthen ethnic inequalities in transfer but counterbalanced them. While the highest overall rates of transfer were found in predominantly white schools, like Kingsborough and LaGuardia, predominantly white schools did not have uniformly high rates, as evidenced by Queensborough. And the highest net effects in both cohorts were found in two colleges with largely minority student bodies. In this sense, the community colleges at CUNY do not appear to have functioned according to the critical view of their role: filtering out students of low social origins from the stream of those progressing to the senior colleges.

In conclusion, the analyses of this section together with those of the last section help to illuminate the considerable disparities in the transfer rates of white ethnic and minority students. The analyses at the end of the last section demonstrated that these ethnic disparities were to some degree a function of differences in high school background, especially those associated with tracking. The analyses in this section explicate greatly the relation between high school background and transfer chances and thereby the comparatively low transfer rates of minority students. Thus, primarily because they were more likely to come from nonacademic high school tracks, minority students were found disproportionately in the vocational curricula, and these were associated with lower rates of transfer. Also, as the year-by-year analyses in the previous chapter revealed, their credit accumulation proceeded at a slower pace than that of white ethnic students, partly because of disparities in high school background, and their slower pace reduced their chances of transfer. On the other hand, the guarantee of transfer with full credit for community-college work to students who completed the associate degree helped those in the career programs and thus minority students. This analysis of transfer shows that ultimate degree aspirations corresponded closely with transfer chances among degree holders and that open-admissions graduates were more likely than regular graduates to transfer. The process of transfer was far more complex than critical analyses of the community colleges suggest.

The Timing of Entry to the Senior Colleges

Questions concerning the role of community colleges in the internal stratification of higher education are not answered conclusively by identifying who transfers and who does not. Equally important is identifying how well students who enter senior colleges are able to make use of that opportunity. If these transfers find themselves overwhelmed by more stringent academic pressures, then guaranteed transfer—however frequent it may be—is a largely empty promise. Transfer, if it is to offer a meaningful chance for community-college students to join the stream moving toward the baccalaureate and possible entry to professional school, must be accompanied by a reasonable chance for academic survival in four-year schools.

The time of transfer to the senior colleges is likely to have an important effect on the use students can make of the opportunity to attain a baccalaureate. Particularly because it determines the age at which transfers are likely to graduate, time of transfer affects the likelihood that the baccalaureate will be completed. Students who enter four-year schools in their fourth or fifth year after starting college—over a third of the transfer students in the 1970 cohort entered in these years—are likely to be somewhat disheartened by their slow progress in the two-year schools. They therefore may tend to become part-time students or to drop out after a minor academic setback. Even should they persist toward the baccalaureate, reaching it will take several more years, thus reducing their chances of entering professional school. Delayed entry to the senior colleges is likely to have even more profound consequences for students who start college at an older age than usual, as was true for many of the minority students entering CUNY's community colleges during the early years of open admissions.

Table 8.6 shows the variation of time of transfer by admissions status and ethnic and racial background for transfers in the 1970 and 1971 cohorts. The semester of transfer is recorded as the first fall or spring semester in which a student appeared at a senior college, and these semesters are numbered consecutively starting with 1 for the fall semester of the freshman year. That a greater proportion of students from the 1970 cohort appeared in the eighth semester, the spring of the fourth year, or later is of course a result of the greater period during which to observe transfer in that cohort. This difference in time periods affects the magnitude of percentages throughout the two subtables but not the basic patterns.

In both cohorts, open-admissions students transferred later than regular students, and there were important ethnic differences in transfer even for students in the same admissions category. In the 1970 cohort, for example,

TABLE 8.6. Percent Transferring in Each Semester, by Ethnicity and Admissions Status

Ethnic Group	REGULAR					OPEN				
	5th or before	6th	7th	8th or later		5th or before	6th	7th	8th or later	
				1970 Cohort						
Jewish	61	19	14	6	(84)	32	28	24	15	(170)
Catholic	42	25	19	14	(264)	33	31	16	20	(233)
Black	25	21	18	36	(28)	18	20	28	35	(80)
Hispanic	35	27	18	20	(49)	18	25	35	23	(40)
				1971 Cohort						
Jewish	56	25	14	5	(96)	47	26	19	8	(126)
Catholic	55	23	17	5	(214)	48	24	24	4	(164)
Black	38	18	24	20	(55)	32	28	25	14	(134)
Hispanic	35	33	21	12	(43)	48	15	28	9	(46)

Source: Sample data.

nearly a third of white ethnic open-admissions transfers made their move by the fifth semester, the fall semester of the third year, but only 17.5 percent of minority open-admissions transfers did so. Among regular students in that cohort, over 60 percent of transfers by Jewish students and over 40 percent of transfers by Catholic students occurred as early as the fifth semester, while a third of transfers by Hispanic students and only a quarter of those by black students were as early. There were also dramatic differences in that cohort between black students and others in late entry to the senior colleges. Over 60 percent of black open-admissions students and nearly 55 percent of black regular students did not enter the senior colleges until the seventh semester or later, i.e., until the fourth or fifth years. The percentages of late arrivals among white students were markedly lower.

The patterns of time of transfer were rather similar in the 1971 cohort, although there were a few differences in detail, in addition to those clearly caused by the different time span during which we observed transfer. Open-admissions Hispanic students were as likely to transfer by the fifth semester as were open-admissions Jewish and Catholic students, although their arrival was slower thereafter. And regular Catholic students were as likely as regular Jewish students to enter the senior colleges by the fifth semester, in contrast to the pattern in the 1970 cohort.

These differences in time of transfer were largely a function of relatively simple academic processes. Table 8.7 presents a straightforward academic model that illuminates the relation of high school and ethnic background to time of transfer. The dependent variable in the model is the number of the semester in which the student first appeared in a senior college. Thus, positive coefficients indicate influences delaying entry and negative coefficients those hastening it. According to the model, the primary academic determi-

TABLE 8.7. Basic Academic Model of Time of Transfer, Unstandardized Co-efficients Only[a]

	1970 Cohort		1971 Cohort	
Curriculum[b]	−.500	p<.001	−.257	p<.001
Credits per semester	−.093	p<.001	−.093	p<.001
Semesters out	.910	p<.001	.868	p<.001
Associate degree	1.878	p<.001	3.451	p<.001
Interaction effect				
Degree × credits per semester	−.111	p<.001	−.222	p<.001
Constant	7.318		6.764	
R^2	.248		.289	

Source: Sample data.

[a]Standardized coefficients are not reported because of the confounding presence of interaction effects.

[b]This is a dummy variable with a score of 1 assigned to liberal arts students.

nants of transfer time were rate of credit accumulation in community college, number of semesters out of school during the community-college career, curriculum, and attainment of an associate degree. The interaction term expresses the simple notion that for those who attained the degree, the rate at which they accumulated credits was especially important for the time of their transfer.

The features of the model indicate some mechanisms that promoted relatively early transfer on the part of white students and those from academic high school tracks. To begin with, students in the liberal arts curriculum, who were disproportionately white and from academic high school tracks, transferred earlier than students in the vocational curricula. The net advantage of the liberal arts students was a half a semester in the 1970 cohort and a quarter of a semester in the 1971 group.

In addition, the student's credit accumulation rate had some effect in delaying or speeding entry to the senior colleges. That rate was determined in part by high school background and varied by ethnicity among students with similar high school backgrounds. According to both equations in table 8.7, the time of entry of a student who transferred without a degree was lowered by nearly a tenth of a semester for each additional credit in his or her accumulation rate. This reduction can be given some concrete meaning by using the equations to predict the semester of entry of liberal arts nongraduates who earned ten credits each semester and were continuously enrolled. Both equations predict a time of entry between the fifth and sixth semesters, the fall and spring semesters of the third year. Thus, some of these students would have transferred in the fifth semester, having completed forty credits of community-college work, and others would have transferred in the sixth, having completed fifty credits.

In general, attainment of an associate degree delayed entry to the senior colleges. For example, the "cost" of an associate degree was three-quarters of a semester's delay for students earning ten credits per semester in the 1970 cohort and over one semester in the 1971 cohort. Only students making rapid progress were not delayed by completing their degree work—for example, a graduate had to be accumulating nearly seventeen credits per semester in the 1970 cohort in order to transfer at the same time as a nongraduate. That completing degree requirements would generally take extra time seems obvious once it is pointed out, but it holds a nonobvious implication for students in the vocational curricula. Since they were less likely than liberal arts students to be able to transfer without an associate degree (see table 8.1), the need to complete a degree added a further delay to their already slower transfer.

The last variable in the model is unsurprising: the student's entry to the senior colleges was delayed by nearly one semester for each semester out of school during his or her community-college years.

This model explains the difference between open-admissions and regular students in time of transfer and most of the ethnic differences as well. Only in the 1970 cohort were there ethnic differences in time of transfer among students equal in terms of the model, but they were strong only in relation to black students. With the model controlled, black transfers still appear to have lagged behind Jewish transfers by .80 semesters, but Hispanic students lagged behind by only .28 semesters.

The unusually late transfer of black students probably had some of its roots in events outside the academic processes with which we are concerned. Black transfers were somewhat more likely than others to have entered the senior colleges after a period out of CUNY. In the 1970 cohort, 30 percent of black open-admissions transfers and 32 percent of black regular transfers appeared in the senior colleges for the first time after a semester or more in which they were not enrolled (compared to 20 percent of the other students in either admissions category). Probably many of these students had left CUNY's community colleges in order to take a job or look for one. Their return as transfer students perhaps should be seen as a sign that their long-term employment prospects were not attractive. Somewhat speculatively, then, the late entry of black transfers can be seen as partly a reflection of their racial disadvantage in New York City's labor markets.

Finally, there were differences in the speed with which students from different community colleges entered the four-year schools. In both cohorts, students from Borough of Manhattan Community College, who were more likely to transfer than were academically comparable students from other schools, were also the earliest transfers when the academic model is taken into account. However, students from another school with unusually high transfer rates, Bronx Community College, were the latest transfers in the 1970 cohort and were only barely faster than students from New York City Community College, the latest transfers in the 1971 cohort. These three schools with earliest and latest transfers all had substantial minority enrollments. The students from those with largely white enrollments—Kingsborough (available only in the 1971 sample data), Queensborough, and Staten Island community colleges—were not unusually early or late in their times of transfer. As in the analysis of college transfer rates, it is difficult to see these college effects as contributing to ethnic and racial stratification at CUNY.

Nonetheless, our analysis of time of transfer adds a second element to a pattern of cumulating disadvantage for minority students in using access to CUNY's community colleges as means for gaining a baccalaureate. Chapter 5 indicated that minority community-college students were, on the whole, nearly as likely as whites to aspire to a postassociate degree. Black community-college students in fact had the same aspirations as white ethnics. But minority students were distinctly less likely than whites to transfer to a four-year school and even when they did transfer they were likely to do so later than whites. To be sure, most of these ethnic differences derived from universalistic academic processes, but these were in turn partly a function of prior inequalities students brought with them to CUNY. Obviously, it is important to see how these inequalities may be reflected in the performance of transfer students in the senior colleges.

The Academic Performance of Transfer Students in the Senior Colleges

The bottom line in any educational accounting of the opportunities created by CUNY's transfer program must be in terms of the numbers of students who ultimately graduated with baccalaureates and those who dropped out after transfer, presumably unable to make satisfactory progress in the four-year schools. To gain a preliminary assessment, table 8.8 presents the graduation, retention, and dropout rates of transfers in the 1970 cohort, tabulated by high school average (categorized to indicate both community- and senior-college admissions status) and semester of entry. For purposes of comparison, the graduation, retention, and dropout rates of students who began at the senior colleges and were enrolled in the fifth semester are shown also. This comparison group is identified as senior-college natives.[19] The table is restricted to the 1970 cohort, as are the remainder of the analyses in this chapter, because many of the transfers in the 1971 cohort had been in the senior colleges only a brief time by the end of our data and thus judgments about their success are risky.

The table shows rather clearly that, overall, senior-college natives did considerably better than community-college transfers with comparable high school averages. The natives were distinctly more likely to have graduated with a baccalaureate by the end of five years and, with the exception of students whose high school averages were below 75, somewhat less likely to

TABLE 8.8. Senior-College Standing of Transfers in June 1975, Overall and by Semester of Transfer, Compared to the Standing of Senior-College Natives, 1970 Cohort

	HIGH SCHOOL AVERAGE								
	80 or above			75–79.9			Below 75		
	Grad.[a]	Ret.	Drop.	Grad.	Ret.	Drop.	Grad.	Ret.	Drop.
Senior Natives[b]	61	12 (7,781)	27	47	21 (2,530)	32	32	24 (1,293)	43
Transfers Overall	39	29 (357)	32	32	31 (839)	37	23	39 (1,919)	38
5th semester or before	56	14 (180)	29	48	12 (385)	40	39	19 (650)	42
6th semester	34	27 (70)	39	36	28 (187)	36	29	30 (477)	41
7th semester	25	39 (56)	36	16	42 (122)	42	13	52 (393)	35
8th semester or later	0	71 (51)	29	0	74 (145)	26	2	70 (399)	28

Source: Population data.
[a]Grad. = graduated; Ret. = retained; Drop. = dropout.
[b]Senior-college natives are defined as students who originally enrolled in the four-year schools and were in attendance in the fall semester of the junior year.

have dropped out. Just where community-college transfers stood at the end of this period depended on when they transferred. Transfers who entered the senior colleges in the fifth semester or earlier were nearly on a par with the natives. In fact, the graduation rate of early transfers with high school averages under 75 exceeded that of comparable students who began there. But the graduation rates of those who entered in semesters later than the fifth fell off sharply with each semester's delay in entry, reflecting parallel declines in the chance of completing the requirements for the baccalaureate by the end of the fifth year. Of course, large numbers of late transfers were still in school at the end of the fifth year and their graduation rates undoubtedly continued to rise in the sixth and seventh years. But given the relatively weak community-college records of these late transfers, many probably dropped out in these years as well.

The impact of time of transfer on chances of graduation by the end of the fifth year implies that minority transfers were less likely than white transfers to graduate speedily. This is confirmed by table 8.9, which shows the graduation, retention, and dropout rates of transfers, classified by ethnicity and community-college admissions status. In each category of admissions status, Jewish transfers were most likely to have graduated after five years and Catholic transfers were next most likely. Black and Hispanic transfers were less likely to have graduated, with Hispanic students the least likely of open-admissions transfers and black students the least likely of regular transfers. However, the disparity between the graduation rates of white and minority transfers was counterbalanced to some degree by disparities in their dropout rates. Among open-admissions transfers, Catholics were most likely to have dropped out and Jews were next most likely. Among regular transfers, Jewish, Catholic, and Hispanic students were equally likely to have dropped out of the senior colleges, but black students were much less likely to have done so. It must be remembered that black students were unusually likely to enter the senior colleges in the fourth and fifth years, thus greatly reducing their chances of either graduating or dropping out by the end of the fifth year.

TABLE 8.9. **Senior-College Standing of Transfers in June 1975, by Ethnicity and Community-College Admissions Status, 1970 Cohort**

Ethnic Group	REGULAR			OPEN		
	Grad.[a]	Ret.	Drop.	Grad.	Ret.	Drop.
Jewish	45	21	33	29	38	32
Catholic	39	28	33	25	39	36
Black	29	57	14	20	56	24
Hispanic	33	33	35	18	58	25

Source: Sample data.

[a] Abbreviations are as in table 8.8.

To understand further the senior-college achievements of transfers, we examined the relationships of four key indicators of senior-college perform-ance to a number of academic variables pertaining to high school back-ground and community-college experience. Table 8.10 reports the results of these analyses, retaining only the significant determinants of these indica-tors of senior-college performance: grade point average;[20] credits per semes-ter; baccalaureate attainment; and dropout.

To begin with, there was only a modest relation between academic per-formance in the community colleges, as indexed by grades and credits, and that in the senior colleges. Credits in the senior colleges were a function of credits and grades in the community colleges, and senior-college grades were a function of community-college grades but not community-college credits. Nonetheless, the variation in grades and credits among similar stu-dents in different community colleges, documented in chapter 7, means that

TABLE 8.10. Academic Determinants of Senior-College Performance of Trans-fers in the 1970 Cohort, Unstandardized Coefficients Only[a]

	Graduation	Dropout	Credits Per Semester	Grade Point Average[b]
High school average[c]	.007 p<.01	_e	_e	_e
Curriculum[d]	.075 p<.01	−.115 p<.001	.920 p<.01	.179 p<.01
Community-college credits per semester	.009 p<.05	_e	.145 p<.01	_e
Community-college grade point average	.084 p<.001	−.122 p<.001	.933 p<.001	.373 p<.001
Associate degree	.587 p<.001	−.072 p<.05	.771 p<.05	_e
Semester of transfer	−.058 p<.001	−.056 p<.001	−.621 p<.001	−.094 p<.001
Semesters out between college	_e	.047 p<.001	−.384 p<.001	_e
Interaction effect Degree × semester of transfer	−.075 p<.001	_e	_e	_e
Constant	.268	1.062	7.757	1.871
R²	.240	.095	.213	.125

Source: Sample data.
[a]The interaction effect in the graduation equation confounds some of its standardized co-efficients. Others are not reported for the sake of consistency.
[b]Students who transferred to Richmond College were eliminated from this equation because they did not receive regular grades.
[c]The zero point of high school average has been moved to 75.
[d]This is a dummy variable with a score of 1 assigned to liberal arts students.
[e]These variables were not retained because they did not make significant contributions.

grade and credit performance in the community colleges was not a precise indicator of how well students would do under the greater and more uniform academic demands of the senior colleges.

The student's community-college record was related to his or her chances of dropout or graduation after transfer, but interestingly grades were the more important part of the record. An increase of a letter grade in community-college grade point average reduced the risk of dropout by 12 percent and increased the likelihood of graduation by over 8 percent. Community-college credits did not affect dropout once the variables reported in the table are taken into account, while each addition of a credit to the community-college credit accumulation rate raised the probability of graduation by less than 1 percent, a very small increase given the guaranteed transfer of credits earned in the community colleges toward the requirements of the baccalaureate.

The greater impact of community-college grades on senior college achievement gives an interesting twist to our earlier analyses. These showed that transfer and its timing were determined largely by the speed of the student's progress through community college, reflected in credits each semester, rather than by the quality of his or her academic performance, reflected in grades. But, once transfer had taken place, the quality of community-college performance took on a much larger role.

Community-college curriculum also had an important effect on senior-college performance. Not surprisingly, students from the liberal arts programs appear to have been better prepared for the academic demands of the four-year schools. Among students with similiar community-college records, enrollment in a liberal arts program in a two-year school was worth an additional credit in each senior-college semester and nearly a fifth of a letter grade in senior-college grade point average. Consequently, transfers from the liberal arts programs were nearly 12 percent less likely to drop out and 8 percent more likely to graduate than comparable transfers from the vocational curricula.

Time of transfer had an impact on senior-college performance that added to the burdens of transfer students with weak community-college records. Time of transfer appears in all four equations, but in the graduation and dropout equations its coefficients indicate what we already know: late transfers had not had enough time either to graduate or to drop out by the end of the fifth year. Its effects on senior-college grades and credits are less obvious and more significant for our analysis of transferring. Even when we control for relevant community-college performance, later transfers earned fewer credits and lower grades than did earlier transfers.[21] While the difference between them in grades was slight, the difference in credits was more substantial. A year's delay in transfer cost 1.2 credits per semester. This cost was added to the disadvantages late transfers suffered because they had weaker community-college records, which predisposed them to slower progress and lower grades in the senior colleges.

Delaying entry to the senior colleges after completing work at the two-year schools also hurt the senior-college performance of transfers. Undoubtedly, a period out of school magnified the shock experienced in a new and more demanding academic setting. A year out of school in between community and senior college cost the transferring student over three-quarters of a credit each semester and raised the probability of dropout by over 9 percent. The credit cost of a school interruption must be added to the cost of a later transfer in order to see its full significance. In other words, the student who transferred after a year out of school actually earned two fewer credits per semester than the otherwise comparable student who went directly from a community to a senior college. Twenty percent of black transfers were out of school for at least as long as a year.

One important finding in support of CUNY's policy of guaranteed transfer to community-college graduates is that possession of an associate degree was generally a help to the transferring student. Even when we control community-college credits and grades along with other relevant variables, degree holders earned more credits and were less likely to drop out. The dropout equation includes semester of transfer and thus takes into account the later entry of graduates to the senior colleges.

The most important effect of community-college graduation was its impact on senior-college graduation. Assuming that transfer was early enough to allow for a reasonable chance to complete the senior-college requirements by the end of the fifth year, the benefit of community-college graduation was substantial, even when graduates are compared to nongraduates with similar community-college records. Community-college graduation increased the probability of senior-college graduation by nearly 14 percent for students transferring in the sixth semester and by 21 percent for those transferring in the fifth. These increases are based on comparisons of graduates and nongraduates who transferred in the same semester. If we allow a semester's delay in transfer for completion of the requirements for the associate degree, in accordance with our previous analysis of transfer time, the benefits of the degree are diminished but remain noteworthy. Thus, the graduate who transferred in the sixth semester was still 8 percent more likely to complete the baccalaureate than the academically comparable nongraduate who transferred in the fifth; the graduate who transferred in the fifth was 15 percent more likely to graduate from a senior college than the nongraduate who transferred in the fourth.

Few other characteristics of transfer students were related to their senior-college performance. High school background exerted an effect on senior-college outcomes for transfer students with similar community-college records only in the case of baccalaureate attainment. Transfers with better high school grades, i.e., regular students, were more likely to have graduated by the end of the fifth year than those with poorer grades, open-admissions students. The virtual absence of high school variables from these equations indicates that students who did well in the community colleges were likely to do well after transfer, regardless of deficiencies in their high school preparation. Ethnicity, moreover, had no significant effect on the senior-college performance of transfers, although transfers who were nineteen or older at entry to CUNY earned one fewer credit per semester after transfer than did younger students.

Finally, the community colleges students attended generally affected their senior-college performance but the senior colleges to which students transferred generally did not. Community-college effects are visible in graduation chances as well as in credits and grades, and sometimes these effects appear to have been substantial. Transfers from Borough of Manhattan and New York City community colleges were over 10 percent less likely to have graduated than were comparable students from Bronx, Queensborough, and Staten Island community colleges. Students from the first two schools also earned lower grades than did students from other schools; their senior-college grade point averages were a third of a letter grade lower than those of comparable students from Queensborough Community College, whose students earned the highest grades and the most credits in the senior colleges. Transfers from Borough of Manhattan Community College accumulated considerably fewer credits than did other transfers—nearly two fewer credits a semester than transfers from Queensborough, for instance.

The effect of the community colleges on the subsequent performance of their transfers bears close scrutiny in the case of Borough of Manhattan Community College. Given their academic characteristics, Borough of Manhattan students appear to have been unusually likely to transfer and to do so early; the analyses of previous chapters showed that they earned unusually many credits and high grades. This last analysis of the performance of transfers strengthens our earlier conclusion of grade and credit inflation at this school. Its transferring students scattered widely over CUNY's senior colleges, so that their senior-college performance cannot be attributed to the special academic circumstances at one four-year school. Their relatively poor performance after transfer could mean only that their earlier grades and credits were the result of comparatively lenient academic standards.

To conclude, this analysis of the senior-college performance of transfers underlines the difficulties faced by minority students and those from nonacademic high school tracks in using the opportunity to attend a community college eventually to obtain the baccalaureate degree. These students were concentrated in vocational curricula and earned community-college credits at slower rates than others, reducing not only their chances for transfer but also their prospects for success if they did transfer. They also transferred later than others, and this, too, reduced the probability they would be successful. On the other hand, the associate degree, which many minority transfers possessed, helped to insure the success of the transferring student.

Conclusion

Overall, the analyses in this chapter testify to the poor prospects for students with weak high school backgrounds entering the community colleges to overcome their initial disadvantages and obtain the baccalaureate. The one bright spot in this portrait lies with CUNY's transfer policy and its guarantee of transfer with full credit to the community-college graduate. Possession of the associate degree added greatly to the open-admissions student's probability of transfer. And transferring among degree holders was to a large extent a function of educational aspirations, making it apparent that upwardly aspiring graduates felt encouraged to go on. Completion of the degree requirements did take time and frequently did delay transfer. But the student who waited often was rewarded after transfer because possession of the degree helped to insure success in the senior colleges and especially helped to insure completion of the baccalaureate within five years of entry to CUNY.

But the limited chances of using access to the two-year schools as a pathway to the baccalaureate are shown with dramatic clarity by table 8.11, which presents the percentages of 1970 community-college freshmen who had completed the baccalaureate or were working toward it by spring 1975, classified by their ethnic background and community-college admissions status. Even though about 70 percent of open-admissions students wanted at least a baccalaureate, in no case does the percentage of senior-college graduates among them rise above 10 percent; among regular students, roughly two-thirds of whom aspired to go beyond community college, only in the white groups does it rise above that figure. About a tenth of each group's 1970 freshmen still were working toward the baccalaureate five years after admission, but most of these students were not within striking distance of the degree. In fact, the average credit accumulation of the persisting students in *every* group was not even midway between the total needed for an associate degree and that needed for the bachelor's. Consequently, although graduation rates would rise somewhat in the sixth and seventh years, it is unlikely that all of the persisting students would graduate eventually. Some of them had arrived only recently in the four-year schools, and given the slowness of their academic progress and the comparatively weak academic records of late transfers, their chances of completing a degree were not great.

As the critical view of the community colleges suggests, attainment of the higher prestige baccalaureate degree was especially limited among mi-

TABLE 8.11. Percentages of Senior-College Graduates and Persisters in 1970 Community-College Cohort, by Ethnicity and Community-College Admissions Status

ETHNIC GROUP	REGULAR		OPEN	
	Graduates	Persisters in Senior College	Graduates	Persisters in Senior College
Jewish	17	8	10	13
Catholic	12	9	6	9
Black	5	10	4	11
Hispanic	9	9	3	9

Source: Sample data.

nority students. In neither admissions category did the number of black senior-college graduates rise above 5 percent, even though the aspirations of black students were no different from those of whites; among Hispanic open-admissions students, whose aspirations were also high, graduates were only 3 percent. Thus, a mere handful of minority open-admissions students were able to take full advantage of the transfer guarantee by spring 1975. Although others were still in attendance in the senior colleges at that point, many of these persisters were older than usual at entry to CUNY and, especially in the case of blacks, had transferred late and after a period out of school. Their prospects for graduation were not good.

A source of minority disadvantage looming large in our analyses were the nonacademic high school tracks from which minority students frequently came. By virtue of their high school tracks, they were more likely to choose the vocational curricula on entry to CUNY's community colleges, and they accumulated credits at a slower pace than did whites. Their curriculum placement and their credit rate worked against their transfer, delaying it at best. Their community-college curricula and academic records and their late transfer reduced their chances for success in the senior colleges.

Beyond the handicaps rooted in high school track lie other, more elusive disadvantages stemming broadly from the situation of racial and ethnic minorities in American society. Thus, in light of the frequency with which they began college at ages of nineteen and older, minority students were probably more likely than whites to have sought employment after high school, but the bleakness of their employment prospects brought them back to school. Many of these students returned intending to gain additional vocational skills that would improve their labor market position. In the case of blacks, some appear to have left school again after community college in order to try their fortunes in the job market only to return as transfer students a semester or more later, with reduced chances for success in the senior colleges. In these respects and many others, white students held a competitive edge over minority students. The magnitude of this edge was generally small in any single instance, but its cumulative impact was large.

In their fundamentals, then, our analyses support the critical view of the community colleges and their role in the stratification of higher education. To be sure, our analyses clearly indicate that the academic processes in the community colleges and the relation of these schools to the four-year colleges were, at CUNY at least, far more complex than the sometimes simplistic writings of the critical analysts would suggest. But, importantly, entry to a community college under open admissions appears to have given the student only a modest chance for transfer to a senior college and a slim one for graduation from a four-year school within five years. And these chances were smaller for a minority student than they were for a white student. Overall, CUNY's transfer program did not reduce the unequal distribution of white and minority students between the senior and the community colleges but added to it.

Notes

1. Jerome Karabel, "Community Colleges and Social Stratification," *Harvard Educational Review* 42 (November 1972): 521–562. See also Samuel Bowles and Herbert Gintis, *Schooling in Capitalist America* (New York: Basic Books, 1976), chap. 8.
2. This characterization is given by Bowles and Gintis, p. 230.
3. *Wall Street Journal*, March 17, 1970.
4. Burton Clark, "The Cooling Out Function in Higher Education," *American Journal of Sociology* 65 (May 1960): 569–576.
5. Karabel.
6. Karabel, p. 556.
7. In the original open-admissions plan, conceived before the City College confrontation, access was in fact to be expanded primarily in the community colleges and noncollegiate skills centers. But the conception of open admissions was changed greatly by the confrontation and its aftermath. Nonetheless, some critics saw the intent of the new plan in terms of ethnic and class stratification. See, for example, Ellen Kay Trimberger, "Open Admissions: A New Form of Tracking?" *Insurgent Sociologist* 4 (Fall 1973): 29–43.
8. The 1970 cohort is the best one from which to estimate the degree aspirations of community-college students. The 1971 and 1972 questionnaires offered "don't know" as a possible response to the question about degree aspirations, and the percentages of students aspiring beyond the associate degree appear lower as a consequence. Probably, some students who wanted to go beyond the associate degree but were not sure how far gave this response.
9. Of course, transfers from the career programs might, if they were not transferring to a parallel senior-college program, have had to take additional distributional requirements to qualify for the baccalaureate.
10. Curriculum is the one to which a student was assigned at entry. Undoubtedly, some students changed from one curriculum to another after entry, but we have no information about how often this happened or who those students were.

Also, the 1972 cohort will not be considered in this chapter because only three years of performance data are available for its students. Necessarily, transfer rates are low according to our limited data for those who entered in 1972.

11. Since the transfer rates of the 1970 and 1971 cohorts are based on different periods, we have not presented the year-by-year accumulation of moves for the latter. With one less year of data for that cohort, the relative frequency of moves in any year is magnified accordingly. The year-by-year pattern in the 1971 cohort is nonetheless similar to that observed during the first four years for the 1970 cohort.

12. Students attending Hostos and LaGuardia community colleges have been dropped from analyses of the 1971 sample because the nonstandard grading practices of these schools are not compatible with the construction of the academic variables that will be used to explain transfer.

13. In conducting the regression analyses reported in this chapter, we moved the zero point of the student's high school grades to 75; in other words, the grades variable was replaced by grades − 75. One consequence of this transformation is that positive values of the new variable indicate regular admissions status and negative values indicate open-admissions status. (The reason for the transformation lies in the statistical instability of some interaction effects reported in later analyses in this chapter.)

14. That is, we have tested for interactions between degree attainment and curriculum, on the one hand, and the remaining determinants of transfer, on the other. The best recent article on interaction effects in multiple regression is by Paul Allison, "Testing for Interaction in Multiple Regression," *American Journal of Sociology* 83 (July 1977): 144–153. Allison establishes that an interaction effect can be represented as the product of two or more variables. There is one difficulty with Allison's results, however. He appears to show that changing the arbitrary zero point of an interval scale does not change fundamental properties of an interaction term that uses that scale as one of its components. However, we have found that this result is true only when the correlations on which the regression is based are derived from the same set of cases. This condition is not met by our regression equations since we have based each of our correlations on the maximum amount of available data by using the so-called pairwise deletion treatment of missing data. Hence any interaction involving an interval component is somewhat unstable. Since this instability is worse as the correlation between the interaction and its component variable is greater, we have transformed one important variable, high school average, to reduce that correlation. With its zero point moved to a high school average of 75, our transformed variable has the nice property that its positive values indicate regular admissions status and its negative values open-admissions status. Also, some of the standardized coefficients in an equation that includes an interaction term are difficult to interpret because of the generally high correlations between interactions and their components. We therefore have omitted standardized coefficients from the remaining tables in this chapter.

15. For the reader unfamiliar with interaction effects, we will use this comparison as an example of how to work with them (also see appendix B).

Involved in the comparison are three kinds of terms: the dummy variables representing degree intentions; the dummy variable representing whether or not the student earned the associate degree; and the interactions between the first two. Written as a single expression, the terms appear as follows:

$$- .028d_1 - .099d_2 + .284d_3 - .033d_1d_3 - .199d_2d_3,$$

where d_1 and d_2 are dummy variables for students aspiring to the baccalaureate and those aspiring to the associate degree, respectively, and d_3 is a dummy variable that is 1 for students who earned the associate degree and 0 otherwise. The comparison involves graduates who did not aspire beyond the associate degree and graduates who aspired to the baccalaureate. For the first group, d_2 and d_3 are 1 and d_1 is 0. Hence the value of the expression, which is added to the value of the remaining part of the equation, is $- .099 + .284 - .199 = - .014$. For the second group, d_1 and d_3 are 1 and d_2 is 0. Hence the expression has the value $- .028 + .284 - .033 = .223$. The difference in probability of transfer between members of the two groups who are the same with respect to the other variables in the equation is therefore $.223 - (- .014)$, or $.237$, which rounds to .24.

16. It should be noted that the negative coefficient of the curriculum variable does *not* indicate that the liberal arts curriculum had some negative effect on transfer. Rather, that coefficient should be seen as a constant correction factor applied to the frequently large differences in favor of liberal arts students created by the interaction between curriculum and credits per semester.

17. Throughout the analyses of this chapter, we have tested the relations of other student characteristics, like gender and the need to work, to the various aspects of transfer. Occasionally, these other characteristics add significantly to our basic academic models, but, even when they do, their influence is generally small. In order not to overburden the text, we have not reported their effects, except in one instance where an effect seemed especially germane.

18. These net effects are taken from the coefficients of dummy variables representing the colleges, which have been added to the basic academic model of transfer. These coefficients have been multiplied by 100 to aid comparison to the overall rates.

19. Since virtually all transfers were enrolled at some point during the third or a later year, senior-college students who dropped out during the first two years were eliminated from the comparison group.

20. Students who transferred to Richmond College, where regular grades were awarded infrequently, were eliminated from the analysis of senior-college grade point average.

21. Some might see the effects of time of transfer on senior-college performance as an indication that transfers need a period to adjust to the academic demands of the four-year schools, implying that the performance of late transfers would eventually improve. We do not believe that in the main these effects should be interpreted in this way. Our belief is based on comparisons of the performance of transfers during their first year in the senior colleges to their subsequent performance. Simply, these comparisons do not show the general improvement in subsequent performance that an adjustment hypothesis would require.

9.   Equipping the Underprepared Student: The Effects of Remediation

FROM 1940 TO 1970 there was a steady rise in the proportion of students completing high school and entering college. The percentage graduating from high school increased from 45 to 75 percent,[1] and the proportion of graduates going on to college grew from 35 to 60 percent.[2] Four main currents account for this growth. In the immediate postwar period, the G.I. Bill swelled the ranks of college goers. Then, during the fifties, there were efforts to identify able students with strong academic records for whom economic resources constituted a barrier to college. Such efforts occurred in the context of a national concern with the identification and utilization of talent that would presumably improve the competitive position of the United States in the race for technological supremacy during the Cold War. This period represented an effort to expand access to college within the framework of a meritocratic principle.

A third and subsequently stronger trend is represented by the expansion of community colleges in response to the surge in demand for postsecondary education. Indeed, the increase in college-going was absorbed primarily in the two-year colleges, whose numbers grew tremendously, particularly from 1960 to 1970.[3]

A fourth source of increased enrollments was related to a growing skepticism about meritocratic values. Many concluded that the meritocracy, with its emphasis upon standardized achievement test scores and related "objective" criteria of ability, succeeded in eliminating all but token representation of minority groups and lower socioeconomic classes from participation in higher education. Largely as a result of this view, the emphasis shifted from the identification of able individuals to an expansion of educational opportunity for those *groups*, notably blacks and Hispanics, under-represented in higher education. This not only added to community-college enrollments but also led to special admissions programs in four-year colleges—programs in which minority groups were primary target populations. Nonetheless, the majority of students who attended college as a result of expanded access were whites.[4]

The newer recruits to postsecondary education generally have had weaker high school records than the traditional college-going population. One result has been the emergence of programs designed to remedy the presumed academic deficiencies these students bring with them. Though remedial courses in college have a long history—the first was offered at Wellesley College at the end of the nineteenth century[5]—they are now the rule rather than the exception. According to one nationwide survey,[6] by the mid-seventies 93 percent of community colleges and 78 percent of four-year colleges were offering remedial courses. Moreover, the need for these courses is not limited to unselective colleges. Even universities such as Stanford and the University of California at Berkeley offer remedial courses serving large proportions of students.[7] The fact that poor preparation in basic academic skills is observed even among students with very strong high school records in the most selective colleges suggests that the problem is symptomatic of broad educational changes.[8]

Nowhere have these trends been more clearly evidenced than at CUNY, where there was an expansion of enrollments during the 1950s and sixties, accompanied by increasingly selective admissions practices in the four-year colleges as a response to the limited supply of seats relative to the increasing demand. Then, beginning in 1970, there was a deluge of students who previously would have been excluded.

Not only have these national trends been accentuated at CUNY, but so, too, have the concerns and controversies accompanying them. In the immediate postwar period, increased rates of college-going raised no significant controversy, for students continued, by and large, to meet the traditional selection criteria for college or were allocated in substantial numbers to unselective junior colleges. When the barriers to attendance at four-year colleges were lowered, the traditional values of academic excellence clashed with the newer emphases upon educational opportunity for all. Concern over academic standards was particularly acute at CUNY both because the move from selective to open admissions was abrupt and because the open-admissions policy sought to affect in a positive way the full course of students' college careers. In aiming to improve the educational chances of those students deemed poorly prepared, substantial programs of remedial education were developed, along with expanded support services such as counseling.

This chapter considers how well CUNY achieved this aim. After a brief overview of the University's compensatory effort, we shall address three major questions. First, after open admissions began, to what extent did entering students need remedial work? An answer provides a picture of the magnitude of the educational task the University faced. Second, what was the relationship between the need for remedial services and their delivery? Since these services were considered an important mechanism for helping underprepared students to succeed, it is obviously important to examine the extent to which these students actually received help. Third, what were the results of the remedial programs? We will examine measures of academic success such as grades, dropout, and graduation in an effort to determine whether exposure to remedial programs made a difference for students' educational careers.

Overview of the CUNY Remedial Effort

As a part of the decision for open admissions, every CUNY campus was expected to develop remedial and compensatory services focusing primarily, though not exclusively, on three major areas: writing, reading and study skills, and mathematics.[9] However, because CUNY is a federated rather than a highly centralized university, the detailed structuring of these services was determined largely by the individual colleges. This led to diversity in program development.[10] Overall, the campuses varied in the intensity of their efforts: one made almost no response to the University's directive that remedial programs be developed; others formulated detailed plans.

The first task facing the colleges was to identify students who needed help. For example, students were typically asked to provide writing samples, which were evaluated by faculty in English and/or academic skills departments.[11] In many cases standardized tests of English usage also were administered. To evaluate competence in mathematics, two sources of information generally were used, either separately or in combination: the high school record and testing. The high school record was an indicator of subject area exposure (for example, it would indicate whether a student had taken high school algebra). Tests (either locally constructed instruments or standardized measures with national norms) provided more precise information about proficiency levels and specific types of difficulties. Standardized tests also were used frequently for diagnosing problems in reading skills.

Criteria for placement in remedial courses varied. One college defined reading skills below the eleventh-grade level as signifying a need for remediation, while a second set the criterion at the ninth-grade level. Placement in remedial courses was sometimes mandatory and sometimes voluntary. Just how voluntary it was depended upon a number of factors. When placement guidelines were clearly specified, the program advisor (a counselor or faculty member) had little discretion in applying them. Indeed, at some colleges students' program cards showed the remedial courses they were supposed to take, and students could not have their programs approved unless they were registered for these courses. In other cases advisors had considerable discretion in helping students plan their programs. The planning process often involved more than the decision to place students in remedial courses. At some colleges students exhibiting very weak preparation were counseled to avoid certain courses until they had completed their remedial work, and they might also be advised to register for reduced credit loads so as to introduce them more gradually to the mainstream of college work.

In order to deal with the variation in student need for remedial work, several colleges introduced sequences of remedial courses. Thus, a student with severely deficient writing skills would be placed at an earlier point in the sequence than one with less severe difficulties.[12] The placement of students in remedial courses was not always hard-and-fast. Early performance could result in reassignment to a higher or lower level remedial course, and students initially placed in regular courses could be reassigned to remedial courses if necessary. Conversely, some initially placed in remedial courses started off very well and were reassigned to regular classes.

Campuses also varied in the effectiveness with which the remediation program was implemented. In some instances assessment data on students were not collated in time for a scheduled program planning session. Moreover, administrative and/or funding inadequacies sometimes resulted in an insufficient number of remedial sections.

The conduct of remedial courses sometimes involved innovative techniques: self-paced courses, computer assisted instruction, and audiovisual technology are illustrative.[13] Remedial coursework was often supplemented by study laboratories and tutoring services, which provided individualized help for students needing extra work. Sometimes the tutoring was a separate service to which students would be referred. In other cases a cadre of tutors was assigned to a specific department offering remedial courses.

Criteria for exit from remedial courses likewise varied considerably. At some campuses, departmentwide exams were administered. Often these consisted of a posttest form of the instrument initially used for placement. In writing courses, a typical evaluation procedure was an end-of-term composition. To pass, students were required to demonstrate improvement to a level defined by the department. At other campuses, exit criteria were set by the individual instructor.

Colleges differed in whether they gave credit for remedial courses. The question of credit was a source of controversy on many campuses. Advocates argued that it was difficult to motivate students if they were asked to spend several hours per week in courses that carried no credit. Others argued that to give credit for work that should have been mastered in high school was inappropriate. In part, this issue turned on the content of the compensatory course. For example, at some colleges underprepared students were placed in credit-bearing freshman composition courses that covered standard material but met for extra hours each week.

The organization of remedial programs is best described in terms of their degree of centralization. In a highly centralized model, all remedial courses were taught within a single department, say, a department of academic skills. In a decentralized approach, compensatory work in writing was under the control of the English department, and remedial math was provided by the mathematics department. In practice campuses varied between these extremes. For example, an academic skills department might teach courses in reading and writing, while the mathematics department ran its own remedial courses.

Each organizational model had potential advantages and disadvantages. The centralized approach facilitated the monitoring of student progress and increased the likelihood of interaction among faculty who had been specially recruited for the remedial effort. On the other hand, these centralized departments were more likely to be isolated from the mainstream of the academic programs. The decentralized model increased problems of coordination and tended to segment the students' experiences in remedial courses. But an advantage of this model was that a wider range of regular faculty became involved in the remedial effort, and, indeed, the involvement of traditional academic departments often signaled a greater willingness of the faculty to commit itself to open admissions.

Under open admissions, counseling services were greatly expanded, and in some respects the style of counseling changed. Counselors were more likely to play an outreach role, actively seeking contact with students rather than waiting for them to initiate interaction. In addition, many counseling services moved away from a traditional psychotherapeutic model toward one designed to help students develop skills for dealing with the college environment.[14] Sometimes counseling services became more closely tied to departments offering remedial courses so that remediation and counseling became part of a joint support effort.

The Need for Remediation

The decision for open admissions was made with the expectation that there would be a decline in the overall academic strength of the entering students. In order to obtain a more precise estimate of the proportions of entering freshmen who would need remedial services in reading, writing, and mathematics, CUNY administered two standardized tests to graduating high school seniors in spring 1970 and 1971 (we shall sometimes refer to this battery as the Open-Admissions Test). The first was a test of reading skill and comprehension; the second was a test of numerical competence.[15] Students' scores classified them in each area as needing intensive remediation, some remediation, or none at all.[16]

Students whose reading scores were below those of the average ninth-grade student (based upon national norms) were defined as needing intensive remediation in language skills (that is, in both reading and writing).[17] Those whose scores placed them below the twelfth-grade level were defined as needing some remediation. Students who scored above this cutoff point were not considered to need remediation. A student was considered in need of intensive remediation in math if he or she scored below the twenty-fifth percentile for end-of-year ninth graders. A student whose score was no higher than the sixtieth percentile for end-of-year ninth graders was deemed in need of some remediation. In functional terms the math test (actually a junior high school level numerical computation test) assessed whether a student had the minimal numerical skills to complete most college courses (other than mathematics courses). A student who needed remediation might have difficulty reading and interpreting simple statistical tables or doing simple computations that might constitute part of the work in a social science course.

The results of the testing are presented in table 9.1, which shows the proportions of students needing remedial work in language skills and in math.[18] It is important to note that we are using the reading test as an indicator of the need for remediation in both reading and writing since no university-wide test of writing skills was administered.[19] It is a reasonable assumption that students with difficulties in reading also have difficulties in writing since the latter is thought to involve a more complex set of verbal skills. Of course it does not follow that skilled readers are skilled writers. Therefore, the reading test undoubtedly underestimates the proportion of students who needed remediation in writing.[20]

In the senior colleges 44 percent of all the 1970 freshmen needed at least some form of remedial work (and in 1971 this was true for 53 percent). Among open-admissions students, a substantial majority, 70 percent, needed help, and about half needed remediation in both language skills and math. The proportion seriously underprepared in language skills was quite low—only 6 percent needed intensive remediation. More students were seriously deficient in math—19 percent needed intensive compensatory work in this area (close to 30 percent in 1971). Regular students were far less likely than open-admissions students to need remediation. Still, about 30 percent needed help, though they were most likely to need it in only one area.

The remedial task facing the community colleges was even more extensive. The great majority of all entering students (over 80 percent) needed at least some help. Virtually all of the open-admissions students (about 90 percent) were deficient to at least some degree, and they were highly likely to be weak in both areas. Large minorities were severely underprepared, especial-

TABLE 9.1. Configurations of Need for Remediation in Language Skills and Math, by Admissions Status

	REGULAR				OPEN			
	Need for Math Remediation							
	Inten-sive	*Some*	*None*	*Total*	*Inten-sive*	*Some*	*None*	*Total*
Need for Langauge Skills Remediation								
			Senior Colleges					
1970 cohort								
Intensive	0%	0%	0%	0%	3%	2%	1%	6%
Some	1	5	13	19	12	18	17	47
None	1	9	70	80	4	14	30	48
Total	2	14	83	(N = 8,520)	19	34	48	(N = 4,807)
1971 cohort								
Intensive	0	1	1	2	6	2	1	9
Some	3	7	12	22	17	21	14	52
None	2	12	62	76	5	13	22	40
Total	5	20	75	(N = 7,471)	28	36	37	(N = 4,625)
			Community Colleges					
1970 cohort								
Intensive	7	2	1	10	12	3	1	16
Some	13	17	14	44	23	24	11	58
None	4	13	29	46	5	10	11	26
Total	24	32	44	(N = 3,052)	40	37	23	(N = 5,397)
1971 cohort								
Intensive	8	3	1	12	16	4	1	21
Some	17	20	13	50	27	22	9	58
None	4	12	23	39	4	8	9	21
Total	29	35	37	(N = 2,556)	47	34	19	(N = 4,091)

Source: Population data.

ly in math, where 40 percent of 1970 freshmen (and almost half of the 1971 group) needed intensive remediation. In language skills the proportion severely deficient was not as high—about a fifth needed intensive remediation. Community-college regular students were only slightly less likely to need remediation than their open-admissions peers. About 70 percent in 1970 (and close to 80 percent in 1971) needed help in some area—most needed it in both language skills and math—though the proportions needing intensive remediation were smaller than among open-admissions students.

Students with academic deficiencies did not always think they needed help. Since underprepared students were not invariably compelled to take remedial work, those who felt they did not need help may have been more likely to bypass these courses. We assessed the relationship between the need for remediation as defined by the Open-Admissions Test and student self-reports given at the time they took these tests in the spring of 1970 and 1971, prior to their enrollment in the University. Table 9.2 reports the percentages who said they needed help in writing, reading, and math, with the level of their performance on the tests controlled.[21] Although students with low test scores were more likely to report that they needed help, more noteworthy is the slippage between the two ways of defining the need for remediation—students were considerably less likely to think they needed help than their test scores would indicate. For example, among students whose scores showed a need for intensive remediation, only about half, and often less, actually thought they needed it. Whether this difference between objective and subjective definitions of need had an effect upon placement in remedial courses is a question we shall consider later in this chapter.

Using standardized tests as the yardstick, CUNY was correct in its expectation that open admissions would bring a substantial need for remedial services. But it is also clear that this need was not entirely a result of open admissions, for in the senior colleges a substantial minority of regular stu-

TABLE 9.2. Perceived Need for Remediation in Writing, Reading, and Math, by Test Level.

	% SAYING THEY NEED HELP		
TEST LEVEL	Writing	Reading	Math
Senior Colleges			
1970 cohort			
Intensive	52	38	43
Some	22	15	17
None	4	2	4
1971 cohort			
Intensive	51	42	38
Some	20	14	14
None	4	2	2
Community Colleges			
1970 cohort			
Intensive	55	49	50
Some	28	18	23
None	8	4	7
1971 cohort			
Intensive	45	42	44
Some	22	18	17
None	7	4	6

Source: Population data.

dents were underprepared and in community colleges a majority of them needed help. Especially with regard to the senior colleges, CUNY reflects what we noted earlier as a national phenomenon: many students with apparently good high school records nevertheless have basic skills deficiencies. Paradoxically, then, many of those who were not, formally speaking, beneficiaries of open admissions became eligible for support services that were primarily intended for others.

Ethnicity and the Need for Remediation

Since CUNY's effort to equalize educational opportunity was directed in a major way toward ethnic minorities, and because remediation was intended as an instrument for enhancing opportunity, it is important to look at differences among ethnic groups in the need for remedial work. These differences are shown in table 9.3, which summarizes remedial needs in two ways. First, it shows the percentage of each group who were seriously underprepared, i.e., those who needed intensive remediation in both language skills and math. Second, it summarizes the proportion of each group who needed any kind of remediation and in any degree.[22] Minority students were more likely to need remedial work even when compared with white students of the same admissions status. As an example, among open-admissions students in the 1971 senior-college cohort, 59 percent of Jews, 66 percent of Catholics, but 88 percent of blacks and 86 percent of Hispanics needed at least some remediation in some skill area. Among regular students, ethnic differences were even sharper. In 1971, less than a third of whites needed at least some help, compared with 60 percent of blacks and three-fourths of Hispanics. The ethnic disparities in academic skills are further highlighted by the fact that the need for remediation among regular admissions minority students was often greater than that exhibited by open-admissions Jews and Catholics. Although very few open-admissions students entered senior colleges with severe deficiencies requiring intensive remediation in all basic skills, these few were represented almost entirely by blacks and Hispanics.

In community colleges heavy majorities of open-admissions students in each ethnic group needed at least some remediation, but minority students were even more likely than whites to need help—about 85–90 percent of the whites but virtually 100 percent of blacks and Hispanics were underprepared. There were dramatic differences among open-admissions students in the need for across-the-board intensive remediation: less than 10 percent of whites but as many as a third of the minority students were seriously deficient. Among Jews and Catholics hardly any regular students entered the two-year colleges needing such intensive remediation, but about 20 percent of minority students did.

TABLE 9.3. Percentage Needing Intensive Remediation in Reading, Writing, and Math and Percentage Needing at Least Some Remediation in any Skill, by Ethnicity and Admissions Status

Ethnic Group	NEED INTENSIVE RE-MEDIATION IN READING, WRITING & MATH			NEED SOME REMEDIATION IN ANY SKILL AREA		
	Regular	Open	Total	Regular	Open	Total
Senior Colleges						
-----1970-----						
Jewish	0	1	0	23	65	34
Catholic	0	1	0	29	62	40
Black	1	5	4	67	87	81
Hispanic	2	7	4	54	81	67
-----1971-----						
Jewish	0	0	0	27	59	34
Catholic	0	1	0	31	66	42
Black	0	15	10	60	88	79
Hispanic	0	5	3	76	86	82
Community Colleges						
-----1970-----						
Jewish	2	3	3	75	85	82
Catholic	1	4	2	54	83	69
Black	22	24	23	94	96	95
Hispanic	19	25	22	89	98	94
-----1971-----						
Jewish	2	7	5	77	88	84
Catholic	1	8	4	65	89	76
Black	21	34	30	95	98	97
Hispanic	21	33	28	97	98	97

Source: Sample data.

These ethnic differences among students with similar high school averages need clarification. They raise a question as to whether other aspects of high school background help explain disparities in academic skills. To examine this more closely, we have conducted a set of regression analyses, including, as independent variables, ethnicity and our three usual measures of high school background: high school average, high school track as indexed by the number of college preparatory courses, and rank in high school graduating class. The results are presented in table 9.4. In the senior colleges, although high school average was the most important determinant, both high school track and rank in the high school graduating class also influenced test scores. As one might expect, placement in nonacademic high school tracks hampered the development of students' academic skills. And among otherwise comparable students, those with lower ranks in their high school class earned higher scores on the Open-Admissions Test. This is undoubtedly a reflection of differences in the academic competitiveness of various high schools. In the most competitive, a given high school average results in a lower rank in class than it does in a less competitive high school. Thus, according to the analyses, students from the most competitive high schools did better on the Open-Admissions Test. In the community colleges, the influence of high school track upon test scores was as great as and in some cases greater than the influence of high school average.

It is striking that in both senior and community colleges, ethnic differences in academic skills remained substantial even after controlling more fully for differences in high school background. When white and minority students were equivalent in all aspects of their high school records, whites still outscored minority students on the reading and math tests. In some cases these differences amounted to a gap of two years or more in terms of the grade level equivalents implied by the test scores. These disparities among students with apparently comparable high school backgrounds suggest that there may be important variations not only in the cultural resources available to youths in different ethnic communities but also in the academic quality of high schools; in particular, they hint at the considerable academic inferiority of the ghetto schools attended by many of the minority students in our samples.

Finally, even when we take objective skill differences into account, minority students were less confident about their preparation for college.[23] In 1971, for example, among senior-college students with comparable high school backgrounds and identical scores on the reading test, blacks were almost 10 percent more likely than Jews to feel they needed extra help in reading and Hispanics were almost 15 percent more likely. Similar differences in academic confidence emerged in community colleges. As an example, among those with comparable high school backgrounds and the same scores on the math test, blacks and Hispanics were about 10 percent more likely than Catholics (and 15 percent more likely than Jews) to think they needed help in math.

The Delivery of Remedial Services

We have seen that the need for remedial services was substantial. Before considering how CUNY responded to this need, some cautionary comments are in order. First, although the CUNY Open-Admissions Test provided an estimate of the proportions of students who would need help, it was actually used as a placement device on only a few campuses. Where colleges administered placement tests, a variety of instruments were used. In addition, our definitions of need for remediation do not coincide exactly with those applied at different colleges. Moreover, as noted earlier, we have used the reading test as an indicator of the need for remediation not only in reading but also in writing. The test probably underestimates the proportion of stu-

TABLE 9.4. Open-Admissions Test Scores as a Function of High School Background and Ethnicity

| | READING TEST | | | | MATH TEST | | | |
| | 1970 | | 1971 | | 1970 | | 1971 | |
	b	beta	b	beta	b	beta	b	beta
			Senior Colleges					
High school average	.828	.504	.847	.515	.480	.397	.557	.414
		$p<.001$		$p<.001$		$p<.001$		$p<.001$
Rank in high school class	-.098	-.209	-.105	-.232	-.032	-.093	-.032	-.086
		$p<.001$		$p<.01$		$p<.01$		$p<.01$
College preparatory courses	.985	.180	.875	.157	.753	.187	.625	.137
		$p<.001$		$p<.01$		$p<.001$		$p<.01$
Ethnicity[a]		.201		.128		.206		.207
Jewish	-2.010		.402		-.010		1.211	
Catholic	-1.876		.093		-.505		-.101	
Black	-4.683		-2.172		-4.192		-2.716	
Hispanic	-6.077		-4.277		-4.483		-5.235	
		$p<.001$		$p<.001$		$p<.001$		$p<.001$
Constant	-27.762		-29.646		-13.669		-20.541	
R^2		.342		.285		.311		.279

Community Colleges

	b	β	b	β	b	β	b	β
High school average	.414	.230	.506	.288	.273	.175	.373	.240
	p<.01		p<.01		p<.01		p<.01	
Rank in high school class	−.056	−.125	−.071	−.155	−.013	−.035	−.029	−.071
	p<.01		p<.01		N.S.		p<.01	
College preparatory courses	1.235	.345	.799	.224	1.032	.333	.819	.260
	p<.001		p<.01		p<.01		p<.01	
Ethnicity[a]		.268		.288		.297		.306
Jewish	−1.144		−.273		−.314		.365	
Catholic	−.118		.995		−.350		1.006	
Black	−5.756		−6.532		−6.497		−5.845	
Hispanic	−7.229		−5.974		−7.096		−5.821	
	p<.001		p<.001		p<.001		p<.001	
Constant	−3.658		−7.855		−3.747		−10.858	
R^2	.363		.298		.340		.319	

Source: Sample data.

[a]The omitted category contains "other whites"; the regression equation contained another category, "other non-whites," which has not been reported.

dents who needed compensatory work in writing (many campuses assessed this need directly by evaluating writing samples). Even though the Open-Admissions Test was not typically used as a placement device, it is an instrument that correlates rather well with other major tests.[24] Thus, it is likely that a student who scored low on the CUNY test would score low on other tests measuring the same academic skill. There are no large differences between our definitions of the need for remediation and those used at the various campuses. We believe that the analyses to follow represent a reasonable approximation of the relationship between need for remediation and the delivery of remedial services.

We begin with an overview of CUNY's attempts to deliver remedial services. In the senior colleges 46 percent of the 1970 cohort and 51 percent of the 1971 took remedial work, and in the community colleges about half the students in each of the first two cohorts took compensatory courses.[25] For the great majority of remedial students in both two- and four-year schools, exposure to compensatory courses was not extensive: about 70 percent took no more than two such courses (though in the 1971 senior-college cohort the figure was closer to 60 percent). By and large remedial experience was confined to the first year. In the senior colleges about 70 percent of remedial students took all of this work in the freshman year, and in the two-year colleges the figure was closer to 80 percent.

Remedial courses were far more likely to carry credit in senior than in community colleges. As an example, in the 1971 cohort, almost three-fourths of the compensatory courses taken by senior-college students carried at least some credit, while this was true for only one-fourth of those taken in the community colleges. One would expect, then, that remedial students' credit production in the freshman year would have been reduced more in community colleges than in senior colleges.

There were also differences between senior and community colleges in the skills to which attention was devoted. In the former, more than half of the remedial courses taken were in writing, compared with less than 30 percent in the two-year schools. In the latter more than 70 percent of remedial work was taken in reading and math. This disparity probably reflects differences in the curricular distribution of students at the two levels of CUNY. In the senior colleges the overwhelming majority of students were found in liberal arts, where writing skills would seem very important for academic success. On the other hand, in the community colleges a high proportion of students were enrolled in career programs of a technical nature, in which expository writing skills would seem less important.

How CUNY's remedial services were delivered in relation to students' needs is portrayed in table 9.5, which shows the percentages of students at each level of need (intensive, some, or none) who received remediation in the major skills areas: writing, reading, and math. In both senior and community colleges,[26] as the need for remediation increased, so did the likeli-

TABLE 9.5. Percentage Receiving Remediation, by Need for Remediation

Need for Remediation	SENIOR COLLEGES		COMMUNITY COLLEGES	
	1970 Cohort	1971 Cohort	1970 Cohort	1971 Cohort
% Receiving Remediation in Writing				
Intensive	67	81	40	33
Some	55	63	26	21
None	21	29	8	9
% Receiving Remediation in Reading				
Intensive	28	75	43	68
Some	22	40	25	32
None	1	2	7	10
% Receiving Remediation in Math				
Intensive	34	44	44	39
Some	17	21	24	24
None	14	8	9	14

Source: Population data.

hood of receiving it. In each area students who were most seriously under-prepared (shown in the table as needing intensive remediation) were more likely to receive help than were students whose deficiencies were only moderate. Because of the greater emphasis upon writing skills in the four-year colleges, students in these schools were more likely to receive help in this area than were students with similar needs in the two-year schools. Indeed, in the senior colleges a relatively high percentage received help in writing even though their test scores indicated no need for it (21 percent in 1970 and 29 percent in 1971).

The process by which students were placed into remedial courses displayed a certain rationality since the tested need for help was correlated with its delivery. Nonetheless, considerable slippage existed in the placement process. Substantial proportions of students did not receive help even though their test scores indicated that they needed it. For example, of those who needed intensive remediation in reading in the 1971 cohort, 25 percent of senior-college students and 32 percent in community colleges received none. Of course, tests were not the only mechanisms for assessing student skills. Other factors such as student self-perceptions about the need for help may well have been ingredients of the placement process.

Sharper insight into this process is provided by a set of regression analyses that, in addition to test scores, assess the influence of high school background, students' perceived needs for help, and ethnicity. The results are presented in table 9.6.

In the senior colleges reading test performance was the major factor determining who received compensatory work in writing and reading. But high school average also had a consistent net effect: even with the same test

TABLE 9.6. Determinants of Placement in Remedial Courses[a]

	WRITING				READING				MATH			
	1970		1971		1970		1971		1970		1971	
	b	beta	b	beta	b	beta	b	beta	b	beta	b	beta
					Senior Colleges							
High school average	−.010	−.118	−.020	−.233	−.004	−.072	−.005	−.101	.004	.053	−.003	−.060
	$p<.01$		$p<.001$		$p<.05$		$p<.01$		N.S.		N.S.	
Rank in high school class	.001	.062	.000	.004	.000	.008	−.002	−.117	.001	.029	−.001	−.089
	$p<.05$		N.S.		N.S.		$p<.01$		N.S.		$p<.01$	
College preparatory courses	−.007	−.025	−.019	−.066	−.002	−.012	−.004	−.027	−.050	−.214	−.019	−.107
	N.S.		$p<.001$		N.S.		N.S.		$p<.001$		$p<.01$	
Open admissions test	−.017	−.333	−.013	−.260	−.011	−.337	−.007	−.246	−.008	−.059	−.003	−.078
	$p<.001$		$p<.001$		$p<.001$		$p<.001$		$p<.05$		$p<.01$	
Perceived need for help[b]	.153	.099	.272	.156	.075	.059	.034	.031	.053	.037	.070	.062
	$p<.01$		$p<.001$		$p<.01$		N.S.		N.S.		$p<.01$	
Ethnicity[c]		.026		.051		.132		.137		.076		.124
Jewish	.009		−.001		−.053		.011		.041		.005	
Catholic	.013		−.042		−.051		−.003		−.001		.017	
Black	−.006		.015		.071		.188		.082		.154	
Hispanic	−.009		−.060		−.004		.013		.066		.110	
	N.S.		N.S.		$p<.001$		$p<.001$		$p<.001$		$p<.001$	
Constant	1.827		2.774		1.005		.956		.708		.780	
R^2		.198		.259		.207		.180		.074		.104

244

Community Colleges

	(1)		(2)		(3)		(4)		(5)		(6)	
High school average	−.006	−.083	.002	.032	−.004	−.048	−.004	−.044	−.007	−.094	−.007	−.092
	$p<.01$		N.S.		N.S.		N.S.		$p<.01$		$p<.01$	
Rank in high school class	−.001	−.029	−.002	−.107	−.001	−.039	.001	.046	.000	.004	.001	.061
	N.S.		$p<.01$		N.S.		N.S.		N.S.		$p<.05$	
College preparatory courses	−.010	−.065	−.026	−.167	−.017	−.103	−.005	−.029	−.028	−.181	−.033	−.202
	$p<.01$		$p<.01$		$p<.01$		N.S.		$p<.01$		$p<.01$	
Open admissions test	−.013	−.303	−.007	−.170	−.015	−.326	−.018	−.372	−.008	−.163	−.006	−.110
	$p<.001$		$p<.001$		$p<.001$		$p<.001$		$p<.01$		$p<.01$	
Perceived need for help[b]	.121	.113	.190	.179	.048	.038	.181	.152	.091	.088	.137	.127
	$p<.01$		$p<.001$		N.S.		$p<.01$		$p<.01$		$p<.01$	
Ethnicity[c]		.081		.069		.081		.079		.061		.132
Jewish	−.076		−.051		.007		−.024		.018		−.143	
Catholic	−.054		−.008		−.070		−.019		.012		−.018	
Black	−.129		−.019		−.065		.066		.022		−.008	
Hispanic	−.025		−.049		.010		.081		.095		.083	
	$p<.001$		$p<.01$		$p<.001$		$p<.01$		$p<.05$		$p<.001$	
Constant	1.372		.686		1.460		1.237		1.343		1.313	
R^2	.192		.166		.220		.271		.219		.177	

Source: Sample data.

[a] Placement in remediation is a nominal variable, with those so placed scored as 1 and those not placed scored as 0.

[b] Those reporting that they needed help were scored as 1 and those who did not think they needed help were scored as 0.

[c] The omitted category contains "other whites"; the regression equations contain another category, "other nonwhites," which has not been reported.

245

scores, open-admissions students were more likely than regular students to take remediation in writing and reading. Although the designation, "open-admissions student," is not one reported to us in our interviews as having a role in the placement process, it appears that in scrutinizing the high school records, students' averages must have been considered in the decisions of academic advisors to place students in language skill remediation. Student self-perceptions also affected the likelihood of taking compensatory language skill courses. Even when students' records were alike in all other respects, the feeling that one needed help generally increased the chance that one would receive it. The influence of ethnicity upon placement in writing and reading courses was an inconsistent one. Because of their weaker high school backgrounds, lower test scores, and lower confidence, minority students were more likely to be placed into remedial courses than were whites. However, when compared with whites who were similar to them in these respects, minority students were no more likely to be placed in writing courses. But in reading, ethnicity played an independent role: among students comparable in other respects, blacks were more likely than other groups to be placed in remedial reading courses.

Unlike placement in writing and reading, placement in remedial math was not determined primarily by scores on the math test but rather by high school preparation: students from nonacademic tracks took fewer math courses in high school and were more likely to be placed in remedial math courses. This finding squares with evidence derived from our interviews with math faculty that the high school record was an important consideration in recommending compensatory work in math. Student self-reports that they needed help in math also added to the probability of actually receiving help, but only in 1971. Among students comparable in other respects, those who felt they needed help were 7 percent more likely to receive it. As we found in the case of reading, there were also net ethnic differences in the probability of placement in remedial math. Among students similar in other ways, blacks, and to a lesser degree Hispanics, were more likely to take remedial math courses than were white ethnic students, but the differences were clear-cut only in 1971. In that year blacks were 15 percent more likely to take remedial math than were comparable whites, and Hispanics were 11 percent more likely.

In the community colleges, just as in the four-year schools, the most important determinant of placement in compensatory reading and writing courses was the score on the reading test. But unlike the senior colleges, high school average generally had no influence on the probability of remedial placement. The educational background factor that most consistently determined placement in the language skill areas was high school track. Students' confidence in their writing and reading skills generally made a difference: those who thought they needed help were more likely to receive it. Ethnicity played a very muddy role as an independent determinant of placement in remedial reading and writing. There are visible differences among groups, but none was consistently more likely or less likely to take remedial work.

Math placement in the community colleges reflects a process not unlike that in the senior colleges. Scores on the math test did influence placement, but their importance was overshadowed slightly by the role of high school background, particularly high school track: students from nonacademic tracks had had less exposure to math and were thus more likely to receive compensatory work. Among students of similar skill in math, those who had less confidence were more likely to be placed in remedial math courses. When we controlled for these factors, some ethnic effects were still discernible. Among comparable students, Hispanics were most likely to take remedial math.

These analyses suggest that the process of remedial placement at CUNY was not a completely mechanical one wherein the receipt of compensatory services was a routine consequence of low standardized test scores. Overall, students' academic preparation (as measured by test scores, high school average, and high school track) did, more than any other factor, affect placement. But since placement was not always mandatory, interaction between an academic advisor or counselor and the student was probably an event of importance: students who did not feel a need for help apparently were able to resist the advice of advisors to register for remedial courses. Because of generally lower scores on the Open-Admissions Test, weaker preparation in high school, and less academic self-confidence, minority students were more likely than whites to be placed in remedial courses. However, there were not many clear instances in which minority students were more likely than similar whites to find themselves in remedial courses. In short, minority students were not—simply as a function of minority status—consistently singled out for remedial placement.

Overall, the placement of students in compensatory work can be predicted only moderately well. In part this is the result of organizational features of the remedial effort. There were inefficiencies in the administration of the assessment and placement functions. Sometimes student's records were unavailable at the time they were scheduled for program planning sessions. In other cases funds were insufficient to hire staff for the required number of sections of remedial courses. For these and related reasons, many students whose records and tested skills showed a need for help nevertheless slipped through the administrative net.

The Impact of Remediation

We turn now to the key question of this chapter: did exposure to remedial courses increase students' chances for success in college? We set the stage for our analyses by briefly summarizing what is known about the effectiveness of compensatory education at the college level. Although such programs were quite common in community colleges by the late 1960s, there was not much research evaluating them, and what little there was generally showed disastrous results.[27] Indeed, Roueche and Snow concluded that these remedial programs seemed designed to insure that the students they served would not succeed in college.[28] In the 1970s evaluation studies were more common,[29] but their findings were inconsistent, largely as a result of variation in success criteria[30] and in study designs. A recent review of evaluative research conducted at some of CUNY's colleges is similarly inconclusive:[31] some studies showed gains by remedial students, others showed no difference between them and nonremedial students, and still others showed the performance of the latter to be superior. In short, even though there is considerable prescriptive wisdom about the desirable features of a remedial program, there is no consensus in the research literature on the most effective components.

We compare the academic performance of those who took remediation and those who did not, controlling for differences in high school background and the level of need for remediation. The performance indices are the ones used in previous chapters: grade point average, credit accumulation, dropout and persistence, and graduation. Assessments of the relationship between remediation and academic performance are made at several points in students' careers: after the first year, the second year, and (in the case of senior colleges) after the fourth year. We shall also analyze the relation between remediation and cumulative academic performance. The significance of remediation varies for each of these time periods. It is important to look at the freshman year because many remedial courses (especially in two-year colleges) offered only partial credit or none at all, and possibly there was an initial cost to remedial students in the form of fewer credits earned. However, if remedial students were more likely to return to college for a second year, this might have partly offset any initial credit loss. Since the great majority of remedial students took these courses only in the first year, analyses of second-year performance provide an assessment of the short-run effects of remediation. An analysis of fourth-year academic performance of senior-college students provides an assessment of long-term effects. Finally, we consider the overall impact of remedial experience through an analysis of students' cumulative college records.

We have conducted our assessments by means of two basic regression analyses. Each includes the usual set of educational background measures as well as the academic skills variables (i.e., the reading and math scores from the CUNY Open-Admissions Test).

Our first analyses capitalize on the fact that the considerable slippage in CUNY's placement process created an approximation to a natural experiment: students who took remedial courses had peers of comparable academic skills and background who took none. In the aggregate, of course, there were still important differences in academic skills and high school background between takers of remediation and nontakers. But the fact that students at all levels of skill and background were found both among takers and nontakers indicates that, with suitable controls, differences between takers and nontakers in college performance may be interpreted as effects of remediation.

However, one feature of CUNY's remedial placement process works against this interpretation and suggests that it will provide an overly negative assessment of remediation. Our campus interviews indicated that early performance resulted in the reassignment of some freshmen both into and out of remedial courses. Such shifts moved unexpectedly successful students out of remediation courses and unexpectedly unsuccessful students into them. We cannot tell from our data how often that happened, though we think this was not a rare occurrence. Such moves confound a natural experiment. Moves into the remediation category selected students with a variety of characteristics, such as poor motivation, that were not clearly measured and hence not controllable but that predisposed them to academic failure. Moves out of the remedial category selected students with other characteristics that predisposed them to academic success. Both moves depressed the apparent academic success of remedial students relative to those who did not take remediation.

The students who were shifted cannot be directly identified in our data. The best we can do is to identify the students who did poorly in remedial courses—the approximately 15 percent who failed all of them[32]— and to presume that this group overlaps extensively with those students shifted into the remedial category. In a second set of analyses, we have separated these failing students from those who passed at least some of their remedial courses, ordering the latter group according to the number passed.[33] The academic performance of each group is compared with that of nonremedial students. In all probability, however, these second analyses yield an overly optimistic picture of remediation's impact since, in effect, we are removing the bottom 15 percent of the remedial group and comparing the remainder with the total group of nontakers. Thus, both our assessments of the effects of remediation must be regarded as tentative; the truth probably lies somewhere in between them.

Results for Senior Colleges

The analyses for senior colleges are presented in table 9.7. To summarize the findings more conveniently, we include only the values for the remediation variables.[34] For the total group of remedial students, the results tell a simple story: exposure to remediation did almost nothing to facilitate aca-

TABLE 9.7. Relationships between Remediation and Academic Outcomes through the Senior-College Career[a]

	Grade Point Average		Credits per Semester		Return Next Fall	
	1970	1971	1970	1971	1970	1971
First Year						
Took Remediation	.024	−.044*	−.055	−.526*	.026*	.006
Failed All Remedial Courses	−.717*	−1.191*	−4.852*	−6.453*	−.278*	−.399*
Number of Remedial Courses Passed	.057*	.059*	.379*	−.009	.048*	.043*
Second Year						
Took Remediation	−.102*	−.035	−.100	.302*	.015	.012
Failed All Remedial Courses	−.509*	−.488*	−2.756*	−3.300*	−.097*	−.175*
Number of Remedial Courses Passed	−.005	.004	.214*	.247*	.022*	.019*
Fourth Year[b]						
Took Remediation	−.140*	−.156*	−.127	.095	−.029*	
Failed All Remedial Courses	−.488*	−.469*	−1.972*	−2.795*	−.072*	
Number of Remedial Courses Passed	−.043*	−.052*	.155*	.175*	.009	

	Grade Point Average		Credits Earned		Graduation		Persistence	
	1970	1971	1970	1971	1970	1971	1970	1971
			Cumulative Indices[c]					
Took Remediation	-.049*	-.123*	4.373*	.286	-.023*	-.064*	.009	.009
Failed All Remedial Courses	-.595*	-.862*	-32.830*	-39.695*	-.189*	-.153*	-.201*	-.293*
Number of Remedial Courses Passed	.022*	.003	6.604*	3.197*	.012*	-.014*	.044*	.033*

Source: Population data.

[a] Values presented are unstandardized coefficients; those starred are significant at the .05 level or better.

[b] Since the files end with the spring 1975 semester, there are no return data in the fourth year indices for the 1971 cohort; for the 1970 cohort return includes those who returned for a fifth year or who graduated.

[c] For cumulative indices, the credits variable is the total number earned during the entire period the student was in school.

251

demic achievement. It is true that remediation does not appear to have cost students very much: in the freshman year, remedial students earned almost the same number of credits as comparable nonremedial students (probably because most remedial courses in senior colleges carried at least some credit). Also, remedial students were about 3 percent more likely to return for a second year of college (though in the 1971 cohort they were no more likely to return than were comparable nonremedial students). But after this first year there were no benefits favoring takers over nontakers. The remedial students were no more likely to stay in college than were comparable nonremedial students and overall they were slightly less likely to graduate. Exposure to remedial courses did not enhance the quality of subsequent academic work as measured by grade point average. Indeed, takers of remedial courses had slightly lower grades than did comparable nontakers: the differences was often equal to about a tenth of a letter grade.

While sheer exposure to remedial courses did nothing to enhance students' subsequent academic achievements, success or failure in these courses did make a difference. Among students who passed at least some of their remedial courses, there were certain positive effects. The major one concerned persistence in college. Each course a remedial student passed made him or her about 4 percent more likely than a comparable nonremedial student to return for a second year of college. Students who passed remedial courses were also slightly more likely to return for a third year, and overall (as shown by the cumulative record) they were, for each course passed, about 3–4 percent more likely to stay in school. Partly because they were more likely to stay in college, students who passed remedial courses earned more credits than did comparable nonremedial students. As shown by cumulative records, successful remedial students earned more than six additional credits for each compensatory course they passed (in 1971 their superiority was on the order of three credits for each course passed). In this way the remedial experience added slightly to educational attainment. More to the point, successful remedial students showed a greater likelihood of graduating after five years (shown by the 1970 cohort) than did comparable nonremedial students. But this superiority was slight: each course passed added about 1 percent to the probability of graduating. Moreover, remedial courses, even for those who passed them, appeared to delay the time of graduation: each course passed decreased the probability of graduating after four years (shown by the 1971 cohort) by about 1 percent.[35]

Though a successful remedial experience helped students to stay in school, it apparently did not enhance the quality of academic performance, as measured by grade point average. Though successful students earned slightly better grades in the freshman year, this slight superiority appears to have been mainly a result of the contribution that the remedial courses passed made to that average, for in the second year of college, after remediation had been largely completed, the grades of students who passed remedial courses were no different from those of nonremedial students. And in the fourth year nontakers actually earned slightly better grades. Of course, since students who did not take remediation were more likely to drop out than were comparable remedial students, the surviving nontakers formed a more select group than did the takers. Because of this possibility, positive effects of remediation on students' grades perhaps are obscured in our data.

Among students who were unsuccessful—that is, who failed all their remedial courses—the subsequent effect on their academic careers was disastrous. Relative to the grades of comparable students who took no remediation, their grades were sharply lower; they also were much more likely to drop out, earned far fewer credits, and, of course, were much less likely to graduate. We suspect that those who started poorly and were shifted into remedial classes comprised a substantial proportion of the students who failed all of their remedial courses. It is probable that these were high risk students, who, partly as a result of poor motivation, were very unlikely to succeed in college.

In summary, sheer exposure to remediation did not add to students' achievements in the senior colleges of CUNY, but success or failure in remedial courses did make some difference. The fate of those who were unable to pass these courses was a gloomy one. They fared very badly in their grades and compared to similar nonremedial students they were far more likely to drop out. As a result there was a gap of more than one year of higher educational attainment between them and comparable nonremedial students. Those who passed at least some of their remedial courses (and this includes the great majority of remedial students) were more likely to stay in school and thus to earn more credits, with a slightly better chance of graduating after five years. Nevertheless, these positive effects of the compensatory effort were very modest.

Results for Community Colleges

The relationships between remediation and academic performance in community colleges are presented in table 9.8.[36] For the total group of remedial students the overall picture, with one exception, mirrors that seen in the four-year colleges. The exception is that remedial students in the community colleges completed their initial year about three credits, or one course, behind comparable nonremedial students. This is a greater deficit than was found in the senior colleges, and it reflects the fact that remedial courses in community colleges were less likely to carry credit than were compensatory courses in the four-year institutions. Relative to comparable nontakers, remedial students were about 5 percent more likely to return to college for a second year. Beyond this greater likelihood of returning, there were no other visible benefits to remedial students in that second year or in

TABLE 9.8. Relationships between Remediation and Academic Outcomes through the Community-College Career[a]

	Grade Point Average		Credits per Semester		Return Next Fall[b]		Earned Associate Degree	
	1970	1971	1970	1971	1970	1971	1970	1971
			First Year					
Took Remediation	-.043	.016	-1.592*	-1.299*	.047*	.048*		
Failed All Remedial Courses	-.833*	-.930*	-5.285*	-5.212*	-.273*	-.299*		
Number of Remedial Courses Passed	.118*	.098*	-.434	-.516*	.086*	.074*		
			Second Year					
Took Remediation	-.104*	-.145*	-.676*	-.807*	.017	.016	-.049*	-.050*
Failed All Remedial Courses	-.447*	-.339*	-3.017*	-1.978*	-.129*	-.068*	-.148*	-.058
Number of Remedial Courses Passed	-.006	-.039*	-.083	-.278*	.028*	.031*	-.017*	-.018*

	Grade Point Average[c]		Credits Earned[c]		Earned Associate Degree		Earned Associate Degree or Transferred		Persistence[d]	
	1970	1971	1970	1971	1970	1971	1970	1971	1970	1971
			Cumulative Indices							
Took Remediation	-.142*	-.044	-.812	-.609	-.023	-.020	.002	-.012	.022	.024
Failed all Remedial Courses	-.645*	-.593*	-20.263*	-20.624*	-.156*	-.126*	-.154*	-.142*	-.162*	-.166*
Number of Remedial Courses Passed	-.003	.017	3.141*	2.003*	.009	.006	.027*	.017*	.043*	.046*

Source: Population data.

[a]Values presented are unstandardized coefficients; those starred are significant at the .05 level or better.

[b]Return includes enrollment in either a senior or a community college; second-year students who graduated are counted as returning.

[c]Cumulative grade point averages and cumulative credits were calculated only on that portion of students' records compiled in community college.

[d]Only students who dropped out of community colleges are defined as not persisting; those who transferred to senior colleges and then dropped out are defined as persisting.

their cumulative records. Their grade point averages were, in general, slightly lower (about a tenth of a letter below those of comparable nonremedial students), they were about 5 percent less likely to graduate after two years, and after four and even five years they were no more likely to have earned an associate degree or to have transferred to a senior college than otherwise comparable students who received no remediation.

Just as in the senior colleges, success or failure in remedial courses, rather than sheer exposure, made a difference. About 25 percent of the students who took such courses did not pass them.[37] These students met with academic disaster on every index of academic achievement. On the other hand, among students who passed at least some remedial courses,[38] there were visible benefits, generated largely by the fact that these students were more likely to persist in college than were comparable nonremedial students. Each remedial course they passed increased the probability that they would return for a second year by about 7–8 percent, relative to similar nontakers (the cost to takers in first-year credits was negligible). Though these successful remedial students were slightly less likely than were their nonremedial peers to graduate from community college after two years, they were more likely to persist in school after the second year and ultimately they were a bit more likely to graduate or to transfer to a senior college—each remedial course passed made them 2–3 percent more likely to graduate or to transfer than comparable nontakers. However, this higher probability of graduation or transfer was not accompanied by a superiority in grade point average. While these students who met with some success in remediation earned higher averages in the freshman year than did comparable nontakers, their second-year grades were no different from those of nontakers (in 1971 they were slightly lower) and their cumulative averages were the same.

To summarize, these community-college results were generally similar to those found in the senior colleges. Sheer exposure to remediation did not add to academic success, but students who passed at least some remedial courses were more likely to stay in college and to graduate or move on to a four-year school. While these are important results, the size of the differences must be counted as quite small.

Other Aspects of the CUNY Effort

We have evaluated several other important aspects of CUNY's compensatory effort. These evaluations addressed the following questions: (1) were the effects of remediation greater in some areas (for example, writing) than in others? (2) did it make a difference whether remedial courses carried credit? (3) was the academic impact of remediation greater for students who thought they needed help than for students who did not think they needed it? (4) were students who needed intensive remediation helped as much as students who needed only a moderate amount of help? (5) were students of some ethnic groups helped more than the members of other ethnic groups? and (6) did the remedial effort of some CUNY colleges have more impact than the efforts of others?

These further assessments add very little to our understanding of the effects of remediation identified in the preceding sections. To begin with, there were no unique effects attributable to the specific area in which remediation was received. That is, the conclusions of our basic analyses of remedial impact are not changed by examining separately remedial experiences in writing, reading, and math.

In analyzing the effects of credit for remedial courses, we distinguished three groups of students: (1) those whose remedial courses carried no credit; (2) those who took a mixture of credit and noncredit courses; and (3) those who took all of their compensatory courses for credit. For senior colleges the results of these analyses may be stated simply: the credit status of remedial courses was unrelated to subsequent academic outcomes. In community colleges, the evidence is inconsistent. In the 1970 cohort credit made no difference, but in the 1971 cohort credit-bearing remedial courses seemed to increase the likelihood of persistence and graduation. The credit issue has been a controversial one at CUNY; our findings do not provide a sound basis for its resolution.

We had thought that student perceptions about their need for help might be an important factor determining the outcomes of remediation. In the senior colleges we found a few effects in the writing area: those who felt they needed help were more likely to perform better later on in college, but these effects were very modest and inconsistent. All in all, remedial students' attitudes about receiving help had little effect upon their subsequent academic performance.

To assess whether students with different levels of need for help were affected differently by the remedial experience, we compared two groups of students who differed greatly in their academic preparedness: students who needed intensive remediation in all skills areas and those who needed only some help in one remedial area.[39] We found no evidence that students at one level of need were helped more than those at another level of need.

Minority students entered CUNY more often weakly prepared than white students, and as a result they were more likely to take remedial courses. However, we uncovered no evidence that students of one ethnic background were either helped or hindered by the remedial experience more than were students of any other ethnic background. Inasmuch as minority students were academically more needy than other students, the fact that the remedial experience yielded only modest benefits obviously hampered these students in their academic efforts at CUNY.

Our field interviews at every CUNY campus revealed substantive differences in the style with which each college responded to the challenge of open admissions. We had thought that the diversity of approaches to compensatory education would be reflected in a diversity of student outcomes. But in our analyses, no college or set of colleges emerged as having a distinctive effect upon students' academic careers.[40] That is, at no college did the outcomes of remediation seem to depart much from the aggregate results in senior and community colleges that we reported earlier in the chapter.

Conclusion

CUNY's compensatory education programs were intended as a mechanism for translating educational access into educational results. Though the majority of open-admissions students were underprepared in at least some ways, the need for these support services was not entirely a result of the open-admissions policy. Among students who would have been admitted even without this policy, many entered with skills deficiencies. There were marked differences among ethnic groups in academic preparation. While the need for remediation was visible in every group, the educational disadvantage of minority students was particularly acute. In senior colleges almost 80 percent needed at least some remedial help, compared with 40 percent or less among whites. In community colleges heavy proportions of every group needed at least some help, but minorities were far more likely to be seriously underprepared than were whites. Even when their academic skills were similar to those of whites, minority students had less confidence in their abilities. Because of their weaker high school backgrounds, academic skills, and confidence, minority students were much more likely to be placed in remedial courses. For example, in the senior colleges blacks typically were 25–30 percent more likely than Catholic and Jewish students to be placed in remedial writing and reading; Hispanics were about 15–20 percent more likely. In community colleges blacks typically were 20–30 percent more likely to take remedial courses than were Catholic ethnics, while Hispanics typically were 25–35 percent more likely.[41] As we noted in chapter 5, there was a widespread perception of open admissions as a minority program. The disproportionate representation of minority students in CUNY's remedial programs undoubtedly served to reinforce that perception.

CUNY's remedial efforts did provide some boost to students' academic careers. Senior-college students whose efforts in remedial courses met with at least some success were, relative to comparable students who received no help, more likely to stay in school and more likely to graduate after five years. And in community colleges students who passed remedial courses were more likely to graduate or to transfer to a four-year college. Nonetheless, these benefits were very modest.[42] A student who needed remedial work but did not receive it was penalized only slightly as a result. This small yield of the remedial effort in the early years of open admissions had disproportionate consequences for minority students. Because they were more likely both to need help and to receive it, remediation's modest effects did not do a great deal to compensate for past educational disadvantages and thus to close the large initial gap in academic skills that separated minority and white students.

If the CUNY remedial programs yielded only small benefits, what conclusions follow? Does it follow that such modest results cannot justify the effort and expense and that remediation should be abandoned? We do not think this necessarily follows. Our analyses cover only the first two classes entering under open admissions, and the early years of CUNY's compensatory effort may not have been a true test of its impact for subsequent classes. Administrative inefficiencies, the sheer magnitude of the task, and the absence of experience in the compensatory education of young adults undoubtedly affected the initial results documented in this chapter.

Moreover, an important limitation of our research may have obscured some of the benefits of remediation. It is quite possible that a small number of faculty were highly effective in helping students to improve their academic skills. Certainly, some students showed clear progress. Examples cited by Shaughnessy[43] illustrate students' improvement in basic writing courses. Here are two essays by the same student on the subject of childhood, the first written at the beginning of the semester, the second at the end of the term:

> Harlem taught me that light skin Black people was better look, the best to suceed, the best off fanically etc this whole that I trying to say, that I was brainwashed and people aliked.
>   I couldn't understand why people (Black and white) couldn't get alone. So as time went along I began learned more about myself and the establishment.

> In the midst of this decay there are children between the ages of five and ten playing with plenty of vitality. As they toss the football around, their bodies full of energy, their clothes look like rainbows. The colors mix together and one is given the impression of being in a psychadelic dream, beautiful, active, and alive with unity. They yell to eachother increasing their morale. They have the sound of an organized alto section. At the sidelines are the girls who are shy, with the shyness that belongs to the very young. They are embarrased when their dresses are raised by the wind. As their feet rise above the pavement, they cheer for their boyfriends. In the midst of the decay, children will continue to play.[44]

Another student wrote, at the beginning of a semester, the following essay about reading and writing skills (quoted in part):

> Adults and children are not reading and writing to their levels. The problems people not reading and writing lies on the instructor and his ability. I been to schools that doesn't have the equipments for teaching.[45]

At the end of the semester the same student wrote an essay on the topic of college and immaturity, a part of which follows:

> While I'am in college I work part time. Not including the enormous responsibilities at home that I try hard to forget about while in school. I have the cooking, cleaning and shopping to do at home. Also I have homework and studying to do. When a person has responsibilities and knows how to cope with them he is apt to be mature.[46]

The first sample displays truly extraordinary change; the second shows clear progress. If such instances (resulting no doubt from the efforts of a few unusual teachers) were not rare, neither were they the rule, for if they were they should have found expression in the academic records assessed in our statistical analyses. That the efforts of a few superb teachers greatly enhanced the academic careers of some students is a possibility we were unable to explore systematically. But it is clearly one that CUNY should address in future research. To identify unusually effective instructors carries the potential for transmitting their teaching methods to others.

Notes

1. These rates are based upon the proportion of any cohort entering the fifth grade that graduates from high school. See U.S. Bureau of the Census, *Statistical Abstract of the United States, 1976* (Washington: U.S. Government Printing Office), p. 140.
2. Calculated from *Statistical Abstract, 1976*, p. 140.
3. *Statistical Abstract, 1976*, p. 141.
4. K. Patricia Cross, *Beyond the Open Door* (San Francisco: Jossey-Bass, 1972), p. 15.
5. K. Patricia Cross, *Accent on Learning* (San Francisco: Jossey-Bass, 1976), p. 24.
6. John E. Roueche and Jerry J. Snow, *Overcoming Learning Problems* (San Francisco: Jossey-Bass, 1977), p. 19.
7. Roueche and Snow, pp. 5, 43–46.
8. That this appears to be a national phenomenon occurring even in selective colleges is noted in "Bonehead English," *Chronicle of Higher Education*, March 17, 1975, p. 3. The broad decline in skills has been much discussed in connection with declining SAT scores. See College Entrance Examination Board, *On Further Examination: Report of the Advisory Panel on the Scholastic Aptitude Test Score Decline* (New York: College Entrance Examination Board, 1977).
9. The terms "remedial," "compensatory," and "developmental," are frequently used in the nation's colleges for programs designed to help underprepared students. While these terms sometimes reflect differences in underlying goals or philosophy, more often than not "compensatory" and "developmental" are euphemisms for "remedial"; the latter is sometimes thought of as stigmatizing to students. This issue is noted by Cross, *Accent on Learning*, pp.

24–45, and Roueche and Snow, pp. 6–14. In this chapter we use the terms "re-medial" and "compensatory" interchangeably.

10. For detailed descriptions of the support services on each CUNY campus see David E. Lavin, *From Selective to Free Access Higher Education: Institutional Responses to Open Admissions at the City University of New York* (New York: City University of New York, 1976) (ERIC ED 129 158).

11. Writing samples were evaluated using several criteria, including spelling, punctuation, subject-verb agreement, and skill in organizing and developing ideas. Sometimes these writing samples were judged holistically; that is, readers evaluated them, keeping in mind criteria such as those noted above and making a summary judgment about the quality of the essay. In other cases the criteria were used to generate quantified scores of writing quality.

12. For students whose primary language was not English, many colleges offered special courses in English as a second language. These were designed to help the student acquire greater facility in written and spoken English.

13. One interesting example occurred in Kingsborough Community College's mathematics department. In one course lectures were presented live, but they had also been previously videotaped. The videotapes were stored in a study laboratory, where they could be viewed and reviewed by students in an effort to facilitate their understanding. Quizzes covering the content of each videotaped lecture were available in the lab. They could be taken and immediately scored by tutors so as to provide feedback on the student's understanding of the concepts and problems presented in the lecture.

14. It was a working assumption that many students entering under open admissions did not bring with them the social skills that are part of the the repertoire of traditional students. The aim of counseling was to provide a better "cognitive map" of the college system. This would include information on how to deal with red tape in registrar's offices, how to deal more effectively with professors, and the like.

15. The actual instruments used were selected from the Stanford achievement test battery. The reading test was the *High School Reading Test, Form W* (New York: Harcourt, 1965). The test of numerical competence was the arithmetic computation section of the *Advanced Arithmetic Tests, Form X* (New York: Harcourt, 1964). The 1972 freshmen are not included in the analyses of this chapter, since CUNY did not administer a University-wide test battery in that year.

16. An analysis of the initial testing and a discussion of the cutoff points defining the need for remediation were presented by Patricia Kay, *Open Admissions Reading and Mathematics Tests: May 1970 General Results, Score Distributions, and Comparisons with National Norms* (New York: Division of Teacher Education, City University of New York, June 1970).

17. More precisely, students were defined as needing intensive remediation if their scores placed them at or below the bottom 30 percent of ninth-grade students. Students whose scores placed them in the bottom 30 percent of college preparatory high school seniors were defined as needing some remediation.

18. Throughout this chapter our analyses include only those who took the Open-Admissions Test. In 1970, 21,776 entering students took this test (75 percent of the students in our population for the 1970 cohort). Among the 1971 en-

trants, 18,743 students took the test (representing 60 percent of that class). The takers were a slightly more able group than the nontakers. For example, in 1970 the mean high school average of senior-college entrants who also took the test was 82.1, while the average for nontakers was 79.1. In community colleges the average of the takers was 73.1, while that of the nontakers was 71.7. Therefore, it is probable that our analyses slightly underestimate the proportions of students who needed remedial work.

19. Of course, most CUNY campuses did assess writing skills directly, by either writing samples or a variety of standardized tests of English usage. However, these results are not included in our data.

20. This was pointed out to us by Professor Max Weiner, Ph.D. program in educational psychology, City University Graduate School.

21. When we speak of self-reports of the need for help in writing, it should be noted that the actual question asked of students was whether they thought they needed help in English. Inasmuch as remedial courses in English were overwhelmingly writing courses, we refer to this item as indicating a recognized need for help in writing.

22. For these analyses we use our samples. As with the total population, those in our samples who took the Open-Admissions Test were a slightly stronger group academically than those who did not take it.

23. For each cohort and for senior and community colleges, we conducted three regression analyses. Student self-reports about the need for help in reading, writing, and math (scored as dummy variables where 1 signified that the student thought he or she needed help and 0 signified no reported need for help) were regressed upon measures of high school background, the appropriate score (in reading or math) from the Open-Admissions Test, and ethnicity. The complete set of results is not presented here.

24. For example, within the CUNY population the reading test correlated at .80 with the verbal section of the Scholastic Aptitude Test, while the math test correlated at .69 with the quantitative section of the SAT.

25. Student remedial experiences were part of our academic performance file. For each student the file contains a list of each remedial course taken, the type of course (whether it was in writing, reading and study skills, math, etc.), whether the course carried credit, whether the student passed the course, and the semester in which the course was taken. Definitions of what constituted a remedial course were based upon three sources: (1) college catalogues; (2) information obtained from registrars; and (3) detailed interviews on every CUNY campus with administrators and key faculty in departments offering remedial work. Notwithstanding these efforts, there are some inadequacies in the remedial files. At two colleges a major proportion of the remedial courses were offered as special sections of regular courses. Since our student data files do not contain information about sections of courses, we cannot identify this type of remedial experience. These campuses have been removed from our analyses. In other cases courses identified as remedial from our faculty interviews or from other sources did not appear in any identifiable form in the computer lists of courses taken. However, this occurred for only a small number of courses. Overall, among the colleges included in these analyses, we were able to identify more than 90 percent of the remedial courses offered at CUNY.

26. At Borough of Manhattan Community College, remedial courses were not offered over the period we examined. In order to assess the relationship between need for remediation and its delivery, we restricted the analysis to colleges that offered remediation. Borough of Manhattan was removed from this analysis.

27. Roueche and Snow, p. 8.

28. Roueche and Snow, p. 9.

29. A summary of these evaluation efforts is presented in Cross, *Accent on Learning*, pp. 36–45.

30. Success has been measured by performance on a posttest version of a standardized test following completion of a remedial course, by grade point averages in regular college courses, and/or by rates of college completion.

31. Judith Piesco, *Research on Remedial Programs at City University of New York: A Review of Evaluative Studies* (New York: Office of Institutional Research, City University of New York, 1978).

32. The great majority of those who failed all of their remedial courses took only one or two. In senior colleges 91 percent in 1970 and 83 percent in 1971 took no more than two.

33. Among students who passed remedial courses, the great majority (over 80 percent in 1970 and about 70 percent in 1971) passed one or two. Overall, students passed most of the remedial courses they took. In 1971, for example, 76 percent of the students who took four remedial courses passed at least three of them.

34. The values presented are the unstandardized coefficients. The variable "took remediation" is a dummy variable, with those who took remediation scored as 1 and those who did not scored as 0. The variable "failed all remedial courses" is also scored as a dummy variable, with failers scored as 1 and others scored as 0. For the variable "number of remedial courses passed," the tabled value is the increment in the academic outcome resulting from passing one remedial course. Our analyses (not presented in table 9.7) showed that the relationship of the number of remedial courses taken to academic outcomes is linear. High school background and Open-Admissions Test scores are excluded from the presentation.

   It should also be noted that three of the senior colleges have been removed from these analyses. Brooklyn and John Jay were removed because they offered a substantial amount of remediation through special sections of regular academic courses. Since we cannot separate courses by sections, we cannot identify the remedial students. Medgar Evers has also been removed since it viewed most of its freshman courses as compensatory. In effect, there were no nontakers of remediation at Medgar Evers.

35. That remedial students were slightly less likely to graduate after four years than comparable nonremedial students does not appear as a function of earning fewer credits over that period. We suspect that remediation possibly had a long-term effect of delaying the completion of distributional requirements.

36. Three community colleges, Hostos, LaGuardia and Manhattan, are removed from these analyses. Hostos had a nontraditional grading system and its student data file did not list many of the courses we had identified as remedial. LaGuardia also had a nontraditional grading system, as well as a unique academic calendar, which did not fit with those followed by other colleges. Manhattan Community College is removed since it offered no remedial courses.

37. Of the community-college students who failed all of their remedial courses, 80 percent in 1970 and 88 percent in 1971 took only one or two such courses.

38. Among community-college students who passed remedial courses, close to 90 percent passed one or two. Overall, students passed at least half of the remedial courses they took.

39. Those who needed some, but not intensive help in more than one remedial area were not included in the analyses.

40. These college effects were assessed by adding college-remediation interaction terms to regression equations containing high school background, Open-Admissions Test scores, remediation variables, and college dummy variables.

41. In the community colleges Catholics were usually less likely to be placed in remedial courses than were Jewish students. Differences between Jews and minority students in the likelihood of taking remedial work were smaller than differences between minorities and Catholics. Nonetheless, Jews were always less likely than minorities to be placed in these courses.

42. Students' cognitive skills increased after one year of college. The open-admissions reading and math tests were administered in a posttest form to some CUNY students. Both open-admissions and regular students improved their scores. After one year the average scores of open-admissions students were about equal to the scores of regular students upon entry to CUNY. While these are important changes, they cannot be interpreted as effects of remediation. For further discussion see Jack E. Rossman, Helen S. Astin, Alexander W. Astin, and Elaine H. El-Khawas, *Open Admissions at City University of New York: An Analysis of the First Year* (Englewood Cliffs: Prentice-Hall, 1975), pp. 50–56.

43. Mina P. Shaughnessy, *Errors and Expectations* (New York: Oxford University Press, 1977).

44. Shaughnessy, p. 278.

45. Shaughnessy, p. 279.

46. Shaughnessy, p. 279.

10. The Success of Open Admissions: Conclusions

THE CUNY OPEN-ADMISSIONS policy represents one of American higher education's most ambitious efforts to provide equality of educational opportunity. In large measure the policy was adopted in response to the demands of educationally disenfranchised ethnic groups, but it did not arise in response to those pressures alone. The University recognized, as did many among the liberal and socially conscious elites in New York City, that grave proportions of the minority groups that had migrated to the city during the postwar period lacked the training to become economically mobile in a changing labor market that increasingly demanded higher levels of skills and educational credentials. Blacks and Hispanics were far more likely to earn low incomes, to hold low-status jobs, and to have limited educations in comparison to members of the city's white groups. Of even greater direct concern to policymaking elites were the higher rates of unemployment of minority group members and their representation on the welfare rolls far in excess of their proportion in the city's population.

A university is not as inappropriate a place as it first may seem to create new opportunities for such disadvantaged groups. A substantial body of social science evidence points to higher education as providing fundamental leverage for social and economic mobility. In one of the most recent studies, Jencks and his colleagues have demonstrated that each year invested in higher education brings considerably greater socioeconomic benefits than each year invested in primary and secondary education. They conclude, in effect, that the principal value of high school graduation is to create eligibility for college entry.[1] The socioeconomic leverage provided by higher edu-

265

cation is potent for the members of all groups but, as Jencks and his co-authors document, its benefits are even greater for minority groups than for whites.[2] The opportunities provided by higher education have led some scholars to implicate it in the widening class disparities within the black community and especially in the increasing size and importance of the black middle class. For example, Wilson notes:

> Access to the means of production is increasingly based on educational criteria . . . and thus threatens to solidify the position of the black underclass. In other words, a consequence of the rapid growth of the corporate and government sectors has been the gradual creation of a segmented labor market that currently provides vastly different mobility opportunities for different segments of the black population. On the one hand, poorly trained and educationally limited blacks of the inner city, including that growing number of black teenagers and young adults, see their job prospects increasingly restricted to the low-wage sector, their unemployment rates soaring to record levels . . . their labor force participation rates declining, their movement out of poverty slowing, and their welfare [representation] increasing. On the other hand, talented and educated blacks are experiencing unprecedented job opportunities in the growing government and corporate sectors, opportunities which are at least comparable to those of whites with equivalent qualifications.[3]

These statements indicate the considerable potential of the open-admissions policy as a social intervention on behalf of economically and educationally disadvantaged minority groups. Enough time has now passed so that we can begin addressing the basic question concerning the policy and its consequences: has open admissions worked? It does well to recognize at the outset that there are different levels at which such a question may be answered. On the one hand, an answer may be given in terms of opportunities for individuals from minority groups, i.e., the number who attended college and received degrees as a result of the policy. In this approach, the fact that open admissions provided opportunities also for whites is of less concern since the policy focused in a major way upon minorities. On the other hand, the question may be answered by the extent to which the program brought about greater equality of educational opportunity among different ethnic groups. In so doing, it is necessary to take into account its effect on white groups; we ultimately wish to know whether open admissions affected the relative positions of the major ethnic groups in the city.

Minority Experiences in New York City's Primary and Secondary Schools

We begin with a review of the minority experiences in New York City's schools, which serve as a backdrop to the open-admissions experiment. These experiences help to make intelligible the ethnic patterns revealed in previous chapters and to give shape to an overall interpretation of open admissions.

From the beginning of their schooling, minority students are subject to a series of cumulating educational disadvantages rooted in the economic positions of their families and in their minority status. They enter school to find themselves already behind many whites in the development of academic skills and leave frequently even further behind than when they entered.[4] The initial disadvantages they bring from their families and communities develop in interaction with teacher stereotypes and expectations and with the organization of schools. The lower levels of school performance by minority students confirm teacher stereotypes and lead to lower teacher expectations, which further inhibit school performance. Their status as low achievers is certified by objective tests, which cause them to be placed in slower tracks in primary school.[5] By the time they reach high school, minority students are far more likely to be tracked into nonacademic programs, which hinder their academic preparation and add new burdens to their self-images as poor students.

Some data for the high school class that graduated in 1970, whose members constituted the first group to enter under open admissions, give a good sense of ethnic disparities in educational experience.[6] For example, of those who were present in this group's junior year in high school, 27 percent of Puerto Ricans, 16 percent of blacks, but only 7 percent of whites were found in vocational high schools.[7] And these figures do not describe all the ethnic differences in track placement since there are track variations within nominally academic high schools. Even within academic high schools, minority students are more likely to be placed in non–college preparatory and academically slower tracks.

The difficulties minority students face in graduating from high school are perhaps the most revealing of ethnic disparities in educational experience. Minority students are much more likely to drop out of high school as a result of tracking, low achievement, and the poor academic self-images engendered by their school experiences. Astonishingly, this is true even for those students who survive into the junior year in an academic high school. Again using the junior year of the class that graduated high school in 1970 as an example, 34 percent of blacks and 38 percent of Hispanics in academic public high schools were not found in the senior class a year later.[8] Some had dropped out; others were left back. In sharp contrast, the attrition rate of whites was only 18 percent. If these minority attrition rates between junior and senior years seem high, estimated ethnic differences in rates of graduation on the part of these juniors are even more striking: only 49 percent of black juniors and 40 percent of Hispanic juniors are estimated to have graduated by the spring of the following year, compared with 73 percent of whites.[9] Others eventually graduated, of course, but undoubtedly the late graduates were less likely to go on to college. Overall, minority students are substantially underrepresented among high school graduates. Their lower rates of school completion are clearly shown by comparing their proportions in the high school–age population of New York City with their proportions graduating from high school. In 1970, for example, blacks comprised 25 percent of the city's high school-age population but only 16 percent of high school graduates; Puerto Ricans were 13 percent of the high school age population but only 8 percent of graduates. In contrast, whites constituted 59 percent of the population but 74 percent of the graduates.[10]

Not only do events occurring in the primary and secondary schools of New York City disproportionately reduce the pool of minority students eligible to enroll in college, but eligible minority students are less likely than eligible whites actually to enroll. Of all city high school graduates in 1970, about two-thirds of minority graduates were enrolled in college the following fall, compared with 78 percent of whites. While this difference is smaller than racial differences in college enrollment nationally[11] (a fact that testifies to the effects of open admissions), it adds to the overall gap in educational attainment between white and minority groups in New York City.

This view of minority students' careers suggests that relative to the size of the minority cohort entering elementary school, those who reach college are, statistically at least, an educational elite. In New York City, the great majority of this group who make it into college—about 70 percent in 1970, for example—attend CUNY.[12] Thus, an examination of CUNY provides a good sense of the overall college-going of the city's minority population as well as a reasonable estimate of the impact of the open-admissions policy on the number of college educated minority men and women. By examining the numbers who entered and graduated from CUNY, we can gain a sense of the benefit of open admissions for minority individuals and of the extent to which the program helped to improve the situation of minority groups vis-à-vis others.

An Overview of Open Admissions and Its Results

To give an overview of the detailed patterns explored in previous chapters, we will follow the class that graduated high school in 1970 through to its graduation from CUNY. The students who entered CUNY from this class formed the 1970 cohort, described at length in earlier parts of the book. These students are a particularly opportune group to follow because we measured their academic progress at CUNY for the longest period of time, five years.

To convey readily the relative sizes of different groups of students, we shall imagine this class as having one thousand students. Our analysis considers how many of these one thousand were from each ethnic group, how many were open-admissions and regular students, how many were placed at senior and community colleges, and how many received degrees. We remind the reader that the 1970 cohort actually contained over thirty-five thousand students, up 75 percent from the size of the entering freshman class the year

before (see table 4.3). Over thirty-one thousand of these students were admitted outside the special programs, SEEK and College Discovery; it is
these students that our data and our proportions of one thousand represent.
We will comment later on the extent to which our estimates are affected by
omission of special program students.

Table 10.1 provides a summary of who came in 1970 and who among
them had graduated by spring 1975.[13] In this first class to be admitted after
open admissions began, 378 of every thousand entrants were Catholic ethnics, 314 were Jewish, 93 were black, and 84 were Hispanic (the remaining
131 not shown in the table were other whites and other nonwhites, but mostly the former). As we described in chapter 4, open admissions added appre-

TABLE 10.1. Number of Entrants and Graduates from Each Ethnic Group for
Every 1,000 Entrants, by Admissions Status and College Level[a]

	Senior Colleges			Community Colleges			Total CUNY	
	Regu-lar	Open	Total Senior	Regu-lar	Open	Total Com-munity		% of Gradu-ates[b]
Number per 1,000 Entrants								
Jewish	173	64	237	23	54	77	314	
Catholic	122	68	190	89	99	188	378	
Black	8	27	35	17	41	58	93	
Hispanic	19	20	39	20	25	45	84	
Graduated Any Level								
Jewish	99	24	123	10	15	25	148	38
Catholic	60	19	79	42	25	67	146	37
Black	3.7	6	10	6	8	14	24	6
Hispanic	6	3.8	10	7	5	12	22	6
Graduated Senior								
Jewish	99	23	122	4.0	5	9	131	45
Catholic	58	19	77	11	6	17	94	33
Black	3.7	6	10	0.8	1.7	2.5	12	4
Hispanic	6	3.7	10	1.7	0.7	2.4	12	4
Graduated Senior with B Average								
Jewish	60	5	65	1.2	0.7	1.9	67	52
Catholic	29	4.0	33	5	1.0	6	39	30
Black	1.1	0.8	1.9	0.4	0.2	0.6	2.5	2
Hispanic	2.7	0.8	3.5	0.7	0.0	0.7	4.2	3

Source: Sample data.
[a]Only students admitted outside the special programs are considered, and estimates from
samples have been weighted to correct for overrepresentation of senior-college students
(see appendix A). One decimal place is reported for each number under five.
[b]Percentages do not add to 100 percent because other white and other nonwhite graduates
are not shown in the total number of graduates.

ciably to the size of each group and proportionately more to the minority groups, but the majority of open-admissions students were whites. Nearly 120 of the Jewish students and nearly 170 of the Catholic students were admitted under the new criteria; these open-admissions students accounted for less than half of CUNY students from their groups, however. By contrast, the numbers of open-admissions students from the minority groups were much smaller: fewer than seventy were black and fewer than fifty were Hispanic. But these students accounted for considerably more than half of those from their groups who entered the University.

The table also displays the unequal distribution of white and minority students between the community and the senior colleges, discussed at some length in chapter 4. As it shows clearly, black and Hispanic students in the senior colleges were outnumbered by those in the community colleges. This was not true for the white groups. Jewish students in the senior colleges far outnumbered those in the community colleges; the numbers of Catholic students were nearly equal at the two levels.

In analyzing how well these students did, we have distinguished three different outcomes in terms of the credentials students receive and the life chances generally associated with them. These outcomes do not exhaust all benefits derived from college education since considerable research has shown that occupational and income benefits stem from partial exposure; that is, they accrue even when no degree is received.[14] It should also be remembered from chapter 6 that some students remained in school for more than five years, still pursuing a degree. These students are not counted in our outcome totals. Five years is nonetheless a reasonable period from which to gain a sense of the opportunities afforded by open admissions.

The most basic question that may be asked of the open-admissions policy in terms of its outcomes is this: how successful were students in acquiring educational credentials of any kind? The answer to this question is given by the number of students who received any degree, whether the associate or the bachelor's. Because many students would not have been able to attend college were it not for open admissions, this outcome is the most fundamental measure of the policy's success. A second outcome concerns the attainment of the baccalaureate degree; students who earned this credential stood to benefit from the advantages implied by the completion of four years of college. A third outcome refers to students who, having done well, stood poised to move still further in the educational system. These were students with baccalaureate degrees whose academic performance was of sufficiently high quality (at least a B average) to indicate a reasonable possibility of entering graduate study or professional training. (We do not, however, have any information about the number of students who proceeded to graduate training.)

In gaining an impression of how groups fared within CUNY, we begin by considering all CUNY entrants without regard for level of entry or admissions status. Especially in evaluating the extent to which open admissions brought about greater equality of educational opportunity, it seems inappropriate to take admissions status and level of entry into account. The program was intended, after all, to bring about greater equality even though groups differed considerably in prior educational experiences and preparation for college.

The table makes clear, when looked at in a variety of ways, the advantages that fell to white groups even under an open-admissions system. White graduates far outnumbered minority graduates—there were six Jewish and Catholic graduates for every black or Hispanic graduate, in fact. Even more to the point are the ethnic disparities in the proportions of entrants who ultimately graduated. Close to half the Jewish students who entered and nearly 40 percent of Catholics received a degree of some kind. By contrast, only a quarter of blacks and Hispanics did. When we consider the numbers who graduated with senior-college credentials, then ethnic disparities reach dramatic levels. White ethnic students receiving baccalaureates exceeded minority students receiving them by a ratio of nine to one. White ethnic students attaining baccalaureates with a B average exceeded minority students in this respect by a ratio of fifteen to one. Over 40 percent of Jewish entrants and nearly a quarter of Catholic entrants graduated with a baccalaureate; only 13 percent of black entrants and 14 percent of Hispanic entrants did so. Over 20 percent of Jewish entrants and over 10 percent of Catholic entrants graduated with a baccalaureate and a B average. Only 3 percent of black entrants and 5 percent of Hispanic entrants did so.

Even among open-admissions students, there were disparities in the proportions receiving credentials. A third of Jewish open-admissions students and a quarter of Catholics received a degree of some kind, compared with a fifth of blacks and Hispanics. Differences are evident also in the proportions earning bachelor's degrees: about 25 percent of Jewish students, 15 percent of Catholics, and 10 percent of minority open-admissions students earned the degree. Only small percentages (5 percent or less) of any group earned a senior-college degree with a B average, but differences still favored the white groups. These differences result partly from the fact that white open-admissions students were more likely to begin in a senior college, but disparities remain even when groups at the same level of college are compared.

Nonetheless, the program was of major significance for minority groups. Open admissions substantially boosted the number of graduates from every group, but its contributions were critical to the proportion of black and Hispanic graduates. Black open-admissions graduates outnumbered black regular graduates, so that the program more than doubled the number of black students who received a degree of some kind and more than doubled as well the number of black baccalaureates. It nearly doubled the number of black students placed on the threshold of graduate or professional school. The policy's impact on the number of Hispanic graduates was not quite as large, but open admissions still increased the numbers of Hispanic graduates from any level and of Hispanic baccalaureates by about two-thirds.

So far we have not focused on minority students in the special programs. While these students were not direct beneficiaries of open admissions as a distinct policy, the special programs were important channels of minority access to the University and therefore must be considered in any assessment of CUNY's significance for minority groups. As we described in chapter 4, the overwhelming majority of students in these programs during the period under consideration were black or Hispanic, but they are not present in our samples and hence we cannot identify the precise proportions of either group among SEEK and College Discovery students. In order to gain some sense of the total number of minority graduates of the University, with special program students included, we must discuss the minority groups without distinguishing between blacks and Hispanics.[15] Therefore we have recomputed the numbers of minority graduates to include special program students, as shown in table 10.2, which also includes the numbers of white ethnic graduates for purposes of comparison.[16]

Essentially, the table shows again the great superiority of the white ethnic groups in numbers of graduates, but of course this superiority is reduced somewhat from that in table 10.1. For every black or Hispanic graduate of the University, there were four Jewish and Catholic graduates (in contrast to the ratio of one to six derived from table 10.1). Among the graduates from senior colleges, the numerical superiority of the white groups is still much greater and, to take the most extreme case, there were over ten Jewish and Catholic graduates whose records seemed to qualify them for entry to graduate school for every one such minority graduate, even with special program students included. To appreciate the significance of these ratios, it

TABLE 10.2. **Number of Graduates in the 1970 Cohort from White Ethnic and Minority Groups, with and without Special Program Students[a]**

		MINORITY	
	WHITE[b]	Without Special Program Students[b]	With Special Program Students[c]
Graduated any level with any average	294	46	66
Graduated senior college with any average	225	24	38
Graduated senior college with B average	106	7	10

Source: Sample and population data.
[a]Based on one thousand as the number of students outside special programs.
[b]The numbers in these columns were derived directly from table 10.1.
[c]Graduation rates of special program students are taken from the population data.

helps to recall that minorities constituted nearly 40 percent of the college-age group in the city's population[17] and that whites constituted just under 60 percent (moreover, our analysis has focused on Jews and Catholics, just a part of the white group). By this reckoning, any ratio of white to minority graduates greater than 1.5 to 1 clearly indicates an underrepresentation of minority group members.

What stands out in this analysis of the first class to enter the University under the open-admissions policy is the small number of minority graduates in comparison to white graduates. To a considerable extent this finding results from the small pool of minority students eligible to go to college and from their less advantageous initial positioning within CUNY—both of which are consequences of events in primary and secondary schools. But an analysis of this class alone is not an adequate measure of the magnitude of open admissions' impact. As we demonstrated in chapter 4, the number of minority students entering the University rose dramatically during the first six years of the policy. Just as important, minority distribution between senior and community colleges became more equal over this period—a significant fact not only because of the greater life chances associated with the baccalaureate but also because graduation rates are higher and dropout rates lower in the four-year schools (see chapter 6). Thus, both of these trends can be expected to have led to further growth in the number of minority graduates in each succeeding cohort.

We face some difficulties in discussing with any precision the numbers of minority graduates in later cohorts: we lack data about these cohorts equivalent to the data we analyzed for the 1970 group. While we know the approximate numbers of minority students who entered the University in 1973–1975, when minority representation grew to over 40 percent of each entering class, and know how these minority students were distributed between the community and the senior colleges, we do not know anything else about them. We do not know their high school averages and how many of them were open-admissions students. We do not know how many of them have graduated, and in fact some of them are still in school working toward a degree at the time of writing this chapter.

What we have chosen to do is to make some rough estimates of the numbers of minority and white students in the 1975 cohort who may have graduated by spring 1980, five years after they entered the University. This cohort is distinguished by the facts that it contained the highest proportion of minority students and had a distribution of minority students between community and senior colleges most nearly equal to that of white students. To make these estimates, we have taken the proportions of graduates from different ethnic groups in the 1970 cohort, by level of entry, and applied them to the numbers of minority and white students who entered the community and senior colleges in 1975.

We concede that these estimates are crude, however, and overly optimistic. As we will describe in the next chapter, the University was shaken by New York City's fiscal crisis within the first year after these students entered. Unfortunately, we do not know with any precision how the fiscal crisis affected student careers at CUNY: we know that many students left the University, but we do not know who they were.[18] Moreover, largely as a result of the crisis, the freshmen who enrolled in 1975 were the last class to be admitted under the original open-admissions criteria laid down in 1970. Beginning in 1976, new admissions standards (described in chapter 11) made it more difficult to qualify for a senior college. The new standards probably hindered minority students more than whites since minority students were undoubtedly less likely to qualify under them and, in any event, many white students could afford the alternative of attending a state or a private college. In short, estimates for the 1975 freshmen may not hold for later classes.

Given the roughness of our estimates, we have tried to keep matters simple by combining blacks and Hispanics into one minority category and by combining all the white groups, including those who are neither Jewish nor Catholic. The results are presented in table 10.3.[19] These estimates make a strong case that later cohorts added greatly to the number of college educated minority men and women in the city. If student careers have developed in the 1975 cohort as they had in the 1970 group, then the 1975 cohort would have yielded by spring 1980 more than twice as many minority graduates in each category as did the 1970 cohort, as a comparison of tables 10.2 and 10.3 shows. Correspondingly, the numerical superiority of white graduates would have been reduced sharply. Were special program students taken into account, white graduates overall would have been less than twice as numerous as minority graduates. The white superiority in senior-college graduation and in eligibility for graduate school would have diminished drastically. The ratio of white to minority graduates would have come con-

TABLE 10.3. Projected Number of Graduates in the 1975 Cohort from White[a] and Minority Groups, with and without Special Program Students[b]

		MINORITY	
	WHITE	Without Special Program Students	With Special Program Students
Graduated any level with any average	250	105	136
Graduated senior college with any average	184	62	83
Graduated senior college with B average	85	17	23

Source: Census and sample data.
[a]All white students are included.
[b]Numbers are scaled to be proportional to those in preceding tables.

siderably closer to the white to minority ratio in the city's college-age population.[20] The rise in the number of minority graduates and the fall in white numerical superiority seem too strong to disappear even if allowance were made for possible errors in our estimates.

In sum, the 1970 cohort yields a conservative portrayal of the numbers of minority graduates from the City University, both in absolute terms and relative to the numbers of white graduates. Subsequent cohorts, containing more minority students and larger proportions of them in the senior colleges, added more and more minority students who were able to take advantage of the City University as a significant lever for social mobility. Although after 1972 our data cannot tell us how many of these minority students were admitted under the open-admissions criteria, it is safe to conclude that most of them were. And, even among those who possessed the high school credentials to enter the City University under the traditional criteria, there were undoubtedly many other beneficiaries of the open-admissions program—students who were encouraged to apply to college because the University's adoption of open admissions signaled to them that it was truly willing to meet their needs.

Open Admissions: An Assessment

How are we to evaluate the success of the open-admissions program? In chapter 2, we presented two different perspectives on the role of education in an industrialized society like that of the United States. One emphasizes education's role in promoting equality of opportunity, in loosening the linkage between the status of the family into which an individual is born and that person's own adult status. This perspective also emphasizes education's importance in integrating culturally marginal groups, like minority groups, into the mainstream of a society and extending to them the opportunities normally proffered to members of the majority. The other perspective, however, emphasizes education's role in the persistence of inequality and the preservation of inequality of opportunity. Even though its adherents recognize that education makes social mobility possible for many, they see educational systems as constricting the full potential for mobility in a society. Schools do this by processing students in different ways according to their social origins and specifically by channeling students from lower status ethnic and class groups away from the educational experiences providing the greatest leverage for adult success.

We believe that both perspectives illuminate aspects of the open-admissions experiment. With respect to the first, the policy carved out at one stroke a pathway to greater opportunity for minority men and women. Thousands of minority students have entered the University as open-admissions students. The numbers in table 10.1 are easily translated to yield the total of minority open-admissions students in the 1970 entering cohort—over thirty-five hundred.[21] Succeeding cohorts undoubtedly have contained even larger numbers of minority open-admissions students. Moreover, through 1975 the flow of minority students entering the University was directed more and more to the four-year schools, unlocking the greater opportunities for socioeconomic advancement that they provide. The patterns of minority access we analyzed for this period (see chapter 4) do not sustain the suspicion that minority open-admissions students would be tracked into the community colleges, thereby preserving the senior colleges as turf for white students.

A substantial proportion of these students graduated from college. Again translating from table 10.1, there were over seven hundred minority graduates among the open-admissions students who entered in 1970. Nearly four hundred of these were students who received baccalaureates. The number of minority open-admissions students who graduated with a record indicating the possibility of entry to graduate school was small, however—well under one hundred in the 1970 cohort. But all these numbers probably were magnified in succeeding cohorts, so that thousands of minority students must be reckoned to have received college degrees as a result of open admissions. These graduates form a critical addition to the pool of college educated men and women from New York City's minority communities. As we noted earlier, 70 percent of the city's minority high school graduates who went to college in 1970 entered the City University. Thus, of those who had graduated from college five years later, open-admissions graduates were a significant proportion of the whole. In terms of its impact on the city's minority communities, measured by the proportion of college graduates it added, open admissions made a noteworthy contribution.

The open-admissions policy probably has altered forever historic patterns of ethnic access to the University. In New York, as in many other northeastern cities where successive waves of immigrants have created large and cohesive communities, local institutions frequently can be characterized in terms of distinctive and self-perpetuating ethnic patterns of recruitment and access, understandable in terms of the cultures and experiences immigrants brought with them as well as the specific opportunities that greeted them. In the case of the City University, Jewish and other white ethnics who had difficulty earlier in the century gaining entry to many private colleges and universities took full advantage of the University and thereby wrote another chapter in the story of immigrant and ethnic success in America. Thousands of CUNY graduates, spread throughout many families, gave the University an enormous symbolic importance within these communities and led to a continual recruitment of students for the University from these groups. The thousands of minority students who have entered and graduated from the University since open admissions was inaugurated insure that black and Hispanic students will, in the future, look to the University as a source of opportunity for them.

But at the same time that many minority students were gaining the opportunity for a college education under open admissions, so were even more whites. Many thousands of white students entered the University as open-admissions students, and thousands graduated. According to table 10.1 approximately nine thousand Jewish and Catholic students entered under the open-admissions criteria in fall 1970, and over twenty-six hundred of them left with a degree of some kind; for over sixteen hundred, it was a baccalaureate. Undoubtedly some of these students would have gone to college and graduated without open admissions. But, even while acknowledging that there is some exaggeration in these figures, it seems clear that open admissions produced more white than minority graduates. And when we disregard their admissions status, white graduates of the University outnumbered minority graduates even more. The numerical superiority of the white groups at the University achieves even greater significance when we consider that minority college students in the city were more dependent upon the University than were white college students. Given this analysis, it seems to us unlikely that open admissions made a deep dent in the competitive socioeconomic superiority white groups enjoy vis-à-vis minority groups.

Moreover, in conformity with the perspective that sees education as helping to preserve ethnic and class advantages, white students appear to have enjoyed considerable advantages at CUNY under open admissions. In the main, their advantages did not derive from policies or actions under the control of the University but rather from the University's position in a society in which race matters very much. Even though minority students were more equally distributed between the community and the senior colleges during open admissions than they had been before, they were still disproportionately located in the two-year schools, even six years after open admissions began. Minority students at the senior colleges were distinctly less likely than whites to be found at the most prestigious campuses, the elite senior colleges.[22] Minority students at the two-year schools were more likely than whites to enter the vocational curricula, reducing their chances of eventually entering a four-year college (see chapter 8).

As we showed in chapter 4, these remaining imbalances probably were a function more of past inequalities than of the mechanics of CUNY admissions procedures. Their most immediate cause lay in ethnic variation in college and curriculum preferences, an outgrowth of the enormous disparities in previous educational experiences, especially in the tracking of students in high school and before. But the fact remains that open admissions did not eradicate ethnic differences in the initial positioning of students—positions that carry different potential for students' educational and occupational life chances.

As we have shown in chapter after chapter, minority disadvantages did not end with the less favorable positioning of minority students but continued throughout their academic careers. If we ignore altogether disparities in educational background and simply compare students at the same level of college, the aggregate differences in performance among groups were quite large in magnitude. At the senior colleges, for example, the cumulative grade point averages of black students in the 1970 cohort were almost a full letter grade behind those of Jewish students and half a letter grade behind those of Catholic students. The averages of Hispanic students were nearly two-thirds of a letter grade behind those of Jewish students and a quarter of a letter grade behind those of Catholic students. Similarly, in their accumulation of credits five years after entry to CUNY, black students averaged thirty-two fewer credits than did Jewish students; this was a gap of considerably more than a year's work, given the slow rates at which CUNY students in general accumulated credits. Black students averaged fifteen fewer credits than did Catholics.[23] The credit accumulation of Hispanic students was only slightly better than that of blacks. Ethnic differences at the community colleges were not as profound as these, and ethnic differences in accumulated credits at the two-year schools were sometimes nonexistent (in the 1970 cohort, for example) as a result of the long period in which students had to complete a normally two-year program and the greater tendency of white students to transfer to the four-year schools without first earning an associate degree. In addition, at both levels white ethnic students were less likely to drop out than were minority students and, if they left CUNY's senior colleges, they were more likely to be transferring; they were also more likely to graduate. White students at the community colleges were more likely than minority students to transfer to the four-year schools.

For the most part, these ethnic differences in success result from great disparities in high school background that CUNY's remedial programs apparently did little to erase. But when high school influences on college performance are taken into account, important ethnic differences, generally in favor of white ethnic and especially Jewish students remain. Thus, even among open-admissions students, whites were more likely to be successful than minority students.

Following conventional social science wisdom about the determinants of academic achievement, we have looked for other characteristics of minority and white students that might explain the differences between them. But, once their different high school backgrounds are taken into account, minority students appear to have been not as different from whites in their characteristics as many thought. As we found in chapter 5 when we compared students of different ethnic origins in the same admissions categories, minority students did come from noticeably poorer families; they were also older and more likely to be female. Aside from these distinctions, there were only a few additional differences that might seem on the surface to be academically relevant. The most important was the greater need of minority students for remedial work, even by comparison with whites of equivalent high school background. In addition, minority students were more likely to have been late to class in high school (and, presumably, their lateness occurred also at CUNY); they were more likely to hand in assignments late; and they were more likely to have a vocational orientation to college. This last point is a frequent complaint among faculty everywhere: students are more interested in getting a job than an education. On the other hand, minority students were also more likely to see their own personal growth as a reason for attending college. With the exception of the lower scores of minority students on the tests used to measure student needs for remediation, none of these ethnic differences in the characteristics students brought with them to college explains much of the differences among ethnic groups in success at college.[24] In the end, substantial ethnic differences remain unexplained.

Undoubtedly these residual ethnic differences reflect inadequacies in our measures. As an example, in the senior colleges, the explanatory power of students' scores on the standardized tests administered to measure need for remediation is probably reduced by the low ceiling of the mathematics test. Because this test was intended to measure differences within a relatively low skill range, many senior-college students, mostly white, scored at or near the top of the scale, and consequently mathematics skill differences among these students are unmeasured. With a fuller scale of mathematics skills, we would probably be able to explain more of the ethnic differences in academic outcomes in the senior colleges. It would not help us in the community colleges, however.

There also are student characteristics not measured in the data available to us that may explain additional parts of the remaining ethnic differences. One is language. It is well documented that ethnic variations in linguistic usage—in spoken and written English—set minority students apart from white students.[25] These variations are not fully measured by the test of reading comprehension, the sole measure of language skills available to us.

Thus, at CUNY, even when a white student and a black student were both deficient in writing, the deficiencies of the white were not packaged in black dialectical usage (as they undoubtedly were for some blacks). And in the case of some Hispanic students, their difficulties were compounded by the fact that English was not their primary language. While there has been much debate about black English and whether it is as "good" or as valuable as standard English, and whether Spanish should be legitimized as an alternative tongue in educational institutions, these controversies are of little relevance for the question at hand—how do we account for remaining ethnic differences in academic success? The fact is that at City University, the "currency of the land" is standard English, and it is against this standard that the academic performance of students was measured.[26] In this light it is possible that their special language problems—problems with which most faculty were unfamiliar and which they found especially troublesome—handicapped minority students in their academic efforts.[27]

Nevertheless, we doubt that all of the ethnic differences in academic success can be explained in terms of student characteristics that are intrinsically linked to academic achievement. Based upon the size of these differences and upon our impressionistic knowledge (as participants in the CUNY community), we believe that to some extent ethnic differences in success also stem from faculty reactions, both to open admissions and to the minority students it brought into the University. This amounts to saying that some faculty may have discriminated against minority students.

We advance this explanation with some hesitation, recognizing its speculative nature. We collected no systematic data about faculty attitudes; we also have no data about what went on in classrooms that would allow us to identify acts that favored white over minority students. Nevertheless, odd as it may seem, in arguing from unexplained success differences among ethnic groups that some discrimination has occurred, we are not doing any more than others have done. The data we lack might bolster the case if we had them; they would not prove it conclusively. In a sense, assertions of discrimination based on statistical data are always only plausible; they can never be demonstrated.

The difficulties inherent in such assertions are documented in Cole's lucid and comprehensive review of the concept of discrimination and the methods of proving it.[28] As Cole notes, most proofs of discrimination are based on residual or unexplained differences and consequently can never be definitive; they are always subject to the challenge that another factor may be adduced that explains the residuum. Quoting Hankins's definition of discrimination as the "unequal treatment of equals," Cole puts his finger on the great difficulty of establishing when people are equal with respect to all relevant characteristics.[29] Consider as an example the difficulty of establishing that two students, one minority and one white, should have received the same grades. Assuming that they took the same courses, one would have to demonstrate that they were equal in all ways that might be relevant to a universalistic academic process—equal, in other words, in intelligence, skill, and effort. Given the complexity of these concepts and the imperfect nature of measurement generally, no matter how many variables one had to control for relevant characteristics the possibility would always linger that other or better variables would contribute to explaining whatever ethnic differences remained. In short, any claim of academic discrimination is open to challenge.[30]

One way of making the assertion of discrimination more plausible is to outline the reactions of many faculty as we perceived them. In so doing, we are relying on impressionistic and hence imperfect evidence.

In order to understand these reactions and the part they may have played, it must be recognized that both within and outside the walls of the

University, there was a frequent equation between open-admissions and minority students. This is not to say that the extent of open admissions' benefits for whites was entirely unknown, but there was a general perception that black and Hispanic students were the "real" open-admissions students, either in terms of the depth of their academic neediness or in terms of the numbers admitted to the University only because of the program. The pervasiveness of this perception is illustrated by an anecdote, possibly apocryphal, that is often told at CUNY: on the first day of class, a professor pointed to some black students seated in his classroom, with whom he was unacquainted, and warned that "you open-admissions students" would have to work extra hard to keep up with the demands of the course.[31] That this perception of open admissions as a minority program was shared by students, including whites who benefited from the program and minority students who did not, is indicated by the magnitude of ethnic differences in attitudes toward the policy (see chapter 5).

The reactions of many faculty to the policy were governed not only by the size of the minority presence but also by the abruptness with which the policy began and initial conditions following its implementation. While other universities in the nation have had a long history of free access admissions policies, none has ever moved so quickly from highly selective entrance criteria to the liberal and relatively unstratified policy on which CUNY embarked. Especially in the senior colleges, the change was sudden and even startling. An early study indicated broad support for open admissions among both faculty and administrators,[32] with attitudes generally more favorable in community than in senior colleges and administrators somewhat more supportive than faculty.[33] However, we suspect that additional faculty exposure not only to open-admissions students but also to the accompanying conditions of overcrowding, increased class size, and the subsequent effects of the New York City fiscal crisis led to a decline in support.

Though many professors expressed concern over a possible erosion of academic standards during the period of conflict immediately preceding open admissions, overriding that concern for many of the essentially liberal and socially conscious faculty was the commitment to social justice intrinsic to the concept of open admissions. While faculty were aware that open admissions would bring to the University many students with weak academic preparation, it was hoped that the remedial and other support services would enable these students after a time to move into the mainstream of college work. The general view of what open admissions would entail was predominantly assimilationist: the new students would enter, remedy their deficiencies, and take their places in the traditional curriculum. Even the delivery of remedial services would not unduly burden the faculty since remediation was to be provided by staff specially hired for the task. In short, we think that a great many of the faculty perceived that, beyond the stresses of a greater number of students, no serious alteration of the professorial role would result. But the reality was sharply different from this expectation.

The minority students who came to the University generally presented a strong contrast to the white ethnics who had come in previous generations. They were cultural foreigners, as earlier students had been, but they often seemed proud of this identity, whereas students from southern and eastern Europe had been eager to assimilate. The earlier attitude was expressed well by one City College alumnus of the class of 1913, a Russian Jew who spoke no English when he arrived in New York at the age of eight. When asked whether he resented the efforts of City College faculty to Americanize him, he replied that the faculty were "the light."[34] And such an attitude was mirrored in a later generation of faculty at CUNY. As one writer (a City College administrator, formerly an English professor) put it:

> We faculty members were whites whose parents had been Irish or Italian or Jewish immigrants out of one ghetto or another. . . . After growing up in the streets of Brooklyn and the Bronx, we had struggled to disembarrass ourselves of every ethnic odor.[35]

In contrast, the late 1960s and early seventies were marked by demands for ethnic studies departments, modifications of curriculum to reflect black and Hispanic cultural experiences, and attacks upon CUNY academics as "cultural imperialists."

For many faculty this new situation presented a stark and gloomy contrast with the earlier days of the University. The different ways in which their expectations were rebuffed created in many a considerable sense of stress.[36] For some, open admissions appeared to signal the imminent collapse of higher education in America. Others felt demoralized by the recognition that the students seemed to know less than in former years, as when a teacher of medieval history complained that students entering his course had never even heard of Charlemagne. In earlier days, when the "proletarian Harvard" was an appropriate label for City College, faculty took great pride in the subsequent accomplishments of the graduates they had "produced." But faced with an influx of poorly prepared and often culturally foreign students, it is understandable that faculty would find the changed situation very threatening to their own sense of status. Perhaps the response of many, especially those with roots in the older era, is best summed up in these words:

> Where were the old liberal arts students who simply wanted to study philosophy or literature or history? Where were those who could not be programmed, who weren't so absolutely certain of their careers, who weren't so utterly nervous about job security, and who came to us with a literacy we took for granted? Gone. Gone to the colleges of the State University. Gone to Queens and to

Hunter. Gone to the suburbs and the exurbs and the hinterlands. And with their flight something faded from our own lives—a passing purpose, a pointed passion.

What really gnawed away at our innards and left us hollow, what began to create a sad yet anxious look in our eyes and a dreadful listlessness in the way we moved through classes or sat at committee meetings, what dulled our lunchroom conversations and made us depend more on each other than on the students—who had always been the great reward for teaching at City College—what coursed in our bodies like an incurable illness was our growing realization that we no longer had a profession.[37]

We sense from our experiences at CUNY that the reactions of some faculty fastened on the minority students; they were the "strangers." They generally were distinguished from white students not only by physical appearance but also by cultural style—dress, manner, and, as noted earlier, language. By contrast, there was nothing to identify whites as open-admissions students unless their academic deficiencies were blatant. We believe that some faculty found it easier to acknowledge the academic talents of white students than they did those of academically comparable minority students.[38] We are not suggesting that all or even most faculty did so. Nor are we suggesting that most faculty who felt discouraged by open admissions therefore favored white students. Moreover, there were many faculty who remained throughout sympathetic to open admissions and strove to find talent expressed in a variety of cultural styles. But, in all probability, the antipathy to minority students was widespread enough to surface in our data. The magnitude of the difference it made may not have been very great in the aggregate—in some analyses in chapter 6 and 7, there were no visible differences among students of different ethnic origins but similar educational background. But we suspect that this antipathy added to the advantages white students possessed by virtue of the better educational opportunities they had received in primary and secondary schools and the cultural and financial resources possessed by their families and communities.

If we are right, this increment to the competitive edge white students enjoyed must be counted as a cost of the open-admissions program. It was a development tending to preserve inequality, occurring in response to policies promoting equality, and thereby it was a cost consistent with the critical perspective on education. Its occurrence would not make the City University unusual, however. The sociological literature indicates that in general the reactions to ethnic newcomers depend on their numbers, the abruptness of their entry to new social arenas, and the status discrepancy between them and others.[39] All of these factors were present in the CUNY situation.

In summing up, we cannot subsume open admissions under either of the major perspectives on the role of education; the tension between the two cannot be resolved. As is true in the analysis of educational systems more generally, each of these perspectives frames a partial and selective view of the consequences of open admissions. In line with the first, which emphasizes education's role in expanding opportunity, open admissions brought substantial benefits to all major ethnic groups in the city. Many minority students entered the University as a result of the program and subsequently graduated. But, in line with the second perspective, which sees education as tending to preserve privilege, more white students took advantage of the program than did minorities. Our analysis of open admissions thus highlights the policy's paradoxical character, one that it probably shares with many other ameliorative reforms. While benefits do flow to those targeted to receive them, they also flow unintentionally to others, and often the latter, possessing more resources than the former, are better able to take advantage of the new opportunities.

Notes

1. Christopher Jencks, et al., *Who Gets Ahead?* (New York: Basic Books, 1979), p. 189. That the benefits of higher education are greater than those of primary and secondary education is also revealed by the major analyses carried out by David Featherman and Robert Hauser, *Opportunity and Change* (New York: Academic, 1978), p. 261.
2. Jencks et al., p. 174.
3. William J. Wilson, *The Declining Significance of Race* (Chicago: University of Chicago Press, 1978), p. 151.
4. This point is made in the well-known Coleman Report. See James S. Coleman, Ernest Q. Campbell, Carol J. Hobson, James McPartland, Alexander M. Mood, Frederic D. Weinfeld, and Robert L. York, *Equality of Educational Opportunity* (Washington: U.S. Government Printing Office, 1966), p. 21.
5. Work on teacher expectations and their consequences is summarized and discussed in Caroline Hodges Persell, *Education and Inequality* (New York: Free Press, 1977), chaps. 7 and 8.
6. To give this picture of the graduating high school class of 1970, we used Robert Birnbaum and Joseph Goldman, *The Graduates: A Follow-up Study of New York City High School Graduates of 1970* (New York: Center for Social Research, City University of New York, 1971). Birnbaum and Goldman discussed graduates of all the city's high schools.
7. Birnbaum and Goldman, p. 42; these percentages are for students in public high schools only.
8. Birnbaum and Goldman, p. 43.
9. Birnbaum and Goldman, p. 43; these figures are projections from the known ethnic rates of attrition between the junior and the senior year and the known overall rate of attrition during the senior year.
10. Figures describing the ethnic composition of the high school age population of

New York City were derived from U.S. Bureau of the Census, *Census of the Population, 1970*, vol. 1 (Washington: U.S. Government Printing Office, 1970), pp. 97, 429. The text reports the percentages of ethnic groups among fifteen to nineteen year olds in the city's population; we were constrained to this age range by the categories in the census tables for Puerto Ricans. Also, since most Puerto Ricans are classified as whites in census tables, we subtracted them from the white group in order to arrive at the percentage of whites noted in the text.

11. Birnbaum and Goldman, p. 119.
12. Birnbaum and Goldman, p. 124; white college goers were somewhat less likely to attend CUNY—about 62 percent did so.
13. We remind the reader that only the sample data can be used as the source for this table since only they provide ethnic information about individuals. However, in constructing the universitywide estimates in the table—i.e., the numbers of students in categories, regardless of level—we have had to correct for the overrepresentation of senior-college students in the 1970 sample (see appendix A).
14. One study that distinguishes the effect of attending college from that of graduating is Jencks et al., chap. 6.
15. We know the proportion of graduates among the special program students from official CUNY records. We do not know, however, whether these graduates were black, Hispanic, Asian, or white. Since not all the special program students were black or Hispanic, our estimates slightly overstate the total number of minority graduates.
16. The numbers in table 10.2 are again scaled to a base of one thousand students admitted outside the special programs. Scaling the total number of special program students to the proportion of this base yields 1,124 as the size of the entering class in 1970.
17. Blacks constitute 25 percent and Puerto Ricans 13 percent. It would seem that one should not add the two figures since there is some overlap between the two categories, but there are also some persons who would be classified as minority in our analysis but are counted in neither census category—namely, white Hispanics who are not Puerto Ricans. Hence the sum of the two figures, 38 percent, is probably a good, even though crude, estimate of the relevant minority population.
18. Students left the University for a variety of reasons—some because they were disheartened by the disruptions on some campuses and by the uncertainties clouding CUNY's future. Others left because they were unwilling to pay tuition, which was imposed in fall 1976. Tuition probably had less impact on minority students than on whites since blacks and Hispanics came more frequently from low-income families and therefore qualified for full financial aid under the state's Tuition Assistance Program. However, this aid was provided for eight full-time semesters, and students who needed more than eight semesters to graduate may have found it difficult to finance the last phase of their college careers. Students who began in community colleges were also eligible for eight semesters of aid, but if they required more than two years to earn the associate degree and then transferred to a senior college, they would exhaust their aid eli-

gibility before completing the B.A. For a full discussion of the tuition question at CUNY see chapter 11.

19. The 1975 entering cohort was larger than that which entered in 1970. In order to convey the relative sizes of the two groups, we scaled the numbers in table 10.3 to be proportional to the numbers for the 1970 cohort, reported in preceding tables.

20. We estimated the ethnic composition of the city's college-age population from the composition of its ten to fourteen year olds in 1970. Among this group, blacks formed 28 percent, Puerto Ricans 16 percent, and whites 53 percent (see also notes 10 and 16 above).

21. Since about 31,500 students entered CUNY outside the special programs in 1970 (see table 4.2), any figure in table 10.1 need only be multiplied by 31.5 in order to yield the approximate number of students to which it refers.

22. This underrepresentation was caused by the small minority presence at two elite schools, Brooklyn and Queens. In contrast, by 1975 minority students comprised more than 50 percent of the freshman class at City College, a fact probably explained by the school's location in Harlem and its symbolic importance in the emergence of open admissions. Minority students were also not underrepresented at Hunter College.

23. These comparisons include all students from these groups who entered the senior colleges in 1970, regardless of whether they dropped out or persisted. The credit accumulations of black students are lower than those of white students for two reasons: black students dropped out earlier and more frequently; they acquired fewer credits for each semester in school.

24. We did not take note of the significance of coming late to class and handing in assignments late until after we had completed the analyses for chapter 7. We did include these two variables in certain subsequent analyses that involved somewhat restricted samples. These later analyses show that these two variables contribute modestly to the explanation of academic performance, adding to that which is explained by the variables discussed in chapter 7. Their addition to equations does not reduce ethnic differences by much, however.

25. For example, see Joey L. Dillard, *Black English* (New York: Random House, 1972); William Labov, P. Cohen, C. Robins, and J. Lewis, *A Study of the Nonstandard English of Negro and Puerto Rican Speakers in New York City* (Washington: U.S. Office of Education, Cooperative Research Project no. 3,288, 1968); William Labov, *Language in the Inner City* (Philadelphia: University of Pennsylvania Press, 1972).

26. Indeed, nonstandard English is often viewed by teachers as a deficit and plays a role in their evaluations of students. See, for example, Lawrence B. Rosenfeld, *An Investigation of Teachers' Stereotyping Behavior: The Influence of Mode of Presentation, Ethnicity, and Social Class on Teachers' Evaluations of Students* (ERIC ED 090172, 1973). That language may be a factor mediating between pupil race and teacher evaluations is also pointed out in Persell, p. 104.

27. This point should not be strongly emphasized. If there were severe language problems that were not measured by the reading tests, then we should expect to see minority students placed in remedial writing classes far more frequently than is indicated by their high school backgrounds and test scores. This did not happen, however (see chapter 9).

28. Jonathan R. Cole, *Fair Science: Women in the Scientific Community* (New York: Free Press, 1979), chap. 2.

29. Cole, pp. 27-28; in this part of his discussion Cole has borrowed from Hubert M. Blalock, Jr., *Toward a Theory of Minority-Group Relations* (New York: Wiley, 1967), pp. 15-18.

30. It might be objected that an experimental method, of the kind used to establish legally discrimination on the part of realtors, could be used to determine conclusively whether discrimination has occurred. Cole, p. 31, seems to advocate experimental procedures. However, they are quite limited in application and are often open to the objection that those treated unequally are not, in fact, equal in all functionally relevant ways. They are most usable when the functionally relevant characteristics are simple and few in number—such as having a middle-class appearance and proof of the ability to pay in the instance of proving realtor discrimination, where whites and blacks are sent to the same realtor in search of an apartment or a house. When the relevant characteristics are complex and difficult to enumerate completely, then experimental procedures are open to the same challenges as arguments from residual differences. No amount of randomization in design can guarantee that groups of white and minority students are equal in all functionally relevant ways if ethnicity is likely to be correlated with the characteristics affecting academic outcomes.

31. This anecdote is cited by Sherry Gorelick, "Open Admissions: Design for Failure?" *Politics and Education* 1 (Summer 1978); 8-13.

32. Jack E. Rossman, Helen S. Astin, Alexander W. Astin, and Elaine H. El-Khawas, *Open Admissions at City University of New York: An Analysis of the First Year* (Englewood Cliffs: Prentice-Hall, 1975), pp. 125-127.

33. That administrators are somewhat more supportive of efforts to increase minority enrollments is not a finding limited to the CUNY setting. Similar results were found in a study of several institutions around the nation. See Marvin W. Peterson, Robert T. Blackburn, Zelda F. Gamson, Carlos H. Arce, Roselle W. Davenport, and James R. Mingle, *Black Students on White Campuses: The Impact of Increased Black Enrollments* (Ann Arbor: Institute for Social Research, University of Michigan, 1978).

34. From an interview by Lavin with Louis Kornfeld, New York City, March 21, 1979.

35. Theodore L. Gross, "How to Kill a College: The Private Papers of a Campus Dean," *Saturday Review*, February 4, 1978, p. 14.

36. Our impressions of these negative reactions seem supported by similar observations at other places. For example, Blauner concludes that at Berkeley faculty found that they did not like to teach Third World students. See Robert Blauner, *Racial Oppression in America* (New York: Harper & Row, 1972), chap. 8.

37. Gross, p. 19.

38. That faculty everywhere may find it easier to discern the academic talents of students who are like themselves in social background is made plausible by analogy with the counselor-student interactions described by Frederick Erickson, "Gatekeeping and the Melting Pot: Interaction in Counseling Encounters," *Harvard Educational Review* 45 (February 1975,): p. 44-70. Analyzing videotaped interactions, Erickson described how the social identities of the participants affected the smoothness of interaction and the amount of help a stu-

dent was likely to receive. While faculty grading depends most heavily on material written by students, the evaluation of this material is still likely to be affected by the character of faculty-student interactions. Moreover, at CUNY the social identities of students may have had special prominence for faculty because of the tensions and controversy arising from open admissions.

39. See, for example, Robin M. Williams, *Strangers Next Door* (Englewood Cliffs: Prentice-Hall, 1964), and Blalock.

11.   New York City's Fiscal Crisis and the Fate of Open Admissions

BETWEEN FALL 1975 and fall 1976 the size of the entering freshmen classes at CUNY plummeted from forty thousand to twenty-nine thousand.[1] Overall enrollment shrank from about 250,000 students to 200,000.[2] Full-time staff decreased by more than five thousand, or 25 percent, of whom about two thousand were instructional staff.[3] More than half of the nine thousand part time teaching positions were eliminated. Such drastic reductions were among the important bottom-line consequences of the most traumatic events in the history of the University. Striking as they are, these cold numbers express only superficially the shocks that reverberated throughout the University during a fifteen-month siege and left the open-admissions policy profoundly changed. This chapter describes these changes, noting the economic, political, and interpersonal processes that gave rise to them.

The Fiscal Crisis of New York City

By late winter and early spring of 1975 the reality of New York City's enormous fiscal crisis began to take shape. Over a long period the city had provided a range of services unparalleled in any other American municipality: a gigantic hospital system; long welfare rolls supported more generously than elsewhere and administered by an extensive social service bureaucracy; labor contracts highly favorable to a vast army of unionized municipal workers; and a largely tuition-free university system consisting by 1971 of

289

nine senior colleges, eight community colleges, one upper-division college, and a graduate school.

During the late nineteenth century and well into the twentieth, the economy of the city had been expanding rapidly. As a major funnel of immigration, New York gained a reputation as a city of great opportunity—stories of spectacular social mobility were legion. Alongside this reputation was the image of New York as supportive of the poor—providing through its many services a buffer to ease the lives of those not fortunate enough to find success.

The drastic postwar demographic transition severely strained the city's economic resources. After World War II the exodus of whites to the suburbs gained impetus along with a slowly increasing movement of corporations out of the city and often out of the state. At the same time, a heavy immigration of blacks from the South and Latins from the Caribbean was occurring. The changing labor market could not support such a large influx of people, who were often poorly educated and unskilled, and the need for municipal services expanded as the tax base to support this expansion was shrinking. New York City turned to the credit markets to finance not only its operating and capital expenses but, more and more, the debt itself. The growth of CUNY was no small contributor to the expansion and increased cost of municipal services. Indeed, the University's budget grew from $67 million in 1960–1961 to $325 million in 1970–1971, the initial year of open admissions.[4] By 1975 the city's budget had reached an astounding $12 billion.

The need to service its debt greatly stepped up New York's forays into the credit markets. The banks that underwrote the city's offerings of notes and bonds found it increasingly difficult to place them, and there was a sharp downgrading of the securities by financial rating institutions. The city's fate was sealed: it was unable to enter the credit markets and the specter of default loomed large. To make matters worse, this critical situation threatened the ability of the state to meet its credit needs.

An early reaction to the crisis was a visit to Washington by Mayor Abraham Beame and Governor Hugh Carey in an effort to persuade President Ford of the necessity for federal loan guarantees so that the city might reenter the credit markets. Not only was the response clearly negative, but somewhere in the discussions the City University received attention. The conversation was reported to have gone as follows:

> "Mr. Mayor," the President said, "I understand you have free tuition in your city university, and you're asking us to provide money for the city. We don't have free tuition in Lansing, Michigan. Why should the federal government provide free tuition for the students in New York City and not in other cities of the nation?"
>
> Mr. Beame, the son of immigrant Jews who traced his rise to the city's highest office from the start provided by tuition-free classes at City College in the

1920's, reduced the issue to a personal level, apparently unconscious of the double-meaning the city's critics would read into his response.

"If we hadn't had free tuition," he said, "I wouldn't be here."[5]

After this meeting it was clear that outside help would depend upon a convincing demonstration by the city that it was taking serious steps to improve its fiscal condition. There was little sympathy for New York as a generous and liberal municipality. The outside view was harsh: the city was profligate. Though Mayor Beame could hardly have been responsible for a crisis that had been many years in the making, there was a general lack of confidence in his determination to take the painful steps that were to be demanded. This was one reason for the establishment of a watchdog agency that played a dominant role in setting the course of fiscal policy thereafter. This agency, the Emergency Financial Control Board (EFCB), was charged with overseeing and approving a wide range of municipal decisions with fiscal implications. It was constituted predominantly by individuals representing the interests of investors and the financial community. With regard to CUNY, the EFCB was to have a strong, if sometimes indirect, hand in determining its fate.

The Crisis Confronts the University

During the late spring of 1975, the city began to make sharp budget reductions. Major cuts were announced for all city agencies. For the coming academic year the University had anticipated a budget of about $650 million. Its share of the cuts was $87 million. In response CUNY increased tuition among those categories of students already paying tuition (graduate students, nonresidents of the city, and part-time nonmatriculated students). Among the much larger group of students who attended tuition-free (full- and part-time matriculated undergraduates), small fees—which had been charged for a long time—were increased by about 50 percent. Both actions recouped about $30 million. The remainder of the cut, $57 million, was distributed to each of the CUNY colleges, which made reductions in areas of supplies and in teaching and administrative staff.

Painful though this large cut may have been, the University hardly expected to escape the city's crisis unscathed. What was unexpected, however, was the announcement by the mayor in August of an additional $32 million reduction in the city's share of CUNY's operating budget for the school year, which was to begin in only a few weeks. To make matters worse, according to a legislated funding formula, any loss of funds from the city would be accompanied by state cutbacks. In this case the reduction in city funds triggered a loss of about $23 million from the state, for a total of $55 million. In short, from a sum of about $650 million, which seemed assured in April, CUNY now faced the academic year with about $510 million to spend. How the University could deal with this last-minute cut was the focal point around which a grim crisis developed. It was to be a crisis that re-awakened many of the conflicts that had accompanied the birth of open admissions and that brought into question the very mission of the University. Eventually, it brought about major changes in the structure and functioning of the open-admissions policy.

To respond to this abrupt and drastic change in its fiscal situation, the University was faced with two broad alternatives: reduce costs or increase income. Of course, it could also have developed a plan combining the two, but these options were frequently seen as mutually exclusive by important actors during the University's crisis. The essential ingredient of the first alternative was to reduce the size of the student body since this would allow reductions of faculty and staff, the major item in the University's budget. Obviously, any effort to pare the student body substantially would involve greater selectivity in admissions and thus a restriction of access to CUNY. The second option could have been implemented only through the imposition of tuition. This was the option favored by public officials. Indeed the August announcement by the mayor was accompanied by the statement that the $32 million reduction was being imposed "in lieu of tuition."[6] This statement reflected a consensus within the EFCB that CUNY's long tradition of free tuition should be ended.[7] In fact, the thinking of the EFCB on the tuition issue was part of a much broader concern over the entire fiscal relationship between the city and the University. As Stephen Berger, then head of the EFCB, later stated with reference to CUNY:

> It is not a municipal service. It's a service the city happens to be providing—it's hardly a municipal service. On what definition is a university a municipal service? What is a city in business to provide? . . . One looked at the major spending areas, and the City University was a major spending area which the city had no business being in.[8]

If the city and the EFCB were at that time contemplating the termination of, or at the very least a drastic reduction in, municipal support for CUNY, then funding would depend upon a major increase in support from the state, which had its own extensive system of higher education, SUNY. This system charged tuition (at that time $650 per year for freshmen and sophomores and $800 for juniors and seniors), but it also provided an extensive program of financial aid known as the Tuition Assistance Program (TAP).

The impact of tuition on CUNY's students can be estimated by considering the income distribution of the 1974 freshman class.[9] More than half of the full-time freshmen came from families with incomes below $10,000. Among this group, the costs of tuition would have been fully covered by TAP and other sources of aid.[10] Indeed, since CUNY charged fees (about $100 per year) that were not subject to financial aid and that would have been abolished under a tuition policy, these low-income students would have experienced a net benefit from tuition.[11] Above the $10,000 level, TAP awards fell off sharply. For the 20 percent of freshmen with incomes above $15,000, a maximum of only $100 in TAP support was available. Overall, it did not appear that the imposition of tuition would have had a heavy short-term impact on the majority of CUNY's full-time students. However, a third of the CUNY student body were part-time matriculated students who had not been paying tuition. These students would not have been covered by TAP, and even though they generally had higher incomes than did full-time students, they obviously would have been more affected by a tuition policy. Tuition also carried a long-term risk: TAP aid was available for a total of only eight semesters. Since many students required longer than this to graduate from a senior college, there was a likelihood that they would approach the completion of their studies at the same time that they were losing tuition assistance. On balance, then, a tuition policy at CUNY promised to have mixed effects, but at least in the short run it did not appear to threaten the great majority of low-income students. In any event, it was a virtual certainty that tuition would be a prerequisite for any major transfer of funding responsibility from the city to the state. This was the context in which the University was asked to impose tuition and to present a plan showing how it proposed to operate on a reduced budget in future years.

Through a good part of the fall, there was no clear response on the University's part. CUNY Chancellor Robert J. Kibbee and his vice-chancellors devoted numerous meetings to consideration of various cost-cutting options, such as the consolidation or merger of certain colleges, increases in faculty workload, and elimination of some programs, but the imposition of tuition was not at that point an alternative given close consideration.

To understand the seeming paralysis of CUNY, it is important to consider the dominant concerns of the Board of Higher Education not only with regard to tuition but also with regard to open admissions. The board had been installed in January 1974. Its chairman, Alfred A. Giardino, a Brooklyn College alumnus, had an intense personal commitment to the maintenance of free tuition. Other members of the board reflected Giardino's sentiments. In this respect the BHE represented a large constituency in the city. Among the hundreds of thousands of students and alumni, an almost sacred significance was attached to free tuition: it symbolized the faith that many generations of New Yorkers had placed in the University as an avenue of opportunity for the poor.

As important as the tuition issue was public concern with academic standards at the University. While the controversy surrounding this topic may have become less vocal after open admissions began, it never disappeared. Media reporting about the open-admissions policy was frequently negative, and the issue of standards was the item most often mentioned.[12] Ethnicity was subtly interwoven with this concern. Because minority group pressure had played such a major role in the initiation of open admissions, the policy was perceived, both within and outside the University, as largely a minority program. As a result, the concern with academic standards, even though genuinely felt by many, served as a lightning rod for deeper and darker feelings about race in the public at large. Although a liberal social climate placed constraints upon the statement of the issue in direct ethnic terms, for many in New York City expressions of concern over standards implicitly identified minorities as the underprepared students and as threats to academic quality.

The perception of open admissions' negative impact upon standards was reflected within the BHE and predated the fiscal crisis. From the beginning of his tenure as its chair, Giardino had been very concerned about the issue. He felt that the open-admissions policy was being undermined by the poor preparation of so many of the city's high school graduates and that remedial services were not an appropriate area for a large commitment of resources at the college level. Indeed, one of his first acts was to arrange a meeting with the president of the city's Board of Education to consider ways of developing and improving basic skills training in the secondary schools.[13] The academic standards issue was addressed with special cogency by another BHE member, Rita Hauser, in a *New York Times* article published in June 1975, even before the fiscal crisis had hit CUNY with its fullest force.[14] Hauser argued that despite the view of free tuition as yet another symbol of New York's profligacy, the real issue was open admissions. Not only was the policy a large financial drain, but it was, she asserted, an educationally unsound approach, though she recognized the political difficulty of reversing it. Concluding that many CUNY students were unequipped for any college work, Hauser proposed that if they could not demonstrate after two years that they had benefited from the University's expensive remedial programs, they should be given an appropriate certificate and dismissed.

A key situational factor undoubtedly contributed to the refusal of the University to yield on the tuition issue. A history of past crises made it credible to many at CUNY that a relatively favorable resolution might occur. Throughout Bowker's chancellorship, CUNY had often found itself in budgetary crises, but they were for the most part resolved on terms reasonably favorable to the University. What was true of CUNY seemed to be true of the city as well. It had had fiscal crises before, but they had never seemed to lead to painful results. With all of the public utterances about the impending disaster facing New York, there was at least some precedent for thinking that matters might be less serious than the statements of public officials would have had one believe. Moreover, even though Mayor Beame publicly affirmed the seriousness of the fiscal crisis, there is some reason to think that he privately encouraged Giardino to believe that if he waited, money would eventually be forthcoming and free tuition could be maintained.[15] Undoubtedly, it was thought that CUNY alumni and students could be a potent political force and that as pressure mounted on the University, they might exert strong counterpressure.

Also hindering the University's ability to act in the face of the crisis was the increasingly strained relationship between Giardino and Kibbee. When Giardino became chairman, he began almost immediately to perform his role in a style sharply different from that of his predecessors on the boards of the preceding few years. He involved himself not only in the broad policy issues facing CUNY but also in day-to-day activities of the University's central administration. He frequently made direct requests for information or gave instructions to staff well removed from the top of the central authority structure.[16] He sometimes became involved directly in writing University news releases in spite of the fact that a public relations office already existed. These activities blurred the demarcation between the role of the chancellor and that of the board chairman. Giardino's usurpation of chancellorship functions was in part an expression of his low estimate of Kibbee's competence. He wanted to dismiss Kibbee, but to do so he needed a clear consensus on the board.

In the fall Giardino had asked the chancellor to produce a plan that would be responsive to the fiscal emergency, but the strain between the two had an immobilizing effect. Kibbee understood that the best chance for a rapid solution would be to negotiate with city and state on the tuition matter.[17] Precisely because both city and state saw tuition as a politically difficult issue, CUNY had negotiating leverage: in return for accepting both the principle of tuition and the responsibility for its imposition, tuition might have been introduced on terms more favorable to the University and the short-run crisis resolved.[18] However, with the board so adamantly opposed to such a course, and in the absence of any public constituency to whom Kibbee could turn for support, any pressure on his part to pursue the tuition alternative might well have given Giardino the votes he needed to oust the chancellor.

November passed with little if any progress toward a resolution of the impasse. In early December the New York State Board of Regents (the governing body overseeing all levels of education in the state) issued a report calling for drastically increased state responsibility for the funding of CUNY, strongly affirming continuation of the open-admissions policy, and presenting a set of long-term and short-run recommendations for stabilizing the University's fiscal crisis.[19] The key recommendation was the call for the imposition of tuition. In this regard the report asserted that through TAP and federal programs, no student would be prevented from attending CUNY because of inability to pay.[20] The regents also laid out a plan for absorbing the $55 million cut during the second semester—a plan that included the immediate imposition of tuition, the foregoing of the equivalent of one week's salary on the part of faculty and staff, and an infusion of state aid to make up the difference. On its face the document appeared supportive and sympathetic to the University and, at the least, provided a basis for further negotiation among CUNY, city, and state officials.

Nonetheless, tuition remained an issue that the board seemed to have no intention of negotiating. It continued to hope that city and state pressure might eventually dissipate—the belief persisted that public officials would never allow the University to collapse. But if the board was unyielding on tuition, it had begun to develop positions that reflected its dim view of open admissions' impact on academic standards. These positions were incorporated in a set of resolutions that the board passed during an important meeting on December 15. The chancellor was directed to develop (1) uniform and strict guidelines defining satisfactory student progress toward a degree and (2) new standards of proficiency in basic skills as criteria for admission to the junior year of college and for admission to senior colleges on the part of those wishing to transfer from community colleges. Kibbee was also directed to develop plans for scaling down the size of the University through the elimination and consolidation of programs and campuses. For dealing with the short-run necessity of cutting $55 million during the second semester, the primary resolution of the board was to furlough faculty and administrators for one month, a move projected to save $32 million.

Of even greater import for the open-admissions policy was another resolution listed on the agenda for this meeting. It read as follows:

> Whereas, The University must continue in its search for more efficient and effective ways of carrying out its educational mission.
>
> Now, Therefore, The Board of Higher Education hereby directs the Chancellor to develop and apply admission standards to assure that future undergraduate matriculated entrants to the University have satisfactorily completed their reading and academic requirements for high school graduation and have demonstrated their readiness for college work by meeting successfully a skills test given by the University in standard reading and standard arithmetic or by meeting other standards to be developed.[21]

The board made known that it would consider this resolution on short notice, a procedure somewhat irregular when policy decisions affecting the community in important ways may come up for a vote. After its public meeting, the board went into private session and passed a resolution specifying that in the future no graduate of a New York City high school would be admitted to the University unless that student could demonstrate at least an eighth-grade level of competence in both reading and mathematics (by performance on a test or similar measure). This board decision was the first attempt to change entrance standards since the 1969 resolution on open admissions. On the surface, it appeared reasonable. It hardly seemed unfair that an eighth-grade skill level should be expected of entering college students. Indeed, to many this level itself appeared ridiculously low. Moreover, a New York City high school diploma was supposed to certify at least this level of academic skill. Since many CUNY freshmen did not meet this standard, it was felt that the University should no longer assume a responsibility for remediation, which by the public school system's own criteria rightfully belonged to the latter.

The board resolution carried enormous consequences for the University. In analyzing these consequences we shall review (1) what effects the eighth-grade requirement would have had upon the size of the student body; (2) how any reduction in the size of the student body would have been distributed across the levels of CUNY (i.e., between senior and community colleges); and (3) the characteristics of the students who would have been eliminated from the University.

We can assess the impact of this admissions requirement by considering what its effects would have been had it been applied to students already enrolled. For example, the 1971 freshman class consisted of about thirty-eight thousand students. Had they been subject to the eighth-grade admission criterion, as indicated by scores on the CUNY Open-Admissions Test,[22] only about twenty-six thousand would have been admitted to the University. Above and beyond any educational justification for this cut, it is clear that over time such reductions in successive freshmen classes would have profoundly reduced the total student body, with an obvious impact upon the number of faculty and staff and, therefore, the CUNY budget.

This reduction would have come primarily from the community colleges. Senior colleges would have lost twenty-five hundred of their roughly twenty thousand freshmen, a proportional loss of about 12 percent, while the community-college freshmen would have declined from around 17,500 to about ten thousand, or a reduction of 42 percent. Whether or not these effects for each level of CUNY were understood by the board when it acted, the resolution had an undeniable monetary implication: with drastic reductions in the community colleges, a much larger share of a shrinking fiscal pie would have been available for the senior colleges—historically the cornerstone of CUNY's academic reputation.

The new admissions standard carried profound implications for the ethnic composition of the University: it would have decimated the minority presence at CUNY. Table 11.1 shows the proportions of whites, blacks, and Hispanics who scored below the eighth-grade level on either reading comprehension *or* numerical competence or both, as measured by the CUNY Open-Admissions Test. In the senior colleges more than 40 percent of blacks, 35 percent of Hispanics, but less than 10 percent of whites would have been excluded if the admissions test had been in effect for the 1971 freshmen. Among community-college students, three-fourths of blacks and Hispanics would have been barred from CUNY, compared with one-third of whites. The admissions resolution also would have struck at the University's traditional mission of serving the economically disadvantaged. Table 11.1 shows that within each ethnic group, students from families with in-

TABLE 11.1. Effects of Proposed Reading and Mathematics Admissions Criteria by Ethnic Group, Income, and Level of College.

INCOME	WHITE	BLACK	HISPANIC
% Excluded from Senior Colleges[a]			
Less than $5,000	8	68	50
$5,000-9,999	8	39	34
$10,000 or more	5	28	21
Total	6	41	35
% Excluded from Community Colleges[a]			
Less than $5,000	41	82	83
$5,000-9,999	37	75	66
$10,000 or more	27	69	61
Total	32	76	74

Source: Sample data for 1971 cohort.
[a]"Excluded" refers to any individual who scored below the eighth-grade level on either test. Under the resolution, students had to score above this level on both the reading and the mathematics test in order to be admitted to the University.

comes of less than $5,000 per year were the ones most likely to have been excluded from CUNY.

The academic success of students comparable to those who would not have been admitted under the new admissions standard is of some note. A surprising proportion of those students in the 1971 group who would have been excluded from CUNY under the board's resolution either had graduated or were still enrolled by spring 1975. In senior colleges 9 percent had graduated and another 36 percent were still enrolled, compared with 27 percent graduated and 35 percent still enrolled among students who would have met the new standard. In the community colleges 23 percent of students not meeting the new standard had graduated and 14 percent were still enrolled; for students meeting the standard, the corresponding figures were 35 percent and 13 percent.

In short, using a device that promised to reduce freshmen classes by a third, the board had in effect chosen to terminate the open-admissions policy as an alternative to imposing tuition. This action moved the University away from a central mission to serve disadvantaged minority students. While the decision had an educational rationale and might have provided some reassurance to those who thought that standards had declined, it was equally, if not more, a response to the fiscal crisis: if the size of the student body could be reduced in the major way the board proposed, then perhaps the support of public officials would be forthcoming. The immediate results were quite the opposite. Neither the admissions resolution nor the plan to furlough faculty and staff for one month was perceived by public officials as an acceptable response to the University's fiscal crisis. Indeed, the idea of a furlough was unacceptable because it would have aggravated the city's already difficult relations with the large municipal unions.

The admissions resolution had another important consequence: it brought competing ethnic interests to the forefront of public consciousness for the first time since the onset of the fiscal crisis. Though the precise ethnic impact of an admissions test was not known beforehand (since the board apparently had not asked for such projections), Chancellor Kibbee had made it clear to the members during their deliberations that any skills test used as a selection device would have a disproportionate effect upon minority students.[23] That the ethnic consequences were understood by the board is suggested by the fact that its two minority members were the only ones to vote against the resolution.[24] Following passage, the theme of conflicting ethnic interests was elaborated publicly, and opposition began to mount. Two days afterward, a set of analyses[25] addressed to the racial implications was conducted and then released to the *New York Times*, where it was the subject of a front-page story on December 19.[26] Subsequently, there was an effort on the part of the minority community to reverse the resolution, including a lawsuit asking that it be overturned.[27]

As the board had directed, the chancellor began to develop a more comprehensive plan for redefining the scale of CUNY. By February 1976 such a plan had been drafted. It included proposals for consolidating campuses and programs, as well as more stringent guidelines for student academic progress and retention. In an effort to close the split between minorities and whites that had developed over admissions standards, Kibbee's plan offered a set of admissions criteria that differed from the board's. These new criteria specified that the minimum requirement for admission to a senior college was a high school average of 80 or rank in the top 35 percent of the high school graduating class (the original open-admissions plan required an 80 average or rank in the top 50 percent of the high school class). For admission to one of the community colleges the minimum requirement was a high school average of at least 70 or rank in the top 75 percent of the high school graduating class. Students who did not meet these community-college criteria could take a basic skills test as an alternative and would be admitted if they showed a level of proficiency to be determined by the chancellor. If they did not meet this level, they would be admitted to a "transitional program," where they would receive remedial instruction to improve their basic academic skills.

This new plan projected effects very different from those of the admissions resolution passed by the board. Whereas the latter would have drastically reduced the size of the student body, the Kibbee plan eliminated very few students.[28] Rather, it greatly cut down their number in the senior colleges, allocating them instead to the community colleges. In its emphasis on reallocation rather than exclusion, the plan moderated the potentially drastic ethnic effects of the board's eighth-grade standard.

Other parts of the chancellor's proposal for restructuring the University were stringent. First, he called for the merger of six campuses and for a change in the status of one predominantly minority college from a four-year to a two-year school. It was also proposed that all programs within CUNY be examined with a view toward eliminating duplication of those with low student demand. A final set of proposals concerned student progress and retention. The two most important recommendations were that (1) withdrawal grades be made more difficult to obtain (under the original open-admissions model, students experiencing difficulty in a course could until quite late in the semester take a withdrawal grade rather than an F, with its depressive effect upon grade point average); and (2) students not be allowed to move to the upper division (i.e., the junior year of college) from the lower division or from community college unless they demonstrated proficiency on basic skills tests. These proposals carried the potential for an increase in attrition and failure rates among students who entered with weak academic preparation. Whereas the BHE eighth-grade standard would have reduced the student body directly through the admissions process, the Kibbee plan might have done so less directly through the academic process. By this means and by the consolidation of programs and campuses, the scale of CUNY could be reduced, allowing the University to operate on a smaller budget.

If the University still clung to the position that its fiscal crisis could be resolved by these steps, public officials remained adamant that emergency funding could materialize only when CUNY imposed tuition. About a month after the Kibbee plan had been drafted, the state education commissioner, Ewald Nyquist, made a speech before the City Club of New York (a civic group with many ties to CUNY) in which he commented upon the proposals and, more broadly, upon the CUNY situation.[29] He pointed out that even though the proposals sought to resolve the University's "academic crisis," the Board of Higher Education still had taken no realistic action to deal with the fiscal crisis. Indeed, Nyquist's remarks strongly reaffirmed the external view of the CUNY situation. Several of his comments are noteworthy in light of board actions that were soon to occur:

> When The City University implemented . . . open admissions . . . it redirected its efforts from serving a relatively small academic elite to its traditional public mission of serving the City's upwardly mobile poor population. That tradition —harking back to 1847—was eclipsed temporarily in the postwar period, when, because of both a shortage of funds and a burgeoning . . . . college-age population, the University set admissions standards that excluded all but the highest achievement students. Since high school achievement and economic circumstances are highly correlated, the effect was that [the] municipal college system, designed to serve the poor, had come to serve the middle class. The poor were systematically excluded.
>
> It was readily apparent to me by late last summer that retrenchment after retrenchment could not be made without finally getting to the point where the

University would be compelled to abandon its mission of extending open access or else allow the quality of academic offerings to fall below acceptable standards. In order to keep this from happening, I recommended to Alfred Giardino . . . that all students attending City University should be charged tuition, beginning with the spring semester this year.

Since the nature and extent of the crisis were made known last summer, the Board of Higher Education has displayed a towering incapacity to make decisions and to implement the hard decisions. . . . Last September and October, I called upon the Board to deal seriously with its fiscal situation; nothing happened. In December, the Regents proposed an academic and fiscal plan for the University; nothing happened.

Time has run out for the Board of Higher Education.[30]

Chancellor Kibbee's restructuring plan formed the agenda for a meeting of the board on April 5, 1976.[31] The agenda did not include the tuition issue. The Kibbee plan was passed largely intact but not before it had succeeded in precipitating violent demonstrations at the University's central administrative offices by minority students protesting the planned merger and downgrading of predominantly minority colleges.[32]

A substantial portion of the academic year had now passed without any change in the positions of the BHE, the city, and the state on the tuition issue. The University still faced its huge deficit. Whether time had indeed run out for CUNY was a question soon to be answered.

The University Collapses

The budget reductions imposed the previous August rendered CUNY's monthly dollar allocations insufficient to meet monthly expenses. In fact the University had been meeting them through advances from the amounts allocated to each succeeding month. In May the University was informed that an advance from its June allocation would not be forthcoming and there was to be no restoration of any portion of the cuts from the previous August. Default was imminent.

It was probably at this point that some of the assumptions in which the board had encapsulated itself began to crumble. It was clear that the city and state would indeed let CUNY go "down the drain"—that the budget crisis scenarios of the Bowker years and the early 1970s no longer applied. Governor Carey, who had promised to preserve free tuition in his 1974 gubernatorial campaign, was ultimately forced by the fiscal realities in both city and state to change his position, and on May 20 he issued a policy statement explaining that

the provision of new aid from the State must necessarily be linked to the generation of additional student revenue. . . . the BHE must give serious attention to the extension of the current tuition policy at State University levels to matriculated undergraduate students.[33]

The next day Giardino and Kibbee met with representatives of both the mayor and the governor for a discussion of the governor's statement. Giardino was dissatisfied with the level of state support that would be provided CUNY above and beyond the revenues that would be generated by tuition. But at this late date there was neither time nor leverage for drawn out negotiations.

On May 25 Giardino submitted his resignation to Mayor Beame, and several other board members also resigned. Three days later the University defaulted on its obligations for the month of May. Chancellor Kibbee was forced to close the entire University—just at the period of final exams and commencement.

During the ensuing two-week period, a frenetic series of conferences and negotiations took place in Albany. The result was a legislative package with the following provisions:

1. A new Board of Higher Education, expanded to fifteen members, with diminished city power and increased state appointments.
2. A requirement that tuition be imposed at the same levels in force at SUNY.
3. Elimination of most of the April board resolution to close or merge campuses (this was inserted as an accommodation to minority legislators, who would have refused to vote for the package without this proviso).
4. The inclusion of CUNY in TAP in order to offset the effects of tuition upon low-income students.
5. A reduced budget of $470 million for the coming academic year (which presumably would be augmented by tuition revenues).
6. The immediate provision of $24 million in state aid, which would allow CUNY to reopen and complete the academic year.

While these events were going on, replacements to the board were made by Mayor Beame for those who had earlier resigned. With these new members taking their seats, the board voted to impose tuition on June 1. On June 14, Governor Carey signed the legislative package, and the University finished out the year.

In September 1976 a sharply reduced freshman class entered. It is difficult to identify precisely the reasons for the decline since it was not caused directly by the mechanics of the modified admissions criteria. Most likely the pessimistic news engulfing the University took its toll. Students heard that there would be a test to qualify for admission, and even though that proposal was later abandoned, it undoubtedly deterred weak students from applying.[34] Then, news that it would henceforth be more difficult to gain admission to a senior college may have discouraged some who preferred these colleges but who would no longer qualify. All through the year there were reports of impending tuition charges but no news that substantial financial aid would be available, especially for low-income students. When tuition was finally imposed, this probably reduced the enrollment of some students who would not have qualified for financial aid (or at least not 100 percent aid). And, of course, the closing of the University just at final exams and graduation could hardly have been reassuring to prospective students. All of these events created a strong impression of CUNY as a very unstable institution and thus a less attractive one. The result was greatly decreased enrollment among all groups.

The Crisis in Retrospect

American higher education in the twentieth century offers other instances of lower status groups gaining sudden access to institutions that previously they had not attended in great numbers. A notable example is that of Jews entering elite eastern universities in the early years of the century. Unmistakably, their entry in large numbers was seen as a threat to the status and privilege, as well as the "cultural purity," of those old-stock American groups that were the traditional clients of these universities. The response of these groups was the development of restrictive quotas, often justified by rationales that had the appearance of fairness.[35] And at the City College of New York, one result of the great Jewish influx at the turn of the century was a flight from the college by those of northern European stock, who had earlier dominated the student body.[36]

In some ways, the events at CUNY in the period from 1969 to 1976 were not unlike these earlier episodes. Poor minorities fought to gain a foothold in the hope that this would create a flow of blacks and Hispanics into the middle class. Those white groups who already occupied middle-class positions viewed the minority efforts with alarm. Students from these new groups differed from the whites in many ways. Their aspirations were not often accompanied by levels of academic skill traditionally associated with CUNY students. And, as noted in earlier chapters, they also differed in nonacademic ways—in taste and style—just as eastern European Jews had appeared different when earlier they sought entry to elite colleges.

We suspect that some whites resented open admissions because it constituted a removal of their own privilege, thus posing a threat to their chances of maintaining and enhancing their social and economic position. In the liberal atmosphere of New York such resentment is rarely expressed publicly. Rather, we think it surfaced obliquely in the debates over standards: the stated concern was that open admissions would lower standards and the CUNY diploma would decline in value. While these fears were never dispelled under open admissions, there was at least an uneasy coexistence between the values of merit and equality. But when the fiscal crisis struck, the conflicts of 1969, still smoldering, ignited with renewed intensity. The

CUNY board's attempt to retrench open admissions was a step that it had probably wanted to take and the crisis presented a good opportunity since a move away from open access would have made CUNY a less expensive university to run. It was also a step that struck at the heart of the minority presence and that therefore aroused their vigorous opposition as they sought to preserve the gains that open admissions represented to them.

On the other hand, the tuition issue did not create ethnic conflict. This may seem surprising since a tuition policy would have weighed less heavily upon minority students: they were far more likely than whites to come from low-income families[37] and thus to qualify for full TAP aid. Even with the deficiencies of TAP—notably the exclusion of part-time matriculated students and the eight-semester limit—a tuition policy should have seemed preferable to the certainty that minorities would have been disproportionately excluded from CUNY under any plan that used an admissions test as a device to reduce the student body. Yet, as a way out of the fiscal crisis, tuition was never seized upon by minorities as an alternative better serving their interests.[38] The tuition aid program was not well understood and it was undoubtedly mistrusted by minorities. Given the state's own financial situation, there were no guarantees that TAP would not be pruned in the future. Moreover, it may have seemed curious that whereas in earlier days the University was free for the relatively select number who qualified, when the minority presence in CUNY grew large, the issue of tuition was raised. Even if the differential consequences of tuition as opposed to admissions standards were clearly perceived, it was difficult to convince anyone that paying for college was better than free education. Therefore, advocacy of tuition on the part of minority members of the board might have subjected them to hostility from the minority community.[39]

We can only speculate about the difference it might have made if CUNY had been able earlier to confront tuition as a policy option. Given the political difficulty that tuition posed for elected officials of both city and state and their desire to see the board take action, it is conceivable that tuition on terms more favorable to CUNY could have been negotiated in fall 1975 than in spring 1976, when the University's leverage had crumbled. Some of the shortcomings of TAP might have been adjusted for the case of CUNY; for example, aid for part-time students might have been an item on which the University could have negotiated favorably. In any event, earlier resolution of the tuition issue undoubtedly would have allowed the completion of the academic year. And with more time to communicate the financial aid possibilities accompanying tuition, CUNY might have averted the sharp decline in applications and enrollments for fall 1976.

The political heat of the fiscal crisis has substantially changed the open-admissions policy. The new admissions criteria now track a larger proportion of CUNY's students into the community colleges. In 1975, the last year the original open-admissions entrance criteria were in force, 53 percent of freshmen were placed in a senior college. In 1976, when the new admissions criteria took effect, only 37 percent were placed in four-year institutions.[40] Our earlier analyses (see chapter 8) suggested that the educational attainment of students initially placed in community colleges was less than that of comparable students who began college in a four-year institution. One would expect, therefore, that the changed admissions criteria would lower the ultimate educational attainment of many students.

As noted earlier, the number of entering freshman declined sharply immediately after the fiscal crisis. Table 11.2 shows that the 1976 freshman

TABLE 11.2. Changes in the Distribution of Minority Freshmen at CUNY, 1975–1978

Cohort	Senior	Community	All of CUNY	Cohort Size
Representation of Minority Students among Freshmen Entering Senior and Community Colleges				
% of Minority Students among All Entering Students				
1975[a]	40.0	46.9	43.3	38,114
1976	44.4	55.5	51.3	29,283
1977[a]	40.6	51.1	47.3	31,940
1978	47.8	57.1	53.3	32,300
% of Minority Students among All Entering Non–Special Program Students				
1975[a]	33.1	41.7	37.3	34,352
1976	31.3	51.6	44.6	25,741
1977[a]	23.3	46.0	38.5	27,364
1978	31.2	52.2	44.5	27,188

Cohort	Senior	Community
Stratification of Entering Minority Students across Senior and Community Colleges[b]		
All Entering Students		
1975	.92	1.08
1976	.86	1.08
1977	.86	1.08
1978	.90	1.07
Non–Special Program Students Only		
1975	.89	1.12
1976	.70	1.16
1977	.61	1.19
1978	.70	1.17

Source: CUNY annual censuses.
[a]Ethnic data were unavailable for Hunter College in these years. The column, "Cohort Size," does not include Hunter students.
[b]Ratios of actual proportions to those expected if minority students were uniformly distributed across the levels of CUNY. Ratios calculated from percentages which appear in the top panels of the table.

class contained about eleven thousand fewer students than did the 1975 class.[41] Though freshmen enrollments rebounded somewhat in 1977 and 1978, they did not rise to precrisis levels. The composition of these classes has also changed. Since the crisis there has been a decrease in the proportion of entrants with strong high school records.[42] Furthermore, while the enrollment decline has occurred among all groups, it has been proportionately greater among whites than among minority students. Quite possibly, some whites, possessing greater economic resources than minorities, have reacted to tuition by going elsewhere to college.[43] As a result of the greater falloff among whites, the proportion of minority freshmen has increased. In 1976 they constituted, for the first time since the inception of open admissions, a majority of the freshman class.

After the fiscal crisis, the special senior-college program, SEEK (composed overwhelmingly of minority students), began to replace open admissions as the mechanism for preserving integration in the senior colleges. SEEK students were not subject to the more stringent criteria governing entry to the four-year institutions. As the table shows, the percentage of minority students in those schools increased somewhat when we include SEEK students. Of course, minority students constituted larger proportions of the freshmen classes after 1975, so that it still could be true that minority representation at the senior colleges declined relative to the numbers of minority students entering CUNY. But with special program students included, this happened only to a very minor degree, as is shown by the bottom panels of table 11.2, which present the ratios of the minority compositions of the senior and community colleges to the overall minority compositions of the different freshmen classes.[44] However, with special program students taken out, minority percentages in the senior colleges did not increase and consequently, as the bottom panels show, minorities were far more underrepresented in senior colleges in 1976 and in each subsequent year than in 1975 (minority freshmen who entered in 1975 were more equally distributed across CUNY than in any preceding year of open admissions). All in all, then, while entering freshmen were more likely to find themselves in community colleges, overall, minorities were not, as a result of changed admissions guidelines, disproportionately more likely to be so placed, but this fact must be attributed to the SEEK program.

Other policy changes may affect students' prospects for academic success. Stricter standards for retention now exist. Moreover, senior-college students must pass basic skills proficiency tests before they will be allowed to enter their junior year, and community-college students must pass these tests before transferring to a senior college.[45] These requirements were put in place at the very time that remedial and counseling staffs were cut back because of the crisis. While proficiency tests can be valuable for monitoring and improving the effectiveness of CUNY's remedial programs, the elimination of students is also a possible—even likely—consequence.

Though open admissions still exists in the sense that CUNY remains open to all high school graduates, the modification in the policy may diminish many students' chances of earning a degree. And given that minority students enter with weaker academic preparation than whites, their chances may be even more diminished. We doubt that these major changes would have occurred in the absence of the fiscal crisis.

On a deeper level, that crisis resurrected the debate over a fundamental question: is access to higher education a privilege or a right? In contemporary American society, as elsewhere, higher education is distinguished from the preceding stages of the educational system because it is normatively a selective stage, to which only some should have the privilege of access. In the general view, this privilege is extended to those who qualify on the basis of previous academic achievements, although the American system has always had places somewhere for those with the financial means to pay tuition, regardless of their academic qualifications. In practice, the combination of academic and financial barriers has tended to exclude youth of lower socioeconomic status and of minority origins despite the growth in rates of college attendance after World War II and the great importance a college education has assumed for the future occupational and financial positions of individuals. As a consequence, the view of higher education as a privilege has had strong ideological overtones, legitimating the increasingly significant role of higher education in overall inequality of opportunity.

Open admissions was based on a new premise: college education is a right, just as grammar school and high school education have come to be accepted. The policy assumed that anyone possessing a high school diploma could benefit from the chance to attend college. Under open admissions, CUNY exhibited the features of a system of universal higher education: like the primary and secondary schools, it was free and publicly supported and it provided a next rung on the educational ladder for those who had advanced beyond the earlier steps. The open-admissions policy attempted to lay to rest the often debated question about who should be educated. This was the question on which selective admissions policies had been based and which in part had led to differences in the educational attainment of various class and ethnic groups.

But the view of higher education as a privilege did not die under open admissions; it merely faded a bit into the background. Six years after open admissions began, the question of who should be educated acquired again a legitimacy derived from older notions of privilege. The assault on open admissions as undermining academic standards emerged from the premise that not all students are "college material." That premise was widely enough shared so that the direction of change in response to the fiscal crisis was in favor of selectivity: more stringent requirements for admission to four-year colleges; skills proficiency tests as the gateway to the upper levels of the four-year colleges; and the imposition of tuition, whose effects were not fully offset by financial aid to those who could not afford to pay. This contraction of opportunity was not the inevitable result of the fiscal crisis. The budgetary axe fell with unequal severity upon different levels of the public education system and with greater force on CUNY than on any other service within New York City, indicating clearly that the concept of higher education as a right is far from universally accepted.

If, under the pressures of the fiscal crisis, the view of college as a privilege regained its ascendancy, we think this happened as a result of attempts by more advantaged groups to maintain their position. One consequence of coming from an advantaged family is the greater chance such origins give to attain the educational credentials necessary for socioeconomic success.[46] The democratization of educational opportunity that the open-admissions program signified threatened to remove or limit this competitive edge. Thus, while CUNY is still a more open institution than other systems of higher education, such as California's, the legacy of the fiscal crisis has been a narrowing of the mission to which the University committed itself in 1969. In the end, it has moved closer to the older view: higher education is a privilege not a right.

Notes

1. City University of New York, *Data Book* (New York: City University of New York, Fall 1976), chap. 2.
2. Office of the Chancellor, *Effects of the New York City Fiscal Crisis on the City University of New York* (New York: City University of New York, 1978).
3. Chancellor, *Effects of Fiscal Crisis*. The estimate of two thousand teaching positions appeared in Larry Van Dyne, "To Fit the Budget: Painful Layoffs, Sweeping Cutbacks—The New York Tragedy-3," *Chronicle of Higher Education*, September 27, 1976, pp. 6-7.
4. The figures for 1960-1961 are taken from Board of Higher Education, *Financial Report of the University* (New York: City University of New York, 1961), p. viii; figures for 1970-1971 were taken from Board of Higher Education, *The Chancellor's Budget Request for 1971-72* (New York: City University of New York, 1970), p. 11. Of course, over this period CUNY was partly supported by state funding.
5. Larry Van Dyne, "The New York Tragedy," *Chronicle of Higher Education*, September 13, 1976, p. 10.
6. This pointed out in Larry Van Dyne, "The Free-Tuition Fight Is Lost: The New York Tragedy-2," *Chronicle of Higher Education*, September 20, 1976, p. 4.
7. From an interview by Jerome Karabel with Stephen Berger, New York, August 2, 1978.
8. Karabel interview with Berger.
9. The income data are reported in Laurence F. Mucciolo, *An Analysis of the Im-*

pact of Charging Tuition at the City University of New York (New York: Office of the Master Plan, City University of New York, December 1975), p. 26.
10. Mucciolo, chap. 7.
11. Mucciolo, p. iii.
12. A good illustration is provided by the nationally syndicated article by Rowland Evans and Robert Novak, "The Wrecking of a College," Washington Post, December 24, 1970.
13. From an interview by Jerome Karabel with Alfred A. Giardino, New York, July 19, 1978.
14. Rita E. Hauser, "Rethinking Open Admissions," New York Times, June 23, 1975.
15. Karabel interview with Berger.
16. His involvement in administrative activities and interactions with staff below the top echelon were reported to Lavin by several members of the University's central office
17. From an interview by Jerome Karabel with Robert J. Kibbee, New York, July 6, 1978. The same view was expressed by Kibbee in an interview with Lavin.
18. One important aspect that might have been negotiable at an early stage pertained to part-time matriculated students. These students were eligible for free tuition at CUNY. However, under the state's TAP part-timers were not eligible for assistance.
19. State Education Department, A Report of the Regents on the City University of New York (Albany, December 1975).
20. In one respect this assertion was misleading. Part-time matriculated students would not have been covered without a change in state policy.
21. Board of Higher Education, Calendar December 15, 1975 (New York: City University of New York, 1975), p. 5.
22. These tests (described in chapter 9) are part of the Stanford achievement test series published by Harcourt Brace Jovanovich. The tests were administered to a large number of freshmen in the 1970 and 1971 cohorts.
23. This conclusion is based on a personal discussion between Lavin and Kibbee in January 1976 and also on a memorandum from Kibbee to the board (dated January 19, 1976) explaining the circumstances under which a study of the ethnic impact of the board's decision had been released to the New York Times.
24. The fact that the resolution was passed in a private rather than a public session also suggests awareness of its controversial nature.
25. David E. Lavin and Richard A. Silberstein, Effects of New Admissions Criteria upon the Ethnic Composition of the City University of New York (New York: City University of New York, December 1975).
26. Iver Peterson, "City U. Plan May Cut Down on Minorities," New York Times, December 19, 1975. The report was developed on Lavin's initiative and was released after consultation with a key member of Kibbee's staff, Vice-Chancellor J. Joseph Meng. Although all of the CUNY vice-chancellors received copies of the report prior to its appearance in the Times, none, except for Meng, had been involved in the decision to release it, and Kibbee was probably unaware that it would appear publicly.
27. This is described in Charlayne Hunter, "City U. Faces Suit over Admissions,"

New York Times, January 9, 1976. The suit was instituted on the technical
ground that the BHE had failed to provide the required minimum of one week's
notice before holding a public hearing. The question of bringing suit on a con-
stitutional issue was, according to Franklin Williams, the black vice-chairman
of the BHE, to be held in reserve. While the suit had an immediate effect of
adding pressure on the University to reconsider the standards resolution, it was
eventually dismissed by the court.

28. The proposal to set up transitional centers was never implemented. All students
who did not meet senior-college admissions criteria were allocated to community colleges, no matter how low their high school average or rank. In practice,
therefore, no students were eliminated under the Kibbee admissions criteria.

29. Ewald B. Nyquist, "The City University of New York: Crisis and Cure," remarks delivered before the City Club of New York, New York, March 15,
1976.

30. Nyquist.

31. Board of Higher Education, *Calendar: April 5, 1976* (New York: City University of New York, 1976). A major item on the agenda dealt with student retention and the implementation of a proficiency testing program. In explaining the
need for these policies, the board stated: "With the inception of the Open Admissions Program, the University and its faculty have liberalized the grading
process so as to maximize opportunities for students. In the process, the grading system has been abused to the extent that very little incentive has been provided the student where he or she is doing less than average work. The intent of
these resolutions is to have students' transcripts accurately reflect their performance." There is no empirical evidence for this assumption that standards
had deteriorated. Indeed, the data presented in this volume hardly suggest that
at CUNY under open admissions, a policy of "social promotion" prevailed.

32. Keith Moore, Richard Brass, and Harry Stathos, "22 Are Hurt as City U. Students Riot," *New York Daily News*, April 6, 1976.

33. Hugh L. Carey, *Program of Responsible Action for the CUNY Crisis* (Albany:
Office of the Governor, 1975).

34. Indeed, a CUNY report shows that the largest single percentage decline in applications and enrollment was among students with college admissions averages
of less than 70. See Barry Kaufman and Robert Terdeman, *Application and Enrollment of CUNY Freshmen: Fall 1975 vs. Fall 1976* (New York: Office of
Program and Policy Research, City University of New York, 1977).

35. Rich anecdotal material, as well as analyses of the attempts of elite universities
to restrict Jewish access, appears in Stephen Steinberg, *The Academic Melting
Pot*, (New York: McGraw-Hill, 1974), chap. 1. An analysis that focuses in
depth upon Columbia University may be found in Harold S. Wechsler, *The
Qualified Student: A History of Selective College Admissions in America* (New
York: Wiley, 1977), chap. 7. In part the use of standards of character such as
"well-roundedness" and "leadership" as admissions criteria was an effort to
invent standards that, it was thought, Jews could not meet. Efforts to recruit
national student bodies were used to justify regional quotas, and one function
of such quotas was to limit the number of Jewish entrants.

36. That older groups stopped attending the college after the Jewish influx is noted

in S. Willis Rudy, *The College of the City of New York: A History* (New York: City College Press, 1949), pp. 292–293.

37. Among 1971 senior-college freshmen, 73 percent of blacks, 77 percent of Hispanics, but only 37 percent of whites came from families with incomes of less than $10,000. Below this income for community-college students were 85 percent of blacks, 91 percent of Hispanics, and 44 percent of whites.

38. There was a precedent for minority support for tuition: in what now seems like a remarkable perception, a black assemblyman in the state legislature asserted ten years earlier that free tuition at CUNY was being used as a means of excluding the city's minority population. This insight was lacking during the 1975–1976 period. See Sheila C. Gordon, "The Transformation of the City University of New York, 1945–1970" (Ph.D. Diss., Columbia University, 1975), pp. 196–197.

39. Mr. Franklin Williams described this difficulty in an interview with Jerome Karabel, New York, July 18, 1978.

40. Calculated from CUNY enrollment reports for 1975 and 1976. In 1977 and 1978, about 40 percent of freshmen entered senior colleges.

41. The number of students shown for the 1975 cohort (40,368) is larger than that shown for that year in table 4.3. In chapter 4 we excluded students enrolled in CUNY evening sessions because we wished to assess the effects of open admissions upon the enrollment of students who began college as full-time freshmen. Evening students were far more likely to enroll on a part-time basis. Subsequent to 1975, CUNY enrollment reports did not distinguish between day and evening students. The 1975 figure was thus changed to achieve comparability with these subsequent years.

42. Office of the Chancellor, *Admissions and Enrollment at the City University of New York through 1990* (New York: City University of New York, October 1979), p. 5 and exhibit 5.

43. Definitive evidence on the number who went elsewhere is lacking. While CUNY's freshman enrollment declined by about eleven thousand between 1975 and 1976, the number of graduates of New York City high schools who enrolled in the State University of New York and in independent colleges in the state increased by only about two thousand. There were only very small percentage increases in enrollments in out-of-state colleges. It appears that somewhat less than half of the 1976 graduates who might have attended CUNY enrolled elsewhere the following fall. Others may have enrolled in college at a subsequent time. Data furnished by Dr. Barry Kaufman of CUNY's Office of Institutional Research.

44. These ratios were calculated in the same way as those in table 4.4. That is, we calculated the ratio of the percentage of minority students at each level of CUNY to their percentage among entering students. This ratio indicates the extent to which minority students were underrepresented or overrepresented in senior and community colleges. A ratio below 1 indicates that minority students were underrepresented relative to their overall proportion in the freshman class. A ratio of above 1 indicates their overrepresentation.

45. Proficiency tests were administered for the first time to the fall 1978 freshmen. As this is written, senior-college students have not yet accumulated enough

credits to be classified as juniors and community-college students have not been in school long enough to earn associate degrees and/or to transfer to senior colleges in significant numbers. Therefore, no data yet exist on the proportions of students, initially below standard on the tests, who passed them at a later point.

46. An important critical analysis of credentialism and its relation to social stratification appears in Randall Collins, *The Credential Society* (New York: Academic, 1979).

APPENDIX A   Quality of the Sample Data

Since many of our analyses are based on samples of student populations, it is necessary to assess the samples' representativeness by comparing them to the populations, using variables measured for both. Some sample and population data are presented in table A.1.

Because the colleges included in the samples vary from year to year, the most basic comparison involves the distribution of students between senior and community colleges. There are large discrepancies between the samples and their populations, but not always in the same direction. Senior-college students are overrepresented in the 1970 sample but greatly underrepresented in the 1971 and 1972 samples. These discrepancies do not affect most of our tables since level of college is controlled in them, but they possibly affect Table 4.7, showing college preferences and admission rates. For example, because the 1971 and 1972 samples contain disproportionate numbers of community-college students, table 4.7 overstates the percentages of students in those years who preferred senior colleges but were placed in community colleges (i.e., those who were placed in senior colleges are underrepresented). Nonetheless, we do not believe that our conclusions from this table are affected because they are based on the pattern of ethnic differences and that pattern is consistent across the three samples even though their biases lie in different directions.

Since most of our tables control for level of college, additional comparisons between the samples and the populations are best done with such a control, and the data for these comparisons are also presented in table A.1. One important variable is ethnicity. Here, the only available population

313

TABLE A.1. Comparison of Sample with Population for Selected Variables, 1970, 1971, and 1972 Cohorts

Cohort	HIGH SCHOOL AVERAGE				RATE OF			MEAN GPA		% Minority	% Senior College	% Community College
	<70	70-74.9	75-79.9	80+	Graduation	Drop-out	Transfer	Drop-out	Other			
1970												
Total population											58	42
Total sample											69	32
Senior population	4	11	24	60	39	47				11		
Senior sample	4	9	23	64	44	42				13		
O.A. – Sr. pop.	11	28	62	0	26	58		1.54	2.44			
O.A. – Sr. sample	10	26	64	0	30	53		1.57	2.43			
Reg. – Sr. pop.	0	0	0	100	48	40		2.34	2.94			
Reg. – Sr. sample	0	0	0	100	52	37		2.43	2.95			
Comm. population	33	34	23	11	28	64				27		
Comm. sample	26	34	27	13	33	59				25		
O.A. – Comm. pop.	49	51	0	0	23	67	24	1.49	2.31			
O.A. – Comm. sample	44	56	0	0	26	65	26	1.40	2.32			
Reg. – Comm. pop.	0	0	68	32	39	54	29	1.89	2.72			
Reg. – Comm. sample	0	0	67	33	43	50	30	1.81	2.74			
1971												
Total population											54	46
Total sample											38	62
Senior population	5	13	24	59	21	44				18		
Senior sample	5	8	24	63	30	35				14		
O.A. – Sr. pop.	13	30	57	0	10	55		1.46	2.34			
O.A. – Sr. sample	13	21	66	0	19	44		1.68	2.49			

314

	1	2	3	4	5	6	7	8	9	10	11	12
Reg. – Sr. pop.	0	0	0	100	30	36		2.28	2.90		55	45
Reg. – Sr. sample	0	0	0	100	37	29		2.40	2.97		30	70
Comm. population	35	32	23	11	25	61				33		
Comm. sample	32	33	24	12	31	54				36		
O.A. – Comm. pop.	52	48	0	0	19	66	18	1.44	2.27			
O.A. – Comm. sample	49	51	0	0	25	59	21	1.68	2.27			
Reg. – Comm. pop.	0	0	68	33	36	51	27	1.93	2.70			
Reg. – Comm. sample	0	0	66	34	43	44	30	2.21	2.74			
1972												
Total population												
Total sample												
Senior population	7	14	24	55	1	40				18		
Senior sample	3	10	23	64	1	33				21		
O.A. – Sr. pop.	14	31	55	0	1	49		1.40	2.21			
O.A. – Sr. sample	9	27	65	0	1	44		1.42	2.23			
Reg. – Sr. pop.	0	0	0	100	1	31		2.20	2.84			
Reg. – Sr. sample	0	0	0	100	1	26		2.43	2.91			
Comm. population	35	30	21	13	21	54				40		
Comm. sample	34	30	22	14	24	52				37		
O.A. – Comm. pop.	54	46	0	0	16	58	12	1.50	2.23			
O.A. – Comm. sample	53	47	0	0	18	56	14	1.50	2.22			
Reg. – Comm. pop.	0	0	62	39	33	45	17	2.00	2.71			
Reg. – Comm. sample	0	0	61	39	37	42	19	1.99	2.73			

Note: O.A. = open-admissions; Reg. = regular admissions; Sr. pop. = senior-college population; Sr. sample = senior-college sample; Comm. pop. = community-college population; Comm. sample = community-college sample.

measure is the percentage of minority students (i.e., the combined percentage of blacks and Hispanics) in each freshman class, taken from the CUNY census. It is clear from table A.1 that sample and population figures agree closely for both senior and community colleges in all three cohorts.

Another important variable is high school average, the basis for distinguishing open-admissions from regular students and also one of the best predictors of academic performance in college. Examination of the population and sample distributions shows that overall the samples contain slightly higher proportions of more able students than do the populations. Broadly speaking, this bias is of small magnitude—usually involving a difference of only a few percentage points in each category of high school average. However, in some instances the discrepancies are larger. In the 1970 cohort, community-college students in the sample clearly show a higher average than the population from which they were drawn; this is also true of senior-college students in the 1971 and 1972 samples. Because of these biases table 4.5 somewhat understates the proportions of open admissions students in the community colleges in 1970 and in the senior colleges in 1971 and 1972. But again our conclusions from the table are based on an ethnic pattern broadly consistent across the three cohorts.

These biases also raise the possibility that the college performance of sample students at CUNY was better than that of the population as a whole. That possibility is best addressed by comparing samples and populations in terms of important performance variables. One of these is movement from community to senior college. As table A.1 shows, sample and population transfer rates closely correspond for all three cohorts.

Another variable is college grade point average. Table A.1 presents the mean averages for students who dropped out and for those who graduated or were still enrolled as of June 1975 (shown as "other"). For the latter category the sample and population figures agree closely. The largest difference occurs for senior-college open admissions students in the 1971 cohort, where the performance of the sample is somewhat better than that of the population. Among dropouts, there are some larger population-sample differences, especially among the 1971 freshmen. Grade point averages in the populations generally are a bit lower than those in the samples, suggesting that the extent to which students identified as dropouts transferred to institutions outside the CUNY system may have been less than the sample data imply.

Graduation and dropout rates are two further outcomes receiving major attention in our analyses. With regard to graduation rates, the comparisons in table A.1 show moderate and consistent differences between sample and population for the 1970 and 1972 cohorts: the sample graduation rates are higher by as much as five percentage points. For the 1971 cohort, the upward bias in the sample is greater than for the other cohorts, especially among senior-college students. With regard to dropout rates, the same pattern holds in reverse: the rates for the samples are lower than for the populations, and the discrepancies are largest for the 1971 cohort. These biases are important because our conclusions concerning dropout and graduation rates involve not only ethnic patterns within our samples but also comparisons of our samples to national data. The superiority of the CUNY record over the national is not as great as that implied by the samples. This qualification is noted in the discussion of dropout and graduation rates (see chapter 6).

While population measures are, of course, not available for every variable measured in our samples, overall these comparisons show a close correspondence between samples and populations. Although the samples contain greater proportions of academically able students and the CUNY performance of these students is in some respects better than that of the corresponding populations, we do not find grounds for skepticism concerning the conclusions we have drawn from the samples.

APPENDIX B Reading the Results of Regression Analysis

Most of the statistical analyses reported in this book rely on regression analysis, currently the statistical procedure most widely used by sociologists for analyzing phenomena that depend on multiple influences. The results of regression analysis pose some hurdles for readers unfamiliar with statistical procedure, but this type of analysis more than compensates for this disadvantage by the numerous advantages it offers overs its nearest competitor, the easily accessible tabular kind of analysis, in which results are expressed in terms of percentages. Thus, regression analysis does not require that intrinsically noncategorical variables, like grade point average, be divided into somewhat arbitrary categories, as tabular analysis does (to form categories, one might have to distinguish between grade point averages of 3.01 and 2.99, if the boundary of two categories were 3.00, even though the distinction is nearly meaningless). More important, the few coefficients of regression analysis allow us to see the effect of any variable on another in a compact and direct way even when a large number of other variables are controlled. By contrast, when a large number of independent variables are involved, tabular analysis requires the analyst to infer the effect of any variable from a large number of percentage differences, generally of varying reliability because of the small numbers of cases many involve.[1]

The purpose of this appendix is to give the reader unfamiliar with regression analysis a few guidelines for reading the tables accompanying the text. We warn in advance, however, that we will ignore many of the statistical details that would appear in even an elementary statistics text, especially those having to do with estimation of coefficients and statistical inference,[2] and focus the discussion entirely on the intepretation of key coefficients.

318

In its simplest form, regression analysis expresses one variable, the one being explained (the so-called dependent variable), as a linear function of others, those viewed as constituting an explanation (the so-called independent variables). The word "linear" in the preceding sentence implies only that a change in the dependent variable induced by a change in an independent variable is directly proportional to the magnitude of change in the latter.[3] Such an equation might look like the following:

$$y = -3.108 + .059x_1 + .002x_2 + .046x_3,$$

where y is the predicted cumulative grade point average (on a scale of 0 to 4) of a student who entered senior college in fall 1970, x_1 is that student's high school average (in points), x_2 is his or her high school rank, and x_3 is the number of college preparatory courses he or she took in high school. In this instance, the dependent variable is cumulative grade point average in senior college, and the independent variables are the components of high school background. Four numbers have been estimated from the 1970 senior-college data to yield a specific equation. The leftmost is the so-called intercept and the others have been referred to in our text and tables as "unstandardized" coefficients (or b's; they are also referred to as "metric" coefficients).

This equation can be used to predict[4] the grade point average of a student with a known high school record. Thus, in the case of a student with a 90 high school average, who stood at the eightieth percentile of his or her class, and who took fifteen college preparatory courses in high school, simple substitution of these values in the equation yields a predicted grade point average of 3.05, almost exactly a B. The usual interpretation of unstandardized coefficients can be illustrated by using the equation to predict the cumulative grade point average of a second student with the same high school record except for an average one point higher. The predicted grade point average of this student is higher by .059, the value of the unstandardized regression coefficient of high school average. Thus, an unstandardized coefficient describes how much we would expect the dependent variable to change if the relevant independent variable changed by one unit, *while the other independent variables remained unchanged.* An equivalent formulation is that the unstandardized coefficient describes the difference in the dependent variable that we would expect to find between two students who differed by one unit in the relevant independent variable but were the same in terms of the remaining independent variables.[5] Often in the text we offer reduced versions of these formulations, saying, for example, that a difference of ten points in high school average resulted in a difference of over half a letter grade (i.e., .59).

As the words "predict" and "expect" in these formulations imply, there is generally not an exact match between the value of a dependent variable predicted by a regression equation and the observed value of that variable.

319

The imperfect fit occurs for a number of reasons: variables are imperfectly measured; relationships are not truly linear; some of the influences on the dependent variable are not included in the equation (and perhaps have not been measured because they are not understood); and, most simply, chance is involved. One of the strengths of regression analysis is that it gives a coefficient that describes the exact degree of fit between predicted and observed values. Hence, this same coefficient identifies the power of the explanation constituted by the independent variables. The coefficient is generally called the R^2, or the square of the multiple correlation coefficient. In the case of the equation above, the R^2 is .313. This number can be thought of as the proportion of individual-to-individual grade differences—in a specific statistical form called the "variance"[6]—that is explained by the independent variables. Thus, the statistically minded social scientist will say that high school background accounts for 31.3 percent of the variance in senior-college grades. This may not seem like a lot—it seems to leave over half of the grade differences unexplained—but in fact it is a lot by the usual standards of social science analysis. Grades at CUNY were substantially predictable from high school records but by no means were they entirely so. Students who had done badly in high school were not doomed to flunk out of CUNY.

Which of the three components of high school background had the most powerful effect on college grades cannot be deduced from the coefficients described up to this point. Although it might seem as though the most powerful variable were the one with the largest unstandardized coefficient, this is not necessarily the case. The magnitudes of the unstandardized coefficients depend on the units in which the variables are expressed and thus change when the variables are rescaled. If we expressed high school rank in terms of deciles rather than percentiles, so that one unit in the new version of the variable corresponded to ten units in the old version, then the unstandardized coefficient of high school rank would be ten times larger than it is in the present equation. In other words, by manipulating the scales of the variables, we can alter the magnitudes of the unstandardized coefficients at will, making any one of them the largest.

To identify the strengths of the influence of the independent variables, we need a version of the equation in which variables have been purged of their natural scales.This version is the standardized version because it assumes that the variables are expressed in standardized form, each with a mean of 0 and a standard deviation of 1.[7] This version looks like the following in the specific analysis we have been using as an illustration:

$$y' = .460x_1' + .044x_2' + .109x_3',$$

where y' is the predicted cumulative grade point average in standard deviation units, x_1' is the standardized version of high school average, x_2' is the standardized version of high school rank, and x_3' is the standardized version of the number of college preparatory courses taken in high school. No intercept is required in the standardized version of an equation. The coefficients are called "standardized" coefficients (or betas) in the text and tables.

Each of the standardized coefficients can be interpreted just as we do an unstandardized coefficient, recognizing that the units in this case are standard deviation units. Thus, the standardized form predicts an increase of .46 standard deviation units in cumulative grade point average for each increase of a standard deviation unit in high school average. Although standard deviation units are not familiar enough for most of us to grasp intuitively a relationship expressed in their terms, this interpretation takes on great importance because the independent variables are now expressed in comparable units and thus their standardized coefficients can be compared to determine their relative influence. In this instance, we see that high school average is clearly the most powerful of the independent variables.

An interpretation of standardized coefficients that is useful for gaining some feeling for their magnitudes, even though it has some important limitations, can be given in terms of the concept of "explained variance," already adduced in relation to R^2. One can view the square of the standardized coefficient of any independent variable as the proportion of the variance in the dependent variable explained by that independent variable. Thus, high school average explains .212, or 21.2 percent, of the variation in cumulative grades, accounting for over two-thirds of the variation in grades explained by high school background (31.3 percent). This interpretation of standardized coefficients is particularly useful in the case of categorical variables, such as ethnicity and gender, because the alternative interpretation depends on standard deviation units but these units do not correspond meaningfully with discrete categories.

But we must repeat the warnings of others that the goal of analysis should not be a partitioning of the explained variance in terms of the independent variables.[8] Indeed, not all of the variance explained by the independent variables jointly can be attributed neatly to them individually. This is so because the independent variables are usually correlated with each other, a phenomenon often called "multicollinearity," and for that reason their individual effects are not entirely distinguishable. Consequently, the sum of the squares of the standardized coefficients in the equation above usually does not equal the explained variance, or R^2.[9]

What has been discussed so far carries us a long way, but one major alteration is required to include variables that are most naturally expressed as categories rather than as values. Examples of such variables are ethnicity, gender, and graduation status. In regression analysis, these variables are typically represented by so-called dummy variables. A dummy variable can take on only the values 0 and 1 and represents membership in a single category. For example, a dummy variable representing membership in the Jewish category (part of the ethnicity variable) has the value 1 for a student who is Jewish and the value 0 for a student who is not. A single dummy variable fully represents a dichotomy (i.e., a variable with two categories) because it provides two values. In the general case, the number of dummy variables required to represent a nominal variable is one fewer than the number of its categories. Thus, five dummy variables are required to represent the six categories of ethnicity. Consequently, one category is in a sense omitted; membership in it is not represented by any of the 1-values of the dummy variables. The omitted category plays an important role in the interpretation of the coefficients of multiple dummy variables, as indicated below.

At the most general level, two uses of dummy variables must be distinguished. In the first they function as dependent variables. In this instance, they are used to represent only substantive variables that are dichotomies (e.g., graduation versus nongraduation), and the resulting equation and unstandardized coefficients have a special interpretation. Consider the following unstandardized version of a simple analysis of senior-college graduation in terms of high school background:

$$y = -1.060 + .013x_1 + .001x_2 + .024x_3,$$

where y is the predicted value of a dummy variable representing graduation, with graduates coded as 1, and x_1, x_2, and x_3 stand as before for high school average, rank, and college preparatory courses, respectively. Imagining the same student as before, with a high school average of 90, rank at the eightieth percentile of his or her class, and fifteen college preparatory courses, and substituting these values in the equation yields a predicted value for graduation of .55. Obviously, this is equal to neither of the two values of the dummy variable. More generally, in the case of a dependent dummy variable, the regression equation does not predict a *value* of the dependent variable; rather it predicts the *probability* of the event represented by the dummy variable. Thus, the equation predicts that the probability of such a student graduating from a senior college within five years is .55; in other words, 55 percent of such students would be expected to graduate. We can also interpret the unstandardized coefficients in terms of probabilities or percentages. For example, the probability of graduation rose by .013 for each additional point in high school average and hence by .13, or 13 percent for each additional ten points in high school average.

The second use of dummy variables is as independent variables; in this case they may represent dichotomies or substantive variables with more than two categories, such as ethnicity.[10] Consider as an example the equation that results from the addition of ethnicity to the equation shown above for cumulative grade point average. The unstandardized version is as follows:

$$y = -2.672 + .056x_1 + .002x_2 + .031x_3 + .089d_1 - .152d_2 \\ - .222d_3 - .274d_4 - .069d_5,$$

where y, x_1, x_2, and x_3 are the same as before and d_1, d_2, d_3, d_4, and d_5 are dummy variables representing membership in the Jewish, Catholic, black, Hispanic, and other nonwhite categories, respectively. The omitted category contains whites who are neither Catholic nor Jewish, and it is helpful to begin the interpretation of the equation with a student from that category. For such a student, all the dummy variables are 0 and hence only the intercept and the terms involving the components of high school background are involved in predicting cumulative grades. if we use the same values of these components as before ($x_1 = 90$, $x_2 = 80$, and $x_3 = 15$), the equation predicts a cumulative grade point average of 2.99, just below a B.

The interpretation of the coefficients of the dummy variables is now easy to explain. For a Jewish student with the same high school background as the student above, the intercept and the terms involving the components of high school background are exactly the same as they were for the student above. Of the dummy variables, only d_1, representing membership in the Jewish category, is non-zero. Since its value is 1, the predicted cumulative grade point average of the Jewish student is $2.99 + .089$, or 3.08 rounded. In other words, the unstandardized coefficient of the dummy variable for Jews is the expected grade difference between a Jewish and an "other white" student with equal high school records. The corresponding interpretation for the coefficients of the remaining dummy variables is obvious, and so, too, is the derivation of the expected grade difference between two students from ethnic categories represented by dummy variables. It is merely the difference between the two relevant coefficients. For example, the expected difference between a Jewish and a Hispanic student with the same high school background is $.089 - (-.274)$, or .363—more than a third of a letter grade. This is the largest ethnic difference between students with similar high school records.

Note that the choice of the omitted category is essentially arbitrary, an important consideration because the specific values of the unstandardized coefficients depend on the precise category chosen. This causes no real difficulty for interpretation as long as it is remembered that unstandardized coefficients are *differences* between members of the categories represented by the dummy variables and members of the omitted category. However, this arbitrariness causes considerable difficulty in the interpretation of the standardized coefficients of the dummy variables since they can be changed simply by choosing another omitted category. (An exception to this statement is a single dummy variable, representing a substantive dichotomy.) In any event, what is needed is a coefficient that represents the explanatory power of the substantive variable (e.g., ethnicity) rather than its categories. A computationally different coefficient—the so-called sheaf coefficient, based on the standardized coefficients of the dummy variables and the correlations between them—can be used for this purpose.[11] Its value does not depend on the choice of the omitted category, and we have used it throughout the book to indicate the explanatory potency of variables, such as ethnicity, family income, and college attended, represented by dummy variables.

Finally, we have occasionally made use of so-called interaction effects, especially in chapter 8. An interaction posits that the effect of one independent variable depends on the value of another. The simplest form for such an interaction, and the only one used by us, occurs when the effect of one independent variable is different for various categories of a second, categorical variable. In chapter 8, for example, we assumed that the effects of some determinants of transfer, such as credits per semester, could vary according to curriculum. Thus, we assumed that curriculum interacts with credits. In regression analysis, these interaction effects are represented by multiplicative terms involving the interacting variables. Consider the following example from the analysis of transfer in the 1970 cohort:

$$y = .007 + .021x_1 - .054x_2 + .029x_1x_2,$$

where y is the predicted value of a dummy variable representing transfer, with transfer coded as 1, x_1 is the average number of credits earned during regular-year semesters in the community colleges, and x_2 is a dummy variable representing community-college curriculum, with liberal arts coded as 1. In this equation, the interaction between curriculum and credit average appears on the far right.

In effect, this equation can be read as containing two equations, one for those in the liberal arts and one for those in the vocational curricula. In the latter case, x_2 and the interaction are 0, so that the equation consists only of the intercept and the term involving credits per semester. Thus, the probability of transfer of a student in the vocational curricula increased by 2.1 percent for each additional credit that he or she earned per semester. However, in the case of liberal arts students, x_2 is 1, simplifying the interaction term in a way that allows it to be combined with the term involving credits per semester. Also, the term for curriculum now appears as a constant that can be combined with the intercept, yielding a simpler form for the equation:

$$y = - .047 + .050x_1.$$

Thus, the probability of transfer of a liberal arts student increased by 5 percent for each additional credit that the student earned per semester. Comparing the coefficient of credit average in the two forms of the equation demonstrates that the interaction term allows one to "model" the effect of curriculum in terms of what the same academic events imply for students in the different curricula. As this brief analysis shows, each additional credit per semester in the community colleges added far more to the probability that a liberal arts student would transfer than it did to the probability that a career student in the vocational curricula would.

Notes

1. To some extent this problem is overcome in log-linear analysis, developed by Leo Goodman and others. For an elementary discussion of log-linear analysis see Stephen Fienberg, *The Analysis of Cross-Classified Categorical Data* (Cambridge: M.I.T. Press, 1979). Still, log-linear analysis requires a contingency table, and when there are numerous independent variables, the numbers of cases in many cells are necessarily small.

2. For discussion of the statistical details of regression analysis see Hubert M. Blalock, Jr., *Social Statistics* (New York: McGraw-Hill, 1979), and Ronald J. Wonnacott and Thomas H. Wonnacott, *Econometrics* (New York: Wiley, 1970).

3. By no means is regression analysis restricted to linear relations. We have generally assumed linear relations throughout the book, however. In a few cases in which that assumption seemed questionable, as in the relation between family income and educational outcomes, we entered the independent variable, i.e., family income, as a series of categories, thus making no assumption about the functional form of the relationship.

4. The word "predict" is used here in a special sense since all the events being predicted have already happened. In any statistical analysis, one is momentarily covering over some information to discover whether it could have been predicted on the basis of other information.

5. One must be cautious about the most literal interpretation of these words. They do not mean that each coefficient was somehow estimated from the data for those individuals who matched on the other independent variables. Such a procedure would use very little of the information since few individuals match on all but one of the independent variables. Nor do the words mean that if we found two individuals who did match on all but one of the independent variables and differed by one unit on that one, these two would differ by the value of the unstandardized coefficient of that variable in their scores on the dependent variable.

6. The variance is the square of the more familiar standard deviation.

7. The standard form of a variable is given by the following formula:

$$x' = \frac{x - \overline{x}}{s_x}$$

where x is any value of the variable, x' is the corresponding standardized score, $\overline{x}$ is the mean of the x values, and s_x is their standard deviation.

8. See, for example, two works by Otis Dudley Duncan: "Partials, Partitions, and Paths," in Edgar F. Borgatta and George W. Bohrnstedt (eds.), *Sociological Methodology, 1970* (San Francisco: Jossey-Bass, 1970); *An Introduction to Structural Equation Models* (New York: Academic, 1975), especially pp. 65–66.

9. Even more troubling for the interpretation of standardized coefficients, however, is the fact that the sum of the squares of the standardized coefficients may in certain circumstances add up to *more* than the total explained variance, or R^2. This may happen when the effects of two independent variables are consistent in direction (e.g., both are positive) but the variables are negatively cor-

related with each other. This fact underlines the limitations inherent in the interpretation of standardized coefficients in terms of explained variance.

10. The interpretation of the dummy variable coefficients that we give rests on the assumption that the categories of the substantive variables are mutually exclusive, i.e., an individual cannot belong to two categories of the same variable. Of course, this is usually the case. But, for the reader who is reading this appendix before the text, we must point out that the categories of the ethnic variable, despite their mixture of religious, racial, and other labels, are in fact mutually exclusive (see chapter 4).

11. The sheaf coefficient is described by David R. Heise, "Employing Nominal Variables, Induced Variables, and Block Variables in Path Analyses," *Sociological Methods and Research* 1 (November 1972): 147–173.

Name Index

Abramson, Harold, 87
Acker, Joan R., 42
Ackerman, Tom, 25, 26
Acland, Henry, 44, 89
Adams, Walter, 27, 67, 88
Agnew, Spiro, 201
Alba, Richard D., 22
Alexander, Karl, 44, 198
Allison, Paul, 227
Alwin, Duane, 43
Anker, Irving, 118
Arce, Carlos H., 287
Armor, David J., 90
Astin, Alexander W., 23, 26, 45, 51,
    56, 155, 156, 199, 264, 287
Astin, Helen S., 23, 45, 56, 199, 264,
    287

Badillo, Herman, 13-14
Baldwin, Alfred, 198
Baltzell, E. Digby, 45
Bane, Mary Jo, 44, 89
Bartlett, Susan, 43, 153
Beallor, Marc, 25
Beame, Abraham, 290, 291, 294, 302
Bell, Daniel, 30, 43
Berger, Stephen, 292, 308, 309
Bernstein, Basil, 44, 198
Biaggi, Mario, 12

Birnbaum, Robert, 284, 285
Blackburn, Robert T., 287
Blalock, Hubert M., Jr., 287, 325
Blau, Peter, 29-30, 42
Blauner, Robert, 287
Bohrnstedt, George W., 325
Boocock, Sarane S., 44, 117
Borgatta, Edgar F., 325
Bourdieu, Pierre, 44
Bowker, Albert H., 5-11, 13-16, 18,
    23, 24, 25, 294
Bowles, Samuel, 33, 44, 134, 156
Brass, Richard, 310
Bronfenbrenner, Urie, 198
Brunner, Seth, 27
Butler, Nicholas Murray, 21

Campbell, Ernest Q., 44, 89, 284
Carey, Hugh L., 290, 301-302, 310
Chandler, Porter, 25
Clark, Burton, 44, 201, 202, 226
Cohen, David, 44, 89
Cohen, P., 286
Cole, Jonathan R., 280, 287
Coleman, James S., 33, 44, 88, 89,
    284
Collins, Randall, 43, 44, 312
Cook, Martha, 44
Cope, Robert G., 153

Copeland, Joseph, 13
Corcoran, Mary, 43, 153
Cosenza, Mario E., 21
Cottrell, Donald P., 24
Covello, Leonard, 22, 117
Creedon, Carol F., 153, 154
Cross, K. Patricia, 91, 92, 117, 260, 263
Crouse, James, 43, 153

Davenport, Roselle W., 287
Daymont, Thomas, 43
DeWitt, Karen, 26
Dillard, Joey L., 286
Duncan, Beverly, 89
Duncan, Otis Dudley, 29–30, 42, 89, 325

Eaglesfield, David, 43, 153
El-Khawas, Elaine H., 23, 45, 56, 199, 264, 287
Elliot, Stephen, 26
Erickson, Frederick, 287
Etzioni, Amitai, 201
Evans, Rowland, 309

Farley, Reynolds, 43
Featherman, David, 30, 31, 42, 43, 284
Feldman, Kenneth A., 153
Fitzpatrick, Joseph, 88
Ford, Gerald, 290
Fowler, Steve, 27
Fox, Sylvan, 26
Freeman, Richard B., 31, 45, 153
Friedman, Milton, 42

Gallagher, Buell T., 9–13, 24, 25
Gambino, Richard, 22, 117
Gamson, Zelda F., 287
Gerzon, Mark, 153
Giardino, Alfred A., 293–295, 301, 302, 309
Gintis, Herbert, 33, 42, 44, 47, 89, 134, 156, 226
Glazer, Nathan, 21–25, 87
Goldman, Joseph, 284, 285
Goodman, Leo, 325
Gordon, Milton M., 87
Gordon, Sheila C., 22–27, 311
Gorelick, Sherry, 21, 22, 287
Greaves, William, 26
Greeley, Andrew M., 22, 87

Green, Robert, 88
Greenspan, Arthur, 26
Griffin, Larry, 198
Gross, Theodore L., 45, 287
Gusfield, Joseph, 45

Halsey, A. H., 44
Hannah, William, 153
Hauser, Robert, 30, 31, 42, 43, 284
Heise, David R., 55, 58, 326
Heller, Louis G., 44
Heyns, Barbara, 44, 89
Hobson, Carol J., 44, 89, 284
Holy, Thomas C., 22
Hunter, Charlayne, 309
Hurn, Christopher J., 42, 198
Hyman, Herbert H., 43, 154
Hyman, Seymour H., 13

Jackson, Gregory, 153
Jaffe, Abraham, 27, 67, 88
Jencks, Christopher, 20, 27, 32, 33, 42–44, 89, 153, 265, 266, 284, 285
Jones, Maldwin Allen, 21
Juola, Arvo E., 45

Kantrowitz, Nathan, 87, 90
Karabel, Jerome, 44, 45, 134, 156, 201, 202, 226, 308, 309, 311
Karmas, Constantine, 198
Kaufman, Barry, 39, 45, 310, 311
Kay, Patricia, 261
Kelly, Sara, 88
Keniston, Kenneth, 153
Kibbee, Robert J., 293, 295, 296, 299–302, 309, 310
Kifner, John, 25
Kim, Jae-On, 199
King, Martin Luther, 7
Kohen, Andrew, 198
Kornfeld, Louis, 287
Kramer, Rena, 39, 45
Kruska, J. B., 89

Labov, William, 286
Lavin, David E., 43, 56, 89, 158, 261, 287, 309
Lewis, J., 286
Lieberson, Stanley, 89
Liebow, Elliot, 118
Lindsay, John V., 8, 12, 14, 16, 18

McClelland, David, 198

McClelland, Kent, 43, 153
McDill, Edward, 44
McNamara, Joseph, 26
McPartland, James, 44, 89, 284
Maeroff, Gene I., 200
Max, Pearl, 156
Mayer, Martin, 26, 37, 45
Medsker, Leland, 154
Meng, J. Joseph, 89, 309
Merton, Robert K., 118
Michelson, Stephan, 44, 89
Mills, O., 153, 154
Milner, Murray, 44
Mingle, James R., 287
Mood, Alexander M., 44, 284
Moore, John, 88
Moore, Keith, 310
Moynihan, Daniel P., 21–25, 87
Mucciolo, Laurence F., 308, 309
Mueller, Charles W., 199
Mueser, Peter, 43, 153

Nerlove, Sara Beth, 89
Nestel, Gilbert, 198
Neumann, Florence M., 1n.
Newcomb, Theodore M., 153
Newman, Frank, 153
Novak, Robert, 309
Nyquist, Ewald B., 300, 310

Olneck, Michael, 43, 153

Pantages, Timothy J., 153, 154
Pareto, Vilfredo, 42
Parsons, Talcott, 42
Passeron, Jean-Claude, 44
Penzer, Jonathan, 25
Persell, Caroline Hodges, 44, 198, 284
Peterson, Iver, 309
Peterson, Marvin W., 287
Pettigrew, Thomas, 88
Piesco, Judith, 263
Podell, Lawrence, 39, 45
Powell, Adam Clayton, 12
Procaccino, Mario, 12, 13

Rainwater, Lee, 118
Ravitch, Diane, 20, 24
Reed, John Shelton, 43, 154
Reis, Howard, 25
Riesman, David, 20, 27, 32, 42, 43, 153
Rist, Ray, 198

Roberts, Donald A., 21, 22
Robins, C., 286
Rockefeller, Nelson A., 11, 16, 23, 27
Romney, A. Kimball, 89
Rondileau, Adrian, 22
Rosen, Bernard, 198
Rosen, David, 27
Rosenbaum, James, 44
Rosenberg, Gustave, 23
Rosenfeld, Lawrence B., 286
Rossell, Christine, 88
Rossi, Peter, 22
Rossman, Jack E., 23, 45, 56, 199, 264, 287
Roueche, John E., 248, 260, 261, 263
Rudolph, Frederick, 21
Rudy, S. Willis, 20–22, 311

Schooler, Carmi, 198
Schumach, Murray, 26
Schumer, Leo S., 22
Schwartz, Joseph, 43, 153
Scully, Malcolm G., 45
Shaughnessy, Mina P., 259, 264
Shepard, Roger N., 89
Silberstein, Richard A., 198, 309
Sklare, Marshall, 117
Smith, Adam, 42
Smith, Marshall, 44, 89
Snow, Jerry J., 248, 260, 261, 263
Solmon, Lewis C., 153
Spady, William G., 153
St. John, Nancy Holt, 89
Stathos, Harry, 310
Steinberg, Stephen, 24, 45, 118, 310
Strodtbeck, Fred, 198
Sutton, Percy, 8

Taeuber, Alma F., 89
Taeuber, Karl E., 89
Taubman, Paul J., 153
Terdeman, Robert, 310
Tinto, Vincent, 153
Treiman, Donald, 42
Trent, James W., 154
Trimberger, Ellen Kay, 44, 87, 88, 226

Valentine, William, 118
Van Arsdale, Harry, 14–15
Van Dyne, Larry, 308
Vecoli, Rudolph, 22
Vesey, Lawrence, 45

Wagner, Geoffrey, 44–45
Ward, Sherry, 43, 153
Weber, Max, 42
Wechsler, Harold S., 21–24, 310
Weiner, Max, 56, 262
Weinfeld, Frederic D., 44, 284
Williams, Franklin, 310, 311
Williams, Jill, 43, 153

Williams, Robin M., 288
Wilson, Logan, 153
Wilson, William J., 266, 284
Wonnacott, Ronald J., 325
Wonnacott, Thomas H., 325
Wright, Charles R., 43, 154

York, Robert L., 44, 284

Subject Index

Ability grouping, 34–37
Academic discrimination, 280
Academic merit, 17–18
Academic outcomes, 30–31, 35, 49–50,
  119–197; *see also* Black students;
  Catholic students; Hispanic students; Jewish students
  college preparatory courses and,
    143–149, 163–165, 167, 172–175,
    177, 180, 184, 187–190, 192, 194
  community colleges, 186–196
    credits, 124–125, 139–140, 148,
      187–189, 191–193, 195–196
    cumulative performance, 130–134,
      194–196
    dropout rates, 125–126, 132–134,
      140–141, 189, 191, 196
    educational background and, 147–
      150, 187–190
    freshman performance, 191–193
    gender and admissions status, 98,
      193
    grade point average, 121–123,
      139–140, 148, 187, 188,
      191–194
    graduation rates, 132–134, 140–
      141, 149, 189–190, 194–196,
      269
    high school tracking and, 188, 190

  persistence, 149, 189–190, 194–195
  return for fall, 187, 189–190
credits, 49, 50
  in community colleges, 124–125,
    139–140, 148, 187–189, 191–
    193, 195–196
  cumulative, 127–128, 131–132
  of ethnic groups, 136–137, 139–
    140, 144, 148, 165, 166, 172–
    175, 177, 181, 183–185, 188–
    189, 192, 278
  in freshman year, 124–125, 179–
    181, 183, 186
  in senior colleges, 124–125, 136–
    137, 144, 164–166, 170–175,
    179–181, 183–186
dropout rates, 20, 36, 49, 119, 120
  community colleges, 125–126,
    132–134, 140–141, 189, 191,
    196
  of ethnic groups, 138–141, 168,
    186, 267
  in freshman year, 125–126
  in senior colleges, 125–126, 129–
    130, 138, 183, 186
educational background and, 142–
  151, 187–190
  community colleges, 147–150,
    187–190

Academic outcomes, *cont.*
  credits, 144, 147, 148, 164–166
  of ethnic groups, 100–105,
    144–150
  grade point average, 144, 147,
    148, 150, 162–164
  graduation rates, 145, 147, 149,
    151, 167–169, 178, 190
  persistence, 145, 146, 147, 149,
    151, 166–168
  senior colleges, 143–147, 150,
    161–176
family income and, 142–143,
    146–149
grade point average, 49
  in community colleges, 121–123,
    139–140, 148, 187, 188,
    191–194
  cumulative, 127–128, 131–132
  educational background and, 144,
    147, 148, 150, 162–164
  of ethnic groups, 136–137, 139–
    140, 144, 148, 162–164, 172–
    175, 177, 181, 183–185, 188,
    192, 195, 278
  in freshman year, 121–123, 179–
    181, 183, 186
  in senior colleges, 121–123, 136–
    137, 144, 162–163, 179–181,
    183–186, 278
graduation rates, 49–50, 120, 130
  in community colleges, 132–134,
    140–141, 149, 189–190, 194–
    196, 269
  educational background, 145, 147,
    149, 151, 167–169, 178, 190
  of ethnic groups, 138–141, 145,
    150, 169, 184–186, 190, 195,
    269, 271, 272, 274
  in senior colleges, 129–130, 138,
    145, 167–169, 183–186
high school average: *see* High school
  average
high school rank: *see* High school
  rank
high school tracking and, 17, 34–37,
    48, 79–81, 85, 87, 143, 146–147,
    164, 166, 169, 188, 190, 267
parents' education and, 51, 53, 79–
    81, 95, 110, 143–149, 185, 207
remediation, 20, 30, 50, 105, 119,
    130, 179, 248–260, 279, 281, 306
  in community colleges, 234–237,
    253–256

credit accumulation, 248, 250–
    252, 254, 255
credit for courses, 232, 233, 242,
    252, 253, 257
grade point average, 248, 250–
    252, 254–256
graduation, 248, 251, 256
persistence, 248, 251, 252, 255
return for fall, 250, 254
in senior colleges, 234–237, 242–
    244, 249–253
retention rates
  in community colleges, 132–133,
    140–141
  of ethnic groups, 138–141
  in senior colleges, 129–130, 138
  of transfer students, 217–222
senior colleges, 15–19, 34, 36–37
  credits, 124–125, 136–137, 144,
    164–166, 170–175, 179–181,
    183–186
  cumulative performance, 127–130,
    183–186
  dropout rates, 125–126, 129–130,
    138, 183, 186
  educational background and, 143–
    147, 150, 161–176
  freshman performance, 179–183
  gender and admissions status, 98,
    179–180
  grade point average, 121–123,
    136–137, 144, 162–163,
    170–178, 179–181, 183–186, 278
  graduation rates, 129–130, 138,
    145, 167–169, 183–186, 269
  longitudinal model of student's
    career, 169–178
  need to work, 180–181
  persistence, 145, 166–168, 171,
    183–186
  retention rates, 129–130, 138
  return for fall, 172–177
  social origin and, 143–147, 150
  stopping out, 170, 177
  year-by-year achievement, 161–169
social origin and, 142–151
  in community colleges, 147–151
  credits, 144, 147, 148
  ethnic groups, 92–97, 144–150
  grade point average, 144, 147,
    148, 150
  graduation rates, 145, 147, 149,
    151
  persistence, 145, 147, 149, 151

Academic outcomes, *cont.*
  in senior colleges, 143–147, 150
  standards, 37–40, 120, 281, 282,
    294, 303
  student characteristics and, 97, 100,
    159–160
  transfer students, 217–224
  welfare students, 142
Academic standards: *see* Standards
Admissions: *see* Open admissions
Affluent families, 32
Age, admissions status and, 51, 99–
  100, 110, 278
American Council on Education
  (ACE), 51, 56
American Occupational Structure, The
  (Blau and Duncan), 29–30
Asian-Americans, 62, 68*n.*, 189
Aspirations: *see* Degree aspirations
Associate degree, 132, 203, 204–205,
  209, 210, 215–217, 222, 224, 254,
  255, 270
Audiovisual technology, 232

Baccalaureate degree, 121, 132, 202,
  203, 210, 217, 219, 223, 224, 270,
  271, 276
Baruch College, 63, 180, 184
Benefits, perceptions of, 52, 109–115
Beyond the Open Door (Cross), 91–92
Black students, 60
  admissions resolution (fiscal crisis),
    297–299
  age and admissions status, 99
  citizenship, 97
  classroom behavior, 104
  college preference, 77–83
  college preparatory courses, 101
  community-senior college transfer,
    206–208, 210, 212
  credits, 136–137, 139–140, 144, 148,
    165, 172–175, 181, 183–185, 188–
    189, 192
  curriculum placement, 84–86
  degree aspirations, 106–107
  dropout rates, 138–141, 168, 186,
    267
  educational background, 100–105,
    144–150
  ethnic stratification, 64–70
  family income, 93, 94
  freshman performance, 181, 183,
    186, 192
  gender and admissions, 98, 100

grade point averages, 136–137, 139–
  140, 144, 148, 162, 163, 172–175,
  181, 183–185, 188, 192, 195
graduation rates (college), 138–141,
  145, 149, 169, 184–186, 190, 195,
  269, 271, 272, 274
graduation rates (high school),
  267–268
language, 279
need to work, 94
Open-Admissions Test Scores,
  240–241
parents' education, 96
perceptions of benefits of open admissions, 109–115
persistence, 145, 149, 167, 184–185,
  195
personal characteristics of, 97–100
post-college job plans, 107
reasons for college attendance,
  107–108
remediation, 237–239, 244–246, 258
retention rates, 138–141
return for fall, 172–175
self-rating, 102
social origin, 92–97, 144–150
transfers, 214, 216, 219, 225
Board of Higher Education (BHE), 3,
  6, 7, 13–17, 18, 293–302
Borough of Manhattan Community
  College, 63, 73, 193, 195, 196,
  211, 216, 223
BPRSC (Black and Puerto Rican Student Community), 11–14
Bronx Community College, 73, 192,
  194, 211, 216
Brooklyn College, 3, 63, 73, 86, 180,
  182, 184

California, University of, 67, 230
California public higher education system, 19, 63, 67
Career programs, 7, 49, 84–85
Catholic school system, 4, 104, 179
Catholic students, 60
  admissions resolution (fiscal crisis),
    297–299
  age and admissions status, 99
  classroom behavior, 104
  college preference, 77–83
  college preparatory courses, 101
  community-senior college transfer,
    206–208, 210, 212
  credits, 136–137, 139–140, 144, 148,

Catholic Students, *cont.*
    165, 172, 173, 181, 183–185, 188–
        189, 192, 278
    curriculum placement, 84–86
    degree aspirations, 106–107
    dropout rates, 138–141, 168, 186
    educational background, 100–105,
        144–150
    ethnic stratification, 64–70
    family income, 93, 94
    freshman performance, 181, 183,
        186, 192
    gender and admissions status, 98
    grade point average, 136–137, 139–
        140, 144, 148, 162, 163, 172–175,
        181, 183–185, 188, 192, 195, 278
    graduation rates, 138–141, 145, 149,
        169, 184–186, 190, 195, 269, 271,
        272, 274
    language, 96
    need to work, 94–95
    Open-Admissions Test Scores,
        240–241
    parents' education, 95–96
    perceptions of benefits of open ad-
        missions, 110–114
    persistence, 145, 149, 167, 184–185,
        195
    personal characteristics of, 97–100
    post-college job plans, 107
    reasons for college attendance,
        107–108
    remediation, 237–239, 244–245, 258
    retention rates, 138–141
    return for fall, 172–175
    segregation, 74–76
    self-rating, 102
    social origin, 92–97, 144–150
    transfer, 147, 214, 216, 219, 225
Citizenship, 97
City College of New York (CCNY),
    70, 73, 180, 182, 184
    confrontation on admissions (1969),
        1, 9–14
    entrance requirements, 3–5
    expansion of, 3
    origins of, 1–2
City College of New York Alumni As-
    sociation, 15
City University of New York (CUNY)
    budget crisis (1969), 10–11
    Commission on Admissions, 16–18
    dual admissions proposal, 13–14
    Faculty Senate compromise, 13–14
    growth of, 290
    open admissions: *see* Open admis-
        sions
    origins of, 1–2
Civil rights movement, 7
Civilian Review Board, 8
Classroom behavior, 103, 104, 279
Coleman Report, 33, 71
College Discovery, 6, 7, 9, 51, 62, 269,
    272
College effects, 31–32
College enrollment statistics, 28, 32
College placement, 61, 76–83
College preference, 76–83, 85, 277
College preparatory courses, 5, 7, 36,
    48, 53, 79, 101, 110, 114, 143–
    149, 163–165, 167, 172–175, 177,
    180, 184, 187–190, 192, 194, 207,
    240–241, 244–245
Columbia University, 7
Committee of Ten, 10–12
Community colleges, 7, 15–19, 34, 36–
    37, 186–196
    age and admissions status, 99
    classroom behavior, 103, 104
    College Discovery, 6, 7, 9, 51, 62,
        269, 272
    college preference, 76–83
    college preparatory courses, 101
    credits, 124–125, 139–140, 148, 187–
        189, 191–193, 195–196
    cumulative performance, 130–134,
        194–196
    curriculum placement, 83–86
    degree aspirations, 106–107, 108
    dropout rates, 125–126, 132–134,
        140–141, 189, 191, 196
    educational background and, 147–
        150, 187–190
    enrollment under open admissions,
        63–70
    first-generation college attendees,
        95–96
    freshman performance, 191–193
    gender and admissions status, 98,
        193
    grade point average, 121–123, 139–
        140, 148, 187, 188, 191–194
    graduation, 132–134, 140–141, 149,
        189–190, 194–196, 269
    growth of, 229
    high school tracking and, 188, 190,
        202
    integration, 71–76

persistence, 149, 189–190, 194–195
remediation, 234–237, 253–256
retention rates, 132–133, 140–141
return for fall, 187, 189–190
and senior college transfer: *see*
    Transfers, from community to
    senior colleges
social buffer view of, 201–202
social origin and, 147–151
student self-rating, 102
students' need to work, 94–95
students' perceptions of benefits,
    109–115
Computer assisted instruction, 232
Cooling out process, 36, 201
Credits, 49, 50
in community colleges, 124–125,
    139–140, 148, 187–189, 191–193,
    195–196
community-senior college transfer
    and, 210, 215–216, 220–221
cumulative, 127–128, 131–132
educational background and, 144,
    147, 148, 164–166
ethnic groups, 136–137, 139–140,
    144, 148, 165, 166, 172–175, 177,
    181, 183–185, 188–189, 192, 278
in freshman year, 124–125, 179–181,
    183, 186
remediation and, 248, 250–252, 254,
    255
in senior colleges, 124–125, 136–137,
    144, 164–166, 170–175, 179–181,
    183–186
social origin and, 144, 147, 148
transfer students and, 220–221, 223
Curriculum placement, in community
    colleges, 83–86

Data analysis, types of, 54–56
Degree aspirations, 51–53, 85, 106–
    107, 108, 181, 182, 185, 192, 194,
    202, 203, 210
Discrimination, 280
Dropout rates, 20, 36, 49, 119, 120
in community colleges, 125–126,
    132–134, 140–141, 189, 191, 196
of ethnic groups, 138–141, 168, 186,
    267
in freshman year, 125–126
high school, 267–268
remediation and, 248
in senior colleges, 125–126, 129–130,
    138, 183, 186

of transfer students, 217–222
DuBois Club, 9, 10

Education, views on role of, 29–37,
    275, 283–284, 307
Educational aspirations, 2–4, 76–82,
    92; *see also* Degree aspirations
Educational attainment: *see* Academic
    outcomes
Educational background, 47–48, 53,
    85, 266–268, 278
academic achievement and, 142–151,
    187–190
community colleges and, 147–150,
    187–190
community-senior college transfer,
    205–208, 222–223
credits, 144, 147, 148, 164–166
of ethnic groups, 100–105, 144–150
grade point average, 144, 147, 148,
    150, 162–164
graduation rates, 145, 147, 149, 151,
    167–169, 178, 190
of open-admissions students,
    100–105
persistence, 145, 146, 147, 149, 151,
    166–168
senior colleges and, 143–147, 150,
    161–176
Educational skills centers, 7
Elite senior colleges: *see* Senior col-
    leges
Emergency Financial Control Board
    (EFCB), 291, 292
Entrance requirements, 3–5, 60
Ethnic balance, 17
Ethnic studies departments, 38, 39,
    282
Ethnicity: *see* Black students; Catholic
    students; Hispanic students; Jew-
    ish students

Faculty attitudes, 35, 267, 279,
    280–283
Family income, 51, 53, 55, 79–81, 92,
    93–94, 97, 110–111, 114, 142–
    143, 146–149, 207
Family size, 93–94
First-generation college attendee,
    95–96
Fiscal crisis in New York City,
    287–288
Fordham University, 4
Foreign-born parents, 97

Fourth-year credits, 170, 176
Four-year colleges: *see* Senior colleges
Free Academy, 1-2
Freshman performance, 121-126
  in community colleges, 124-125,
    179-181, 183, 186, 191-193
  credits, 124-125, 179-181, 183, 186
  of ethnic groups, 181, 183, 186, 192
  grade point average, 121-123, 179-
    181, 183, 186
  in senior colleges, 179-183
Freshmen, changes in the distribution
  of minority (1975-78), 298,
  305-306

Gender, admissions status and, 51, 97-
  98, 100, 110, 179-180, 278
G.I. Bill, 229
Grade inflation, 39
Grade point average, 49
  in community colleges, 121-123,
    139-140, 148, 187, 188, 191-194
  cumulative, 127-128, 131-132
  educational background and, 144,
    147, 148, 150, 162-164
  of ethnic groups, 136-137, 139-140,
    144, 148, 162-164, 172-175, 177,
    181, 183-185, 188, 192, 195, 278
  in freshman year, 121-123, 179-181,
    183, 186
  remediation and, 248, 250-252,
    254-256
  in senior colleges, 121-123, 136-137,
    144, 162-163, 170-178, 179-181,
    183-186, 278
  social origin and, 144, 147, 148,
    150
Graduation rates, 49-50, 120, 130
  in community colleges, 132-134,
    140-141, 149, 189-190, 194-196,
    269
  educational background and, 144,
    147, 149, 151, 167-169, 178, 190
  of ethnic groups, 138-141, 145, 149,
    150, 169, 184-186, 190, 195, 269,
    271, 272, 274
  high school, 267-268
  remediation and, 248, 251, 256
  in senior colleges, 129-130, 138,
    145, 167-169, 183-186
  social origin and, 145, 147, 149, 151
  success of open admissions, 269-276
  of transfer students, 217-222

Guidance counselors, high school, 79,
  81, 85

Hidden curriculum, 35
High school background: *see* Educational background
High school average, 3-5, 7, 17-19,
  47-48, 53, 77-78, 80, 81, 110,
  114, 143-145, 147-149, 162-169,
  172-177, 180, 184, 187-190, 192,
  194, 207, 217-218, 240-241,
  244-245
High school rank, 17-19, 48, 53, 77-
  78, 143-145, 147-149, 162, 163,
  165, 167, 172-175, 180, 184, 187,
  189, 190, 192, 194, 207, 240-241,
  244-245
High school tracking, 17, 34-37, 48,
  79-81, 85, 87, 100-101, 110-111,
  143, 146-147, 164, 166, 169, 188,
  190, 267
Hispanic students, 5, 6, 60
  admissions resolution (fiscal crisis),
    297-299
  age and admissions status, 99
  citizenship, 97
  classroom behavior, 104
  college preference, 77-83
  college preparatory courses, 101
  community-senior college transfer,
    206-208, 210, 212
  credits, 136-137, 139-140, 144, 148,
    165, 166, 172-175, 177, 181, 183-
    185, 189, 192, 278
  curriculum placement, 84-86
  dropout rates, 138-141, 168, 267
  educational background, 100-105,
    144-150
  ethnic stratification, 64-70
  family income, 93, 94
  freshman performance, 181, 192
  gender and admissions status, 98,
    100
  grade point average, 144, 148, 162-
    164, 172-175, 181, 183-185, 192,
    195, 278
  graduation rates (college), 138-141,
    145, 149, 150, 169, 184-185, 190,
    195, 269, 281, 272, 274
  graduation rates (high school),
    267-268
  language, 279
  need to work, 94

Open-Admissions Test Scores and, 240-241
parents' education, 95
perceptions of benefits of open admissions, 109-115
persistence, 145, 149, 150, 167, 184-185, 195
personal characteristics of, 97-100
post-college job plans, 107
reasons for college attendance, 107-108
remediation, 237-239, 244-247, 258
retention rates, 138-141
return for fall, 172-175
segregation, 74-76
self-rating, 102
social origin, 92-97, 144-150
transfer, 214, 216, 219, 225
Hostos Community College, 63, 73, 211
Hunter College, 2, 63, 180, 182, 184

Index of Dissimilarity, 71
Industrialism, education and, 29-33
Inequality (Jencks), 33
Integration, 70-76
Irish Americans, 3, 4, 14-15; *see also* Catholic students
Italian Americans, 3, 4, 14-15; *see also* Catholic students

Jewish students, 60
admissions resolution (fiscal crisis), 297-299
age and admissions status, 99
classroom behavior, 104
college preference, 77-83
college preparatory courses, 101
community-senior college transfer, 206-208, 210, 212
credits, 136-137, 139-140, 144, 148, 165, 166, 172-175, 177, 181, 183-185, 188-189, 192, 278
curriculum placement, 84-86
degree aspirations, 106-107
dropout rates, 138-141, 168, 186
educational background, 100-105, 144-150
ethnic stratification, 64-70
family income, 93, 94
freshman performance, 181, 183, 186, 192
gender and admissions status, 98

grade point average, 136-137, 139-140, 144, 148, 162-164, 172-175, 177, 181, 183-185, 188, 192, 195, 278
graduation, 138-141, 145, 149, 150, 169, 184-186, 190, 195, 269, 271, 272, 274
language, 96
Open-Admissions Test Scores and, 240-241
parents' education, 95
perceptions of benefits of open admissions, 110-114
persistence, 145, 149, 150, 167, 184-185, 195
personal characteristics of, 97-100
post-college job plans, 107
racial tension, 8-9
reasons for college attendance, 107-108
remediation, 237-239, 244-245, 258
retention rates, 138-141
return for fall, 172-175
segregation, 74-76
self-rating, 102
social origin, 92-97, 144-150
transfers, 147, 214, 216, 219, 225
Jewish Defense League, 12
Job market prospects, 31
John Jay College, 63, 180, 184

Kingsborough Community College, 63, 73, 193, 211, 212, 217

LaGuardia Community College, 63, 211, 212
Land-grant colleges, 19
Language skills, 231, 233-247, 259-260
Languages, 96, 279, 283
Lehman (Herbert H.) College, 63, 73, 180, 184
Liberal arts curricula, 36-37, 49, 83-85, 191, 205, 209, 210, 212, 215, 221
Listwise deletion, 55, 56
Longitudinal model of a senior-college student's career, 169-178

Manhattan College, 192, 194
Mathematics, 48, 197, 231, 233-247, 279
Mayoral primary (1969), 12

Medgar Evers College, 73
Morrill Act of 1862, 19

Need to work, 52, 94, 180–181, 185, 192, 195
New World Coalition (NWC), 10
New York City, fiscal crisis in, 281, 287–308
New York City Community College, 73, 192–194, 211, 212, 216, 223
New York State Board of Regents, 295
Non-elite senior colleges: see Senior colleges
Normal School, 2

Occupational position, 30–31, 35–37
Open admissions
  academic outcomes: see Academic outcomes
  beginnings of, 5–9
  in California, 19, 63, 67
  confrontation at CCNY (1969), 1, 9–14
  critical perspective on education and, 33–37
  industrialism, thesis of, and, 29–33
  national attention to, 19
  New York City's fiscal crisis and, 281, 287–308
  research background and procedures, 46–59
  roots of, 19
  students: see Black students; Catholic students; Hispanic students; Jewish students
  success of, 265–284
    assessment of, 275–284
    educational background and, 266–268
    faculty attitudes, 279, 280–283
    graduation, 269–276
    overview of, 268–275
  uniqueness of, 19–20
  working out, 15–18
Open-Admissions Test, 48, 52, 53, 56, 180, 183, 184, 192, 194, 233–236, 238–242, 247, 297
Opportunity and Change (Featherman and Hauser), 30

Pairwise deletion, 55, 56
Parents' education, 51, 53, 79–81, 95, 96, 110, 143–149, 185, 207
Particularism, 29

Pennsylvania, University of, 40
Persistence, 49
  in community colleges, 149, 189–190, 194–195
  educational background and, 145, 146, 147, 149, 151, 166–168
  of ethnic groups, 145, 149, 150, 167, 184–185, 195
  remediation and, 248, 251, 252, 255
  in senior colleges, 145, 166–168, 171, 183–186
  social origin and, 145, 147, 149, 151
Personal characteristics of open-admissions students, 97–100
Postgraduate degree, 202, 209, 210
Postindustrialism, 30
Postwar baby boom, 6
Preference, college, 76–83, 85, 277
Professional schools, 3
Proficiency tests, 306, 307
Public Education Association, 15
Puerto Ricans: see Hispanic students

Queens College, 3, 70, 73, 78, 86, 180, 182, 184
Queensborough Community College, 63, 73, 192–194, 196, 211, 217, 223

Racial tension, 8–9
Reading, 48, 197, 231, 233–247
Recency of migration, 97
Religion: see Catholic students; Hispanic students; Jewish students
Remediation, 20, 30, 50, 105, 119, 130, 179, 229–260, 279, 281, 306
  in community colleges, 234–237, 253–256
  credit accumulation, 248, 250–252, 254, 255
  credit for courses, 232, 233, 242, 252, 253, 257
  delivery of, 239–247
  ethnic groups and, 237–239, 244–247, 258
  grade point average, 248, 250–252, 254–256
  graduation and, 248, 251, 256
  history of, 230
  impact of, 247–256
  need for, 231–239
  overview of CUNY effort, 231–233
  persistence, 248, 251, 252, 255
  return for fall, 250, 254

in senior colleges, 234–237, 242–244,
  249–253
Residence, college preference and,
  81–83
Residential segregation, 82–83
Retention rates
  in community colleges, 132–133,
    140–141
  of ethnic groups, 138–141
  in senior colleges, 129–130, 138
  of transfer students, 217–222
Return for fall
  in community colleges, 187, 189–190
  ethnic groups and, 172–175
  remediation and, 250, 254
  in senior colleges, 172–177
Richmond College, 63

Scholastic Aptitude Test, 13, 36
School decentralization, 8
Schooling in Capitalist America
  (Bowles and Gintis), 33
Second-choice college, 76
SEEK (Search for Education, Eleva-
  tion, and Knowledge), 6, 7, 9, 17,
  18, 51, 62, 64–67, 72, 73, 76, 100,
  269, 272, 306
Segregation, 71–76, 82–83
Self-image, 181–182
Self-paced courses, 232
Self-rating, 52, 53, 102, 181–182, 194
Senior colleges, 15–19, 34, 36–37
  age and admissions status, 99
  classroom behavior, 103, 104
  college preference, 76–83
  college preparatory courses, 101
  community college transfer to: *see*
    Transfers, from community to
    senior colleges
  credits, 124–125, 136–137, 144, 164–
    166, 170–175, 179–181, 183–186
  cumulative peformance, 127–130,
    183–186
  degree aspirations, 106–107, 108
  dropout rates, 125–126, 129–130,
    138, 183, 186
  educational background, 143–147,
    150, 161–176
  enrollment under open admissions,
    63–70
  family income and admission status,
    93, 94, 97
  first-generation college students,
    95–96

freshman performance, 179–183
gender and admissions status, 98,
  179–180
grade point average, 121–123, 136–
  137, 144, 162–163, 170–178, 179–
  181, 183–186, 278
graduation rates, 129–130, 138, 145,
  167–169, 183–186, 269
integration, 71–76
longitudinal model of student's career, 169–178
persistence, 145, 166–168, 171,
  183–186
remediation, 234–237, 242–244,
  249–253
retention rates, 129–130, 138
return for fall, 172–177
SEEK program, 6, 7, 9, 17, 18, 51,
  62, 64–67, 72, 73, 76, 100, 269,
  272, 306
social origin and, 143–147, 150
stopping out, 170, 177
student self-rating, 102
students' need to work, 180–181
students' perceptions of benefits,
  109–115
Sex-role socialization, 97
Social origin, 30, 32–35, 51, 53, 55,
  110–111
  academic achievement and, 142–151
  community colleges and, 147–151
  community-senior college transfer,
    205–208
  credits, 144, 147, 148
  of ethnic groups, 92–97, 144–150
  grade point average, 144, 147, 148,
    150
  graduation rates, 145, 147, 149,
    151
  persistence, 145, 147, 149, 151
  senior colleges and, 143–147, 150
  transfers, 202, 205–208
Socioeconomic outcomes of college education, 31–32, 121
Special program students: *see* College
  Discovery; SEEK (Search for Education, Elevation, and Knowledge)
  program
Standardized tests, 35, 36, 231
Standards, 37–40, 120, 281, 282, 294,
  303
Stanford University, 230
State University of New York (SUNY),
  16, 292, 302

Staten Island Community College, 63,
    73, 193, 196, 211, 217
Stopping out, 49, 130, 170, 177, 181
Student characteristics, 97, 100,
    159-160
Student surveys, 51-54
Students for a Democratic Society
    (SDS), 9
Study laboratories, 232
Supportive counseling, 20, 119

Teacher attitudes, 35, 267, 279,
    280-283
Technical-vocational curriculum, 36-
    37, 83-86, 191, 192, 200, 209,
    210, 212, 215, 221, 223, 225
Top 100 Scholars program, 17
Tracking: see High school tracking
Transfers
    to colleges outside CUNY, 124, 130,
        138, 146-147, 151, 168, 171, 176
    from community to senior colleges,
        36, 49, 203-226
    academic performance, 217-224
    basic academic model of, 208-213
    basic aspects of, 203-205
    credits, 210, 215-216, 220-221
    curriculum and, 209-210, 212, 221
    degrees, 202-205, 217, 219,
        223-224

educational background and, 205-
    208, 222-223
ethnic groups and, 147, 206-208,
    210, 212, 214, 216, 219, 225
grade point average, 220-221
rates by curriculum, degree, and
    admissions status, 204
social origin and, 202, 205-208
timing, 213-217, 219, 221-222
within CUNY, 49
Tuition Assistance Program (TAP),
    292-293, 295, 302, 304
Tutoring devices, 232
Two-year colleges: see Community col-
    leges

United Federation of College Teach-
    ers, 15
Universalism, 29

Welfare students, 142
Wellesley College, 230
White flight, 82, 177
Work, students' need to, 52, 94, 180-
    181, 185, 192, 195
Writing, 231, 233-247, 259-260

York College, 63, 73